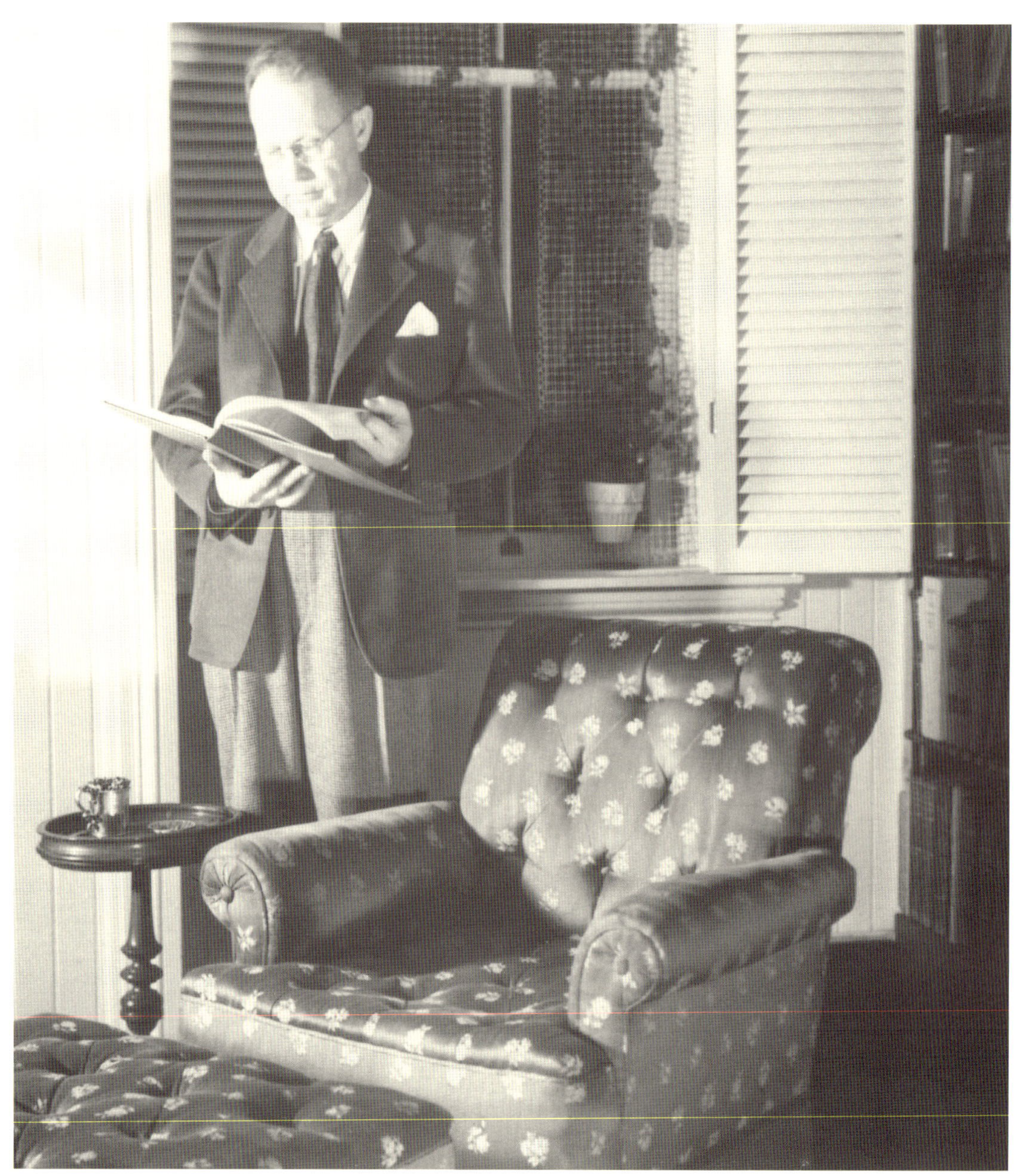

Grant Wood in his Iowa City home (detail), c. 1937.
State Historical Society of Iowa–Iowa City.

Grant Wood's Main Street

Art, Literature and the American Midwest

Lea Rosson DeLong

With contributions by
Henry Adams - Sally E. Parry - Kent C. Ryden

Brunnier Art Museum
University Museums
Iowa State University
Ames, Iowa

Published by University Museums, Iowa State University, Ames, Iowa
Printed by Sigler Printing and Publishing Incorporated, Ames, Iowa
Distributed by University Museums and
Sigler Printing and Publishing Incorporated, Ames, Iowa

University Museums, Iowa State University
290 Scheman Building, Ames, Iowa 50011
Phone: 1-515-294-3342
Fax: 1-515-294-7070
Web: www.museums.iastate.edu

Printed on acid-free paper.

First edition, 2004

Library of Congress Cataloging-in-Publication Data
DeLong, Lea Rosson.

Grant Wood's Main Street; *Art, Literature and the American Midwest* / Lea Rosson DeLong;

with contributions by Sally E. Parry … [et. Al.] - 1st ed.
p. cm.
Exhibition catalogs.
Includes bibliographical references and index.

Library of Congress Control Number: 2003114990
ISBN 1-888223-54-5

Dedicated to all the memories
of our Main Streets
that we carry with us through our lives.

This book is published on the occasion of the exhibition
Grant Wood's Main Street

At the Brunnier Art Museum
University Museums
Iowa State University, Ames, Iowa
13 January - 7 August 2004

Grant Wood's Main Street is organized by the Brunnier Art Museum, and sponsored by Howard F. and Roberta Green Ahmanson and Hometown Perry, Iowa.

Henry Adams received his B.A. from Harvard University and Ph.D. from Yale University. He is currently chair of the Department of Art History at Case Western Reserve University.

Lea Rosson DeLong received her B.A. from the University of Oklahoma and her Master's and Ph.D. from the University of Kansas. She is currently guest curator for the Brunnier Art Museum, University Museums, Iowa State University.

Kent C. Ryden received his Ph.D. from Brown University. He is associate professor of American and New England Studies at the University of Southern Maine.

Sally E. Parry received her Ph.D. from Fordham University. She is currently associate professor of English at Illinois State University.

Table of Contents

Grant Wood's Main Street

"I am glad you like the *Main Street* drawings. A man takes a good deal for granted when he tries to interpret in drawings what has been so adequately done in words. Nonetheless, in spite of some misgivings on that score, I got a great kick out of trying to capture the essence of that story we all admire. I hope you can make it out to Iowa before long....A few days here might prove restful to you, and also, if you have any point of dispute on the illustrations, that would be a good time to give me hell."

Wood to Sinclair Lewis.
July 10, 1937

"These drawings are not to be illustrations for the book; they will stand on their own feet as individual pictures..."

Wood to Maynard Walker.
October 21, 1935

Letter from Grant Wood to Sinclair Lewis, July 10, 1937. Yale Collection of American Literature, Beinecke Rare Book and Manuscript Library, Yale University.

Letter from Grant Wood to Maynard Walker, Archives of American Art, Maynard Walker File, reel 2025, frame 987-988.

Preface

Each of us started out somewhere. We were all born in one, very particular place. Some of us stayed there, may live there still. Others of us moved before we got to know our birthplace or perhaps when we were older, after high school, or later still. But, whether we know it or not, we are shaped by the places that have formed the context for our lives.

For me, the realization came in my early **thirties**. Born in Perry, Iowa, in 1949, I grew up riding my bike all over town. Such freedom! The town was mine, the seemingly endless fields, all that space, never more than a few blocks away. Later, I learned to drive, and my space grew from blocks to miles. In my twenties, I worked summers as a corn-detasseling **foreman**, and the fields became a kind of home. Some of that rich, black earth clung to my shoes and walked back into town with me.

Like many in my generation, I left the state to go to college and wound up as a journalist living in the endless suburb that is Southern California. In the early 1980s, I lived an hour from any open space, from the ocean or the desert — no cornfields here. Some nights I simply **had** to get in my car and drive; I needed room. And I didn't know why. Then I read Susan Allen Toth's *Ivy Days: Making My Way Out East*. She had grown up in Ames, Iowa, just 30 miles from my **hometown** and then had gone East to Smith College, where the world seemed somehow cramped:

> **My Iowa landscape was mostly earth and air, plants and** sky....everywhere my mother drove me I absorbed the same sense of space. Outside the towns was a reassuring repetition of fields and farm, fields and farm.... That unconscious assumption of space was part of what made my confinement in Northampton difficult.

Exactly. Yes. Northampton, Massachusetts, wasn't quite Orange County, but the effect was the same.

Not only did I not understand the importance of growing up in big physical spaces until much later, but I also missed the importance of growing up in a place filled with equally large interior spaces — places deep within each of us. There was room to think, to roam in my mind **as well** as on my bike. And there was space for people to be different. Not until my father died did I hear a story of how he and his fellow railroaders could differ over profound issues (in their case, religion), and yet laugh together and respect each other in deep ways. And, even after that, I learned that in my small town of about 7,000 souls, there were many ethnic, as well as religious, differences. **Yet** we lived together. It hadn't always been easy, but impassable rifts were indeed bridged and festering wounds healed. That story has yet to be written.

Grant Wood, too, grew up in Iowa. He knew those spaces, inside and out. We know him for his unforgettable images of wide fields and silent towns, for farm faces, and for portraits from the town. His towns were Stone City, Cedar Rapids, and Ames. In 1937, he illustrated a special edition of *Main Street*, Sinclair Lewis's classic indictment of the smallness of small towns.

As ever, Wood found more in the assignment than Lewis's caricatures. Wood knew the irony of the small town from inside out. And you see it in these images: *The Main Street Mansion* (an Arts and Crafts bungalow); *The Perfectionist*; *The Sentimental Yearner* (ah, yes;) *The Radical*; *General Practitioner* (this portrayed with a firm hand taking a pulse — no face at all;) *The Good Influence* (if only we had listened;) *The Practical Idealist* (she with the unmistakable gleam in her eye); *Booster*. Through Wood's eyes we not only see them, but we see ourselves in them.

In America, people in small towns (just like people in big cities) all came from somewhere else. In the Midwest, they came in large numbers in the late 19th and early 20th centuries, but they continue to arrive today; they come from Ireland, Wales, Denmark, Norway, Bohemia, the Netherlands, Sweden, Greece, Germany, Italy, England, Cuba, Laos, Vietnam, China, Russia, Sudan, Somalia, Mexico, Central and South America, and elsewhere.

We know the stories of how they settled cities. We have yet to connect their immigrant journeys with how they settled and built communities in small towns. **Both yesterday and today, very different people have had no choice but to know each other's names and experience each other's lives on Main Street and in Every Town.** It is our loss that Grant Wood is no longer here to paint the images of that story. But we have those he captured in the first half of the 20th century.

My hope for those who see Grant Wood's *Main Street* images for the first time is that the experience becomes a starting point, a jumping-off place to discover the meaning of difference in small towns set in large spaces, a kind of closeness with room to maneuver. My suspicion is that we are on to something here. **And, given the conflicts around the world between people who seem unable to bridge the chasms created by their differences, it is time to listen to the stories told by these small town faces and the lives behind them.**

Roberta Green Ahmanson
Corona del Mar, California
10 May 2003

Director's Foreword and Acknowledgements

Grant Wood became a historic figure while he was still making art history. After *American Gothic's* national acclaim in 1930, millions knew Grant Wood's painted Midwestern faces and rolling Iowa landscapes. Only six years later, he was drawing his masterpiece illustrations for Sinclair Lewis's *Main Street,* published by the Lakeside Press in Chicago.

University Museums is pleased and proud to be part of this long overdue publication and accompanying exhibition that will allow scholars and art lovers everywhere to make their first extended acquaintance with Grant Wood's capacity, talent, and gifts as a master drawer.

In addition to drawing the *Main Street* illustrations, in 1936-37 Grant Wood was also directing and designing the creation of his second major mural cycle, *Breaking the Prairie Sod* at Iowa State in Ames. Under the Public Works of Art Project (PWAP), he had previously completed the first cycle of nine panels, *When Tillage Begins, Other Arts Follow* in 1934. It was Grant Wood's and Christian Petersen's artistic legacies from the Depression era that founded the public art program at Iowa State. Today, Iowa State's more than 450 major public works in its Art on Campus Collection serve as a strategic educational asset for students, scholars, and the public.

The exhibition and book, *Grant Wood's Main Street,* reflect the passion and commitment of its organizers and those who will experience it. The project is the vision of Roberta Green Ahmanson, whose passion and determination to meld world-class quality with Midwestern expression equals that of Grant Wood. Knowing of Iowa State's enduring interest in Grant Wood and American arts and letters of the Depression era, she approached us as a partner. Iowa State is honored to be an arts partner. After all, that is part of our land-grant heritage – arts with practice. After planting the exhibition seed, Roberta allowed the germination and fruition of the project to flourish under the scholarship of guest curator Dr. Lea Rosson DeLong. The citizens of Iowa State University, the State of Iowa, and the nation are grateful to Roberta Green Ahmanson for her inspired leadership to uncover our past, explore our future, and live and work in a creative and peaceful world. By rediscovering Grant Wood's and Sinclair Lewis's *Main Street,* we can rediscover how the ultimate resiliency of individuals, families, and communities allows us to endure. On behalf of the University Museums, Iowa State University, we extend our sincere appreciation to Roberta Green and Howard F. Ahmanson for inspiring and funding this investigation of American arts and letters. Perhaps it seems obvious, but the substantive role that Roberta Green Ahmanson played in this project cannot be overemphasized. The opportunity to explore an intriguing historical perspective that bears significant relevance in the contemporary world is an unparalleled stimulus for curators and scholars. Mrs. Ahmanson's conversations and observations helped shape this exhibition and publication and resulted in deeper understandings.

Grant Wood's drawings for *Main Street* have never been publicly exhibited together until this exhibition. When this project began, some of the drawings' locations were known, and some were not. The journey from visionary concept to solid exhibition and book publication was possible only because of the scholarly research and determined, historical detective-work of Dr. Lea Rosson DeLong. Dr. DeLong's sensitivity has distinguished her previous publications, including the book *Christian Petersen, Sculptor*. Her museum and academic career have been devoted to the arts of the Depression era and her insights, interpretations, and analyses are provoking, intriguing, and thoughtful. *Grant Wood's Main Street* is her latest scholarly undertaking and is an important contribution to the field of American art history.

All major projects have significant, and sometimes invisible, partners. These *Main Street* project partners worked regularly with Roberta Green and Howard F. Ahmanson and were only a phone call away. I am deeply grateful to Elaine Hirshl Ellis, who thoughtfully and thoroughly assisted the exhibition project. William Clark, president of Hometown Perry, Iowa has become a new and valued museum colleague, as he and his associates work towards opening a new museum in Perry and invigorating their Main Street Perry with a cultural renaissance. Pam Jenkins, sociologist, recommended authors for inclusion in this publication and provided insights into the issues and times portrayed in Sinclair Lewis characters. Kathy Lenz and Jeff Spence of Hotel Pattee coordinated educational programming and exhibition promotions. And Ann Hirou, project manager for the Ahmansons, answered our detailed inquiries with patience, diligence, and thoughtfulness.

As we uncovered some of the roots of discourse in American arts and letters of Grant Wood and Sinclair Lewis, we gained insight from some of the nation's best writers and critical thinkers in regionalist art, letters and culture. I am grateful to Sally E. Parry, associate professor of English at Illinois State University; Kent C. Ryden, director and associate professor of American and New England Studies; and Henry Adams, department chair and professor of American Art at Case Western Reserve, for their essay contributions to this book. Their reflections of the 1930s, when nationalist rhetoric flourished and artists across the country laid passionate claim to making a true American art, have given us a clearer vision of America, its ideals, and its people.

I am grateful to the public and private lenders to this exhibition. Without their cooperation *Grant Wood's Main Street* would not have had the depth and comprehensiveness that so clearly distinguishes it. The lenders are: Fine Arts Museums of San Francisco; Roberta Green and Howard F. Ahmanson; Peter Brady; The Davenport Museum of Art; Hunter Museum of American Art; Edward Lenkin; Minneapolis Institute of Arts; Pennsylvania Academy of the Fine Arts; Smithsonian American Art; and Vance Jordan Fine Art.

To Ron McMillan, Sigler Publications, Ames Iowa, I offer my appreciation for the masterful design and production of this book. Karol Crosbie skillfully assisted with the copy editing, and Ken Burditt, customer relations specialist for ISU Publications, provided invaluable expertise in shepherding the publication process. And I extend my sincere appreciation to Keith Bystrom, University Counsel, for his advice.

And finally, I would like to thank the staff of the Brunnier Art Museum who worked in so many capacities to present the exhibition. They truly are the inspired energy and force of the museum. Rachel Hampton worked diligently on loans, publications, and promotions; Matthew DeLay and Allison Sheridan coordinated educational programs; Janet McMahon provided administrative support; Susan Olson guided volunteer membership activity; and, Eleanor Ostendorf provided installation and collections support. Dana Michels DeRoin began this exhibition journey with us, and I am grateful for her initial curatorial support.

I am pleased and honored to acknowledge the gracious help, commitment, and expertise of all these people in presenting this book and exhibition.

Lynette L. Pohlman
Director and Chief Curator
University Museums, Iowa State University

Curator's Acknowledgments

Working on this exhibition has given me a deepened regard for both Grant Wood and Sinclair Lewis and for those aspects of America that they both represent. Whether in resentment or reverence, these two artists insist that we look at ourselves — as Midwesterners, Americans, and as individuals. The ideas and the stories and, most of all, the human nature that both portray are as revealing, as uncomfortable, and as inspiriting today as they were in the 1920s and 1930s. The *Main Street* of their work is changed and, at the same time, unchanged.

The research on Grant Wood's *Main Street* drawings was productive in many satisfying ways. But it was frustrating in regard to the search for primary documents for the series which, to date, remain unlocated. The publisher of the Limited Editions Club, George Macy, corresponded with Wood and Lewis, and those files were maintained long enough to be examined by James M. Dennis in his seminal monograph, *Grant Wood: A Study in Art and Culture* of 1975. Most of Macy's archives are now found at the Ransom Humanities Center at the University of Texas, and a microfiche file of Macy's records on the many books he published remains at the Easton Press in Norwalk, Connecticut. I would like to express my thanks to the Easton Press, notably Michael Hendricks and Jay Crutcher, for allowing me to search their microfiche records and for facilitating my work in Norwalk. Unfortunately, the records on the *Main Street* commission are not to be found in either place.* I thank the many scholars and librarians who made suggestions and aided me in my search. I am hopeful that one outcome of this catalogue will be the rediscovery of the Macy-Wood-Lewis papers. Anyone attempting to understand Grant Wood must rely, first of all, on the two major studies by James M. Dennis (*Grant Wood: A Study in American Art and Culture*) and Wanda Corn (*Grant Wood: The Regionalist Vision*), both of which remain as standards of scholarship on the artist. Having consulted their work many times in numerous contexts, I appreciate the foundation they have laid in the literature on Wood. I thank them both personally for responding to my questions, especially in regard to the location of materials.

This study draws a good deal on the Scrapbooks compiled by the sister of Grant Wood, Nan Wood Graham. The materials that she kept over the years: newspaper clippings, articles, exhibition catalogues, and a variety of other documents are now an invaluable resource for anyone researching Wood. Not everything is identified or credited completely, but there is an abundance of clues to follow. Aside from the information itself, the editorial comments Mrs. Graham added to her Scrapbooks are always interesting and often well founded. She was a tireless and thorough defender of her brother and his art, and her advocacy of his reputation has led her to be somewhat discredited as a good source for art historians. She made no pretense of being a scholar or archivist (or of being impartial), but she did have a familiarity with the details of her brother's life that no one else could match. Her first concern was to keep the record as accurate and complete as possible, and her memory was reportedly strong. Keeping in mind her partisan position and applying appropriate discretion, her records, memories, and observations about Grant Wood are a creditable source for the art historian. These Scrapbooks and much other material have been entrusted to the Davenport Museum of Art (the Scrapbooks are available on microfilm through the Archives of American Art), where, despite their fragility, I was allowed to look at the Scrapbooks themselves. My very sincere thanks is extended to Michelle Robinson, Curator of Collections and Exhibitions, and their knowledgeable Registrar, Patrick Sweeney, for all their assistance and cooperation.

I am deeply grateful to Lynette Pohlman, Director of the University Museums, for giving me this and many other opportunities. I appreciate her knowledge, her vitality, her generosity, and her resourcefulness. My special thanks goes to Roberta Green Ahmanson, both as patron and collector, and to her staff at Hometown Perry, including Elaine Ellis, Pam Jenkins, Ann Hirou, and Bill Clark, for entrusting us with this project and giving us the support to carry it out. The staff at the Brunnier Art Museum is a marvel of competence and devotion, and I thank them all, Janet McMahon, Allison Sheridan, and most especially, Rachel Hampton, for their good work and congeniality; they have all been delightful to work with. A special thanks goes to Matthew DeLay, who read *Main Street* along with me and who discussed it with me nearly daily, offering useful, insightful, and amusing commentary.

In addition, I would like to thank Andrew Thompson of the Owen Gallery; Jane Milosch and Teri Coate Salle of the Cedar Rapids Museum of Art; Debra Evans and Karin Breuer of the Fine Arts Museums of San Francisco; Mark Hain of the Pennsylvania Academy of Art; Joanne Moser and Lynn Putney of the Smithsonian American Art Museum; Ellen Simak and Elizabeth Le of the Hunter Museum of American Art; Dennis Jon of the Minneapolis Institute of Arts; Elizabeth Buschor of the Upper Midwest Conservation Association; Kathi Kaminski of the Lenken Companies; Roger Howlett of the Childs Gallery; Carol Irish and Kendall Scully of Vance Jordan Fine Arts, Inc.; Mrs. Samuel Kravitt and the Candace Perich Gallery; James H. Maroney, Rose Wood and Amy N. Worthen of the Des Moines Art Center; Joan Liffring-Zug Bourret; and Vivian Torrence (also, like Wood, an American artist in Munich). Librarians are a blessing in this and any research project, and

I would like to thank those at the Special Collections of the University of Iowa Library, especially Archivist David McCartney, the Rare Books and Special Collections at the Beinecke Library at Yale, the library staff of Norwalk (Connecticut) Community College, and the always reliable staff at the Art Institute of Chicago, especially Bart Ryckbosch.

I would also like to acknowledge my nephew, Sgt. John Michael Phillips, Jr., 101st Airborne Division, United States Army, whose deployment to Iraq coincided with the period when I was writing this catalogue and with whom I frequently corresponded. Perhaps the reality of his challenges and my comments on art, literature, and Main Street helped us both keep our lives in perspective.

Finally, and as always, I thank my husband, Harris Coggeshall (Tim) DeLong, for his faithfulness during the period of this project. Unfailingly indulgent and generous, he seems to know what to overlook and what to notice, and I appreciate his judgment.

Lea Rosson DeLong
Guest Curator, *Grant Wood's Main Street*

*The Macy-Wood-Lewis papers were found after this exhibition catalogue was in press. After study and further research, their information will be presented in future publications. The author thanks the Easton Press and Jay Crutcher for assistance in locating these important documents.

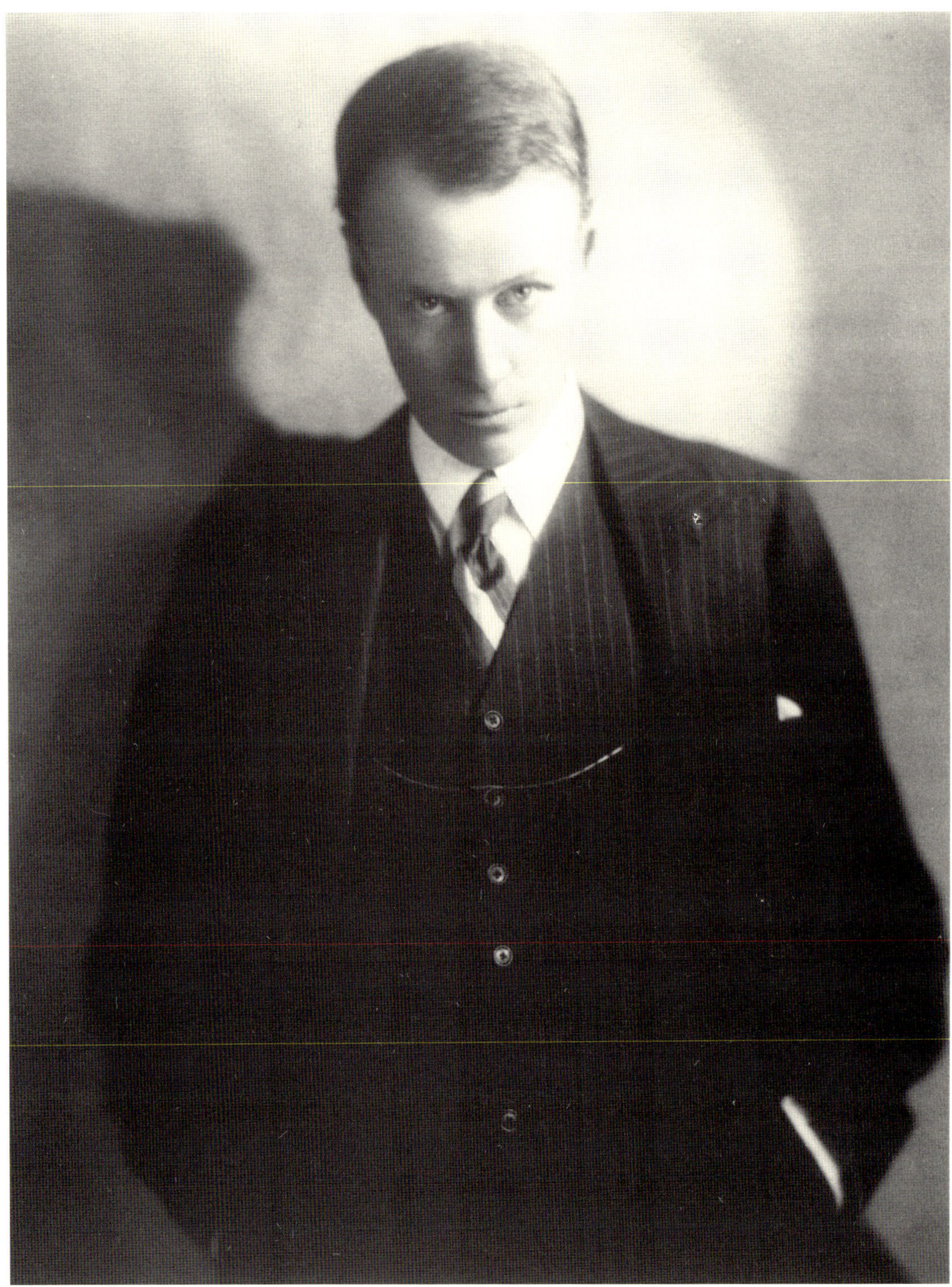

Figure 1 Sinclair Lewis, c.1915

Chapter 1
Sinclair Lewis

Sinclair Lewis (1885-1951) caused a public furor when *Main Street* was published in 1920. In it, he exploded the notion that the small town represents that which is best about American life, or, as he put it, "that the American village remains the one sure abode of friendship, honesty, and clean, sweet, marriageable girls." [1] He became a part of what Carl Van Doren would identify as "The Revolt from the Village" movement, a direction in literature presaged by Hamlin Garland's harsh portrayal of hard-scrabble rural Midwestern life in *Main-Travelled Roads* in 1891. This movement gathered strength prior to World War I, with Edgar Lee Masters's *Spoon River Anthology* (1915) and continued with Sherwood Anderson's *Winesburg, Ohio* (1919) and Zona Gale's *Miss Lulu Bett* (1920), all of which protested conformity in speech and behavior and "standardized dullness." [2] "The village represented what Americans thought they were, what they sometimes pretended (to themselves as well as others) they wanted to be, and if the small town was typically American, the Midwestern small town was doubly typical." [3] Because of this identification, many Americans saw these attacks on the small town as an attack on American civilization. Mark Schorer, Lewis's first biographer, wrote, "No reader was indifferent to *Main Street*; if it was not the most important revelation of American life ever made, it was the most infamous libel upon it." [4]

Lewis relished the controversy brought about by *Main Street*. It was the best-selling novel of 1920, put him on the literary map for critics and readers alike, and was considered for the Pulitzer Prize. [5] It made a financial success of the fledging publishing firm of Harcourt, Brace, and Howe, a company that would go on to publish Lewis's novels throughout the 1920s. And it set the stage for an incredibly productive decade that ended with Lewis becoming the first American to win the Nobel Prize for Literature. Schorer summed up the opinion of many of the leading critics of the day—including H. L. Mencken, William Allen White, Carl Van Doren, Franklin Adams, and Heywood Broun—by noting that *Main Street* "marked the end of American complacency." [6]

Although many people were angered by this caustic view of small-town life, Lewis was writing from experience. He was born in the small town of Sauk Centre, Minnesota, and did not leave the state until he went off to Oberlin College in 1902 to prepare for admittance into Yale University. [7] He felt ambivalent about his hometown, and, like Carol Kennicott, despaired about the lack of cultural awareness and open minds. He was a dreamy, awkward boy, not much approved of by his father, Dr. E. J. Lewis, who hoped that Harry (Sinclair's real first name) would become a doctor like himself and his brother Claude. But Lewis had bigger ideas. He studied English at Yale, traveled on cattle boats to England, worked as a maintenance man at Upton Sinclair's utopian community, Helicon Hall, as well as a reporter, literary secretary, and eventually worked in publishing in New York. He wrote poetry and short stories from his Yale days onward and in 1912 wrote his first novel *Hike and the Aeroplane*, a juvenile adventure story published under the name of Tom Graham.

His first novel under his own name was *Our Mr. Wrenn: The Romantic Adventures of a Gentle Man* in 1914, the story of a young man trying to break away from routine, inspired by the writing of H. G. Wells. Wells's social commentary was vital to Lewis's outlook on the world, an influence so important that Lewis named his first son after Wells and later dedicated a novel to him. The next year found another Lewis novel, *The Trail of the Hawk: A Comedy of the Seriousness of Life* (1915), focusing, like *Hike*, on pioneering efforts in air transportation and also exploring young married life. Lewis had met Grace Hegger, a writer for *Vogue* magazine, in 1912, and married her in 1914. Aspects of her personality infuse Lewis's female characters through the end of the 1920s. Both *Our Mr. Wrenn* and *The Job* (1917) are dedicated to her. Grace's independent attitude and work ethic enrich the portrayal of Una Golden in *The Job*, a story of an ordinary woman who needs to make a living to support her widowed mother and later herself after her husband abandons her. Unlike abandoned women in many older novels, who must sacrifice their honor or die in poverty, Una is a contemporary woman who faces her problems in a practical manner. She works as a secretary for many years and eventually becomes a successful business executive. Even at the end of the novel, when she has a romance with one of her staff, she decides that their impending marriage will not mean the end of her business life. Lewis also wrote two shorter novels before 1920, *The Innocents: A Story for Lovers*, also in 1917, about an older couple in love; and *Free Air*, in 1919, a romance loosely based on an automobile trip that Lewis and his wife took across the Midwest.

Lewis achieved his full artistic potential with *Main Street*, creating a novel that expresses his ambivalence about his hometown and America. His opening claim is bold: "This is America—a town of a few thousand, in a region of wheat and corn and dairies and little groves. The town is, in our tale, called 'Gopher Prairie, Minnesota.' But its Main Street is the continuation of Main Streets everywhere. . . .Main Street is the climax of civilization." The Main Street that protagonist Carol Kennicott finds in Gopher Prairie is an ugly, dreary place where conservative values and a rigid social hierarchy reign and new thoughts—about culture, education, and behavior—have no place. It is only new ideas about business that are prized. Carol's experiences reflect some of what Grace encountered when Lewis brought her home to meet his father and stepmother. But Carol was Lewis as well. He told his friend Charles Breasted that in many ways "Carol is 'Red' Lewis: always groping for something she isn't capable of attaining, always dissatisfied, always restlessly straining to see what lies just over the horizon, intolerant of her surrounding, yet lacking any clearly defined vision of what she really wants to do or be." [8] Lewis revealed strong feminist sympathies, showing the limited choices available to women at the beginning of the twentieth century and how frustrating it was for them to be thinking human beings with only a very small stage on which to exercise their intelligence. Ann Douglas notes that Lewis "was almost alone among this generation of male white writers in using female protagonists as autobiographical stand-ins in his fiction." [9]

Main Street marked only the beginning of an artistically satisfying decade for Lewis: he wrote six more novels, four of them best-sellers, and all of which helped, as E. M. Forster noted, "to lodge a piece of a continent in our imagination." [10] *Babbitt,* a study of a middle-aged, middle-class businessman in the Midwestern city of Zenith, was published in 1922. Lewis picked up on the enthusiasm for real-estate speculation that Dr. Kennicott and Honest Jim Blausser espoused and set it in a much larger and more developed city. The portrayal of the everyday life of a businessman capitalized on the excessive consumerism of the 1920s, a decade in which President Calvin Coolidge declared, "The business of America is business." Lewis did copious research for this novel, visiting Midwestern cities, attending meetings of such business clubs as the Rotary and Elks, and picking up slang, rhythms of speaking, and the discourse of "boosterism." He even drew maps and wrote biographies of his characters before he started the novel, in order to make it seem true to life. Maxwell Geismar contended that Zenith was "Gopher Prairie come of age," while Sally Parry called it a "prototypical American city, representing enthusiasm, growth, and progress, as well as the worship of business and the profit motive." [11] Lewis's critique of this obsessively capitalist culture and the incipient fascism it can engender distressed many readers, but the novel sold well, giving the world the term "Babbitt" as synonymous with the average man whose life is defined by his business. Lewis's satire on businessmen continued with an extended character study, *The Man Who Knew Coolidge: Being the Soul of Lowell Schmaltz, Constructive and Nordic Citizen* (1928), which started as a short story in the H. L. Mencken magazine *American Mercury* earlier that year.

Arrowsmith (1925) focused on another major aspect of American society: the medical profession. In young Martin Arrowsmith, Lewis explores notions of idealism versus practicality in choosing one's life's work and also pays homage to the profession of his father and brother. Arrowsmith works as family doctor, a public health official, and later as a medical researcher. His concerns about research are tested when he is sent to a Caribbean island to help stem an outbreak of plague. Although his mentor, Dr. Gottlieb, urges him to keep scrupulously to research conditions in order to contribute to science, Martin gives in to his humane side after his wife dies of the plague and gives the serum to all those infected. The novel is notable for portraying black doctors as being as professional as white doctors. This interest in race in society would be further explored in *Work of Art* (1934) and more notably in *Kingsblood Royal* (1947).

Among the most controversial novels that Lewis wrote was *Elmer Gantry* (1927). Turning from medicine to religion, Lewis created a character that was larger than life and a challenge to the religious establishment. Although Lewis was interested in religion and considered becoming a missionary when he was at Oberlin, he generally believed that organized religion supported the status quo at the expense of society's marginalized. Gantry is a football player who finds God, or at least finds that cheerleading for God is an easy way to make a living. Lewis again did copious research, visiting churches throughout the Midwest and speaking with groups of ministers. At a Sunday evening forum in a church in Kansas City he shocked the group by saying, "If God is striking agnostics down, let him strike me down." [12] Newspapers across the country denounced him, but it was great publicity. Gantry moves from one evangelical religion to another with his refrain of "Love is the morning and evening star," weathering a variety of scandals. In the first half of the novel he hooks up with a female evangelist, modeled after Aimee Semple MacPherson, His female protagonist – played by Jean Simmons opposite Burt Lancaster in a 1960 movie —, dies in a fiery blaze of glory. [13]

The last major novel of the 1920s was *Dodsworth* (1929) about an industrialist who retires while in still vital middle age so that he can see more of the world and experience art and culture. His European education does not turn out the way that he expects, as his wife leaves him to socialize with minor aristocracy. Sam Dodsworth was in some ways an autobiographical stand-in for Lewis. They were the same age and with similar marital problems. Lewis and Grace had separated, and he met Dorothy Thompson, a world-renowned journalist and foreign correspondent. By the time *Dodsworth* was published, Lewis had gained a divorce from Grace and married Thompson, whose character becomes part of the divorcée Edith Cortwright in *Dodsworth*. Lewis felt a good deal of affinity for Dodsworth. In what turned out to be his final novel, *World So Wide* (1951-published posthumously), Sam and Edith make another appearance as an older couple that have settled down in the expatriate American community in Rome, ironically where Lewis would die of a heart attack.

Lewis started off the next decade as the most heralded American writer in the world, the first American to win the Nobel Prize for Literature. Although many writers complained that he was more a critic than a booster of America and thought that there were other, better candidates, Lewis seized the opportunity to call for truly American forms of literature. The award commended him for "his vigorous and graphic art of description and his ability to create, with wit and humour, new types of people." In his Nobel Prize speech Lewis generously recognized a number of other important American writers including Theodore Dreiser, Sherwood Anderson, Willa Cather, Ernest Hemingway, Thomas Wolfe, John Dos Passos, and William Faulkner. He ended by saluting many of his contemporaries, thanking them for "their determination to give to the America that has mountains and endless prairies, enormous cities and lost farm cabins, billions of money and tons of faith, to an America that is as strange as Russia and as complex as China, a literature worthy of her vastness." [14]

The 1930s were a time of immense social and political upheaval, reflected to a certain extent in Lewis's writings, which ranged greatly in quality and success. His most important novel of the decade was *It Can't Happen Here* (1935), which fantasized about American fascists taking over the country. The novel hit close to home for many people, since he populated his story with such actual threats to America's security as Huey Long and Father Coughlin, as well as the fictional thugs of Buzz Windrip and his Minute Men. Dorothy Thompson contributed to his sense of urgency in creating the book. She had been covering the rise of fascism in Europe and in 1934 was one of the first journalists to be expelled from Germany by Hitler. The Federal Theatre Project seized on this compelling idea of homegrown fascism, commissioned J. C. Moffitt and Lewis to write a dramatic version, and on October 27, 1936, 23 productions of the play opened simultaneously in 18 cities. [15] Lewis's other novels of the 1930s included the best-selling *Ann Vickers* (1933), featuring another strong feminist heroine who was loosely based on Dorothy Thompson; *Work of Art* (1934), an intriguing if not totally successful novel which contemplated the notion of what art really consists of—belles lettres or something as mundane as managing a fine hotel; and *The Prodigal Parents* (1938), a slight work in which members of the older generation find their children pretentious and superficial and run off on a holiday.

In the 1940s Lewis's life was often in turmoil due to such factors as his serious alcoholism, Thompson's involvement in national and international affairs, and the uneven reception of some of his recent writing. By the late 1930s his marriage to Dorothy Thompson was shaky; he separated from her several times and later divorced her in 1941. His companion for much of the decade was Marcella Powers, a woman 36 years his junior. He met her while acting in summer stock and used some of her experiences in the creation of *Bethel Merriday* (1940), the story of a young girl who is learning to be an actress. Lewis enjoyed working in the theater, partly because he was able to use his gifts of mimicry, and also because he wanted to be around young people. He wrote *Gideon Planish* in 1943, a return to his satiric writing but with a dig at Thompson as the "Talking Woman." Greater success came later in the decade with *Cass Timberlane* in 1945. He saw it as a study of modern marriages with all the compromise that implies. One of the interesting fictional experiments in this novel was the creation of interchapters where he would write in detail about a marriage, usually one that had a pleasant façade but that underneath had serious problems.

The setting for *Cass Timberlane*, Grand Republic, also became the site of his last important novel, *Kingsblood Royal* (1947). Neil Kingsblood is in many ways a descendent of some of Lewis's earlier idealists, like Carol Kennicott and Martin Arrowsmith. A decorated World War II veteran, Neil comes home to Grand Republic and in the course of genealogical research on his ancestors, discovers that one of his great-great-great-grandfathers was black. He finds his ancestry fascinating and sets out to discover more. But in 1947 America, the common belief was that "Everybody having a *known* trace of Negro blood in his veins—no matter how far back it was acquired—is classified as a Negro." [16] Most of Kingsblood's family and community feel threatened by this information, driving him out of his job, nearly breaking up his marriage, and eventually forcing him at gunpoint to leave his home. Two more novels followed *Kingsblood Royal*, but Lewis seemed to lose touch with his reading public. *The God-Seeker* (1949) was his only historical novel, with a focus on a carpenter in pioneer Minnesota who seeks religion. *World So Wide*, his final novel, echoed *Dodsworth*, with Americans trying to find some sort of purpose in life by traveling to Europe.

Sinclair Lewis loved America, but was, in Dorothy Thompson's words, "a disappointed democrat." As Richard Lingeman notes in his recent biography of Lewis, "His fiction functioned at its highest pitch when galvanized by anger at some banality or stupidity or injustice. His iconoclasm chimed with America's coming of age after World War I, but he wrote with a real moral passion. *He really cared*." [17]

Sally E. Parry

Chapter 1 Notes

1. Sinclair Lewis, *Main Street: The Story of Carol Kennicott*, New York: Harcourt, Brace, and Howe, 1920, p. 264.

2. See Anthony Channell Hilfer, *The Revolt from the Village, 1915-1930*, Chapel Hill: University of North Carolina Press, 1969, pp. 3-34, for a discussion of this movement. In *Main Street*, Carol muses on "an unimaginatively standardized background, a sluggishness of speech and manners, a rigid ruling of the spirit by the desire to remain respectable. . . . It is dullness made God." Lewis, p. 265.

3. Hilfer, p. 4.

4. Mark Schorer, *Sinclair Lewis: An American Life*, New York: McGraw-Hill, 1961, p. 269.

5. *Main Street* was recommended by the jury for the Pulitzer in 1921, but the Trustees of Colombia University overruled them, contending that the novel did not represent the best aspects of American culture, and the prize instead went to Edith Wharton for *The Age of Innocence*. Another jury selected *Babbitt* in 1923, but was again overruled, and the prize went to Willa Cather for *One of Ours*. By the time that Lewis was awarded the Pulitzer Prize, for *Arrowsmith* in 1926, he turned it down, partly out of frustration, partly because he said he did not approve of contests, and partly for the publicity. See Lewis's "Letter to the Pulitzer Prize Committee," *The Man from Main Street: Selected Essays and Other Writings, 1904-1950*, ed. Harry E. Maule and Melville H. Cane, New York: Random House, 1953, pp. 18-20.

6. Noted by Schorer, p. 285.

7. After that, Lewis never came back home for any period of time. He epitomized wanderlust, traveling throughout the United States and Europe, and living in California, New York, Vermont, Washington, D.C., and several places in England and Italy, eventually dying in Rome in 1951. He lived in Minnesota for several years in the early 1940s while doing research for *Kingsblood Royal*. See *Minnesota Diary 1942-46* by Sinclair Lewis, edited by George Killough, Moscow, Idaho: University of Idaho Press, 2000, for his later and somewhat gentler view of his home state.

8. Charles Breasted, "The 'Sauk-Centricities' of Sinclair Lewis," *Saturday Review* Aug. 14, 1954, 7+, p. 8.

9. Ann Douglas, *Terrible Honesty: Mongrel Manhattan in the 1920s*, New York: Farrar, Straus and Giroux, 1995, p. 82.

10. E. M. Forster, "Our Photography: Sinclair Lewis," *Abinger Harvest*, 1936, rpt. in *Sinclair Lewis: A Collection of Critical Essays*, ed. Mark Schorer, Englewood Cliffs: Prentice Hall, 1962, 95-99, p. 95.

11. Maxwell Geismar, "Sinclair Lewis: The Cosmic Bourjoyce," *The Last of the Provincials: The American Novel, 1915-1925*, Boston: Houghton Mifflin, 1947, 69-150, p. 88; Sally E. Parry, "Gopher Prairie, Zenith, and Grand Republic: Nice Places to Visit, But Would Even Sinclair Lewis Want to Live There?," *Midwestern Miscellany XX* (1992): 15-27, p. 21.

12. Richard Lingeman, *Sinclair Lewis: Rebel from Main Street*, New York: Random House, 2002, p. 277.

13. *Elmer Gantry* won a number of Academy Awards in 1960, including Best Picture, Best Actor, and Best Supporting Actress for Shirley Jones who played the part of Lulu Baines, a girl ruined by Gantry who becomes a prostitute and attempts to blackmail him. *Elmer Gantry* has also been turned into two different musicals, one on Broadway in 1970 with Robert Shaw and one more recently in Chicago in 1998.

14. Sinclair Lewis, "The American Fear of Literature," *The Man from Main Street: Selected Essays and Other Writings, 1904-1950*, ed. Harry E. Maule and Melville H. Cane, New York: Random House, 1953, pp. 3-17. The first quote is from the introduction, p. 3, and the second quote from p. 17. Many critics felt that Dreiser should have won the Nobel over Lewis.

15. Schorer, p. 624. See also Hallie Flanagan's *Arena*, New York: Duell, Sloan, and Pearce, 1940; and Tony Buttitta and Barry Witham, *Uncle Sam Presents: A Memoir of the Federal Theatre, 1935-1939*, Philadelphia: University of Pennsylvania Press, 1982, for a discussion of the turmoil leading up to this production.

16. Gunnar Myrdal, *An American Dilemma: The Negro Problem and Modern Democracy*, 1944, 2nd ed., New York: Harper, 1962, p. 113.

17. Lingeman, p. 554.

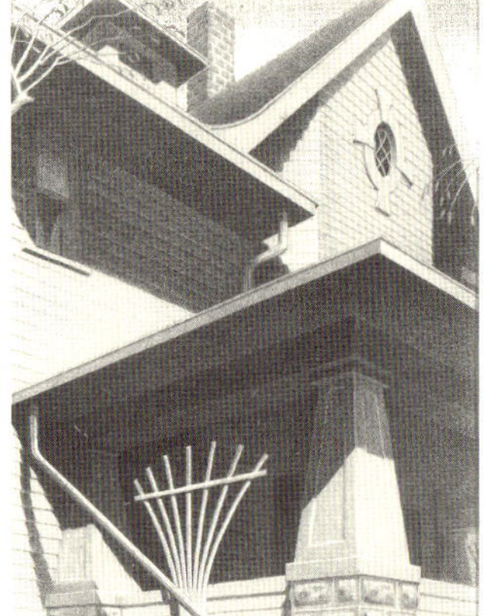

Figure 2 Main Street Mansion

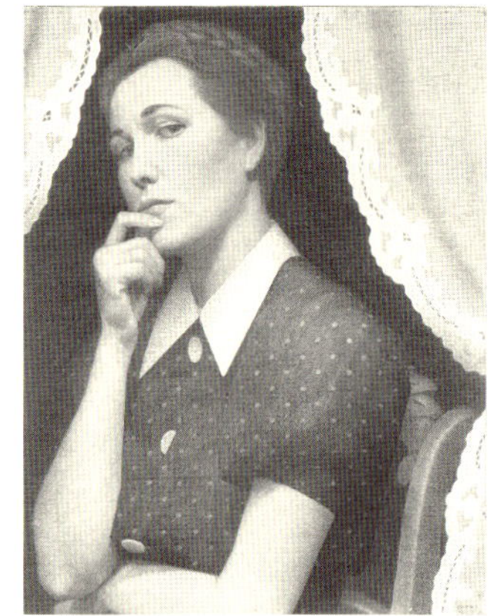

Figure 3 The Perfectionist

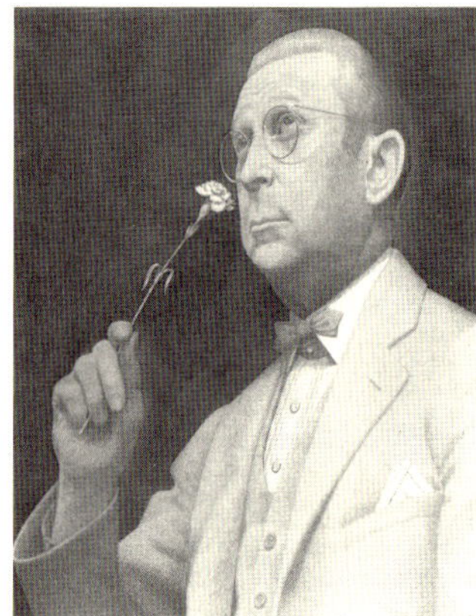

Figure 4 Sentimental Yearner

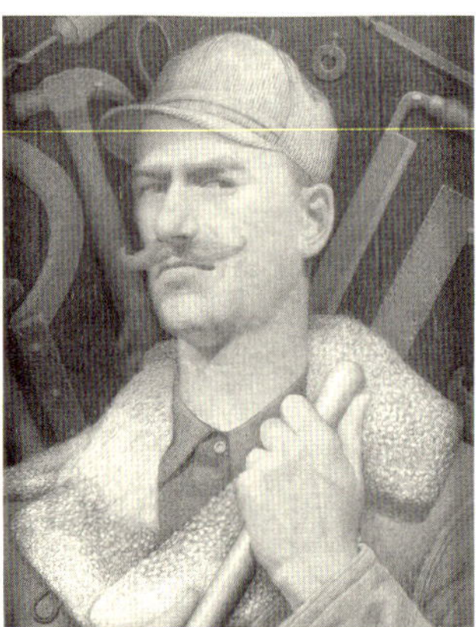

Figure 5 The Radical

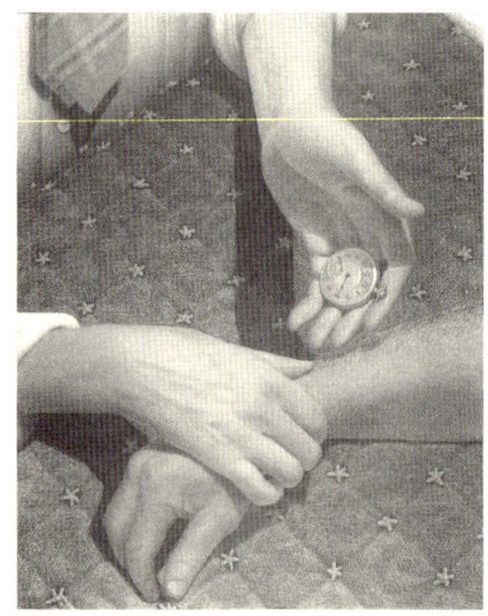

Figure 6 General Practitioner

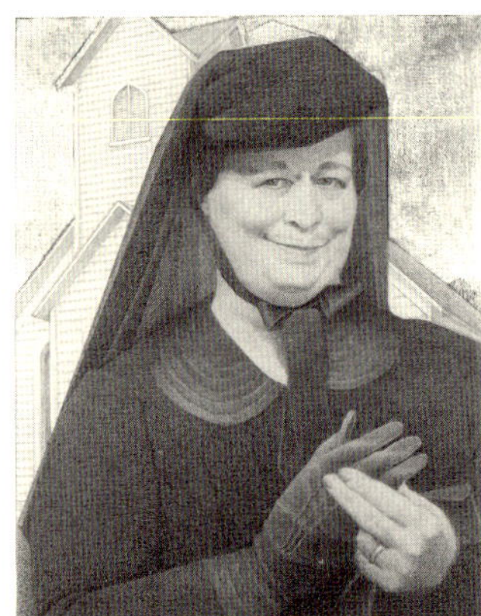

Figure 7 The Good Influence

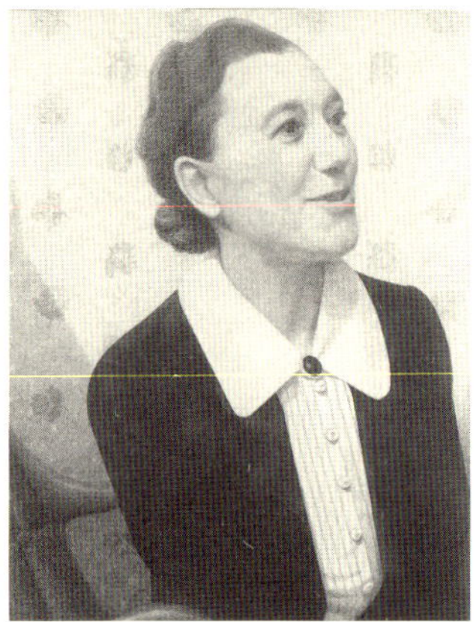

Figure 8 Practical Idealist

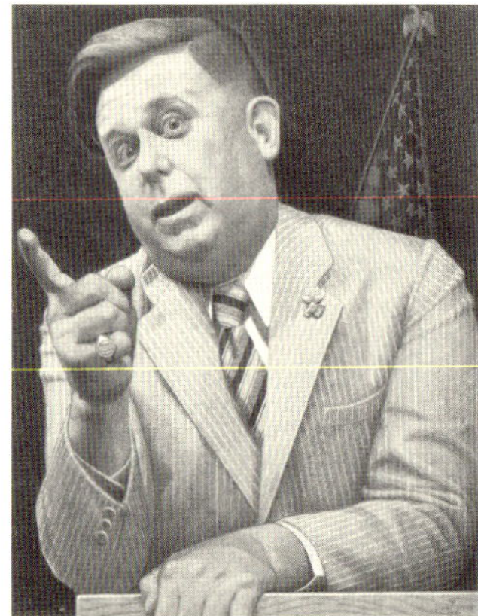

Figure 9 Booster

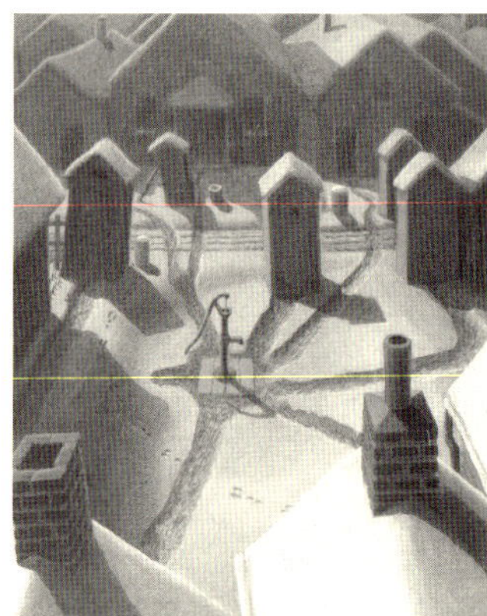

Figure 10 Village Slums

Chapter 2 Grant Wood's *Main Street*

In 1936, Grant Wood (1891-1942) did something he'd been urged to do for several years. Soon after his sudden rise to fame as the creator of the 1930 painting, *American Gothic*, observers noted the affinity between his art and Sinclair Lewis's writing and, since then, had encouraged a collaboration between the two Midwesterners. People could see that both men were insightful interpreters of the American Midwest, though Lewis had been well known since the publication of his novel, *Main Street*, in 1920 and Wood's fame was much more recent. And, since both were themselves Midwesterners, their commentary on their region and the sorts of people to be found there was regarded as authentic. Their work was both serious and entertaining, appealing to the cognoscenti as well as the folk. Both had their detractors, of course, who seemed to figuratively hold their noses as they read Lewis's accounts of Midwestern existence or looked at Wood's depictions of ordinary Iowans in their undramatic landscape. But for many Americans, whether highbrow critics, businessmen, or clubwomen, Wood and Lewis represented the cultural emissaries of, from, and to the Midwest. They were very popular.

What was regarded as a natural coupling was accomplished by New York publisher George Macy when he proposed a special edition of Lewis's signature work, *Main Street*, illustrated by the drawings of Grant Wood, to be offered by his Limited Editions Club. Both men were amenable to the project, so it went forward. Wood agreed to produce illustrations (nine were published) to be interspersed throughout the book, and Lewis agreed to write a new introduction. Further, Macy and his printers, the Lakeside Press of Chicago, allowed Wood to contribute to the design of the book. His drawings were produced mainly in 1936, with the last arriving in New York in March of 1937, and by May, the book was published and being favorably reviewed. The complete series of the *Main Street* drawings has never been shown together until this exhibition at the Brunnier Art Museum. Prior to the publication in the Limited Editions Club book in May of 1937, five of the drawings (*General Practitioner*, *The Good Influence*, *Main Street Mansion*, *The Perfectionist*, and *Sentimental Yearner*) were exhibited at the Art Institute of Chicago's yearly exhibition of works on paper.[1] Eight of the drawings were exhibited at the Memorial Union at the University of Iowa in May of 1937, [2] and then they were dispersed, not to be together again for almost seventy years, even in the retrospective exhibition organized by the Art Institute of Chicago in the fall of 1942 after Wood's death in February of that year. [3]

The drawings were occasionally exhibited individually, but like Wood's art and reputation in the 1940s, '50s, and '60s, they seemed to have become invisible in the American culturescape. Like most pre-World War II realists, Wood (who had been the most widely known of these painters) nearly disappeared from the literature, the market, and the consciousness of the art world. [4] Not until the 1970s, with James Dennis's well-illustrated book, *Grant Wood: A Study in American Art and Culture* (1975, reprinted 1986), did the artist receive a serious and scholarly examination. He benefited further from the overall renewed interest in art of the Depression era, as scholars and an American public who had not struggled through the Depression and World War II became willing to examine that part of our history more closely. Wanda Corn's exhibition *Grant Wood: The Regionalist Vision* (which appeared in cultural showcases like the Whitney Museum of American Art in New York, the Minneapolis Institute of Arts, the Art Institute of Chicago, and the deYoung Memorial Museum in San Francisco) finally ended most of the official art historical sneering and scorn Wood had endured for years. By far the most complete display of Wood's *oeuvre*, Corn's exhibition included seven of the original *Main Street* drawings.

Since Corn's exhibition, there has been no comprehensive Wood exhibition or study, although several smaller ones have expanded the literature on his work and affirmed the critical assessment of his stature as an artist. Notable is Brady Roberts's *Grant Wood: An American Master Revealed* of 1995 that reproduced a number of drawings and contributed important information on the artist's materials and techniques. James Dennis's 1986 *Grant Wood* reproduced more of the artist's drawings than any other publication, but the author's main topic was the paintings. Little has been written specifically about his drawings, even about those which are not preparatory to other works but are intended as finished and complete works of art, like the *Main Street* series. Part of the reason for this lack of commentary is that the drawings are much less well known than the paintings, and they have generally not been studied as sources for evaluating the final painting. In fact, there exists no reliable listing of Wood's drawings. His careful, disciplined approach to his mature compositions (after 1929) suggests that he made many sketches, studies, and finished drawings. A photograph from 1941 (Figure 11) suggests the extent to which he relied on drawings in the development of his paintings. In the photograph, Wood draws a large sketch for his 1941 painting, *Spring in the Country*. Tacked to an adjacent board is a large image of its companion painting, *Spring in Town*. [5] Above *Spring in Town* are four smaller drawings of three figures and a building that are clearly studies for the two paintings. The photograph confirms that in at least two paintings, Wood worked out his compositions precisely before setting brush to canvas. (The prominence of the sketches in this photograph may also, in some measure, be Wood's response to comments disparaging his drawing skills.) The high level of development in these sketches reveals an investment of time and attention that

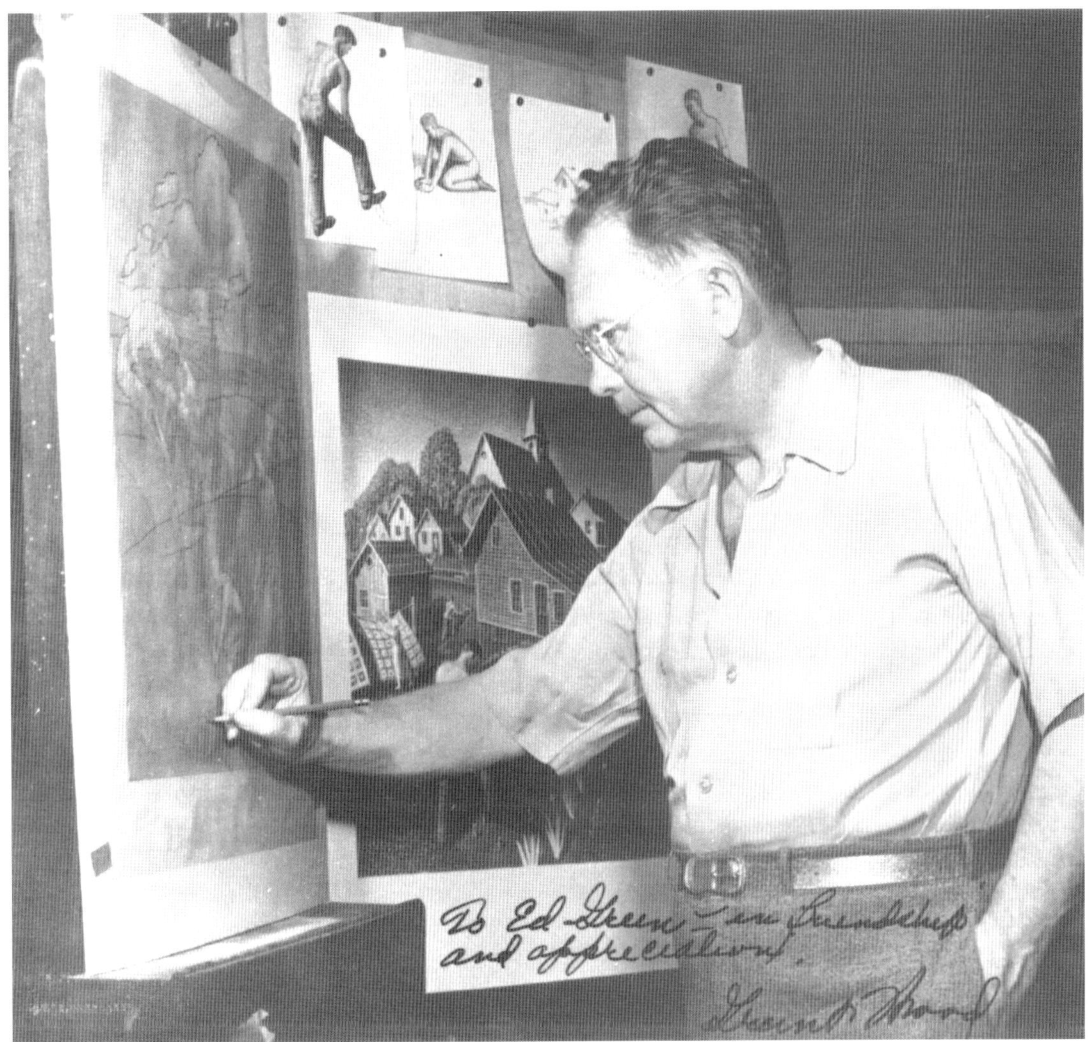

Figure 11 Wood making studies for Spring in the Country*, c. 1940-1941.*

would negate the practice of simply throwing away this preparative material. It is curious, then, how few drawings are actually well known (and reproduced) in the literature on the artist. It might be expected that there would be stacks of drawings and sketchbooks in which he recorded the abundant ideas that came from his visual imagination, but they seem to be missing. We know that he planned to paint more pictures than he actually did paint, and surely some of those projects were sketched out in some form, but if so, these drawings are largely unlocated. When unknown drawings do come to light, they, along with those we already know, suggest how prolific Wood must have been as a draftsman and how important the drawing process was to his artistic being.

As will be discussed, Wood saw these drawings not as preparatory works but as finished works of art, complete in themselves. He also made it clear that he did not regard them primarily as illustrations. The *Main Street* drawings were not intended as mere enrichment to Sinclair Lewis's novel, but were Wood's interpretation of those characters and of the "types" of small towners they represented. He was not just making pictures for Lewis's story, but presenting an artistic and intellectual, if not literary, testament of his own. Wood did produce illustrations and book jackets, but his aim in those was fundamentally different from that of the *Main Street* series. These illustrations, while important and worth exploring, are not the topic of this exhibition catalogue. The exclusion of these illustrations is primarily out of respect for Wood's own characterization of the *Main Street* drawings: he did not want them to be seen as illustrations merely, but as works of art on their own, to be valued separately from the role they played the 1937 Limited Editions Club publication.

All of the *Main Street* drawings are the same size (approximately 20 x 16 inches) and all are on the brown kraft paper that was a trademark of Wood's practice. Most of his works on paper (except his lithographs) are on this support. He encouraged the other artists who worked with him on the New Deal art programs to employ this paper, and he required it of his students. The critic Thomas Craven, in his discussion of Wood's teaching methods, wrote, "There is no formality in his teaching, and no nonsense. His pupils are put to work and trained to follow the old precept of trial and error. They are also initiated into the virtues of brown wrapping paper, which, he swears, is the best of all surfaces for drawing. 'I use nothing else,' he explains. 'It has a fine tone, and it is free from impurities, and for the classroom, you can't beat it. My pupils use it by the roll — it is dirt-cheap. Thus they form the habit of experimenting boldly, whereas the fear of spoiling an expensive paper would cramp their style.'"[6] This cheap brown paper has held up amazingly well and has presented no overwhelming conservation problems so far.[7] Wood affixed the *Main Street* drawings to masonite, probably with gesso; some of the drawings have been detached from this support.

As for the media used in the drawings themselves, the exact materials cannot be definitively established without further examination and analysis. Where analysis has taken place, it appears that the primary medium is not graphite, but wax crayon. In several of the drawings, there appears to be a base of black-blue ink for some areas (the blouse in *Practical*

Idealist, for example). Graphite, charcoal, and chalk were used incidentally (and are not found in every drawing), and gouache may have been sparingly applied. It is impossible to convey in reproduction the complexity of the surfaces of the drawings. They are worked over with thousands of small marks to build up the form and, most intriguingly, to nuance the color. Actually, when examined closely, there is no "color" in the drawings except for the brown color of the paper. [8] In several of the drawings, a distinct blue tone is observed (*The Perfectionist*, *General Practitioner*) and in others, yellow or even reddish tones appear to be present (*Booster*, *Main Street Mansion)*. Upon closer examination, however, these pigments are not apparent. There is only Wood's layering of black and white marks, sometimes broken, sometimes blended. In some early exhibitions of the drawings, the media is listed only as "black and white pencils." [9] While confusing and apparently incorrect, this information may be essentially accurate in that black and white *are* the only colors used, and the term "pencils" may have been employed in a loose, generic sense. In a few instances, pentimenti occur that indicate Wood reconsidered certain aspects while the drawing was under way (the church steeple in *The Good Influence*, for example). It is nearly certain that Wood would have developed his compositions through several phases with numerous sketches. With the exception of *Village Slums*, however, none of these drawings have come to light. In any case, the drawings are marvels of technique and reflect a level of skill and pictorial authority that may not always have been attributed to Grant Wood. It is hoped that the search for more Wood drawings will quicken and that they will become more widely available through exhibitions and publications. His drawings, as supportive material or as independent works, merit more research and more recognition. (Where possible and appropriate in this catalogue, the drawings for the paintings have been reproduced rather than the paintings; for example, *Adolescence*.)

This exhibition does not remedy the paucity of study on Wood's drawings, but it does begin to correct the situation by examining his best known and — we would argue — most accomplished drawings: those for a special edition of Sinclair Lewis's quintessential American novel, *Main Street*. As pointed out earlier, these two artists were natural collaborators; they both created "images" of the Midwest that still define the region and its inhabitants. Whether Lewis's and Wood's interpretations are right or wrong, whether Midwesterners or outsiders still regard them as authentic, and whether their work is recognized as the Midwest of yesterday rather than today, the ubiquitous presumptions about Midwestern character and Midwestern lives are still active and still represented somehow by *Main Street*.

Information on DeLong Citations

NWG: Nan Wood Graham, the artist's sister and compiler of the Scrapbooks housed now at the Davenport Museum of Art. Each Scrapbook is numbered, as are the pages within it.

Reel and frame numbers refer to microfilm from the Archives of American Art (AAA).

Numbers in parenthesis {1} refer to page numbers in the 1937 Limited Editions Club edition of the novel. These numbers also appear in the 1965 edition by The Easton Press (MBI, Inc.), Norwalk, Conn.

Chapter 2 Notes

1. *The Sixteenth International Exhibition. Water Colors, Pastels, Drawings and Monotypes*. Art Institute of Chicago, March 18-May 16, 1937. #508 *General Practitioner*; #509 *The Good Influence*; #510 *Main Street Mansion*; #511 *The Perfectionist*; #512 *Sentimental Yearner*. The medium of all of the drawings is given as pencil. Unless these are the sketches provided in January of 1936 to George Macy — and there is no reason that they would be since Wood had completed eight final drawings and sent them to Lakeside Press by December of 1936 — all of these drawings use media besides pencil. What is termed "pencil" is likely wax crayon. Because the drawings were in Chicago at Lakeside Press by December, 1936, it would have been convenient to submit them to the Art Institute's jury for the March exhibition. *The Good Influence* is given a full-page reproduction in the exhibition catalogue. My thanks to Bart Ryckbosch of the Art Institute for supplying materials related to this exhibition.

2. No exhibition catalogue or printed material of any sort has emerged from this exhibition at the University of Iowa Memorial Union. Information about the exhibition comes from accounts of it in the student newspaper, the *Daily Iowan*, especially the articles by Audrey Hamilton: "Wood Draws for 'Main Street;' Iowa Artist Illustrates Special Edition of Lewis' Novel," May 22, 1937, 5 and "Professor Grant Wood Illustrates 'Main Street,'" June 16, 1937, 5. *Village Slums* was not included in the exhibition. My thanks to David McCartney, University Archivist at the University of Iowa, for his assistance in researching this exhibition.

3. Of the nine *Main Street* drawings, only *The Good Influence* was in this retrospective exhibition of 48 works. It was loaned by Mr. and Mrs. George Gard De Sylva of Los Angeles and was illustrated (plate III) in the catalogue. *Fifty-third Annual Exhibition of American Paintings and Sculpture*, October 29-December 10, 1942, Art Institute of Chicago.

4. A pioneering study of these artists was Howard E. Wooden's aptly named exhibition catalogue, *The Neglected Generation of American Realist Painters: 1930-1948*, Wichita (Kansas) Art Museum, 1981. Wooden included work by Alexandre Hogue, Gordon Samstag, Edward Lanning, William C. Palmer, and other such artists who had become somewhat obscure, but whose careers have been reassessed in the past decades. Wood was not included in the exhibition, although his Regionalist compatriots, Thomas Hart Benton and John Steuart Curry, were.

5. See McDonald, Julie Jensen with Joan Liffring-Zug Bourret, *Grant Wood and Little Sister Nan*, Iowa City: Penfield Press, 2000, 110.

6. Craven, Thomas, "Grant Wood," *Scribner's Magazine*, vol. CI, no.6, 1937, 16-22, 22.

7. Wood's practice of using brown paper was carried on by at least one of the artists with whom he worked on the Public Works of Art Project. John Vincent Bloom (1906-2002) drew full-scale cartoons on brown kraft paper for both of his post office mural commissions: DeWitt, Iowa, 1937-1939; and Tipton, Iowa, 1939-1940. When these large works (48 x 160 inches and 48 x 145 inches) were rediscovered after being stored in Bloom's attic for over fifty years, they were in remarkably stable condition. They were able to be unrolled and displayed in his retrospective exhibition before undergoing restoration. See DeLong, Lea Rosson, *John Bloom: An Eye for Life*, exhibition guide, Ames, Iowa: Brunnier Art Museum, 2002.

8. I am grateful to Debra Evans, conservator at the Fine Arts Museums of San Francisco, for sharing her knowledge and, especially, for alerting me to Wood's media and the lack of pigmentation (other than black and

white) in *The Perfectionist*. I am also deeply appreciative of the tutorial provided to me by Elizabeth Buschor, paper conservator at the Upper Midwest Conservation Association, in the examination of *Sentimental Yearner*.

9. In the catalogue for *The Sixteenth International Exhibition* at the Art Institute of Chicago in 1937, "pencil" was given as the medium for all five drawings shown (See Note 1). In the *Daily Iowan* articles by Audrey Hamilton, the media were given as "black and white pencils." If this information on the media was seriously inaccurate in the Art Institute's catalogue, Wood could have had the opportunity to correct it before it appeared in the *Daily Iowan*. The fact that "black and white" were the only terms added to the media description suggests that Wood recognized the use of the term "pencils" in a generic sense.

16

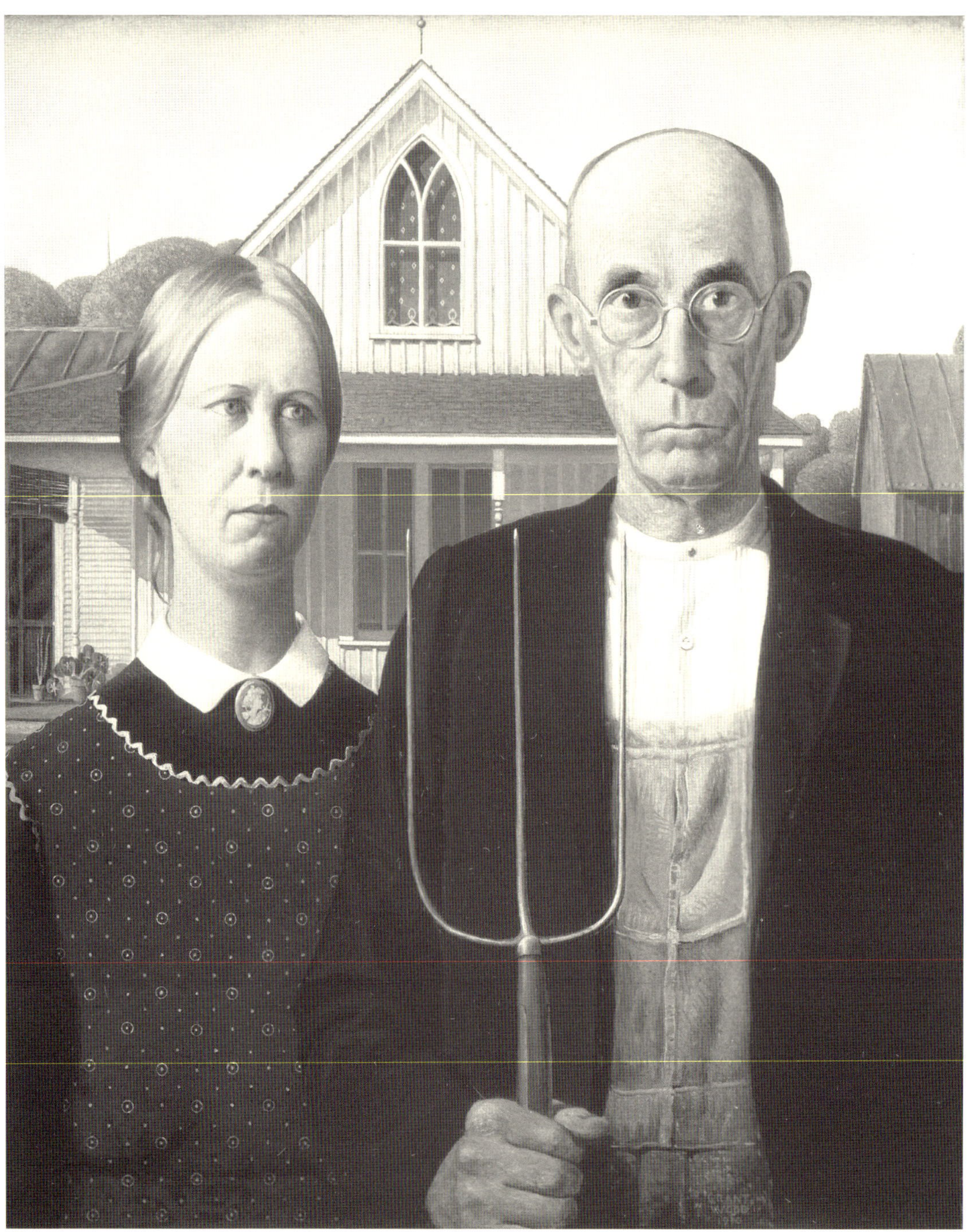

Figure 12 American Gothic, *1930*

Chapter 3
Midwestern Affinities: Art and Literature

The earliest connection made in print between the paintings of Grant Wood and the novels of Sinclair Lewis is found in an editorial in the Boston *Herald* just after the Art Institute of Chicago awarded its Norman Wait Harris medal (and a $300 prize) to *American Gothic* (Figure 12). The instant popularity of this painting elevated Wood from a well-liked local painter in Cedar Rapids, Iowa to a national art star. As far away as Boston (whose residents we might assume to be unsympathetic to — and uninterested in — the Midwest), *American Gothic* was regarded as encapsulating *something* (it is still ill defined) about America's heartland, indeed about America's essence. The two figures in the painting were seen by critics as "a portrait less of two individuals" than as the embodiment of a distinct state of mind: "The longer you look at them, the more you realize they might come from many parts of this country — but from no other [country]." Characterizing the painting as "social satire," the writer suggested, "Sinclair Lewis ought surely to purchase [*American Gothic*] out of his Nobel Prize money."[1]

In 1930 — the same year that Wood's art won fame and a place in the permanent collection of the Art Institute of Chicago — Sinclair Lewis became the first American to receive the Nobel Prize for literature. Many commentators felt Lewis had won because his novels confirmed European condescension towards Americans as untutored, acultural boobs (or, to use a term Lewis brought into common use: as "Babbitts"). By some critics, Lewis was considered less a substantial literary figure and more as merely a satirist who had a knack for "reporting" American speech and the ersatz, materialistic values it communicated. When Wood appeared with *American Gothic* the same year Lewis won a Nobel, it seemed that Lewis's word picture of American life had found a visual counterpart. Or, perhaps we might say, Wood "illustrated" what Lewis "reported." Critics recognized from the beginning that both artists were conflicted about the America they presented in their work, but that seemed to make them even more compatible. The Boston writer ended his commentary by disparaging the "modernistic" paintings that surrounded *American Gothic* in the Chicago exhibition and wondered why anyone would look at them when they could see the Old Masters elsewhere in the museum. "If you happen to have passed the El Grecos on the way to the gallery, why bother to look at the modernistic canvases? El Greco did it all, and so much better. But El Greco couldn't have painted *American Gothic* any more than Cervantes could have written *Main Street*." [2] This belief that both Lewis and Wood had captured something that was distinctively American (though largely negative) was to be often repeated over the next years.

The year following *American Gothic*, 1931, Wood solidified his position as an important new artist and a sharp commentator on the American scene, particularly the Midwest. He followed his picture of the sober farmer and his wife with *Appraisal* (Figure 13), showing an encounter between a country woman and a city woman in which the city woman "appraises" the hen being sold by the country woman who, in turn, is making her own assessment of the city visitor. The subtle study of character, emotional state, and social class that Wood later infused into his *Main Street* portraits is presaged here (as is his comparison of hens and certain types of women). *The Birthplace of Herbert Hoover*, *Victorian Survival*, *Fall Plowing*, and *Young Corn* were all important paintings of 1931 that showed the flowering of Wood's visual imagination and his competence as the standard bearer of a new kind of American imagery. With *The Midnight Ride of Paul Revere*, he expanded his purview beyond the Midwest and into the stories and fables that lay at the foundation of American culture. It is not surprising that so many observers felt that Wood was a unique figure who could combine distinctly American subjects with a style that was both "readable" and accomplished. The year 1931, then, was an *annus mirabilis* [3] for Wood, with the production of so many major paintings and a happy kind of fame.

As his fame grew, the Cedar Rapids artist went beyond his locality to make speeches and judge competitions where he explained his own art and expressed his hopes for a springing of "regional" art throughout the country. During a visit to Omaha in November, 1932 to judge the Joslyn Memorial Museum's exhibition of Nebraska and Iowa artists, Wood was questioned about a recent painting which had caused almost as much of a sensation as *American Gothic*. His painting, *Daughters of Revolution* (Figure 14), chuckled at the pretenses of the Daughters of the American Revolution (D.A.R.), an organization whose members proudly trace their ancestry back to soldiers who fought in the American Revolution (1775-1783). The painting had its genesis in a 1928 incident when the local Cedar Rapids D.A.R. took offense at Wood's use of German craftsmen to fabricate stained glass windows for a war memorial (Germany had been our enemy in the Great War of 1917-1918, the ladies reasoned). The artist in turn took offense at their petty parochialism and, in 1931, produced an image that, beneath its genial first impression, was as caustic and barbed as any painting in American history. In *Daughters of Revolution*, Wood confirmed that he was not just a "booster" of the regional scene, but had the intelligence and honesty to see both sides of his fellow citizens.

He explained to the *Omaha World-Herald* that the flaccid, but opinionated women in *Daughters of Revolution* were not actually portraits, but were composites derived from studying "scores of faces to arrive at what...was typical of the genre." With statements like this and

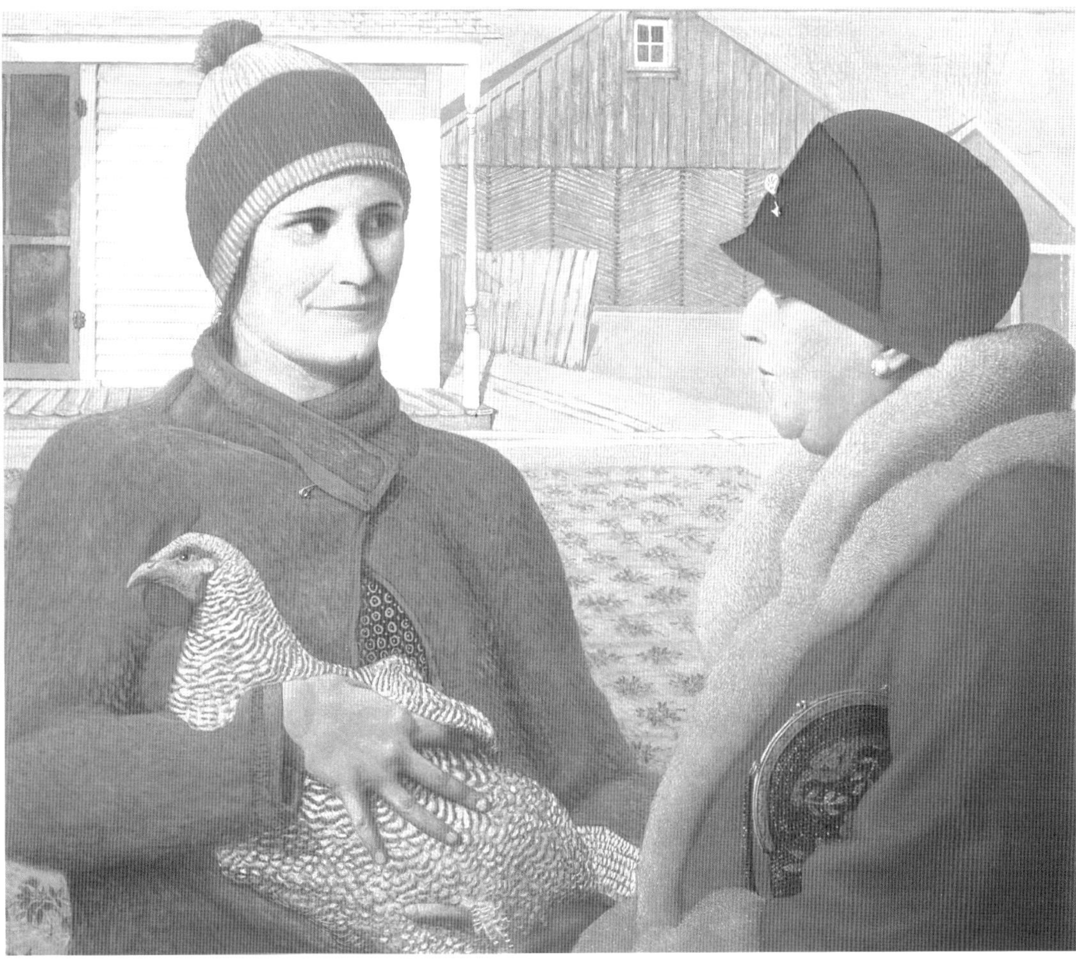

Figure 13 Appraisal, *1931*

20

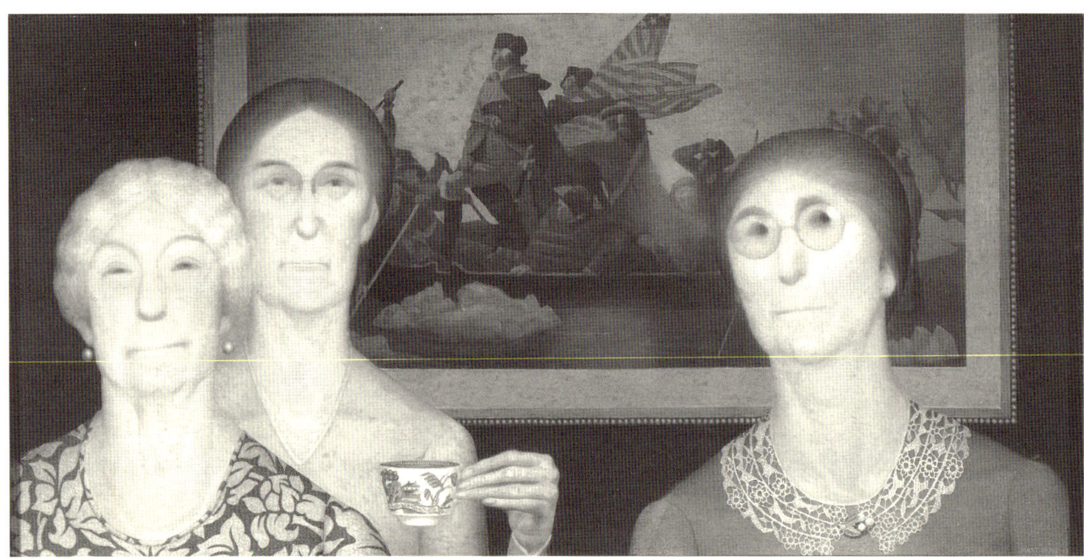

Figure 14 Daughters of Revolution, *1932*

the evidence of the painting itself, Wood began to be regarded by some as a satirist. Without denying *elements* of satire in his work, he shied away from that label, perhaps because he thought of it as too confining and "easy" and because he didn't want to be seen as simply a critic of his own kind, dealing in clichés about the Midwest. "Satirist" was indeed too single dimensional for an artist who had revealed his complexity and ambition. The newspaper reported Wood's assertion that his painting "has no other source...except his desire to portray realistically, with a dash of his native satire, various aspects of American life. He has no grudge and does not set himself up as a critic." Grudge or not, at that point in his career, Wood planned to continue making studies of the types of people around him although he was determined to avoid the obvious, over-parodied ones: "Next in the series, he plans to do a painting of a Shrine quartet and of a group of little theater workers. Then, perhaps, a college fraternity group." [4] These ideas for future subject matter suggest that Wood not only knew Lewis's work (he was well read and especially knowledgeable about literature about the Midwest), but also knew that he had already been linked with the writer as a purveyor of Midwestern stereotypes.

When *Daughters of Revolution* was selected for the first Whitney Biennial Exhibition of American Contemporary Painting in 1932, it was widely discussed, and its notoriety continued to build over the next year. It was seen as a clever, good-natured, and painfully accurate depiction of a comfortable narrowness that had come to be associated with the Midwest. Wood had taken the complex idea of snobbish, complacent women who were incapable of entertaining notions of revolution of any sort and put it into a visual form that could be understood by anyone. Having created a painting embodying complicated issues, he rejected the oversimplified label of "satirist"— even though the public embraced him as a visual satirist on a par with the creator of *Main Street* and *Babbitt*. When it was shown at the Carnegie International exhibition in the Fall of 1933, the poet and critic Louis Untermeyer, who "dote [d] on the satirical in either art or literature," [5] declared it a "complete Sinclair Lewis novel." [6]

Wood often fared better with literature critics than with art critics. Just a few weeks after Untermeyer's praise, the prominent art critic and Princeton University art professor, Frank Jewett Mather, also lectured in Pittsburgh on the Carnegie International, but he did not rank *Daughters of Revolution* highly. "'It isn't a very good picture, but it is excellent satire.'" Mather's instructions to his Pittsburgh audience on how to assess artists (Wood, for instance) are similar to the way Lewis had been judged as a writer. There were two classes of artists, he said: one was "'the observer and reporter' who discovers themes in nature, plucks out the interest, paints what he sees — valuable because his precise, vivid insight enriches duller souls with the 'miracles' of every-day experience (such reporting is Artist Wood's *Daughters of Revolution*)." The second was "the 'creator or constructor' who shows you something you could never see yourself by putting things and colors together to show the way he feels." [7] One of the most common and persistent criticisms of Lewis was and still is today that his work is more "reporting" than true creation, a charge that Wood has also endured.

Numerous literary figures, even ones as unlikely as the expatriate modernist Gertrude Stein (1874-1946), thought highly of Grant Wood. The news of her good opinion was conveyed to the University of Iowa in the summer of 1934 by Rousseau Voorhies, a representative of the Macmillan Publishing Company for whom Wood had designed the book jacket of Sterling North's novel, *Plowing On Sunday*. According to local news reports, Voorhies had recently returned from "a two years' stay in Paris, most of which was spent in Miss Stein's famous studio around which revolves and evolves the most progressive contributions to the world of art and letters." [8] There, he learned that Stein "loves America, but only the Midwest group" and that, for her, Wood was "the first artist of America." The good news, reported the student newspaper, "comes to this cornfield campus through Rousseau Voorhies, American writer and lecturer and friend of Miss Stein: [she] believes that [Wood] is first from the standpoint of time, because there was never really any other American artist before — the others were really imitators of Europe. She believes he is the first from the standpoint of quality, because his is true art — the others...ape Europe." Voorhies elaborated on Stein's reported esteem for the Iowan: "'Grant Wood,' she told me 'is not an imitator, but a creator. He is not only a satirical artist, but one who has a wonderful detachment from life in general which is necessary to create the best of art.'" [9] In relaying these remarks, perhaps Voorhies hoped to counter opinions such as those of Professor Mather; certainly they seem calculated to lift Wood's recognition beyond a simple regional satirist and "reporter" into the ranks of true creators — an elevation that Stein would have surely accorded to herself. Later in 1934, Stein planned to present a lecture at the University of Iowa and meet Grant Wood, but bad weather prevented her appearance. [10]

Voorhies's promotion of Wood's reputation was probably not without self-interest. As a literary agent, he may have been negotiating with Wood for the publication of *Return from Bohemia*, a proposed autobiography. (In the following year, Wood contracted with Doubleday Doran to publish the book.) Perhaps Voorhies was also hoping to arrange for future book illustrations or jacket designs; certainly part of his job on this visit must have been publicizing Macmillan's soon-to-be published *Plowing on Sunday*.

One of Wood's champions in the literary world was Christopher Morley (Figure 15) of *The Saturday Review of Literature*, who became a personal friend of the artist's after meeting him in Iowa City in 1934. [11] In his regular column, "The Bowling Green," he often wrote about Wood and drew attention to literary and artistic events in Iowa, applauding the regional movement in both art and literature. [12] He was also the author (under the name of P.E.G. Quercus) of "Trade Winds," a weekly column of news from the publishing industry in which Wood and other Iowa matters occasionally appeared. Another editor at the *Review* was William Rose Benet (Figure 20) who had a weekly column on poetry and who also kept in touch with Midwestern developments. [13] Morley was converted to Regional-

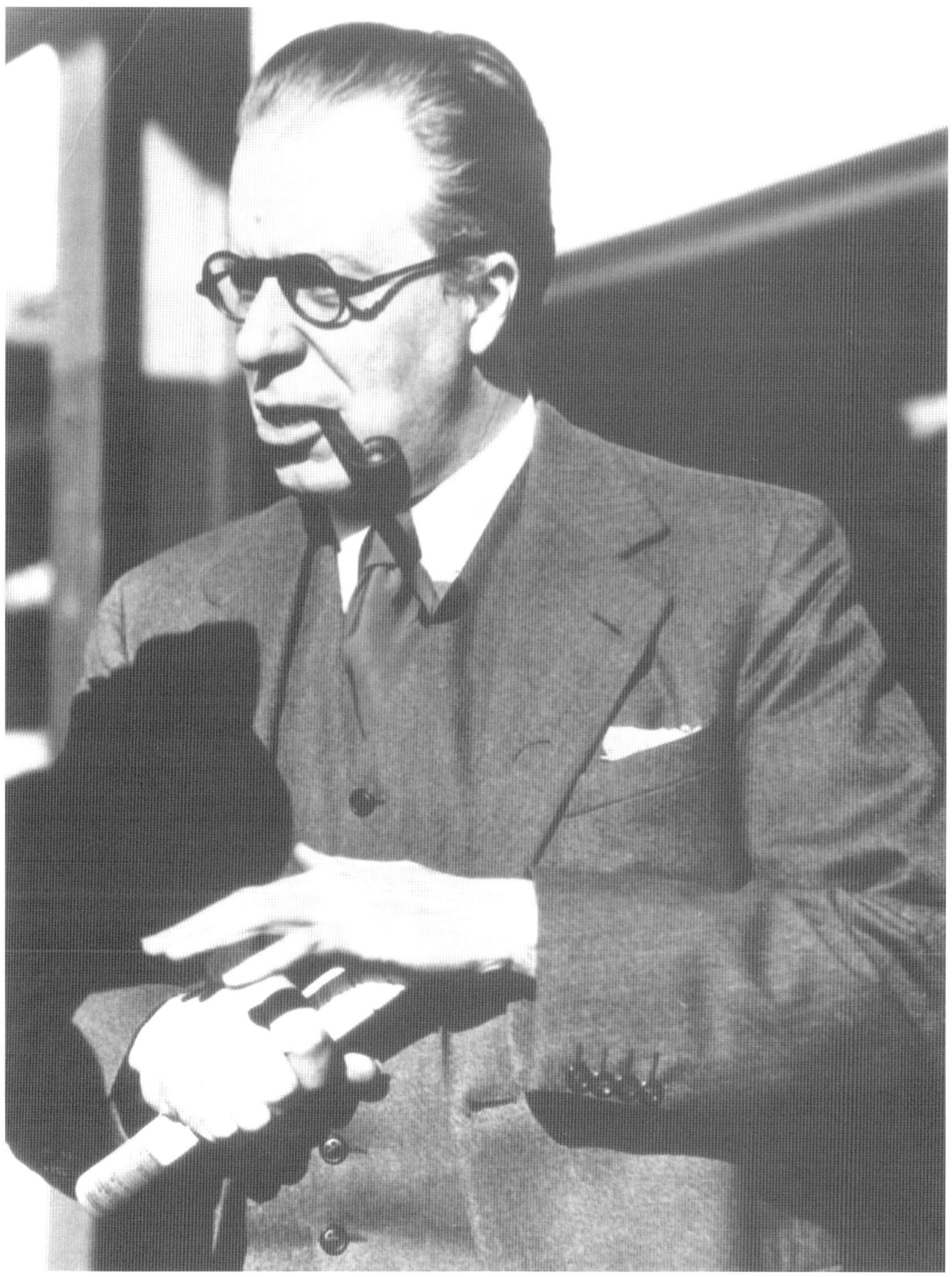

Figure 15 Christopher Morley, an editor at The Saturday Review of Literature, *c.1934*

ism after his 1934 visit during which he was struck by the beauty of the countryside and, especially "the enchanted village of Waubeek, where Jay Sigmund, poet and story teller and insurance official, has preserved an old family cottage exactly as it was seventy years." [14] Sigmund, a friend of Wood's from his Cedar Rapids days, was among the regional literary figures who had most influenced Wood's thinking and whose investment in Waubeek, like Wood's in Stone City, was physical evidence of the idea among regionalists that indigenous culture should be treasured and maintained.

Morley was also delighted by the Society for the Prevention of Cruelty to Speakers and its clubroom which had been decorated by Wood. (Figure 16) Part of the Times Club at the University of Iowa, the S.P.C.S. invited cultural figures of all sorts, but especially writers, to visit Iowa and lecture to students and the public. After his visit, Morley reminisced, "The Times Club of the University of Iowa has had the good heart and good sense to organize a Society for the Prevention of Cruelty to Speakers. When a visitor is due to speak in that town they send him a questionnaire to find out his tastes and preferences in the matter of hospitality. Does he wish to be met, 'entertained,' dined and dress-shirted? or does he prefer to meditate until the dreadful hour? It would be well if many other clubs and hosts had as delicate a sense of kindness as this." [15] A few months later, Morley published a photograph of the clubroom, commenting on its decor. "The Times Club, ...remarking the fact that visiting mandarins were given insufficient chance to collect their wits before appearing in public, set aside a suite in the most comfortable style of the Flying Trapeze era as a paregoric influence upon any traveling spellbinder. Professor [Frank Luther] Mott reports that it has recently been enjoyed by Thomas Benton, MacKinlay Kantor, Stephen Benet, Gilbert Seldes and others." [16] (Figures 17-20) Wood apparently enjoyed a cordial relationship not only with Morley but with *The Saturday Review*, in whose pages he and his activities were often mentioned. His visits to their offices during his New York trips were reported, [17] and when his Regionalist pamphlet, *Revolt Against the City*, was published, that also was noted. [18] Perhaps one indication of Wood's influence at the magazine is the fact that he was able to persuade them to use an image by one of his students, Richard Gates, on the cover of the April 4, 1935 issue. [19]

Wood's art, as we have seen, aroused a remarkable amount of comment from literary figures. They were engaged by his subject matter, his style, and his ability to make his art meaningful to such a wide range of people. From his first shower of fame with *American Gothic*, his skills as a storyteller were judged to far exceed those of just an illustrator. Even when he did illustrations — and made no pretense of creating anything loftier — he was still seen as an artist with a compelling subject (and style) and not merely an "illustrator" of other peoples' ideas and characters. In the art world, on the other hand, there were those who persistently saw him as nothing more than a glorified illustrator. Perhaps part of Wood's appeal to literary figures was the way he presented himself and his art in literary terms. He often spoke of writing and painting in the same breath (especially in the context of region-

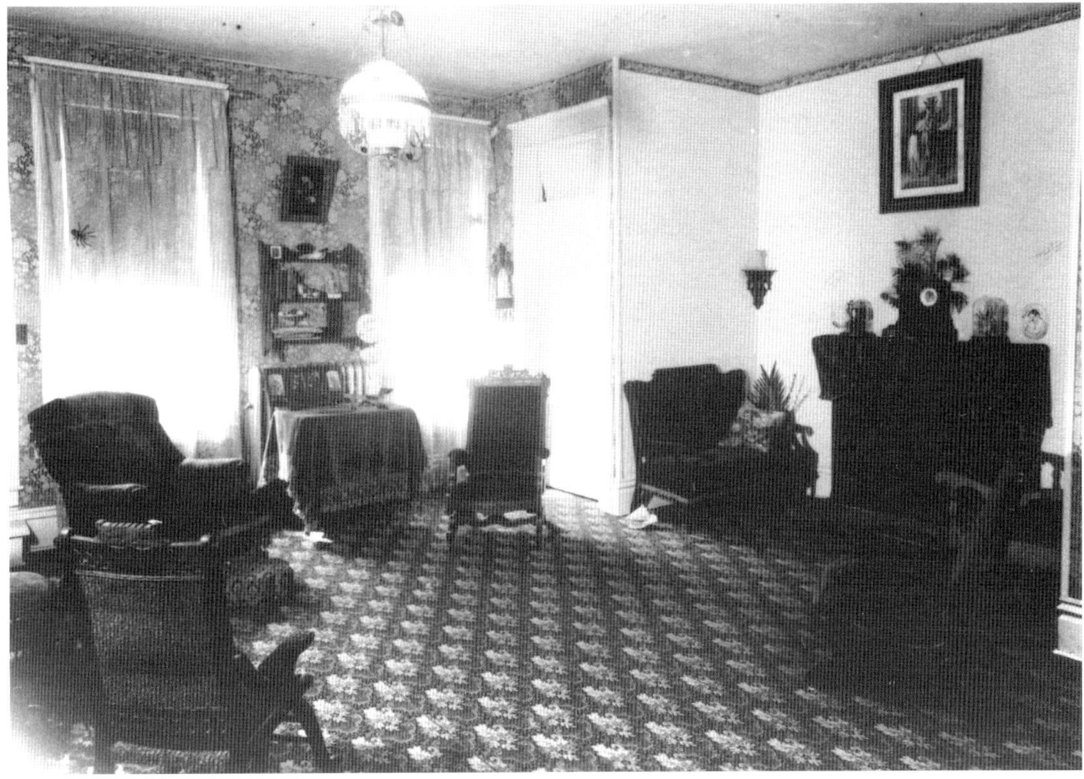

Figure 16 The Wood-designed clubroom of the Society for the Prevention of Cruelty to Speakers, Iowa City, c.1934

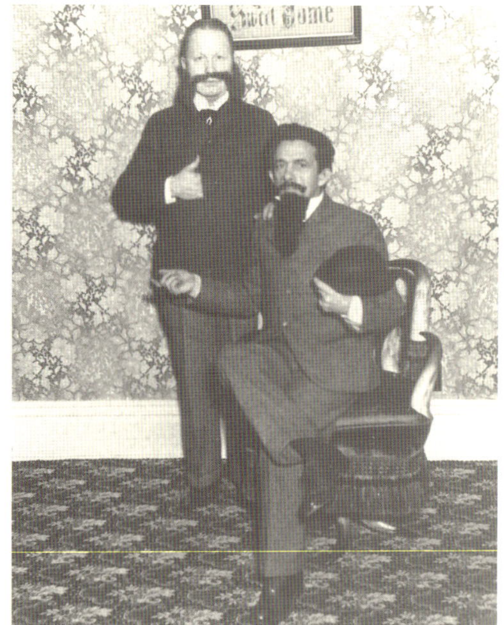

Figure 17 Grant Wood (standing) and Thomas Hart Benton (sitting)

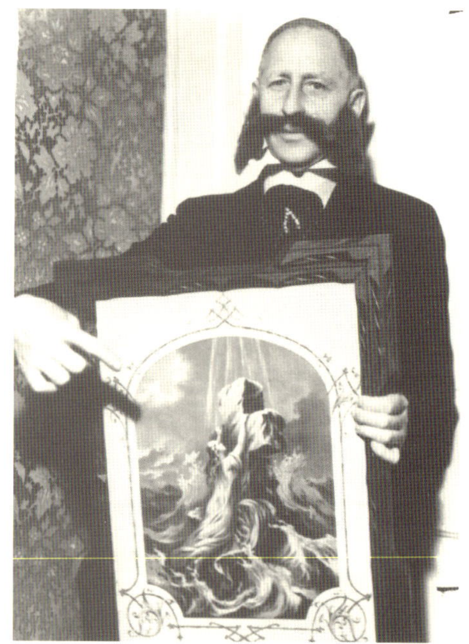

Figure 18 Thomas Craven

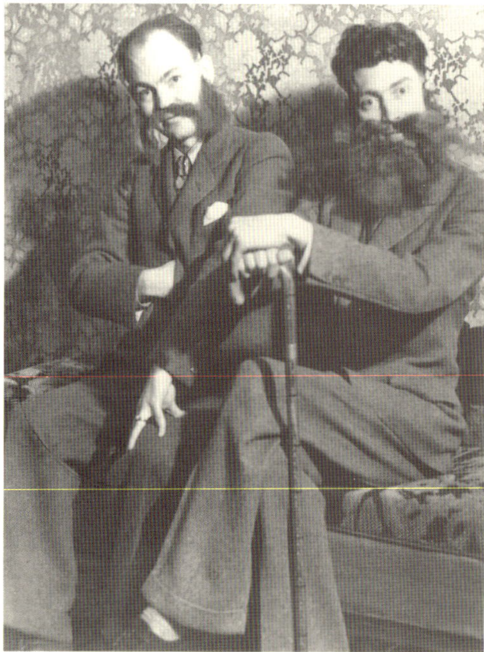

Figure 19 Thomas W. Duncan (left) and MacKinlay Kantor (right)

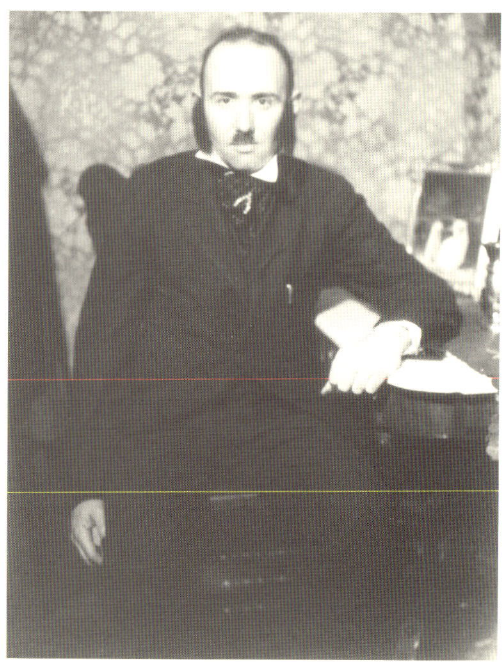

Figure 20 William Rose Benet

alism) and used terms like "editorial comment" and "storytelling" in discussing his own work. It is often noted that his personal associations were as likely to be with writers (from poets to journalists) as with artists. As a younger artist known only locally, he formed friendships with nearby writers, notably Jay Sigmund, and admired those who, like Ruth Suckow, had a wider reputation. When he became a celebrity himself, his encounters were with figures (such as Sinclair Lewis) who enjoyed national and international recognition. Wood's presence at the University of Iowa during the 1930s was regarded as a "draw" for famous writers as well as (perhaps more than) famous artists. His activities as a charter member of the Society for the Prevention of Cruelty to Speakers are well known. It appears that Wood was proactive in establishing himself in literary circles; his recognition among people of letters was not incidental: he himself encouraged it.

In the spring of 1931, just a few months after *American Gothic* had burst on to the scene, Wood presented a lecture in Des Moines about his art and his budding Regionalist philosophy. He told the Iowa Artists' Club that Midwestern artists who wanted their distinctive art about their distinctive region to be recognized needed to be "editorial writers." He warned them to be aware that Eastern critics were inclined to think, "that anything originating west of the Mississippi river [sic] must be crudity itself." He championed the "story telling picture," but cautioned that regional artists must not be content with just telling the story of their culture. To be taken seriously, their stories must be well chosen and their style reflect their understanding of modern styles, particularly abstraction. According to a newspaper article covering his lecture, "The new art [of the Middlewest] embodies a literary feeling, he said. But it must also be decorative if it is to be truly artistic, Mr. Wood declared....'The story telling picture is the logical reaction to the abstractions of the modernists....But the new art must not be merely a tinted photography[sic], it must also be decorative if it is to be truly artistic.'" [20] According to James Dennis, Wood's use of the term "decorative" should usually be interpreted to mean "abstract," reflecting the art education theories the artist absorbed in his earliest training. [21] When Wood used the term "abstraction" in the preceding statement, he was probably not referring to the fundamentals of form that he himself incorporated into his art. He was probably referring to styles such as cubism, which moved beyond the simplifying and reducing of visual form into what Wood would regard as distortion. The abstracting and simplifying stylizations of European artists such as Picasso and Matisse were not always judged as attempts to hone form to its simplest, most fundamental essence, but as simply misshapen nonsense. When Europeans such as Mondrian and Kandinsky moved past abstraction into non-objectivity, many Americans regarded their art as obviously ludicrous and not fit to be called art at all.

Wood may have found modernism's lack of narrative, subject, or story even more unsatisfying than its abstracted and simplified form. By exhorting his fellow heartland artists to infuse stories and editorial comment (a kind of literary component) into their art, he hoped to provide an alternative to what many Americans regarded as incomprehensible "ultramodernism." It has long been noted that Regionalism cannot be identified as truly a *style* of art, except in the broadest sense of simply realism. The definition of Regionalism has mainly to do with subject matter. As an early and prominent exponent of it, Wood showed that his Regionalism was at least as much grounded in literature as in art. Today, the precedents in literature for Regionalism are acknowledged. But perhaps it has been insufficiently recognized how much Wood saw himself as a quasi-literary figure.

If we may judge from one critic's comments on the career-making painting *American Gothic*, Wood succeeded in combining art (with an appropriate level of disguised sophistication) and literature. Writing in 1932 about an exhibition of "contemporary Eastern paintings" in San Diego, critic Arthur Millier probably had novels like *Main Street* and *Babbitt* in mind when he assessed the effect of *American Gothic.*

> You can't imagine a crowd of excited citizens carrying one of these [modern] pictures in a procession to honor the artist, as the Florentines were wont to do.
>
> But you can imagine a crowd of angry Iowans carrying Grant Wood's American Gothic to a bonfire for the man has done something that touches the uninitiated. Here are portraits as relentlessly real as the Flemish portraits by the Van Eycks which he doubtless sought to rival.
>
> The authenticity of this social document (it is no less) comes from Wood's recognition of the long American story which made these firm Iowa people....He was face to face with something real — with such material, in other words, as a good novelist would use.
>
> That does not make it a literary picture. To describe forms and colors in words is one thing, but to organize them in a meaningful picture is a painter's job. And presto — initiate and Philistine both like it. As in the case of a novel, the portrayed are probably the only people who resent it — it is too convincing! [22]

Despite the frequency with which his work was discussed in literary terms (as those above) and despite his camaraderie and even identification with writers, Wood cannot be considered much of an author himself. His ideas and commentary were so widely reported and disseminated that it is surprising how little he actually wrote. Much of what we know about his life and his philosophy comes from newspaper and magazine reports of his lectures and accounts of conversations with critics such as Thomas Craven. The two main written works associated with Wood are his unfinished autobiography, *Return from Bohemia*, and the statement of his Regionalist philosophy, *Revolt Against the City*, both dating from 1935 and neither actually written entirely by the artist. Wood contracted with the Doubleday Doran Company to publish the autobiography and did draw two versions of a "self-portrait with Iowans" that would have been the book cover (both entitled *Return from Bohemia*). But it was his secretary, Park Rinard, who drafted a manuscript that covered only Wood's early life and not his post-*American Gothic* career. These early chapters of the proposed book later (1939) served as Rinard's Masters' thesis at the University of Iowa. *Return from Bohemia* was never published. [23]

Wood's famous Regionalist manifesto, *Revolt Against the City*, espoused his commitment to the idea of artists painting what they knew from their own direct experience rather than adapting themselves to foreign styles and subjects. By this, he did not mean that everyone should paint as he — an Iowan — did, but that each should strive for "genuineness," or "the sincere use of native material by the artist who has command of it." [24] The essay undoubtedly contained Wood's ideas and his hopes for the art of his own time, but Wanda Corn has pointed out that the essay also featured attitudes and phrasings associated with Frank Luther Mott, who may have ghost-written it. [25] At the time of its publication, however, it was assumed to be Wood's writing and was welcomed as an intellectual, artistic rationalization for the still-popular Regionalist movement. Thomas W. Duncan, whose 1934 novel *Plowing On Sunday* boasted a Wood illustration on its book jacket, reviewed the publication and concluded, "I have a hunch this little volume will become a collector's item that will fetch many times its present modest price" (which was 90 cents). [26]

Both *Return from Bohemia* and *Revolt Against the City* were large endeavors that would have taken a considerable amount of time — time that was difficult for Wood to find in the busy year of 1935. There are, however, a few shorter pieces that Wood himself probably did write. [27] An essay, "The Writer and the Painter," appeared in the October, 1935 issue of *American Prefaces; A Journal of Critical and Imaginative Writing*, an Iowa City-based magazine that celebrated and encouraged Midwestern culture. Asked by the editor to comment on "the relation of literature and painting, as it appears to a painter," Wood characterized his article as "rambling notes" but focused on two main concerns. One was the importance of both art and literature in bringing "art back to real life." The other was the necessity for both painter and writer to "see below the surface" so that their creations would achieve universality. "We have to work from the inside out!" he emphasized. To achieve these goals, Wood outlined two necessities: "a definite mental image" and organization of the raw material ("No random 'slice of life' is art"). To show how far an artist might go in securing his mental image in the preparatory stages of a work of art, he offered the example of Thomas Hart Benton's construction of clay models for his painted compositions. For another example: "Sinclair Lewis...spares no pain in his concrete visualization, even going to the extent of building complete models of the houses in which the action of his stories transpires."

His brief essay probably reflects some of Wood's preparation, mental or otherwise, to carry out the commission for the illustrations to *Main Street*. In comments about portraiture specifically, he also seems to be answering the sort of criticism voiced earlier by Mather ("reporters" as opposed to "creators") that had been growing over the years and would soon intensify in a bitter conflict with the University of Iowa Art Department. Perhaps he was sensitive to the fact that his production of paintings had slowed down markedly, and much of his work involved figure drawings and portraits that were to be used as illustrations. Acknowledging the importance of "surface accuracy," he prized more the seeing "below the surface. There, for instance, are two kinds of portrait painters. One kind can paint anybody — any time....The other kind has to acquaint himself profoundly with his subject, or have a personal knowledge of him as a type, and has to know what his subject thinks and feels as well as how he looks. This second kind of painter puts a whole philosophy into his picture, not just a set of features and a complexion. His work has depth." [28] Wood's comment suggests that he had already decided to concentrate on portraits of Midwestern small town types as his illustrations for *Main Street*, and he must have been thinking about how he could bring a fresh, but valid, interpretation to his subject. Further, it provides an idea of how fully Wood gave himself license to interpret the characters in the novel for himself and his drawings.

Not long before his death in 1942 and after he had completed the *Main Street* illustrations, Wood contributed an introduction to a book, *Young Sam Clemens,* which gives some perspective on the importance of literature in his intellectual development. In addition, it presents a good idea of Wood himself as a writer. There is no reason to believe that he did not write it completely himself: it is short and highly personal; it deals more with intellectual matters than biographical ones and thus would be more challenging for another person (such as Rinard or Mott) to convey exactly; no one else has ever claimed to have had a role in producing it; and the style is similar to that found in his correspondence in which he often combines a certain plain-spokenness with vivid, precisely phrased descriptions. Letters that undoubtedly came from his hand show that Wood was an engaging writer who was well able to express himself and be persuasive. That he was quite a well-read person has never been in dispute, and it is clear that he prized good writing.

Young Sam Clemens was written by the son of Samuel Langhorne Clemens (1835-1910) whose pen name, of course, was Mark Twain. In his introduction, Wood declared the eminence that Twain's writing — *The Adventures of Tom Sawyer* (1876) and *Huckleberry Finn* (1885) specifically — had held for him throughout his life. It contains insights into the development of the artist's eye for the world around him and about the internal processes for making judgments about it. His introduction is testimony to the enduring significance in American culture of these two novels for both children and adults. Both are nineteenth century novels, and Wood has often been cited for the nineteenth century, nostalgic, anti-modernist tone of many of his works. Yet, what he reveals in his introduction is that, while the novels did represent a way of life for which Wood had affection, they also alerted him to falsities of Victorian culture. He seems to make four primary points in his discussion. First, he begins with a remembrance of his father that he also included in

Return from Bohemia, recounting how he made the boy return *Grimm's Fairy Tales* because "'we Quakers can read only *true* things.'" [29] The references to his father in his unfinished biography have been read as depicting a repressive parent who cowed the young Grant. [30] That is a reasonable interpretation, but it is also true that in *Return from Bohemia* Wood expresses as much love and reverence for his father as fear. Acknowledging in the 1942 introduction the "narrowness" that forbade the reading of fairy tales, Wood also credits his father with "a rich and tolerant wisdom" since he did not forbid his son to read *Tom Sawyer* and *Huckleberry Finn* although he knew they were fiction. Wood explains, "Some intuition must have informed him that in a broad sense they were 'true things.'" Thus, through this memory, he establishes his solid (sanctioned by his father) belief that literature (and by implication, art) are indeed "true things."

His second point has to do with the "reality" of fiction in the mind of the reader and how that verification is established. As a boy reading about Tom and Huck ("Pity the boy who had to grow up without them!"), Wood recalls how completely he was absorbed into their world. "The world those books created was almost as real to me as that of my mother, ...the collie [dog] Dewey and the...patterned prairie which I knew so well." This conviction was created through the vivid descriptions of both common and uncommon things and through Twain's understanding that for children and certain sorts of adults "everything had a special meaning." Surely this idea is given form in the *Main Street* drawings where every object, every accessory, every item of clothing is a clue for understanding the characters and what Wood wants us to know about them. Thorough description is a constant in the painted stories that Wood tells from *Stone City* to *Main Street*, and we can rely on him to observe (and record) each little revealing detail. The precision and "richness" of Twain's descriptions brought his tales to life for Wood, and that kind of descriptive power is, for many viewers, a quality Wood exhibited in his own art. Yet, interestingly enough, one of the things Wood most appreciated in Twain is the fact that he gave, as Wood remembers it, "no detailed physical description of either" Tom or Huck. "That," he says, "helped." It helped because it freed Wood's imagination to see them variously and to see himself in both Tom and Huck — two very different boy characters. Perhaps the practice he had formed of picturing the characters for himself (and he read the books many times, he tells us) gave him confidence for taking Lewis's people and interpreting them for himself. None of the *Main Street* figures are portrayed in Wood's portraits in a way that parrots Lewis's characterizations. Obviously, Wood felt comfortable presenting them according to his own readings and then solidifying his interpretations by the concrete, meaningful details that gave them authority.

The third point Wood makes in his appreciation of Twain's two novels is that there was no moral in them (as Twain declared in his *Notice* prefacing *Huckleberry Finn*: "Persons attempting to find a moral in it will be banished."). The grand adult sense of "morality" often evades children and, in general, is a surefire way to deaden a spellbinding tale. "Yet,"

Wood instructed, "children can be depended upon to have a keen, penetrating sense of fairness, and if the books had contained anything that went against this, they could never have retained their popularity the way they have." [31] Can the same thing be said of Wood's paintings, especially those that deal directly with human interactions, like *Daughters of Revolution* and *Parson Weems' Fable*? In few of his works do we see a heavy-handed, judgmental moralizing. (Perhaps *The Perfectionist* comes closest to having this tone.) But Wood does make judgments, and we can usually tell what side he is on. He is never a zealot; instead, he is indulgent about human foibles and not bitter. Fairness and proportionate responses are his standards in assessing humans and their deeds. Even in *Daughters of Revolution*, a painting that resulted from a breach of his sense of fairness (and maybe common sense), his light-handed course was to make the narrow minded ladies look trivial and just plain silly. If he had been inclined to pass judgment and moralize, he had abundant opportunity to do so in the *Main Street* illustrations. Yet, even in the instance of Mrs. Bogart (*The Good Influence*), whose behavior in the novel comprises an insidiously damaging immorality, Wood does not damn her. All of the characters he chose to illustrate are guilty of something that could be seized on to provide "the moral to the story" — from Raymie Wutherspoon's provincial censorship to Dr. Kennicott's adultery to Vida Sherwin's duplicity and her glee in telling Carol the gossip about her. Yet, only in his portrayal of Carol, the most unrelentingly and deeply unhappy person in the novel, does he display a lack of sympathy. As discussed here later, Wood's evenhandedness, tolerance and sense of fairness may have been compromised because of his association of this discontent woman with events in his own life. Even in *The Perfectionist*, however, Wood doesn't entirely lose his sense of humor: her cheap lace curtains and her errant button bring her haughty snootiness down to earth.

As for his fourth point, we are not surprised to learn that Wood enjoyed Twain's humor. What the artist gleaned from the novels was more than just a smile but was "one of my earliest realizations of the humorous." From Twain, he learned what humor was and recognized its ability to erase pretense and reveal the untrue. Specifically, the creator of Tom and Huck discredited the sentimentality that was a mainstay of Wood's upbringing and of popular Victorian culture in general. Remarkably, Wood remembered the exact incident in *Huckleberry Finn* in which Twain robbed sentimentality of any seriousness. According to Wood, "It was the part wherein Huck, staying with the Grangerfords, describes the sentimental pictures a daughter in the family had painted before her premature death." Reasonably, what catches Wood's eye, so to speak, is the fact that the incident deals with visual art. There are numerous passages in Twain's writing that ridicule sentimentality, but when he described it in these paintings by the deceased Grangerford girl, Wood "got it" and remembered it. "As I look back on it now, I realize that my response to this passage was a revelation. Having been born into a world of Victorian standards, I had accepted and admired the ornate, the lugubrious, and the excessively sentimental naturally and without question.

And this was my first intimation that there was something ridiculous about sentimentality." Wood does incorporate sentimentality into his art, but usually for the purpose of trivializing it or putting it into its deflated place. One of Wood's most insightful comments is his compliment to Twain for "the brave way...he lashed out against the artificialities and false standards of the time." [32] Perhaps, in a lesser vein, he saw Sinclair Lewis doing the same thing in his novels. More importantly, perhaps he hoped that he had made some advances in that regard himself, as he gently, humorously chided the good influences, the daughters of revolution, the boosters, the shrine quartets and the Victorian survivals.

Chapter 3 Notes

1. "Grant Wood's Painting Lauded In Boston Herald Editorial," undated, unidentified clipping in NWG Scrapbook No.1, 98. The editorial is by Walter Prichard Eaton, "American Gothic," Boston *Herald*, November 14, 1930, 26.

2. Boston *Herald.*

3. My thanks to Monsignor Orr at the Catholic Diocese of Des Moines for help in the grammatical use of the Latin term meaning a "year of miracles" or "year of wonders" in this context.

4. "Grant Wood's New Picture Causes Talk; 'Daughters of Revolution' No Portrait, but 'Composite' Work Says Cedar Rapids Artist," *Omaha World-Herald*, November 23, 1932; NWG Scrapbook No. 1, 81. Of these proposed subjects, only the Shrine quartet was actually carried out. In 1939, Wood produced a lithograph for Associated American Artists entitled *Shrine Quartet*.

5. "Poet Visitor at Art Show Says Culture Heads West; Cathedral of Learning? Well, It Is Ideally Located, So Louis Untermeyer Decides," *The Pittsburgh Press*, October 24, 1933, 4. Untermeyer believed satire was becoming more important in American life. "Satire in novels is on the upgrade, according to Mr. Untermeyer, who dotes on the satirical in either art or literature. The novels of Sinclair Lewis and the short stories of George Milburn show that reading America has come to accept the element of satire, he said, and he added that Milburn is the logical successor to Lewis in that field."

6. "Author at Exhibit Sees Sinclair Lewis in Paint," Pittsburgh *Sun-Telegram*, October 24, 1933; NWG Scrapbook No.1, 72. For additional comments on *Daughters of Revolution* and other works in the Carnegie International exhibition, see Naylor, Douglas, "Canvas Depicting 'D.A.R.' Provokes Most Chuckles," *The Pittsburgh Press*, October 25, 1933, 9. Not everyone immediately equated Wood's interpretation of the Midwest with Sinclair Lewis's. The author, Edna Ferber, seemed to discount Lewis while praising Wood in her comments during a visit to her hometown of Ottumwa, Iowa. "Grant Wood, Cedar Rapids, Iowa artist, has Miss Ferber's unqualified enthusiasm. 'I'd like to see someone write the Midwestern scene as Grant Wood paints it,' she said. "He stands far above anything I've seen.'" Grant, Donald, "Edna Ferber Revisits Iowa; Here to Get New York 'Out of My Bones,'" unidentified, undated clipping in NWG, Scrapbook No.1, 75.

7. "Daughters of Revolution," *The Bulletin Index; Pittsburgh's Weekly Newsmagazine*, November 16, 1933; NWG Scrapbook No.1, 104.

8. Taylor, Adeline, "He Heard Grant Wood Praised in Paris By Gertrude Stein, Comes Here To Meet Him," unidentified clipping (probably from the Cedar Rapids *Gazette*) in NWG Scrapbook No.1, 134B. Another report

explained that Voorhies had met Stein through Bernard Fay, her editor for *The Making of Americans*. "Rousseau Voorhies, Traveler, Lecturer, Visits at Montrose," *Montrose Mirror* (the magazine of the Montrose Hotel in Cedar Rapids), July 1934, in NGW Scrapbook No.1, 134A.

9. "Wood 'Best, Best,' Gertrude Stein Picks Iowa Professor as 'First' Artist in United States," *Daily Iowan*, July 8, 1934; NWG Scrapbook No.1, 134A. Voorhies also relayed Stein's opinion in a lecture at Drake University in Des Moines, arranged by the Drake Department of English and the Iowa Authors' Club. "Gertrude Stein Admires Grant Wood, Iowa Artist; Rousseau Voorhies, New York Critic, Tells of Interview," Des Moines *Register*, June 17, 1934, NWG Scrapbook No.1, 134A.

10. Mott, Frank Luther, "The S.P.C.S.," *The Palimpsest* 43, March 1962, 113-132. Also related in Corn, 46. Wood apparently was not impressed with Stein's approval of his work and may not have been overly disappointed by her failure to appear (or else was angered by it). When he wrote *Revolt Against the City* in 1935, he observed, "Gertrude Stein comes to us from Paris and is only a seven days' wonder." Wood, Grant, *Revolt Against the City*, Iowa City: Whirling World Series, 1935; reprinted in Dennis, James M., *Grant Wood: A Study in Art and Culture*, Columbia: University of Missouri Press, 1986, 231.

11. Taylor, Adeline, "Christopher Morley Gives His Admirers New Food for Thought In Iowa City Talk," Cedar Rapids *Gazette*, n.d. Clipping in NWG Scrapbook No.1, 134B. The caption for an accompanying photograph of Wood and Morley described them as "mutual admirers" who had "spent Monday together in Cedar Rapids and Waubeek." Waubeek was a small town where the Cedar Rapids poet Jay Sigmund sometimes lived and found inspiration for his writing. Wood referred to Morley's visit in his 1935 pamphlet, *Revolt Against the City*: "When Christopher Morley was out in Iowa last Fall, he remarked on its freedom, permitting expansion 'with space and relaxing conditions for work.' Future artists, he wisely observed, 'are more likely to come from the remoter areas, farther from the claims and distractions of an accelerating civilization.'" *Revolt*, reprinted in Dennis, 232. Among the books in Wood's library left by Nan Wood Graham to the Davenport Museum of Art is a copy of *White Jacket* (1892) by Herman Melville with the inscription: "For Grant Wood to remind him of a visit to Morris Sanford's bookstore — with affectionate regards from Christopher Morley, Cedar Rapids, November 10, 1934." Files of the Davenport Museum of Art, inventory number B.65.61. Morley also signed a copy of his own book, *Human Being* (1932). Inventory number B.65.29.

12. Among the articles in which Wood is mentioned (other than those cited elsewhere here) in *The Saturday Review of Literature* are "The Bowling Green," February 25, 1933; "News from the States," June 17, 1933; "Trade Winds," vol. XI, no.32, February 23, 1935; "The Passing of the Patched Parasol," vol.XI, no.36, March 23, 1935; "State Fair," vol.XII, no.1, May 4, 1935; "Trade Winds," vol.XI, no.17, November 10, 1936.

13. His brother, the poet Stephen Vincent Benet, was in Iowa on several occasions. The sculptor-in-residence at Iowa State University, Christian Petersen, produced a portrait head of the poet in 1943. The sculpture is now in the collection of the Brunnier Art Museum.

14. Morley, Christopher, "The Folder," in "The Bowling Green," *The Saturday Review of Literature*, vol.XI, no.23, December 22, 1934, 387. In a later column, Morley published a photograph of a lintel on a Waubeek stone house with anchors carved above it — testimony to the New England backgrounds of early settlers. Commenting on Wood's *Revolt Against the City*, Morley found in Waubeek a good incentive for deserting the city. "What I have in mind...is his allusion to the sturdy old village of Waubeek, near Cedar Rapids; one of the most thrillingly American places I have ever seen....Jay Sigmund, the poet, who spends all his spare time in Waubeek, kindly sent me a snapshot of an old stone doorway where the carved anchors, so far from the sea, show the long memory of the New England race." vol.XII, no.15, August 10, 1935, 13.

15. P.E.G. Quercus (Morley), "Trade Winds," *Saturday Review*, vol.XI, no.25, January 5, 1935.

16. Morley, "The Bowling Green," vol.XII, no.4, May 25, 1935, 15.

17. Morley, "Trade Winds," vol.XII, no.2, May 11, 1935, 29; vol.XIV, no.4, October 20, 1936, 232.

18. Morley, "Trade Winds," vol.XII, no.9, June 29, 1935, 21 ("Grant Wood's vigorous appeal for regional stimulus in the arts"); "The Bowling Green," vol. XII, no.15, August 10, 1935, 13: ("Grant Wood, the Iowa painter, in his pamphlet *Revolt Against the City*...makes a strong appeal for the encouragement of non-urban and regional art. Privately I couldn't take altogether seriously Mr. Wood's anxious suggestion that the Rhodes Scholarships are just one more British 'attempt to control our culture.'")

19. Cover, *Saturday Review*, vol.XIII, no.23, April 4, 1936. On the contents page, the circumstances of the cover art were explained. "The drawing on the cover is the work of Richard Gates, a young Iowa artist, introduced to *The Saturday Review* by Grant Wood. Mr. Wood, who saw the drawing before we did, writes us: 'It is, in my estimation, a beautiful job, and I hope that you are as pleased with it as I am. Gates is a young artist with a world of talent and as soon as I get a little time, I want to write you about him at some length.'" Gates painted a New Deal mural, "The Farmer Feeding Industry," in Harlan, Iowa in 1937.

20. "Discusses Rise of Midwest Art; Grant Wood Sees Need of 'Editorial Comment,'" unidentified newspaper clipping, April 8, 1931; NWG Scrapbook No.1, 52.

21. As Dennis stated, "In the nomenclature of leading American art educators during the first decades of the twentieth century, pictorial abstraction was equated with decorativeness." Dennis, James M., "Grant Wood's Native-Born Modernism," in Roberts, Brady, *Grant Wood: An American Master Revealed*, Davenport (Iowa) Museum of Art, 1995, 42-63, 47. Among these educators were Ernest A. Batchelder whose work Wood read while still in high school and to whose summer course in Minneapolis Wood traveled the very night of his graduation in 1910. Others were Denman W. Ross, Arthur W. Dow, and Ernest F. Fenollosa. Representation (recording phenomena observed by the eye) and design (the discretionary arrangements of formal elements such as line, shape and composition) were, as taught by these educators, two entirely different things. The ability to use design was what distinguished one artist from another or, in other words, separated a creative artist from an illustrator or "reporter." In addition to the Davenport essay, Dennis earlier explored these and other themes related to Wood's understanding and use of modern stylizations in his catalogue for an exhibition he curated in 1985: *Grant Wood: Still Lifes as Decorative Abstractions*, Elvehjem Museum of Art, University of Wisconsin-Madison.

22. Millier, Arthur, "Layman and Critic Hail 'Grass Roots' Portrait; 'American Gothic' Pleases All Comers to San Diego's Show of Contemporary Eastern Paintings," Los Angeles *Times*, July 17, 1932, NWG. Scrapbook No. 1, 77.

23. It has been widely assumed that Wood played a small role in actually writing *Return from Bohemia*. However, if the writing style is compared with that found in Wood's letters and other documents (such as the foreword to *Young Sam Clemens*), there are enough similarities to warrant some reconsideration of this position. In addition, correspondence indicates that he was spending a good deal of time on this autobiography and that he did, at least at first, regard the writing of it as his obligation. The exact conditions of his contract with Doubleday Doran are not now known nor are the arrangements made with Rinard. On the other hand, it can be argued that if it were primarily the work of Wood, the essay would not have been accepted as Rinard's Masters thesis. It is probably not possible to know how to precisely attribute authorship. *Return from Bohemia; A Painter's Story, Part I*, by Park Rinard. Thesis for MA in Dept of English, State University of Iowa, August 1939.

24. Wood, Grant, *Revolt Against the City*, Iowa City, reprinted in Dennis, 232.

25. Corn, Wanda, *Grant Wood: The Regionalist Vision*, Minneapolis (Minnesota) Institute of Arts, 1983, 153, n.85.

26. Duncan, Thomas W., "New Books By Iowans," unidentified clipping, April 1935, NWG Scrapbook No.2, 30.

27. Wood was credited with co-writing a play, *They That Mourn*, with Jewell Bothwell Tull, published in *Stage: Forty-minute prize plays*, New York: 1936. His sister, Nan Wood Graham, gives this account: "When Little Theaters all over the country announced a contest to see who could write the best play, Grant and Jewell Bothwell Tull, wife of a professor at Cornell College, Mount Vernon [Iowa], became co-authors. Their play, *They That Mourn*, was eliminated in local competition, but without their knowledge, Professor Tull entered it at the national headquarters, and it won the national first prize. When Grant received a $1.65 check from a play service for lease of the play, he was as pleased as if he had gotten a thousand dollars." *My Brother, Grant Wood*, Iowa City: State Historical Society of Iowa, 1993, 72. Wood himself gave the most reliable report of this play and also explains how slight his role in it was. To his dealer, Maynard Walker, he wrote on March 16, 1936: "Stop your worrying. I haven't gone in permanently for writing. I didn't, for instance, write the one-act play Roudebusch told you about. I simply furnished the idea to a lady play-write[sic] of this vicinity and she put it into shape. The whole process, as far as I'm concerned, took less than half an hour. I'm not surprised though that you are all mixed up again. Anyone would be if he tried to keep track of all the things I get in on in one way or another." AAA. Maynard Walker Gallery file, reel 2025, frame 991.

28. Wood, Grant, "The Painter and the Writer," *American Prefaces*, October 1935, 3-4. Wood's description of his preparation as a portraitist sounds much like an actor's preparation for his role. In the 1920s, Wood had been active in local Cedar Rapids theater (usually as a set designer) and maintained an interest in the dramatic arts. One of the projects he hoped he and his University of Iowa students could carry out was the decoration of the new theater building on campus. Sinclair Lewis also was involved in drama, writing one of the signature plays of the Depression era, *It Can't Happen Here*. He himself acted in plays and had many close associations with theater people, especially later in his life. The appearance of *American Prefaces*, the new regional literary magazine at the University of Iowa, was praised and discussed on the editorial page of *The Saturday Review of Literature*. "A new weekly magazine called *American Prefaces* has been launched from the University of Iowa under the pilotage of Wilbur Schramm and Norman Foerster. Its avowed purpose is to be a voice for the younger writers of America, especially, one supposes, of mid-America." vol.XIII, no.4, November 23, 1935, 8. Wood continued to make comparisons between writing and painting as late as the summer of 1941. "'Painting is much like writing,' said Grant Wood, Iowa's noted artist, as he paused in his work for a moment to speak of his companion pictures *Spring in Town* and *Spring in the Country*, now being completed in his improvised studio on the north shore of Clear Lake. 'One writes best out of his own experiences and so does one paint best. I do not choose Iowa landscapes because I think them more beautiful than any others but because I am more familiar with the scenes of Iowa. Why should I attempt to paint pictures of some distant land where I may have been but once when the hills and slopes of Iowa are a part of my very life?'" "Grant Wood Says Painting, Writing Are Much Alike," Mason City *Globe-Gazette* July 1, 1941. NWG Scrapbook No.4, 34.

29. Clemens, Cyril, *Young Sam Clemens*, foreword by Henrik Willem Van Loon and introduction by Grant Wood, Portland, Maine: Leon Tebbetts Editions, 1942, introduction unpaginated. All subsequent quotations from this essay are contained in the seven pages of Wood's introduction to the book.

30. For example, see Corn, 1-3.

31. Throughout his career, Wood showed great sensitivity to children. At the beginning of his career, he taught art in the Cedar Rapids public schools, becoming one of the most popular teachers in the system. Children who were considered difficult were sometimes sent by the principal, Miss Frances Prescott, to Mr. Wood's class to have their naughty impulses channeled into productive activities. At the University of Iowa, he participated in the Tenth Iowa Conference on Child Development and Parent Education from which was issued the pamphlet *Art in the Daily Life of the Child*, Iowa City: University of Iowa Publications, New Series No. 1057, Child Welfare Pamphlets No. 73, May 1939. A news clipping, quoting portions of Wood's address to the conference, relates how sophisticated was his view of the art of children. "'It is as natural for children to draw as it is for them to breathe,' he said. 'They are very serious about their earliest efforts. Here is a great test for parental patience. Don't criticize these early gropings. Don't laugh at them. They are important to the children who make them.' The speaker deplored the world's association of art and painting with the work of trained artists. 'Everyone should experience this joy of creation.'" Pownall, Dorothy Ashby, "Iowa Parents Hear Artist; Wood Makes Plea for Children," Des Moines *Tribune*, June 18, 1936. NWG Scrapbook No.2, 57.

32. Clemens, unpaginated introduction.

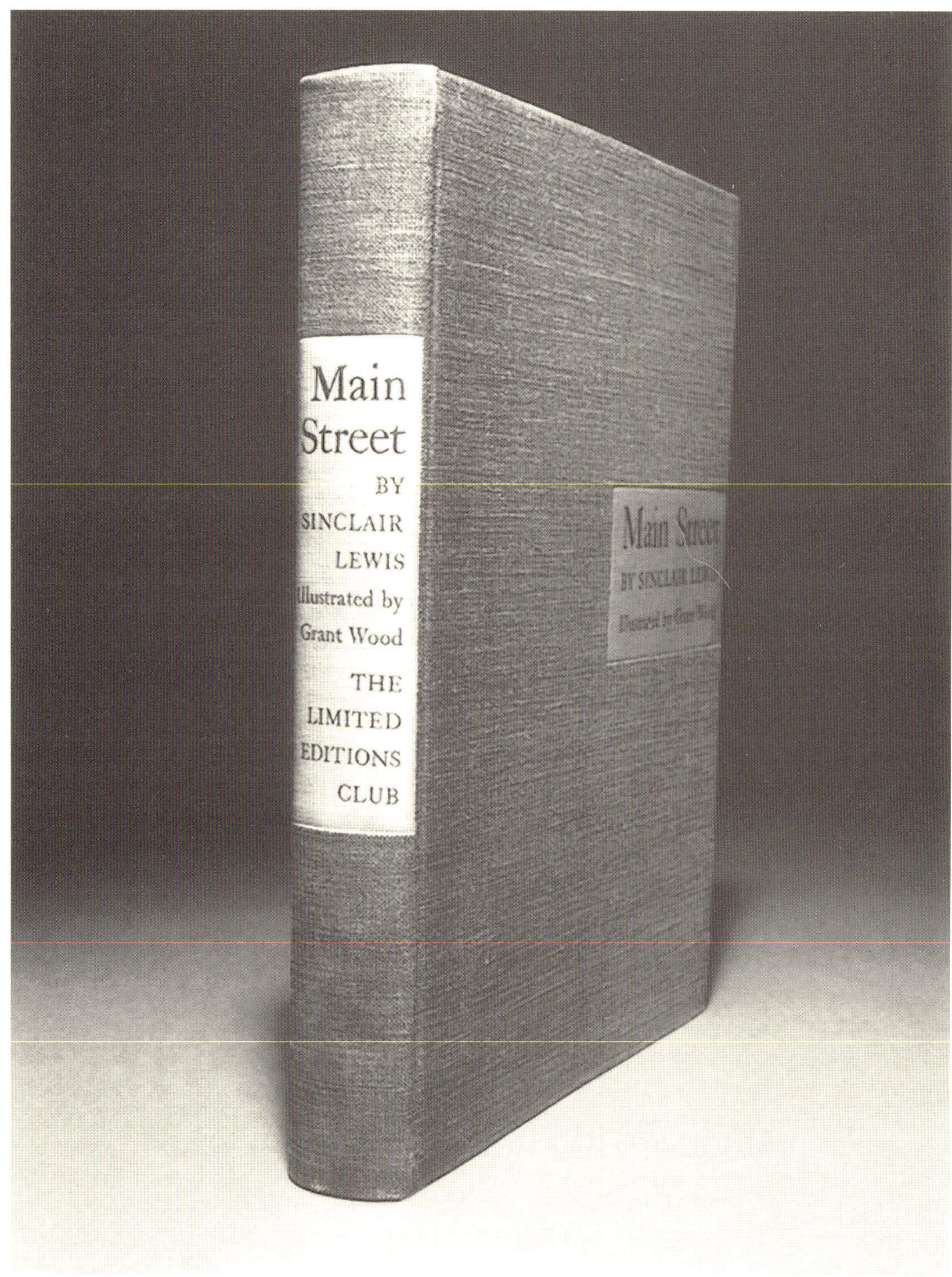

Figure 21 The Limited Editions Club Main Street, *1937*

Chapter 4
The 1937 Illustrated Edition of *Main Street*

Grant Wood is not known to have expressed a desire to illustrate Sinclair Lewis's *Main Street* (or any other book) despite the associations made between himself and Lewis by others. (Figure 21) Accusations of being just an illustrator had arisen soon after the nationally recognized success of his mature style (as shown in *American Gothic*), but Wood seemed to be clear in his own mind about the difference between being an artist interested in "story-telling" and an artist giving form to someone else's stories. Yet, he did not refuse illustration and had carried out several commissions. [1] His associations with literary figures, especially those of his own region, were well established and, in addition, he was frequently mentioned on the pages of the Eastern "high-brow" literary journal, *The Saturday Review of Literature*. The publisher of the New York-based Limited Editions Club, George Macy, would likely have had opportunity to encounter Wood as both an artistic and a quasi-literary figure. According to a review of the book when it was published in May of 1937, Macy was interested in commissioning illustrations from Wood, but hadn't decided what to ask him to illustrate when a correspondent from the Midwest suggested *Main Street*. "The idea of [*Main Street*] originated...in the Middle West. George Macy, director of the Limited Editions Club, received the suggestion in his mail, just when he was trying to think of a book for Wood to illustrate. He forgets who sent it — wishes now he could reward the suggestor with a copy, but the correspondent's name is lost in the files." [2] Who in the Midwest would know Macy's business well enough to think of suggesting the pairing of the two Midwesterners? Possibly it was one of Wood's literary comrades at the University of Iowa, such as Norman Foerster, Paul Engle, or Frank Luther Mott. Perhaps it was someone connected with the Lakeside Press, part of the publishers R.R. Donnelley, headquartered in Chicago. In February and March of 1935, Lakeside Press had sponsored a large exhibition of works by Wood and had published a catalogue with short essays by Park Rinard and Arnold Pyle. [3] It was this Press which Macy called upon to print his special edition of *Main Street* and which afterwards continued to collaborate with him on books illustrated by Midwestern artists.

Archives now unlocated but available to earlier writers, notably Dennis in the first scholarly monograph on Wood, indicate that both Lewis and Wood were pleased about the new edition that Macy proposed. The first requirement was to obtain Lewis's permission, which Macy asked for in a letter that caused him some worry — needlessly, as it turned out. Having asked to reprint the text, Macy remembered, "'I completely failed to add the statement that we would pay some hundreds of dollars for the privilege. Having read in newspapers many stories of 'Red' Lewis's wrath, and being certain of the fact that the omission could give him good cause to wax angry, I spent an entire day frantically — and vainly — attempting to reach Lewis on the telephone so as to avoid the receipt next morning of a blistering letter. The next morning there *was* a letter from him. He said that he would be glad to let us do an edition of *Main Street*; he wondered why he had never joined the Club himself, and attached a check for a year's subscription. Now, nobody speaks ill of Lewis in *my* presence.'" [4] According to this source, Wood's 1932 *Daughters of Revolution* cemented the perception of him as a Midwestern satirist so that Macy naturally "asked the American master of satirical art to illustrate the work of the American master of satirical fiction. Since, as it turns out, *Main Street* was one of Wood's favorite books, he was delighted with the idea. So...was his fellow Midwesterner, 'Red' Lewis." [5]

This same source dates the commission of the drawings in 1936, but a letter from Wood to his dealer, Maynard Walker, in October of 1935 indicates that he was already working on drawings for the novel. Wood's relationship with his dealer was erratic: occasionally cordial, often argumentative, and sometimes accusatory. He never seemed satisfied with whatever financial arrangements the dealer was making, and it is possible that he never truly understood the business aspects of the art world. In this letter, he was resisting sharing any profits from projects that came to him on his own without the agency of the dealer, as the *Main Street* commission apparently did. "Here," he argued, "is a case to illustrate the point. I am making four paintings or drawings to be used by the Limited Editions Club in a De Luxe edition of Sinclair Lewis' Main Street. These drawings are not to be illustrations for the book; they will stand on their own feet as individual pictures and will be saleable as such. However, the Limited Editions Club are [sic] willing to pay me well for the use of them in the book. Their dealing was directly with me and I do not believe that I should pay you one-third commission on them." [6] Obviously, the job evolved over the next months since, in the end, there were nine drawings and no known paintings at all. It is also clear that Wood intended from the beginning for these drawings to be finished works of art, his first such instance of that practice. He had made many drawings before this, of course, but they likely were preparatory works for paintings and, whatever their reason for being, were not intended to be sold as "individual pictures." Drawings done for the purpose of book illustration had been offered for sale (*Farm on the Hill*, for instance), but they had been presented *as illustrations* and not as works able to "stand on their own feet as individual pictures." In April of 1936, while he was working on the *Main Street* drawings, he held an exhibition at the Ferargil Galleries in New York in which the drawings for *Farm on the Hill* were announced as "decorative" works, as if to ensure that no one would assume that Wood thought them the equal of his paintings. [7] Wood makes the point that the *Main Street* drawings were "not to be illustrations for the book;" however, there is no evidence that he did them for any reason other than the Club commission or that he would have taken up the subject of "Main Street" otherwise. What is suggested is that he used this assignment to produce drawings on a higher level than he had theretofore done. The precision and complexity of the completed drawings is evidence that he addressed this task with the same attention he brought to his painting.

Dennis records that Wood had furnished sketches to Macy by January of 1936 and that William Kittredge, book designer at The Lakeside Press in Chicago, had the finished drawings in December of 1936. The final drawing in the book, *Village Slums*, truly was the last drawing, not arriving until March of 1937. [8] It is not known why Wood lagged in producing this final illustration. Possibly it was not part of his original plan for his series and was added after the other drawings were completed. Perhaps it was not even his idea, but Macy's or someone else's. Maybe Wood felt that the overall body of illustrations needed more balance, since he had begun with an architectural image in *Main Street Mansion*. How the sequence of illustrations in the new edition was determined is not known. It does more or less follow the introduction of or the narrative prominence of the characters except, of course, for *Village Slums*. With the addition of this last illustration, the sequence is perfectly balanced pictorially with architecture at both ends and three portraits on each side of the middle image, *General Practitioner* — the "hands" picture. Probably Macy had a good deal to say about sequence since he attended to every detail of his editions. In a 1940 letter to Thomas Hart Benton when he was illustrating *The Grapes of Wrath*, he emphasized to the artist how dependent the success of the book was on the reader's initial perception of the illustrations. "I think you may not realize how people usually pick up illustrated books. If they really wanted their money's worth, people should pick up their illustrated books and begin to read from the first page, so that they will not see any of the illustrations until they reach the parts of the text depicted in the illustrations. But people don't do this; they pick up their illustrated books, and leaf through them quickly in order to look at the pictures. If a set of book illustrations, therefore, is designed to please the customers, then these pictures must tell the whole story to a customer who looks at them quickly. If the customer doesn't find portraiture, the complete background, dignity and cartoon, pathos and melodrama, he decides only too quickly that the artist hasn't done the book properly." [9] If we do what Macy says we should not (but what customers inevitably will), and look quickly through the *Main Street* illustrations, we do receive a brief survey of the book and its major characters as well as some idea of the narrative's tone. (Figure 22)

Wood's commission from Macy to illustrate *Main Street* must have been known in New York publishing circles since it was discussed even before the 1937 edition appeared. As mentioned earlier, Wood's illustrations for *Farm on the Hill* had been exhibited at the Ferargil Galleries in New York and were generally favorably reviewed in the art press — but

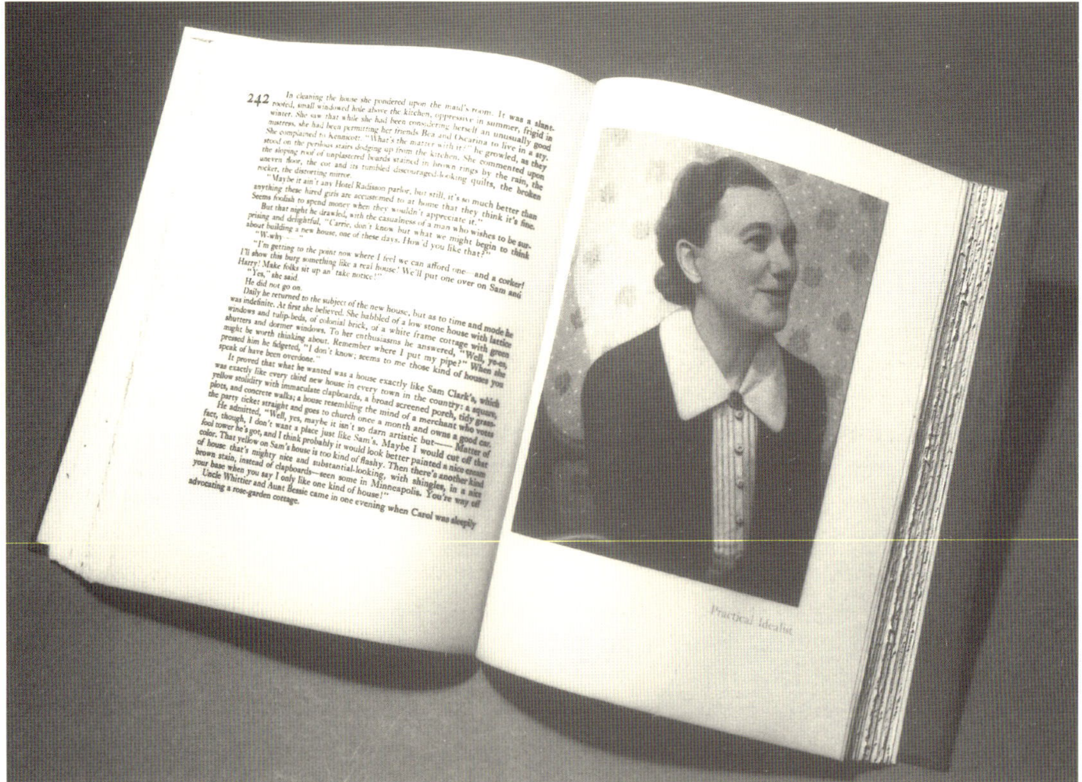

Figure 22 The Limited Editions Club Main Street, *open to the illustration of* Practical Idealist

strictly as illustrations (as Wood intended they should be). In that same year of 1936, Wood's abilities as an illustrator were recognized by the Museum of Modern Art's exhibition *Modern Painters and Sculptors As Illustrators*, curated by Monroe Wheeler. Among works by Picasso, Matisse and Delacroix, Wheeler included *Boy Taking a Bath*, one of the illustrations from *Farm on the Hill*. In his catalogue, Wheeler debated the apparent inconsistency of major modern artists using their talents for book illustrations. "Many people still believe that modern art is or should be non-literary; that the best modern painters feel...repugnance [for] the pictorial treatment of dramatic or poetic subjects." Not true, he declared: "In this exhibition we have evidence that the great men of modernism...have not consistently held this opinion, nor felt any real repugnance to the forbidden themes. On the contrary, with obvious enjoyment, they have welcomed opportunities to try their skill at legend and symbol and sentiment." [10] Therefore, he reasoned, he had "restricted [his exhibition choices] to the work of painters and sculptors of note *as such*," and not to artists whose reputations were built primarily on illustration. In the collaborations between the artists and writers of his exhibition, he found "no evidence of anyone's having thought of himself as shamefully hired, or as working at a disadvantage in harness, or as compromised either by literary or commercial taste." [11] Wheeler also seemed to be thinking specifically of artists like Wood and writers like Sinclair Lewis when he announced that "the highest type of illustrated book is the joint work of author and artist who are contemporaries, working as in equal collaboration; inspired by similar feeling; approaching the same subject-matter from opposite directions; dealing with it twice within the covers of the one volume." [12] But the pairing of contemporary figures did not always work out, he noted, as proven by the Limited Editions Club *Ulysses* by James Joyce, which Henri Matisse had illustrated with images that related more to the *Odyssey* than to the twentieth century masterwork. "It was a great idea to bring them together...[but] there must have arisen practical difficulties, or some misunderstanding. A nobler undertaking than most of the Limited Editions Club's publications, it is by no means satisfactory." But Wheeler had higher expectations for an upcoming Club project, one that bumped Iowa's Grant Wood up into an unaccustomed artistic stratosphere occupied by the likes of Matisse — an elevation that surely pleased Wood and his patron, George Macy. "That same organization has announced another almost equally exciting project: *Main Street* illustrated by Grant Wood. It might be the most interesting American illustrated book up to date." [13] Wheeler must have been disappointed, however, for when the book was revised, his comment about Wood had been excised; he retained the illustration of *Boy Taking a Bath*, but there was no mention of Wood. [14]

In May, just two months after *Village Slums* was finished, the Limited Editions Club's *Main Street* was published and was being reviewed. Among the good opinions expressed was that of Sinclair Lewis himself who "apparently accepted Wood's interpretations [of his characters], for he wished to buy at least two of the original drawings." [15] The drawings were for sale and why Lewis did not acquire them or Wood did not sell them to him isn't known. In addition, because the contract between Macy and Wood is currently unlocated, we do not know exactly what were the commission's requirements nor the fee paid to the artist. Macy's contracts for similar commissions paid the artists $2000, [16] and in her memoir of her brother, Nan Wood Graham reported that he received that amount. [17] As discussed elsewhere, Lewis's relations with Macy remained cordial enough that he was willing to work with him on subsequent proposals for new editions of his novels. As for Wood, Dennis records that he was asked to illustrate another Midwestern classic, *Spoon River Anthology* by Edgar Lee Masters. "For over two years [Macy] pleaded with the artist, urged on by Masters himself, who had previously refused to allow his poems to be illustrated. Although Wood expressed interest in the possibility, he finally declined in early 1941, not wishing to interrupt an active period of painting." [18]

Two months after publication, Wood wrote to Lewis, then living in Stockbridge, Massachusetts, to acknowledge the author's compliments. Addressing him as "Mr. Lewis" and signing his full name (suggesting a formal, not a familiar, relationship), Wood wrote, "I am glad you like the *Main Street* drawings. A man takes a good deal for granted when he tries to interpret in drawings what has been so adequately done in words. Nonetheless, in spite of some misgivings on that score, I got a great kick out of trying to catch the essence of that story we all admire. I hope you can make it out to Iowa before long. My wife and I would like very much to have you and Mrs. Lewis as our guests....A few days here might prove restful for you, and also, if you have any point of dispute on the illustrations, that would be a good time to give me hell." [19] Lewis, in fact, did not come to the University of Iowa right away and had to be persuaded to do so even then. The Times Club (and its subsidiary, the Society for the Prevention of Cruelty to Speakers) had invited him in the Fall of 1940, but Lewis had abruptly left the Midwest and his residency at the University of Wisconsin at Madison in early November and moved back to New York. Perhaps he was reluctant to come again so soon into the region for he wrote Professor Frank Luther Mott that he would come the next Spring if he could. [20] In addition, he undoubtedly held a grudge against the University of Iowa. Earlier that year, Norman Foerster, professor of literature, had invited Lewis to Iowa for a residency and the author consented to come. The president of the University was, however, uneasy about Lewis's reputation for drinking and referred the decision to the Regents who declined the appointment. [21] Finally, due largely to pressure from friends at Iowa, including Wood, Lewis did visit the University in December of 1940.

When *Main Street* appeared in May of 1937, the reviews of the new edition were mostly positive. These illustrations were less noticed by the art press than those for *Farm on the Hill* had been, perhaps partly because the *Main Street* drawings were not exhibited in New York as the earlier ones had been. Five from the series were shown in a major exhibition at the Art Institute of Chicago that Spring: *The Sixteenth International Exhibition. Water Colors, Pastels, Drawings and Monotypes.* [22] As he prepared to send these five drawings to the Art Institute, Wood wrote to his dealer in New York, Maynard Walker, that he had had to matte, frame and price them "hurriedly" while they were at Donnelley. With guidelines suggested by Walker in mind, he had assigned prices to each drawing before they were sent for the exhibition, but since he was unhappy with the framing, he wanted a chance to reconsider everything before he arrived at the final prices. "I want to see them all together and satisfactorily framed before giving you my ideas on prices for them." He apparently had forgotten the preliminary prices he had proposed and asked his dealer to supply them for the Art Institute. With this letter was a separate sheet whose prices, we may assume, were those he had proposed: *General Practitioner*, \$500; *The Good Influence*, \$750; *Main Street Mansion*, \$400; *The Perfectionist*, \$350; and *Sentimental Yearner*, \$500. [23] How had Wood arrived at these valuations? Why was *The Good Influence* worth over twice as much as *The Perfectionist*? Was it based on the amount of effort involved to produce the image, or on Wood's opinion of his own success in capturing the characterization he wanted? Did it reflect his personal preferences among the drawings or his idea of which drawings would be more appealing to buyers? Did it have solely to do with what Wood judged to be the intrinsic quality of the images, an assessment only he, as the artist, could determine? *The Perfectionist* seems fully as complicated a drawing as any of the others, its media handled with at least equal adeptness, and its composition as carefully designed. Does its lower price reflect Wood's lack of satisfaction in the final image? This drawing and *The Radical* are the least nuanced characterizations of the series in that they are nearly totally negative views of figures who, in the novel, have significant shares of tragedy in their lives. *The Radical* at least has its useful tools in the background to denote Miles Bjornstam's skills, but Carol Kennicott has only her flimsy curtains as a prop.

The Art Institute's exhibition was the first public viewing of any works from the *Main Street* series, and their good review in Chicago set the tone for the reception of the book. Singling out *The Good Influence*, the reviewer found that "again our fancy is tickled by the original manner in which Grant Wood transposes his subject through the prism of his artistic imagination." Wood's background is appreciated as good preparation for interpreting Lewis's story of a Midwestern small town. "Wood was born in the little town of Anamosa, twenty-five miles from Cedar Rapids, where he has always lived. His work has brought it into the limelight, until today it is one of the most sought-out art spots in America. It might be said that in art Grant Wood reveals Americans to themselves as Sinclair Lewis does in literature." [24]

One of the earliest commentaries came from a reviewer in Wood's hometown, Cedar Rapids, where people were enjoying the new book and Wood's illustrations. The Cedar Rapids *Gazette* article praised the Limited Editions volume for being "beautifully bound...printed on paper of distinction, set in exquisite type" and overall, a "de luxe edition" in which "all the illustrations by Mr. Wood are equally fascinating." [25] Later on in the month, the University of Iowa student newspaper published an article on the *Main Street* series based on an exhibition at the Memorial Union. Only eight of the drawings were exhibited, but the article listed the titles of nine drawings, eight of which are identical to the illustration titles in the new 1937 edition; perhaps *Village Slums* was the missing drawing since the article mistitles it as "City Slums." Wood was one of the University's stars as far as the media was concerned (though the Art Department didn't think so, as increasingly nasty disputes proved), and the book was regarded as one more in his roster of achievements. "Professor Grant Wood, who looks at American life with both aesthetics and humor, has done it again. This time it is a set of nine illustrations for a special edition of Sinclair Lewis' *Main Street*." Terming it "an American publishing 'natural,'" the article reported that the drawings "represent Professor Wood's conception of rural American types as inspired by Sinclair Lewis' novel of the Middlewest." Incorporating Wood's comment that "'I didn't try to make likenesses, but adapted them to my material,'" the article nevertheless notes the models as it describes several of the drawings. Observing that *General Practitioner* is "a striking portrayal of hands rather than [Dr. Kennicott's] face," the writer finds that "the other pictures are clearly recognizable as characters of the book....Journalism students, who are hard to fool, have detected a convincing resemblance in the features of *The Booster* to Prof. Frank Luther Mott. The drawings, which Prof. Wood completed in January, were done in black and white pencils on brown wrapping paper. In *The Perfectionist*, we see Carol Kennicott, sitting in a window, looking out with somewhat precious disdain on Gopher Prairie. (Figure 23) It is significant that she is shut away from the sordidness of the town by lace curtains. In *The Good Influence*, Mrs. Bogart, dressed in black and with saintly veil, stands in front of a church. But from her smile, the set of her eyes, and the way she draws on her black glove, it is clear that she is meditating the latest town scandal. *Booster* is caught at a dramatic moment in an oration — possibly a Fourth of July speech; there is an American flag in the background. (Figure 24) In striped suit, with lodge button flashing in his lapel, he wags a forefinger at his audience and gives them a 'Bible Belt' platitude....Incidentally, those same students who see a resemblance to Prof. Mott in *Booster* declare that a microscope is not required to discover a resemblance to Prof. Charles Sanders in *Sentimental Yearner*." [26] (Figure 25)

Within a month of *Main Street*'s publication, the St. Louis *Post-Dispatch* ran a full-page story on Wood and his illustrations. "The notion of reprinting Sinclair Lewis' novel *Main Street* with Grant Wood illustrations is so pat one automatically wonders why nobody thought of it before now. The novelist and the painter have become so well known for their studies of rural America that such a collaboration seems more than just appropriate." Wood's illustrations were praised as being the "spotlight" of the publication, partly because they reflected so much of the artist himself, not just the novel's characters on which they were based.

> Even their titles are enough to indicate that these are no footnotes or appendices, but a thoughtful, perhaps even inspired commentary on their own. 'I had great difficulty boiling down any adequate conception of the book into nine drawings,' Wood said. Obviously he solved the problem by going back to the book's origins for a selection of emphasis. The frontispiece is entitled *Main Street Mansion* and the characters chosen are described as types, not called by name. *The Perfectionist* is obviously Carol Kennicott, the heroine of the novel, and *General Practitioner* is, of course, her physician husband — his portrait being the more striking for the whimsical choice of a pair of hands rather than a face as the subject. One recognizes the other characters as the book is recalled or read. But clearly these are intended to be neither portraits nor mere sidelights on Lewis' homely characters. They are Grant Wood's own conception of American village types and they are the fruit of his years of concentration on such people. As such they go a

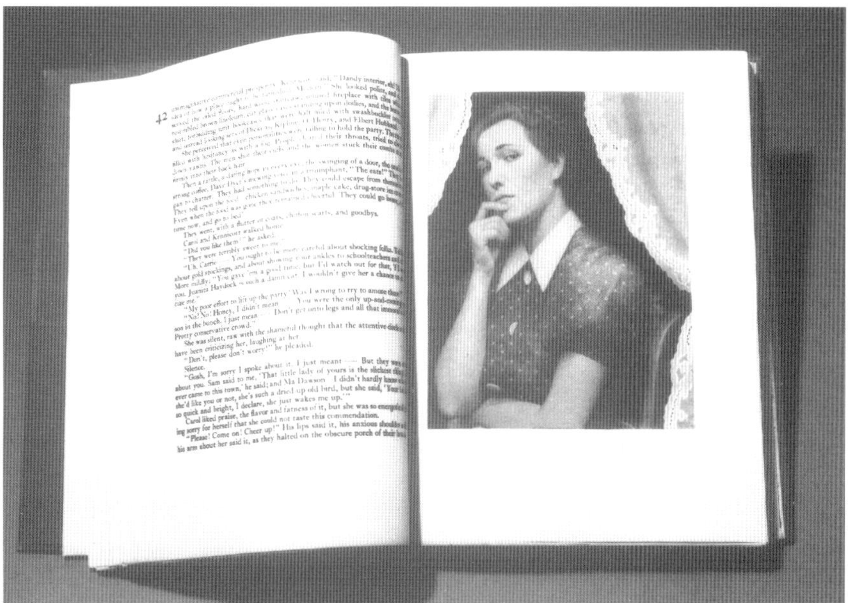

Figure 23 The Limited Editions Club Main Street, *open to the illustration of* The Perfectionist

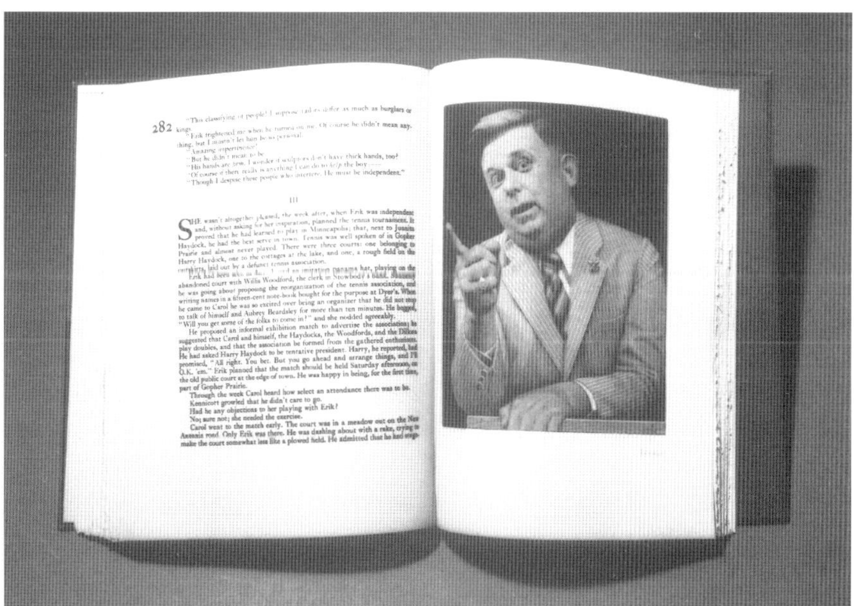

Figure 24 The Limited Editions Club Main Street, *open to the illustration of* Booster

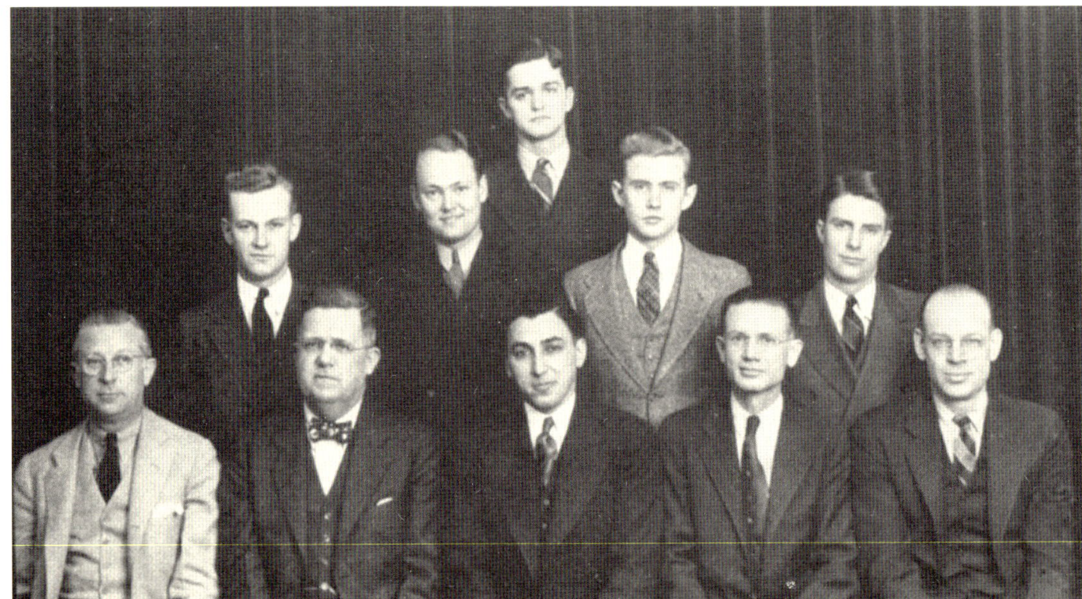

Figure 25 Charles L. Sanders (bottom row, first from left) and Frank Luther Mott (bottom row, second from left). The Hawkeye, *1939*

> good deal beyond the scope of ordinary illustration and have a place of their own, possibly as prominent as the novel itself. [27]

This unsigned article dealt with the illustrations more seriously and extensively than any other review, for it sought to address the relationship between the artist's and the author's concepts of character. It also recognized that Wood's goals were to complete something that could function with or without reference to the novel, something that would "stand," as the artist put it, "on their own feet as individual pictures." Though, as discussed elsewhere, the newspaper lamented the price of the volume, rendering it out of reach for most Midwesterners, it lauded the quality of the publication, careful to note that it had been produced in the Midwest. "Not the least important Middle-Western contribution is the format. The Lakeside Press in Chicago, which became prosperous by printing the mail order catalogues that are such a choice item among rural Americana [sic], is responsible for the actual printing and William Kittredge of Lakeside was its designer. Printed on coarse tan rag paper and bound in neat blue gray and yellow linen, intended to harmonize with Wood's palette, the whole is obviously the darling of everyone who handled a single detail of its construction." [28]

The following month, in June, the critic Thomas Craven, a strong supporter of Wood and other American Scene artists, published an article, "Grant Wood," which included three illustrations from *Main Street*: *The Perfectionist*, *The Good Influence* and *Booster*. Primarily biographical, Craven's article did not mention the drawings directly. They were referred to only in a footnote explaining that this article was their first publication and that all were executed in "black and white pencils on brown wrapping paper." [29] Craven did, however, talk about the strength of Wood's portraiture, claiming that "not since Copley has America seen his equal in the delineation of people. [And] in subtle analysis of character and inventive design, he surpasses the colonial master. By dealing unreservedly with local psychologies, he has created characters which, though rooted in the Iowa soil, belong in the gallery of American types — men and women as native and as faithfully studied as those of Sinclair Lewis, and much more affectionately fashioned." Craven championed Wood's portraiture and figure painting and, in contrast to today's valuation, found that his landscapes "expresse[d] little." [30] By using the term "affectionately," Craven may have intended to acknowledge that Wood's characterizations of Midwestern types were less caustic and more generous than Lewis's. As a high-profile supporter of the Regionalist idea in American art, he might be expected to appreciate Wood's discretion in criticizing Midwesterners.

Wood preferred that his *Main Street* drawings be seen as studies of character with the kind of dimension and contradictions found in real people; as an artist, he did not want to be seen simply as a satirist. His own characterization as a "satirist" was something Wood argued against in many instances. For instance, during a visit to Kansas City almost nine months after the special edition appeared, Wood was disputing that label which kept surfacing in regard to *Daughters of Revolution*, a painting many saw as a prime example of Midwestern satire. The 1932 painting had become "a source of considerable annoyance to Wood. 'Because I have painted a few satirical things,' he says, 'the classifying school of critics have labeled me a satirist. And they go on to find satirical meaning in things that don't have any satire in them. Of course I have been satirical; but I have to keep insisting that I am not a satirist so that people won't get an easy and incorrect notion of what I am about.'" [31] The only other works discussed in this article were the *Main Street* drawings so it seems possible that his comments were prompted by misinterpretations of those drawings. The article includes ruminations about Wood's process in depicting the *Main Street* types.

> Into every painting and drawing of Grant Wood goes a tremendous amount of thought. The illustrations for *Main Street*, for instance, required a great deal of consideration. When you look at the portrait of *The Good Influence*, the smiling woman, you know perfectly well that the smile is the smile of a hypocrite. Wood's problem was to make the smile that of a hypocrite. After he explains it, it is all very simple: but he had to find out

> how to do it. The mouth smiles benignly. But cover up the mouth and look at the eyes; the eyes are hard, cold, unsmiling.
>
> Dr. [Samuel] Johnson, commenting on Swift's *Gulliver's Travels*, remarked that once you had thought of little men and big men the rest was easy. He omitted to mention that no one else had thought of little men and big men. Perhaps genius consists in large part, after all, in finding the right things to think about. Certainly Grant Wood finds the right things to think about; and it is hard work.
>
> It is hard work to think about those things, too, once they are found. And it is hard work to get them portrayed so that the beholder understands what the artist wants him to understand. The hypocrite must be a hypocrite, for every one to see. And not only that: every character must be not only an individual, but also a type in whom every one can see some one he knows. [32]

For all the admiration the *Main Street* series elicited soon after their publication and despite Wood's ambitions for these drawings, they lost ground over the next decades as Wood's reputation declined, and the drawings were overlooked. Even his old dealer, Maynard Walker, could find nothing positive to say about them. In 1954, twelve years after Wood's death, he replied to a collector about a *Main Street* drawing owned by her that "I always thought [the *Main Street* series] among the less interesting of his works. I would not want to acquire the drawing myself and I regret that I cannot suggest anyone who might be interested in acquiring it." [33] Four years later when the University of Kansas Museum of Art was organizing a Wood exhibition, Walker wrote to the curator just as bluntly about his low opinion. "Wood did some largish drawings for a book or two. Many of them are bad....The drawings for *Main Street* are terrible." [34]

In 1959, when the Limited Editions Club published a commemorative volume, *Quarto-Millenary*, two critics, Edward Alden Jewell and Thomas Craven, assessed the 1937 Lewis-Wood *Main Street* favorably, though both called Wood's style "photographic," implying that this quality was a limitation or a weakness in his work. Perhaps the criticism was affected by the hegemony of Abstract Expressionism, the post-war rejection of realism overall, and the late-1950s' disdain of any relationship between photography and serious painting. Even Thomas Craven, despite his championship of Wood in the 1930s and despite his enduring anti-modernism, may have become uncomfortable with Wood's supposed over-reliance on strict verisimilitude. In a survey of the Limited Editions Club books published between 1929 and 1939, Jewell singled out Matisse (*Ulysses* by James Joyce) and Wood (*Main Street* by Sinclair Lewis), as two artists from whom "much might reasonably have been expected." He recognized how "right" the pairings would seem, but, in the end, found the illustrations by both artists disappointing. "Something, in both instances, at once 'clicks.' Yet I feel that the results themselves, while interesting, are not exceptional." Matisse's work he judged to be "rather sparse" and, as for Wood's drawings, they had strengths, but still had "shortcomings." The *Main Street* drawings were "in themselves, ever so devastating and shrewd, as well as quite revelatory of the artist's well-known photographic style; at the same time they seem somehow hardly robust enough in spirit, or broad enough in suggested scope, to match the text. Yet it must be conceded that in this case text and illustration are...essentially of our age, quintessentially American." [35]

Craven appreciated the Americanness of Wood's concept for his *Main Street* illustrations and attributed their "native flavor" to "the conditioning influences" of the artist having grown up in a milieu similar to Lewis's. "Wood was an artist of definite genius — shrewd, patient, a remarkable craftsman, and a painfully slow performer. His delineations of the inhabitants of Main Street are so appropriate, so searchingly observed, and so close to actualities that it is possible to say that in no other book did George Macy publish pictures which so convincingly embody the author's verbal conceptions." His failing, however, was to make the *Main Street* characters hew too much to his own artistic predilections and to encase them too much in his deliberate, carefully delineated style, as Craven explained. "I have, however, a reservation to make. It was Wood's custom, after his first literal studies, to refine and rework his conceptions until they were generalized into his own particular family of mortals — to strike, in other words, the golden mean between the actual experience and the abstract pattern. His *Main Street* personalities are a shade too literal, too close to photographic renderings." [36] This criticism may be based mostly — and reasonably — on the appearance of the drawings in the reproductions of the book. When seen directly in the actual drawings, this "photographic" quality is much less pronounced.

By 1972, another writer commented on the series, not as dismissively as Wood's old dealer Walker had but, similar to Craven, with reservations. Earle Davis, who had known Wood just before his death, was considering the extent to which Wood's art was a valid expression of American, especially small town, culture. In the *Main Street* drawings, he saw Wood balancing humor (or satire) with a thoughtful exploration of character that would transcend a brief comic impression.

> He labels each of his impressions 'types' rather than named persons, nor does he attempt some narrative illustration of the story. His best satiric portraits are probably *The Sentimental Yearner* (eyes uplifted and smelling a single rose); *The Good Influence* (self-satisfied fleshy woman apparently just finished with some charitable action, smiling hypocritically in her black Sunday-cape and veil against a background of a country church which also has a semi-Gothic window); *The Practical Idealist* (strong female nose and chin, hair brushed back, fine encouraging smile, the woman who means well, obviously); and most damaging of all *The Booster* (Babbitt-like face

> and flashy striped business-suit, making a booster-point with a Chamber of Commerce forefinger). The two general scenes which share Lewis's point of view are the artistically horrible *Main Street Mansion*, and *Village Slums*, the latter picture showing the village pump surrounded by out-houses and regular ugly buildings, everything outlined by paths in the snow. [37]

Davis, not deigning even to describe them or to justify his censure, did not detail what was so "artistically horrible" about *Main Street Mansion* and *Village Slums*. It is also not clear why the two architectural studies "share Lewis's point of view" any more than the other pictures. The writer mused as well about how Wood's painting, especially his portraiture, was to be rated as fine art that endured and rose above the particulars of its own time and the subjects portrayed.

> We cannot help concluding, when we examine the vast range of Wood's paintings, that he loved and admired Americans, even while he selected ridiculous examples for satiric laughter. Great portraits usually imply more than the average photographic or prettified copy of the person being painted. America has always had examples of this capacity. Our first great painter, John Singleton Copley, sometimes broke out of the paint-for-pay pattern and gave us the type as well as the individual. Remember the fat, smug Mrs. Ezekial[sic] Goldthwait reaching for an apple or a peach, or the ultra-sophisticated Mrs. Thomas Gage? These people may have lived in 1771, and we may never have heard of them, but the paintings have achieved immortality by what they convey of the human character. [38]

According to Davis, Wood was able to achieve that kind of permanence in some of his portraiture, notably in *Woman with Plants* and, to some extent, in the *Main Street* series where he "aided" Lewis's accomplishment of presenting "the small-town mind...frighteningly preserved"

The *Main Street* drawings were Wood's major artistic effort during the years from 1935 through 1938, and they seem to mark a watershed in his later career. Earlier comments on the appearance of his paintings noted that they appeared "modeled out of hard candy." [39] This description reflects Wood's smooth application of paint in which hardly a brushstroke is evident, a characteristic of the works by which he won his reputation in the early 1930s. By the later 1930s, however, his approach seemed to change, and it is tempting to wonder if it was sparked in part by the *Main Street* drawings. (His work in lithography may have also been a factor in his altered approach to form.) The *Main Street* drawings are painstakingly executed, precise in every detail, and made up largely of thousands of small marks layered one on top of the other. Although perhaps not easily discerned in the

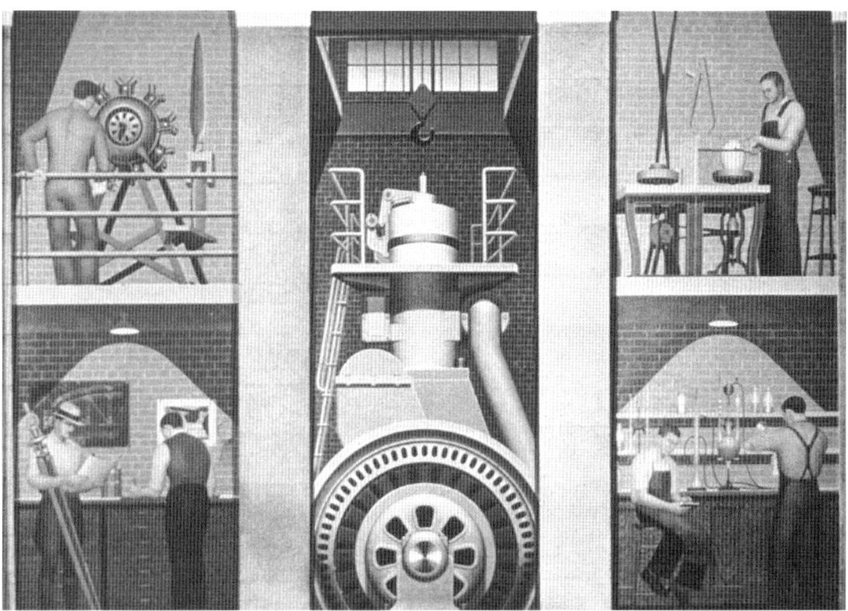

Figure 26 Engineering *(detail of* When Tillage Begins, Other Arts Follow*), 1934. Parks Library, Iowa State University*

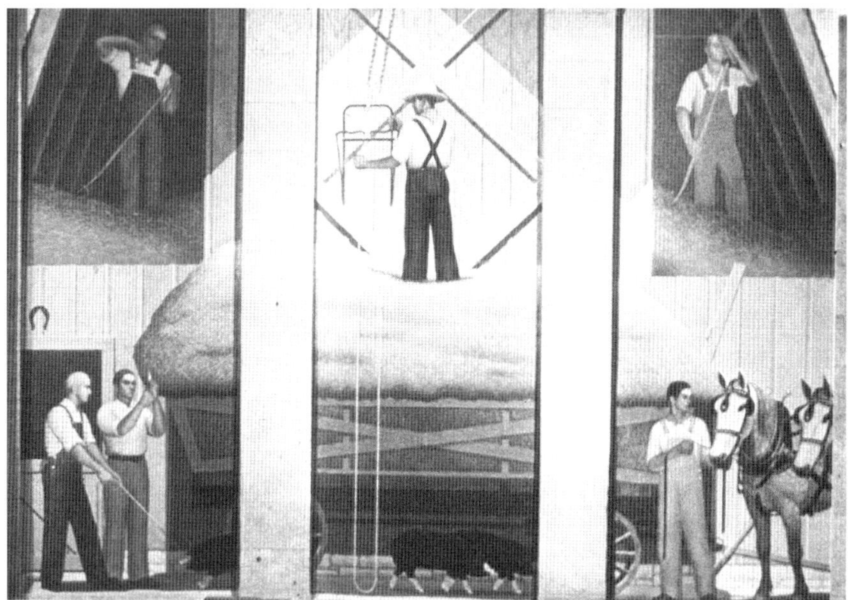

Figure 27 Agriculture *(detail of* When Tillage Begins, Other Arts Follow*), 1934. Parks Library, Iowa State University*

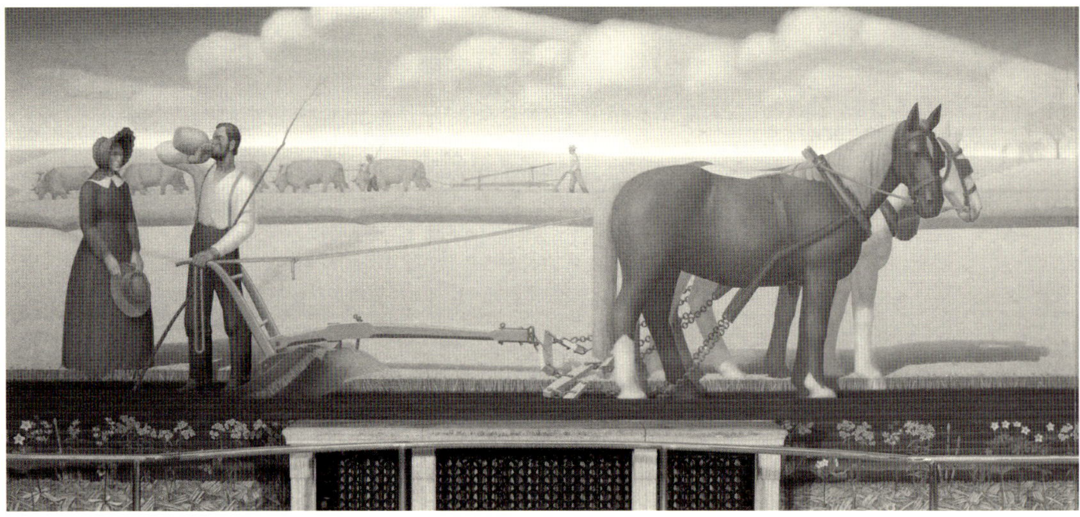

Figure 28 Breaking the Prairie Sod, *1936-1937. Parks Library, Iowa State University*

reproductions of the 1937 *Main Street* edition, the drawings themselves (and we know that Wood intended they should be seen and judged as separate works of art) show an intricate, complex surface in which individual marks are not only evident, but striking. The change in style can also be seen to some extent in the comparison of his Iowa State University murals. The sections depicting the Engineering (Figure 26), Agriculture (Figure 27), and Home Economics colleges, installed by Wood's students in 1935, are smoothly, almost flatly painted. The mural panel installed in 1937, *Breaking the Prairie Sod* (Figure 28), is notable for its multitude of short, abbreviated brushstrokes (seen most clearly in the prairie grass and the woodland ground).

When he resumed easel painting around 1939 (between 1935 and 1938, Wood produced only two major paintings: *Death on the Ridge Road* of 1935 and *Spring Turning* of 1936), the brushstroke had become more broken, with form built up through many small, short strokes of different colors. In his paintings before 1938, some areas did display discernible individual strokes because of his relentless detailing. But in the late 1930s, these kinds of brush marks were used almost exclusively to render the form and were laid down in different colors, as if to constitute the form as much through color as through line. The technique reminds us of a painting from his European days, *The Spotted Man*, created in 1924, but later reworked by the artist. [40] *Parson Weems' Fable* (1939), *Haying* (1939) (Figure 29), *New Road* (1939), *Spring in Town* (1941) (Figure 30) and other paintings from

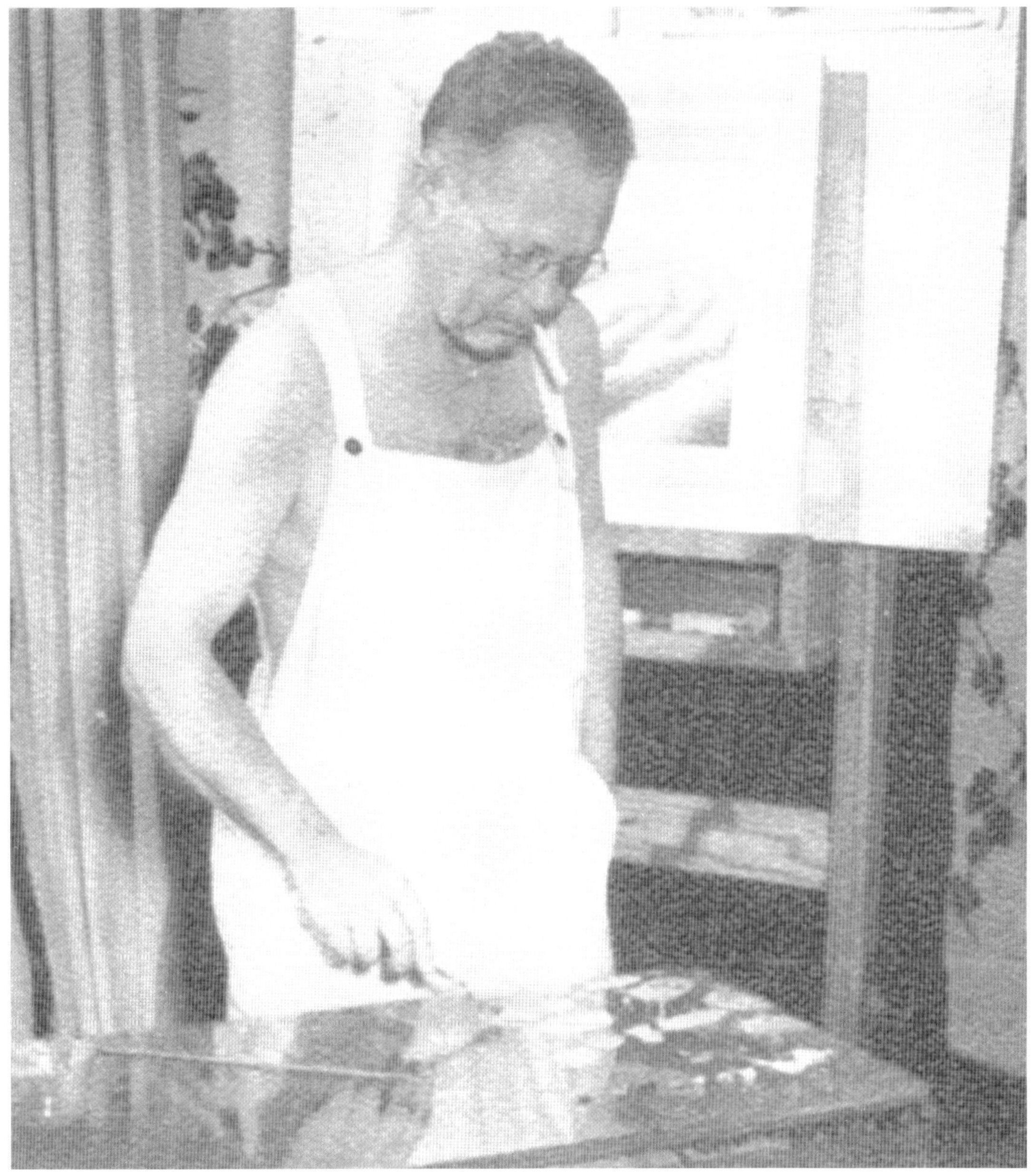

Figure 29 Wood at work on his painting Haying, *c.1940-1941.* The Hawkeye, *1941*

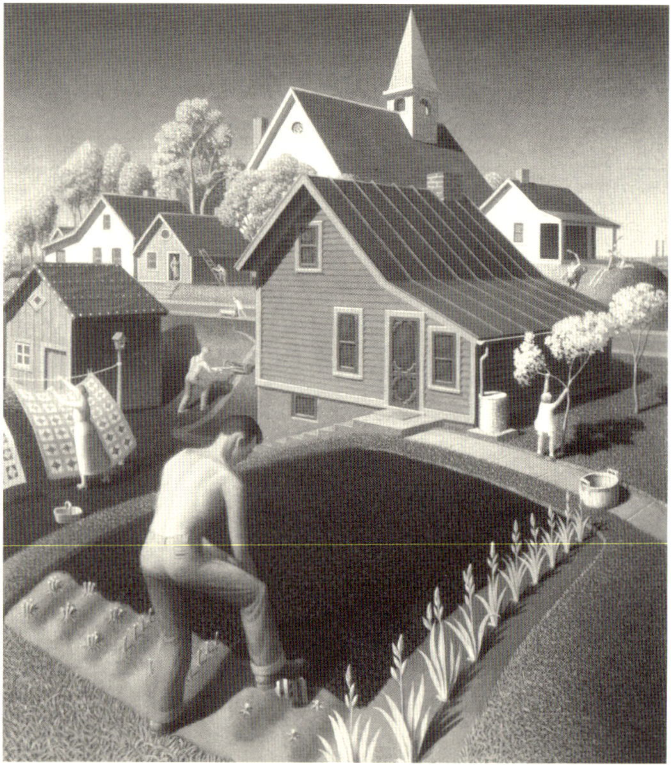

Figure 30 Spring in Town, *1941*

this period display a highly refined brushstroke, with form broken down into specific and small color marks. Though there are several factors involved, the change seems at least partly related to the years of drawing he had been doing, both for lithographs and for *Main Street.* [41]

By the early 1940s, Wood recognized that his Regionalist philosophy and his painting were increasingly coming under fire. It would have been difficult for him to avoid acknowledging the declining esteem for his art, particularly since some of the most disrespectful opinions originated in his own department at the University of Iowa. After the divorce from his wife and the nastiness of the departmental quarrels, Wood seemed ready to embark on a new phase in his life and art. Before long, however, ill health intervened, and death came before he could make much progress in his new direction. When Thomas Hart Benton visited Wood during his last illness, Wood talked to him about creating a new identity for himself and starting anew as an artist. This is a puzzling report and one that could be discounted as a symptom of Wood's terminal illness. [42] Yet, it is possible that Wood, weary of all the publicity and inflated expectations surrounding his art and, anxious about his development as an artist, was indeed planning to create what F. Scott Fitzgerald said American lives never had: a second act.

Main Street: Munich and Gopher Prairie

There has been speculation as to the relationship, if any, between Wood's work and that of a contemporary (1920s and 1930s) German style known as Neue Sachlichkeit (New Objectivity). Since many of the comparisons arise because of similarities in portraiture, a discussion of this issue cannot be evaded in a study of the *Main Street* series. The primary German artists of the style are Otto Dix (1891-1969), Christian Schad (1894-1982), Max Beckmann (1884-1950) and Georg Grosz (1893-1959), all of who were about the same age as Wood (born in 1891) and came to artistic maturity around the same time as he. Also like Wood, they worked in other styles (they had the advantage of much longer lives), but only Neue Sachlichkeit and Wood's Regionalism of the 1930s will be addressed here. Neue Sachlichkeit arose after World War I and was seen partly as a reaction against modernism (especially abstraction). [43] To some extent, it was also a reaction against German Expressionism although, since most of the artists had employed that approach in earlier work, Expressionism was sometimes blended with Neue Sachlichkeit (especially in the case of Dix). As it first developed in the 1920s, it was not associated with Nazism and the bland, soulless style that was preferred by the Third Reich after its rise to power in 1933. [44]

The association between Wood and this German style was first argued by H.W. Janson in his famous 1943 article "The International Aspects of Regionalism." The most damning part of Janson's writing was his contention that Wood's style was "similar to some of the artistic developments accompanying the rise of nationalism in Europe." [45] But his writing contained other observations that were less inflammatory and more objective. The often repeated story of Wood's change in style holds that it occurred as a result of a 1928 trip to Munich, Germany in which he was affected by late medieval Northern European painting by artists such as Jan Van Eyck (c.1390-1441), Rogier van der Weyden (c.1400-1464) and Hans Memling (c.1430-1494). Janson reasonably points out that there is no need to assume that this encounter was Wood's first with this kind of painting since he could have seen examples of it at the Art Institute of Chicago, in New York, and in various European museums during his three earlier trips (1920, 1923-1924, and 1926). In his discussion, Janson differentiates little between Wood's development of his Regionalist philosophy and the actual stylistic change that resulted from this German experience. Questions of philosophy aside, it is clear that something pushed Wood into a new style. Even if intimations of a new development are seen in his paintings of the later 1920s, the new approach found in his portraits of 1929-1930 is striking. Janson's contention is that the American artist was more influenced by the contemporary German Neue Sachlichkeit than by late medieval painting. "During the late 1920s,...Neue Sachlichkeit was so well represented in the art life of Munich that Grant Wood could hardly have escaped from it." [46]

Wood was not in Munich as a tourist, but as a worker, finishing his stained glass windows for the Cedar Rapids Veterans Memorial Building and dealing with challenges in the execution of his design. Part of the difficulty in fabricating the stained glass panels was that the Bavarian artisans painted the faces of Wood's figures as if they were medieval saints (they were accustomed to making stained glass for churches), requiring him to learn the glass craft so that he could draw them himself. [47] He was confronted, then, with a situation that juxtaposed modernism with medievalism and, obviously, he chose modernism. Or, at least he chose to paint in his own style, which hadn't, at that time, any traces of medievalism. Is it possible that he might have had a particular interest in looking at contemporary German art, especially portraiture, which would reinforce his goals for the modern stained glass faces that would eventually be installed in Cedar Rapids? Whether that is the case or not, we do know that Wood's main intention in his previous European trips was to look at and produce art and, since this was his first trip to Munich, it seems safe to propose that he would have spent as much time as possible in the museums and galleries of the city. His language facility was notoriously poor, so he would have had few incentives for socializing, and pictures required no translation. Thus, there is little basis for arguing with Janson that "we may assume that he visited the local exhibitions of contemporary German art."[48] He could also have seen reproductions of German paintings in newspapers, art journals and exhibition catalogues both in Europe and the United States. What is a more difficult question is not whether he saw Neue Sachlichkeit painting, but what, if anything, he took from it. In the end, it is a question that cannot be answered definitively since Wood is not known to have commented on the subject. Nevertheless, the visual affinities are there, and they are intriguing.

It is easy to see what the two kinds of painting have in common: realism, of course, but an especially unsparing kind of realism located in the precise, linear approach to the form. The colors are clear, disposed in broad sections and applied with a blended, unflamboyant brush. The compositional space is distinctly layered with planes that recede in an orderly, unhurried fashion. Stasis is the rule, with few exaggerated gestures or movements. In both Weimar Germany and the American Midwest, portraiture seemed to possess a particular capacity to articulate the cultural tone of the time and place. Also found in both Wood's art and Neue Sachlichkeit is a sort of iconography endemic to both European capitals and American small towns: flowers (hot-house and prairie), clothing (sheer and calico), dishes (wine glasses and Blue Willow tea cups), interiors (night clubs and kitchens), architecture (urban skylines and barns). (Figure 31-32) The light is clear, not nuanced, and sometimes even harsh, revealing the flaws seen in real faces. In *The Good Influence* (1936) (Figure 33) and the face of his sister in *Portrait of Nan* (1933), (Figure 34) Wood demonstrated that he

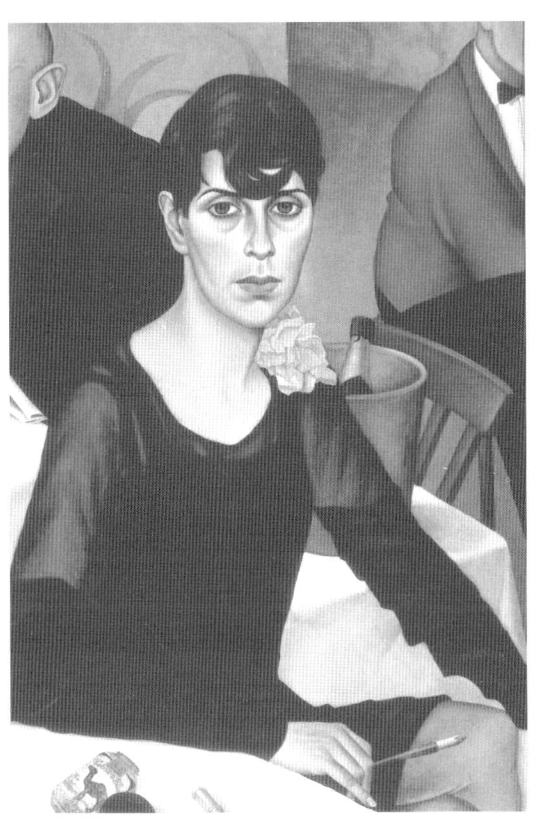

Figure 31 Christian Schad. Sonja, *1928*

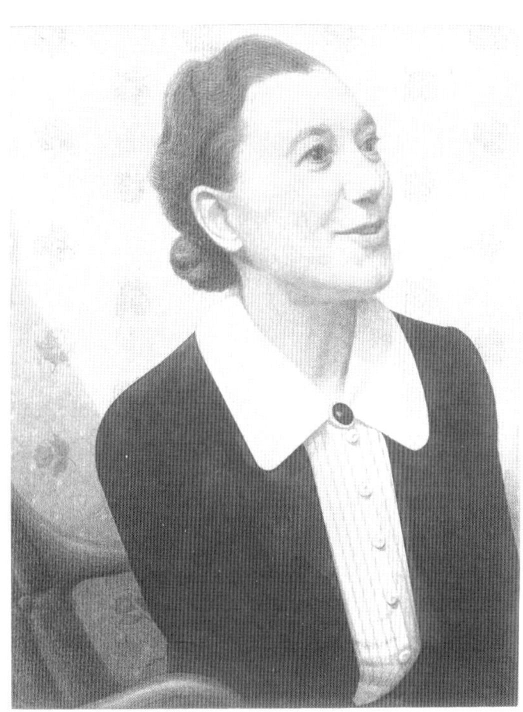

Figure 32 Practical Idealist

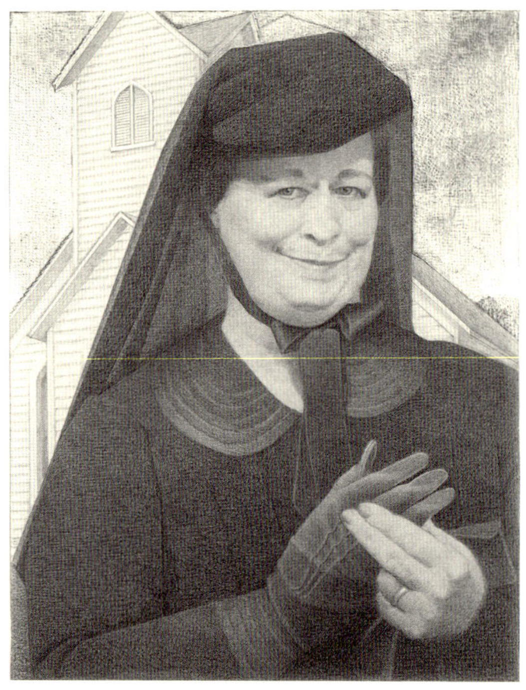

Figure 33 The Good Influence

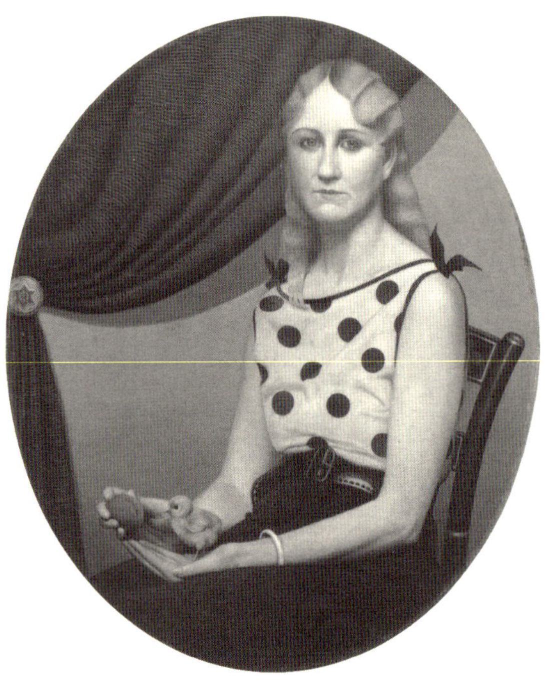

Figure 34 Portrait of Nan, *1933*

could be disarmingly frank about the unbeautiful in a human face. While physical imperfections may be spotlighted, the emotional state of the subjects is more circumspect. For both the Germans and the Americans, their portraits are often marked by a lack of emotional engagement (in the case of Neue Sachlichkeit of the 1920s and early 1930s, it seems the only modesty of the subjects is in their lack of emotional revelation). There is a sobriety about the portraits that edges into grimness, though surely it arises from different sources: perhaps license in Germany, conformity in Iowa.

Interestingly, one of the best examples of this reticent, rather joyless tone is found in the self-portraits of Wood and Schad. In Schad's 1927 *Self-Portrait* (Figure 35) with the nude figure behind him, he turns his head and looks directly out at the viewer, moving his eyes to the right. Wood's *Sketch for Self-Portrait* (Figure 36) and his *Study for Self-Portrait*, (Figure 79) places the artist in the same pose of head and upper body (although he includes only his shoulders), a similar angle on the face, eyes also shifted to the right and looking at the spectator. Both unsmiling men appear very grave, their deliberate, self-aware stares confronting us with their discontent, almost like an accusation. [49] To Schad's left is the torso of an aggressively delineated female nude while on Wood's left is a tall, Midwestern windmill. Schad's background is a bedroom (or a brothel) and urban rooftops; Wood's is an expanse of rolling, ordered Iowa countryside with a few grain stacks: two very different scenes, but ones similarly composed and equally revealing of the artist's ambiance and source of inspiration.

The possibility of stylistic influence from Neue Sachlichkeit cannot be dismissed, but in terms of social comment, few if any convergences can be found. Wood did not enjoy perfect happiness with the Midwestern society around him, as *Daughters of Revolution*, *Return from Bohemia*, and even the *Main Street* drawings show. But the viciousness and despair found in the works of Dix and Grosz especially is absent in his art. His critiques of society, while barbed and well aimed, do not approach the level of revulsion found in, for example Dix's *Big City (Triptych)* of 1927-1928 (Figure 37) or Beckmann's *Departure* (1932-1933). Wood was very much part of a society that would not have countenanced that kind of expression; in addition, he was popularly regarded as a paragon of his society; he was a success in it. One telling point is the fact that caricature is not a major element (if it exists at all) in Wood's art, as it was in Neue Sachlichkeit. He may stand accused of being illustrational, shallow or overly simplified, but even his critics could not realistically make the charge that his portraits were caricatures. Caricature is useful to artists like those of Neue Sachlichkeit who want to express disgust with their society, but not to someone like Wood who saw his society as fundamentally positive and decent. Robert Storr has observed in his writing on Schad and Neue Sachlichkeit that "although reprehensible in social terms, hatred, and the fears that prompt them, are sometimes the root of aesthetic invention, and especially so in the cruel realm of caricature." [50] The hatred and fear that animated the German artists was not present in Wood's psyche — at least not to the degree that would

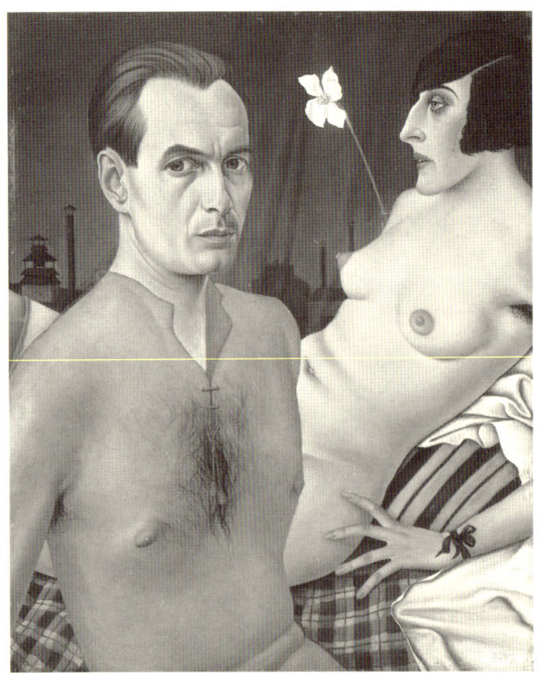

Figure 35 Christian Schad. Self-Portrait, *1927*

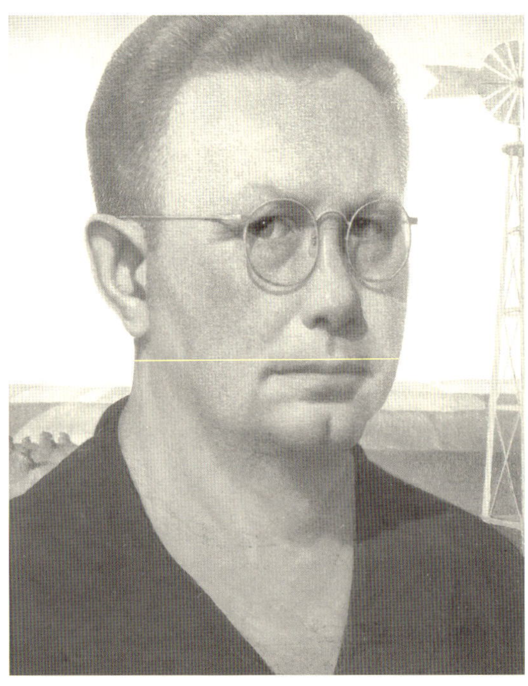

Figure 36 Sketch for Self-Portrait, *1932*

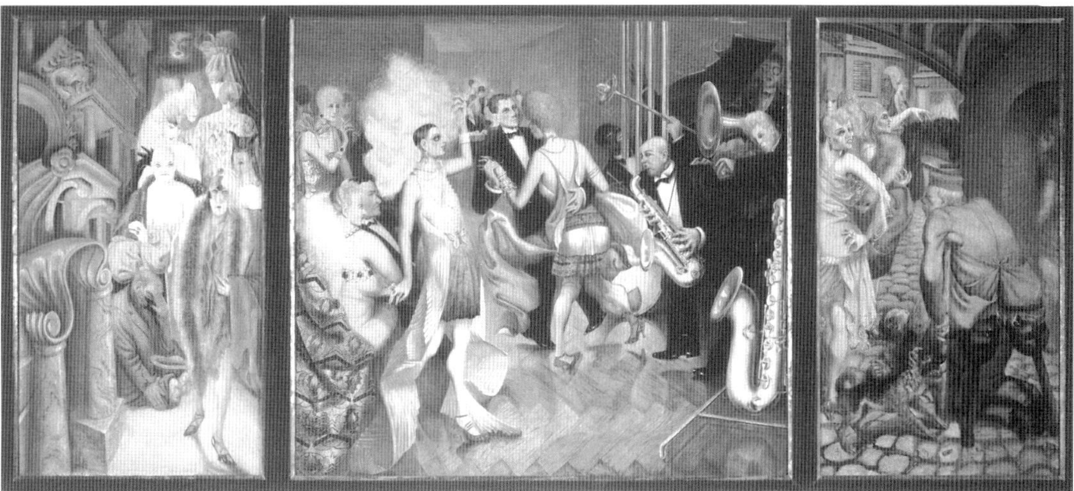

Figure 37 Otto Dix. Großstadt (Triptych) (Big City (Triptych)), *1927-1928*

lead him to create an image like *Big City (Triptych)* (1927-1928) or *The Seven Cardinal Sins* (1933) by Otto Dix or *Republican Automatons* (1920) by Georg Grosz. There remain many today who would fault Wood's "aesthetic invention," but in this context, he hadn't enough anger to follow the Neue Sachlichkeit artists into their subject matter. Consider someone as morally corrupt as Mrs. Bogart and how she might have been treated by Dix or Grosz. Wood does not present her in outrageous terms because he is not outraged by her, nor is he threatened by her. He exposes her no less thoroughly than Schad might have, but he handles the subject with indulgence, good humor, and what might almost be called Midwestern good manners. What Wood might have drawn if he had been less well mannered and more willing to plumb the depths of his own emotional and artistic conflicts is something on which we can only speculate. And, if he had decided to emulate the Germans in their assessment of their society, would even Sinclair Lewis have stood for it?

In the end, as we look at the *Main Street* series, we wonder if the German artist with whom Wood has the most affinities is not these painters at all, but the photographer August Sander (1876-1964). Sander provides us with an unflinching look at German society at

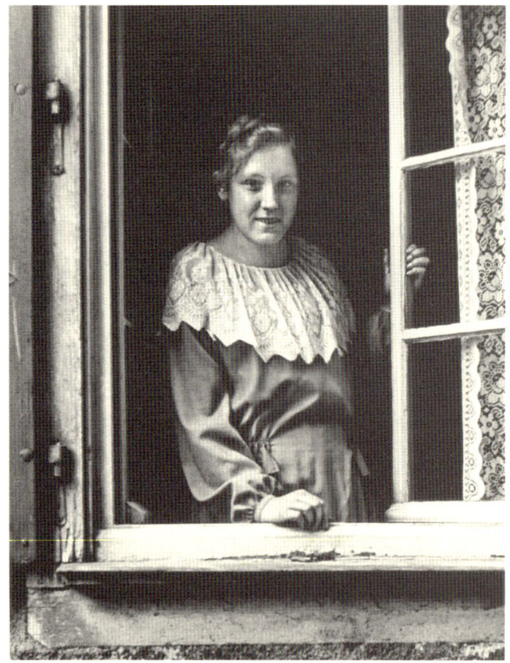

Figure 38 August Sander "Kleinstädterin" (Small-town girl), *1927*

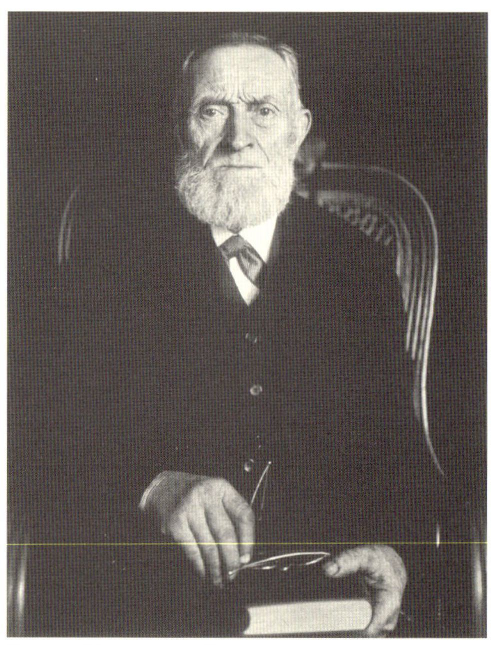

Figure 39 August Sander "Der Stürmer oder Revolutionär" (The Fighter or Revolutionary), *1925*

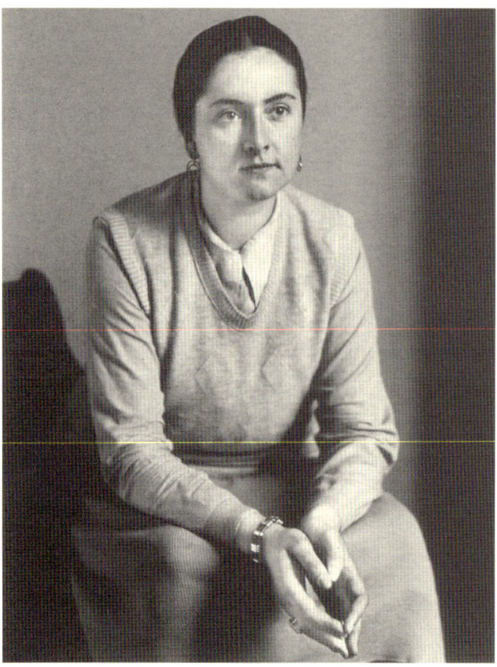

Figure 40 August Sander "Bildhauerin [Ingeborg von Rath]" (Sculptress [Ingeborg von Rath]), *1929*

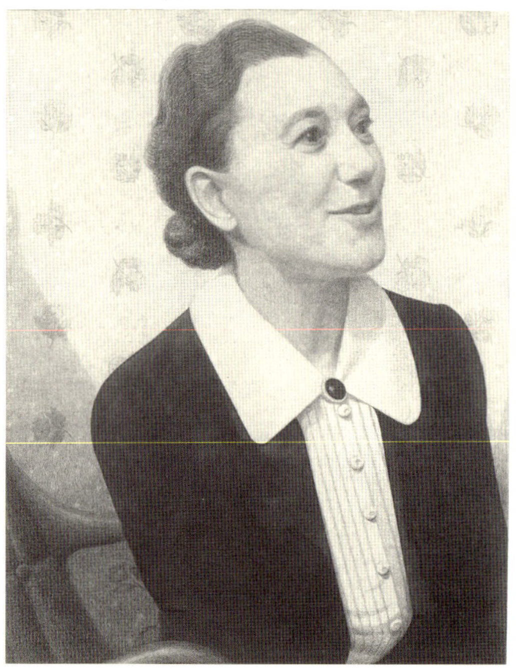

Figure 41 Practical Idealist

several levels but without the obvious judgment and revulsion found in other visual imagery of the time. Sander (Figures 38-40) was committed, as Wood was (Figure 41), to working with "types," believing that in recording people straightforwardly, it was possible to open up dimensions beneath the surface of reality. His photographic survey, entitled *People of the Twentieth Century*, has commonalities with Wood's survey of the citizens of *Main Street* (although the scale of their examination of society's types is quite different) and, in fact, the subject of one of Sander's portfolios is inhabitants of small towns. [51] Sander and Wood, in both their art and their lives, have several similarities. They lived at a time when the national populations of their countries shifted from largely rural to urban areas, a change that was reflected in their own lives. (Sander was born in a rural/small town community in western Germany, but spent much of his adult life in Cologne although, like Wood, he frequently returned to the country for visits and continued to mine it for subject matter.) Both artists were increasingly interested in a relatively "hard" sort of expression. Around 1925, Sander's development of that approach was shown in his major work, *People of the Twentieth Century*, in which his sharply focussed portraits could be seen as "straight" photography, or as Sander termed it, "exact-photography." [52] Wood also abandoned his softly brushed impressionistic style for a hard-edged, precisely realist vision, although this rejection did not occur, interestingly, until after his 1928 visit to Germany. As mentioned earlier, neither artist was as interested in individuals as they were in types (in Wood, shown most clearly in his choice of titles for his *Main Street* drawings: *The Radical*, *General Practitioner*, etc.; in Sander, by broad social appellations such as "Farmers," "Doctors"). Both tended to be emotionally neutral in their portraiture, registering no great extremes of feeling one way or the other (in either their subjects or in their approach as artists). Their central concern appears to be less involved with the individual personality than with temperaments. [53] Dealing in broader social types and more serious sociological commentary, Sander's work does not possess the satire, irony or, more simply, the humor with which Wood invests his portraits. Yet neither artist seems to dislike or be disgusted by their subjects (as were the Neue Sachlichkeit painters), no matter how unsparingly they portray them. [54] The discernment of similarities of Wood's life and art to Sander's aside, the question remains as to whether the American actually knew of the German photographer's work. As with the issue of influence from German painters, no compelling evidence has come to light to prove Wood knew or did not know their work. Though not widely exhibited, [55] Sander's work was recognized and could be seen in Germany or Wood might have encountered it in publications. In 1929, just months after Wood left Munich, Sander published a portfolio of sixty photographs, *Faces of the Time* (*Antlitz der Zeit*) in which his distinctive vision of portraiture reveals many intriguing correspondences with Wood's, especially the *Main Street* portraits. Oddly enough, as with Wood's depictions of Midwestern society, Sander's work was reviewed variously by critics, some of whom believed it affirmed the society he recorded, others that the portraits criticized society, especially the rural aspects. [56] Wood made no more trips to Europe after the 1928 Munich visit, so any influence from contemporary German art on the *Main Street* drawings would have come through revived (or enduring) memories of what he had seen there or through publications available in the United States. Memories, new encounters or no influence at all — Wood has left us very little solid information on the issue of his influence from contemporary German artists. But the visual affinities keep the question alive.

Chapter 4 Notes

1. These were mostly book jackets: *In Tragic Life* (1933) and *Passion Spins the Plot* (1934) by Vardis Fisher, *O'Chautauqua* (1935) by Thomas Duncan, *Plowing on Sunday* (1938) by Sterling North and *Oliver Wiswell* (1940) by Kenneth Roberts. These were likely done for financial reasons or as a favor to the author. *Farm on the Hill* (1935-1936), a children's book by Madeline Darrough Horn, had Wood's illustrations throughout its pages.

2. "A Midwest Artist Views *Main Street*," St. Louis *Post-Dispatch*. Sunday Magazine. May 23, 1937, A1.

3. *Catalogue of a Loan Exhibition of Drawings and Paintings By Grant Wood, with an evaluation of the artist and his work by Park Rinard and Arnold Pyle*, Chicago: The Lakeside Press Galleries, February and March, 1935.

4. The Easton Press, *Notes from the Archives*, insert for The Collector's Library of Famous Editions; the 1965 reprint of the 1937 Limited Editions Club. According to a letter of November 5, 1945 from Macy to S. Spencer Scott at Harcourt, Brace and Company, the Limited Editions Club paid $500 for permission to reprint the *Main Street* text. Microfiche archives of Easton Press.

5. *Notes from the Archives*. In 1939, Wood listed this and four other books that had "most deeply influenced his thinking: 1. *The Grapes of Wrath* 2. *Main Street* 3. *All Quiet on the Western Front* 4. *Manhattan Transfer* 5. *The Autobiography of Lincoln Steffens*." "What Thinking People Read," *Boston Evening Transcript*, July 22, 1939. NWG Scrapbook No.2, 105. Wood and Lewis, in their mutual admiration, had apparently decided to overlook Wood's (or Mott's) comment in *Revolt Against the City* of 1935 in which he deplored the "contempt" Lewis and others had engendered toward the Midwest. "The feeling that the East, and perhaps Europe, was the true goal of the seeker after culture was greatly augmented by the literary movement which Mr. Van Doren once dubbed 'the revolt against the village.' Such books as *Spoon River Anthology* and *Main Street* brought contempt upon the hinterland and strengthened the cityward tendency. H.L. Mencken's urban and European philosophy was exerted in the same direction." Obviously, Wood (or Mott) were countering the "revolt against the village" by their *Revolt Against the City*. Reprinted in Dennis, 231.

6. Letter from Wood to Maynard Walker, October 21, 1935. AAA, Maynard Walker files, reel 2025, frame 987-988.

7. "Wood in the Frank Role of Illustrator," *Art Digest*, vol. X, no.14, April 15, 1936, 8. According to this article, "these are the first book illustrations made by the famous Iowan." The reviewer goes on: "As usual, Wood's draughtsmanship and close attention to details produce recognizable characters; the artist's sly humor and understanding observations make them genuine farm folks." The review is generally positive, but the headline, "Wood in the Frank Role of Illustrator," implies that Wood is finally being honest about what is the true level of his art: illustration. The exhibition of the drawings at the Maynard Walker Gallery (April 14-May 4, 1936) was accompanied by a brochure entitled *Decorative Drawings by Grant Wood.*

8. Dennis, James M., *Grant Wood: A Study in Art and Culture*, Columbia: University of Missouri Press, 1986,

239, n.21. The December delivery of the drawings is perhaps corroborated by an article on the occasion of Wood's visit to the Joslyn Museum at Omaha. "With artistic success have come fat commissions for the Iowan. He recently completed a set of drawings for a limited edition of Sinclair Lewis' *Main Street*. He has nothing on canvas now, this being what he calls an 'in-between' period." "Grant Wood Praises 'Friends of Art,'" *The Omaha Bee-News*, January 28, 1937. NWG Scrapbook No.2, 68. An article of January, 1936 indicates that Wood was at work on the *Main Street* commission by that time: "Iowa Cows Give Grant Wood His Best Thoughts;" New York *Herald Tribune*, January 23, 1936. NWG Scrapbook No.2, 46. "He wants to continue his own easel painting, and especially to illustrate a new edition of Sinclair Lewis's *Main Street*." A 1940 article must have been based on the *Herald Tribune* one of January 1936 since it inaccurately states, "He says that he would like to illustrate Sinclair Lewis's *Main Street* and continue his easel painting." Hanson, Eleanor, "Grant Wood," *The Wellesley Review*, vol.XIV, no.5, March 1940, 13-17; NWG Scrapbook No.4, 16.

9. Letter from Macy to Thomas Hart Benton, June 3, 1940. Easton Press microfiche archives.

10. *Modern Painters and Sculptors As Illustrators*, ed. by Monroe Wheeler, New York: Museum of Modern Art, 1936 (1st edition), 11-12. The exhibition was held April 27-September 2, 1936.

11. Wheeler,10-11 (1936 edition).

12. Wheeler, 16 (1936 edition).

13. Wheeler, 17 (1936 edition).

14. *Modern Painters and Sculptors As Illustrators*, ed. by Monroe Wheeler, New York: Museum of Modern Art, 3rd revised edition, 1946 (copyright 1947 by Museum of Modern Art), 15. The Museum of Modern Art issued Wheeler's catalogue in three editions: 1936, 1938 and 1946. The illustration from *Farm on the Hill* is reproduced on page 96 in the 1946 edition.

15. Dennis, 240, n.34.

16. Letter from Macy to Boardman Robinson, October 14, 1943. For that fee, Macy wanted Robinson to provide sixteen color portraits. Easton Press microfiche archives.

17. Throughout his life, Wood was not attentive to financial matters. In the 1930s during and after his marriage, his economic pressures made him acutely concerned with the amount of money produced by his art. According to his sister, as Wood was autographing pages before the binding of the 1500 copies of *Main Street*, he commented, "'I hope my writing won't improve so much by all this practice that the bank won't recognize my signature on a check.'" Graham, Nan Wood, *My Brother, Grant Wood*, Iowa City: State Historical Society of Iowa, 1993, 139-140.

18. Dennis, 129.

19. Letter from Wood to Lewis, July 10, 1937. Yale Collection of American Literature, Beinecke Rare Book and Manuscript Library, Yale University. My thanks to Laurie Klein of the Library for locating and furnishing this letter to me.

20. Letter from Lewis to Frank Luther Mott, November 16, 1940. Letters of Frank Luther Mott, Special Collections, University of Iowa Library. The letter was written from New York.

21. Schorer, Mark, *Sinclair Lewis: An American Life*, New York: McGraw-Hill Book Company, 1961, 662. Norman Foerster was the model for one of the two tall academicians in Wood's 1937 lithograph, *Honorary Degree*.

22. *The Sixteenth International Exhibition. Water Colors, Pastels, Drawings and Monotypes*. The Art Institute of

Chicago, March 18-May 16, 1937. The five drawings were *General Practitioner* (#508), *The Good Influence* (#509), *Main Street Mansion* (#510), *The Perfectionist* (#511), and *Sentimental Yearner* (#512). My thanks to Bart Ryckbosch at the Art Institute for providing me with materials on this exhibition.

23. Letter from Wood to Maynard Walker, March 11, 1937. AAA. Maynard Walker files, reel 2025, frame 1005.

24. Pynchon, Adeline Lobdell, "Dinner Table Art," *Chicago Journal of Commerce and Law*, March 20, 1936. *The Good Influence* is mistakenly identified in this article as a watercolor. NWG Scrapbook No.2, 61.

25. Montz, Wanda, "'Booster' — By Grant Wood; From Special Edition Of 'Main Street,'" Cedar Rapids *Gazette*, May 9, 1937.

26. Hamilton, Audrey, "Wood Draws for *Main Street*; Iowa Artist Illustrates Special Edition Of Lewis' Novel," *Daily Iowan*, May 22, 1937. Illustrated are *Booster*, *Sentimental Yearner*, *The Good Influence*, and *General Practitioner*.

27. *Post-Dispatch*. Several years before, in 1934, the newspaper had run a substantial article with reproductions on Wood's book jacket for Vardis Fisher's *Passion Spins the Plot.* "How Grant Wood Made a Book Cover," St. Louis *Post-Dispatch*, January 28, 1934.

28. *Post-Dispatch*. A similar palette is found in the 1934 Wood-designed murals for Parks Library at Iowa State University. In this case, the muted yellow tone harmonizes with the color of the stone pillars that surround the murals.

29. Craven, Thomas, "Grant Wood," *Scribner's Magazine*, vol.CI, no.6, June 1937, 16-22; 16. Elsewhere, the media of the drawings was described as pencil (*Sixteenth International Exhibition*...at the Art Institute of Chicago and Hamilton, "Wood Draws..."). If by "pencil" these identifications mean graphite, they are incorrect; however, some wax crayons could have the appearance of a pencil, causing some confusion. The important point is that no other media such as charcoal or chalk is given and the colors are listed as black and white only.

30. Craven, 21.

31. S.A.N., "The Happy, Busy Toiler In Overalls Who Is Grant Wood," Kansas City *Times*, February 14, 1938. NWG Scrapbook No.2, 81. Another article which mentions in passing the *Main Street* drawings is Selby, John, "'I'm Not a Torchbearer,' Says Wood;" Des Moines *Register*, undated clipping, NWG Scrapbook No.2, 84.

32. S.A.N. A month earlier, during a visit to the Rhode Island School of Design, he again tried to counter the label of satirist. In a newspaper article headlined "*American Gothic* Artist Denies Attempt at Satire; 'It's Only Interpretation,' Grant Wood Tells Interviewer," the reporter observed, "He has drawn some satirical illustrations for a special edition of *Main Street*, but generally,...he simply pictures the rural life and people of Iowa. And he likes to tell a story in his pictures. He thinks the United States is too large and diverse a territory to be adequately understood and expressed in a single work of art or even by a single artist in many works of art. He approves that 'cross-section' method taken by Sinclair Lewis, for example, in which the field is narrowed to some typical phase or typical manifestation." G.Y. Loveridge, unidentified Providence newspaper, January 1938. NWG Scrapbook No.2, 90.

33. Letter from Maynard Walker to Mrs. V.R.D. Kirkham, January 21, 1954. AAA. Maynard Walker Gallery files, reel 2025, frame 964.

34. Letter from Walker to Edward Maser, July 25, 1958. AAA. Maynard Walker Gallery files, reel 2025, frames 991-994.

35. Jewell, Edward Alden, "The Books: As Illustrated Books, Part One 1929-1939," (Section One: Critique),

in *Quarto-Millenary, The First 250 Publications and the First 25 Years 1929-1945 of The Limited Editions Club; A Critique; A Conspectus; A Bibliography; Indexes*, New York: The Limited Editions Club (The George Macy Companies), 1959, 21.

36. Craven, Thomas, "An Appraisal," in *Quarto-Millenary*, 34.

37. Davis, Earle, "Grant Wood: He Painted America," *Kansas Quarterly*, vol.4, no.4, Fall 1972, 5-11, 10.

38. Davis, 10.

39. "Iowa Detail," *Time Magazine*, September 5, 1932. NWG Scrapbook No.1, 74.

40. For a discussion of this and other early paintings and the techniques and materials used by Wood, see Roberts, Brady, *Grant Wood: An American Master Revealed*, Davenport Museum of Art, 1995; on *The Spotted Man*, see 2.

41. For a discussion of Wood's late style, see Corn, 610-62 and Roberts, 2-3.

42. Benton recounts Wood's deathbed declaration in his article "What's Holding Back American Art?" *Saturday Review of Literature*, vol.XXXIV, no.50, December 15, 1951, 9-13, 38. In her memoir of her brother, Nan Wood Graham saw Wood's comments to Benton as an example of his indefatigable hope. "After Grant had been told that he had cancer, and that there was no hope, Grant asked to be left alone for a while in order to adjust to the idea. Later, he told...Park Rinard that he was going to shut it out of his mind (a power which Grant seemed to have) and said he was going to go on just as he had before his illness, making plans for the future." She added, however, that she believed that, as his condition worsened, much of his talk was largely a result of the pain management medication. *My Brother, Grant Wood*, 121-122.

43. Many artists who had experimented radically with form before the war drew back from that approach and produced more classical works. Compare, for example, Picasso's cubist work of 1909-1914 with his classicizing drawings such as *Ambroise Vollard* (1915) and *Portrait of Igor Stravinsky* (1920) and paintings such as *The Pipes of Pan* (1923). (Of course, Picasso continued at the same time to create synthetic cubist works.) This return to more traditional forms can also be seen in other arts. Compare Stravinsky's *The Rite of Spring* (1913) with his *Pulchinella* (1919-1920).

44. For a recent discussion of Neue Sachlichkeit in its various branches and manifestations, see Karcher, Eva, *Otto Dix*, Cologne: Taschen, 2003, especially the chapter "'Sachlichkeit' — Objectivity and the Age," 7-16. See also Roberts, Brady, *Grant Wood: An American Master Revealed*, Davenport Museum of Art, 1995, 24-40.

45. Janson, H.W., "The International Aspects of Regionalism," *College Art Journal*, vol.II, no.4, May 1943, 110-115, 114. This and other writings by Janson concerning Wood and Regionalism are usually regarded as reflecting his personal antagonism toward the artist. Wood and Janson crossed paths in 1939 at the University of Iowa when Janson was a young instructor in the art department and Wood was a prominent, if beleaguered, professor. The artist was enmeshed in conflicts, both personal and professional, within the department that were deep, unpleasant, and unresolvable. Special Collections at the University of Iowa contains extensive information related to this conflict in its files on Wood and other parties involved in the quarrels. The possible relationship between Wood and the Neue Sachlichkeit painters is also discussed in Dennis, 75-77.

46. Janson, 113.

47. Nan Wood Graham gives an interesting account of her brother's work in Munich on the Veterans Memorial Building window. *My Brother, Grant Wood*, 60-65. Another appeared in Christopher Morley's column in *The*

Saturday Review of Literature, not long after Morley's 1934 visit to Iowa. "Mr. Wood's fine War Memorial window in the Cedar Rapids City Hall — the largest stained glass in the United States, I believe — was thrilling with morning sunlight streamed against it. The glass was colored and fixed in Germany, which troubled some patrioteers; it seems to me to add the touch of fulfillment to so fine a memorial of the useless tragedy of War. And, as Grant Wood amusingly told me, the firm of glass-workers in Munich had always worked on religious windows so that they made each American soldier face look too messianic. He had to learn the difficult art of glass-painting in a hurry in order to redraw the faces himself. I am always impatient with those who imagine some necessary intolerance between business and the arts; so I was pleased to learn that the only place in Cedar Rapids which was big enough for the artist to spread out his full-size drawing for the window was in the Quaker Oats factory." vol. XI, no.19, November 24, 1934, 311.

48. Janson, 112.

49. This disdainful, almost accusatory stare of the artist can be traced back to the self-portraits of the German Renaissance artist Albrecht Durer (1471-1528), who was an important source for the Neue Sachlichkeit painters.

50. Storr, Robert, "Of Talent, Ambivalence, and the Worst of Times: *Christian Schad and the Neue Sachlichkeit*," ed. by Jill Lloyd and Michael Peppiatt. New York: Schirmer/Musel verlag, Munich, in association with Neue Galerie, New York, 2002, 66.

51. For reproductions and discussions of Sander's photographs see *August Sander: Citizens of the Twentieth Century; Portrait Photographs, 1892-1952*, ed. by Gunther Sander, text by Ulrich Keller, trans. by Linda Keller, Cambridge: The MIT Press, 1986. Much new research has been accomplished on Sander since this 1986 publication. For a more complete and current study of the photographer, see *August Sander: People of the Twentieth Century*, edited in seven volumes by Die Photographische Sammlung/SK Stiftung Kultur, Cologne, revised and newly compiled by Susanne Lange, Gabriele Conrath-Scholl and Gerd Sander, New York: Harry N. Abrams, 2002 and August Sander: People of the Twentieth Century, text volume edited by Die Photographische Sammlung/SK Stiftung Kultur, Cologne, revised and newly compiled by Susanne Lange, Gabriele Conrath-Scholl. Munich: Schirmer/ Mosel 2001 (English edition to be published by MIT Press, New York. The complete series entitled "Small Town Dwellers" is in Volume I: I/6/1-13. The photographs range in date from 1911 to 1935. The author acknowledges the cooperation and suggestions of Die Photographische Sammlung/SK Stiftung Kuitur in Cologne.

52. Keller, Ulrich in *August Sander*, 1986, 15.

53. This characteristic in both Wood and Sander may perhaps be reminiscent of the centuries-old division of human beings into four temperaments, or humors, as shown in the German painter Albrecht Durer's *Four Apostles* of 1526, found in the collection of the Alte Pinakothek in Munich.

54. In Germany, especially in the 1920s and 1930s, there were a number of photographic surveys that purported to document the social "types" of society, mostly in the service of ideological or political agendas with which Sander's work had little in common. Books of photo-portraiture included *Everyday Heads* (1931) by Helmar Lerski, *German Folk Faces* (1930) by Erna Lendvai-Dircksen, *Men at Work* (1930) and *Those of the Soil* (1931) by Erich Retzlaff. For a discussion of these sorts of photographic surveys, see the essay by Ulrich Keller in *August Sander*, 1986, pp. 8-11.

55. Keller, Ulrich in *August Sander*, 1986, 3.

56. Keller, Ulrich in *August Sander*, 1986, 54-55.

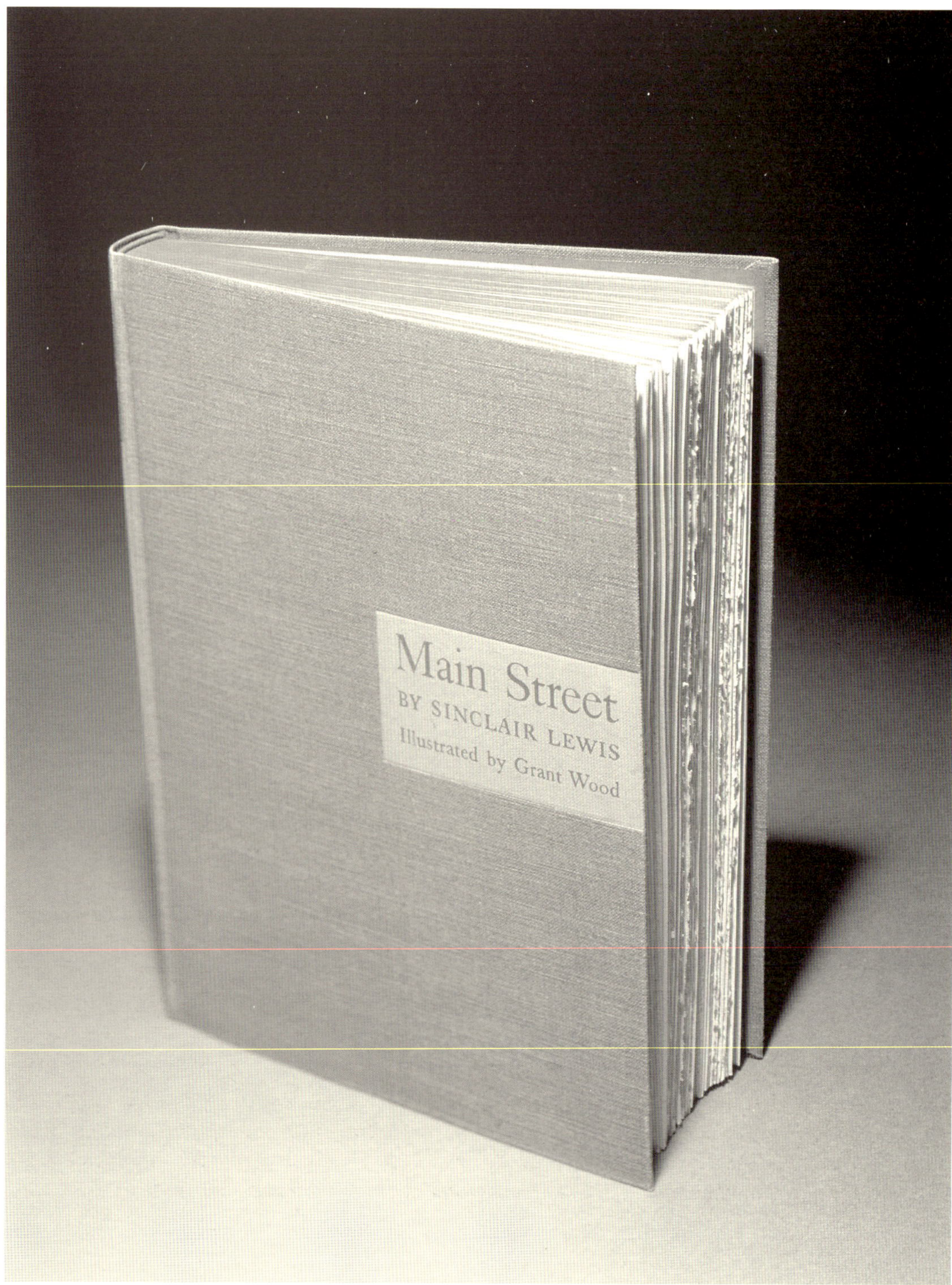

Figure 42 The Limited Editions Club Main Street

Chapter 5
The Limited Editions Club

The Limited Editions Club was created by George Jesse Macy (1900-1956) in 1929, a year that might have seemed a disastrous choice if he had realized that his first book would be released the same month as the Wall Street Crash that precipitated the Great Depression. Yet, the Limited Editions Club was a success and has remained in existence in some form until today His idea was to produce fine publications of classic literary works on high quality paper with distinctive bindings and illustrations by contemporary artists, mostly Americans. Printed by various presses, Macy's books were issued in "series" of about a dozen titles. [1] His most important books were two in which he secured the services of Pablo Picasso (*Lysistrata of Aristophanes)* in 1933-34 and then Henri Matisse (*Ulysses* by James Joyce) in 1934-35. [2] Most of the time, however, he selected American artists for his illustrators, especially those who might be termed American Scene practitioners. Thomas Hart Benton and John Steuart Curry were given multiple commissions by Macy: John Steinbeck's *The Grapes of Wrath*, Mark Twain's *The Adventures of Tom Sawyer*, *Huckleberry Finn*, and *Life on the Mississippi* were illustrated by Benton, and John Steuart Curry was given *The Prairie* by James Fenimore Cooper and *The Red Badge of Courage* by Stephen Crane. [3] Grant Wood's *Main Street* (Figure 42) appeared in the 8th Series (November 1936 - October 1937) along with *Le Morte d'Arthur*, John Milton's *Paradise Lost* and *Paradise Regain'd*, the autobiography of the Italian Renaissance artist Benevenuto Cellini, and the childhood classic, *Pinocchio*, among others. [4]

The books were restricted to a printing of 1500 copies, and each was signed by the artist who illustrated it. Wood signed and numbered *Main Street* at the back of the book in blue-black ink. Printed above the artist's signature was this information: "Of this edition of "Main Street," fifteen hundred copies have been printed for the members of the Limited Editions Club at the Lakeside Press, Chicago, under the supervision of W.A. Kittredge; the illustrations having been drawn by Grant Wood, who here signs." The book was further described as "set in monotype Caslon; Arak paper; flexible binding of full gray linen, printed tan and blue; 406 pages, 7 1/2 x 9 1/2 inches." [5] Beginning with *Main Street Mansion* as the frontispiece, the illustrations were sequenced as *The Perfectionist, Sentimental Yearner*, *The Radical*, *General Practitioner*, *The Good Influence*, *Practical Idealist*, *Booster*, and *Village Slums*.

These titles were printed in brownish-yellow ink beneath each illustration. [6] This and Macy's other Limited Editions Club books were available to subscribers only and were not sold individually or in bookstores. The Club prided itself on the high quality of all its materials, on the selection of the titles and, certainly, on the caliber of artists who contributed illustrations. An advertisement for the 8th Series appeared in the October 17, 1936 issue of *The Saturday Review* announcing that this series was being "printed and illustrated by the most famous book artists in the world" and advising readers to "act quickly" since all the other series had been "fully subscribed." No titles or artists were named nor were any prices quoted. [7]

Macy felt that his books were, considering their quality, of reasonable cost. [8] But soon after the publication of *Main Street*, a St. Louis newspaper commented that the Club's new book was out of reach for most Midwesterners. "[*Main Street*] is issued by (and for) the Limited Editions Club, a tight little society that prints books for members only; members being restricted to 1500. Hence its circulation will be confined to collectors able to afford $108 a year for the satisfaction of being exclusive. Gopher Prairie (the fictitious average village where the book is set) won't see many copies of this edition. Nevertheless the limited edition, whatever its public, must be regarded as an important work of art. And the fact that it will circulate largely in the East makes it worth pointing out that the work originates in every respect save in demand, in the Middle West." [9]

No less a Midwesterner than Sinclair Lewis himself, however, felt justified in associating with — and promoting — the Limited Editions Club (Wood had no known hesitation either). In an excerpt of an essay for the Club's Seventh Series, he declared that the collecting of books was a worthy endeavor, particularly if they were acquired because they were "fine and memorable in themselves" and not just "rare." "The collection of books that are distinguished in themselves, that are a delight to the hand as they are to the eye, that are masterful in paper, in binding, in the arrangement of the page, this is not so very different from the collection of superior paintings — and it is a hundred times or so more possible for purses that are none too fat." [10] The St. Louis *Post-Dispatch* to the contrary, Lewis apparently felt that $108 a year for ten or more books such as those he described was a valid expenditure, even during the Depression. Wood may have joined him in the attitude that, for those who could not afford one of his paintings or drawings, the Club's edition of *Main Street*, with nine illustrations, was rather a bargain. [11]

At Macy's request, Lewis wrote a new introduction to the 1937 *Main Street*. He discussed why he had written the book, the circumstances of its writing in 1919-1920, and the reactions of readers from high school students to the English novelist John Galsworthy. The motivation for the novel came in 1905 after his sophomore year at Yale University when the young man became convinced that American small towns were usually "a respectable form of hell."[12] That was how he had come to feel during a summer spent in his home town of Sauk Centre, Minnesota when he kept "overhearing the villagers none too softly wonder, 'Why don't Doc Lewis [Lewis's father] make [him] get a job on a farm instead of letting him sit around readin'?" The "neighborliness that was the glory of the small town...was a fake," he decided, and he began a novel called "The Village Virus." In this early version, the central character was a young lawyer who was "spiritually starved" in a little town. Eventually Carol Kennicott was shifted into place as the main character and the young lawyer devolved into Guy Pollock.[13] It is not known when in the chronology of publishing this 1937 edition Lewis wrote his new Introduction. He did not mention Wood's illustrations or even acknowledge the reason for writing this Introduction (the publication of a new, deluxe, *illustrated* edition). Lewis speaks only of himself and not of Wood. If he had any opinion of the illustrations or had even seen them, he did not say so. If he possessed any sense of shared affinity with Wood or his art, he failed to mention that as well. In contrast to Wood's demonstrated affection for Midwestern small towns, Lewis did not feel obliged, after nearly twenty years, to soften his view that they were, and remained, a "respectable form of hell."

Macy would have liked to illustrate more novels by Lewis (Thomas Hart Benton for *Elmer Gantry* and John Steuart Curry for *Dodsworth*, he proposed). During World War II, he tried to launch his project with a new edition of *Babbitt* which he proposed to have Boardman Robinson illustrate with sixteen portraits. In his letter offering the commission, he informed Robinson that in his earlier publication of *Main Street*, Grant Wood's illustrations "were all portraits, and some very good ones" and added, "I think you could do a splendid job...since Babbitt and his colleagues require to be portrayed with the same degree of tenderness with which Red [Lewis's nickname] Lewis wrote about them in the novel."[14] Perhaps the idea of depicting personalities rather than narrative scenes, as Wood had done, was something Macy planned to continue in subsequent editions of Lewis's novels. Lewis was delighted at the possibility of another edition: "Yes! I think *Babbitt* with Robinson illustrations would be superb and yes, I'd write an introduction....The prospect of [*Elmer*] *Gantry* with Benton is equally glorious. Wouldn't it be a good idea to have both of these of the dimensions as *Main Street*?"[15] In the end, wartime conditions and budget concerns led Macy to drop the *Babbitt* proposal, and his plans for a series of Lewis novels illustrated by Regionalist artists was never realized.

But Macy was able to enlist the two other major Regionalist artists, Benton and Curry, as illustrators for important American novels. The same year that *Main Street* was published (1937) found Macy negotiating with both artists and with Lakeside Press in Chicago (who had printed *Main Street*). John Steuart Curry had expressed interest in Willa Cather's tale of Nebraska, *My Antonia*, but Cather and her publisher both declined the offer.[16] Lakeside Press was eager to continue working with artists as they had with Wood, and they proposed two more volumes to be done in a format similar to *Main Street*'s. "Really, George," wrote Lakeside's William Kittredge, "I believe that if you can get [Thomas Hart] Benton to do *Life on the Mississippi* and John Steuart Curry to do *The Virginian*, or some such American title, you will have three of your most lasting titles from the point of view of American text, American scene and American painter." [17] Kittredge was proactive in gaining the confidence of the artists about his Press and lining them up for more illustrated books in the vein of *Main Street*, though the titles did change to *Tom Sawyer* for Benton and James Fenimore Cooper's *The Prairie* for Curry. Macy was reluctant to work again with Lakeside because he had found them to be "the most expensive book printer in America," difficult to work with and had been disappointed with their work on *Main Street.* [18] As noted earlier, Macy continued to commission illustrations from these artists, though not all of them were published by Lakeside. Perhaps the most famous ones were Benton's pictures (1940) for *The Grapes of Wrath* by John Steinbeck in which Benton's travels, particularly to California, supplied him with subjects and characterizations which translated into images for the book.[19]

Macy continued producing his special editions until his death in 1956. Afterwards, his wife and then his son maintained the business until it was sold to Boise-Cascade Company in 1970. In 1979, Sidney Shiff became the owner of the Limited Editions Club and has continued the tradition of publishing important books containing illustrations by significant contemporary artists. The focus has been adjusted to emphasize more the artists and the contemporary medium of artists' books. [20] Occasionally, the Easton Press has reissued the editions produced by Macy. [21]

Chapter 5 Notes

1. A complete listing of all the books in all the series is found in Newman, Ralph Geoffrey and Wiche, Glen Norman, *Great and Good Books: A Bibliographic Catalogue of The Limited Editions Club, 1929-1985*, with a preface by Mortimer J. Adler, Chicago: Ralph Geoffrey Newman, Inc., 1989, unpaginated beyond introduction. Each publication is given a number. Newman's introduction states that "many of the twentieth century's most gifted artists brought their magnificent talents to these significant works" and includes Grant Wood among others such as Reginald Marsh, Rockwell Kent, Edward Steichen, Thomas Hart Benton and, of course, Matisse and Picasso. For more information on George Macy and the Limited Editions Club, see Grossman, Carol, "East Side Story: Two Faces of the Limited Editions Club," *Biblio*, March 1999, 30-39.

2. Newman and Wiche. Picasso's *Lysistrata* was in the 5th Series (October 1933 - October 1934), No. 54; this work was translated and introduced by Gilbert Seldes, a writer for *The Saturday Review of Literature*, a magazine with which Wood had close ties. Matisse's illustrations for *Ulysses* (No.71) were in the 6th Series (November 1934 - October 1935). Matisse's illustrations seemed to be more appropriate for Homer's classic *The Odyssey* than Joyce's twentieth century masterpiece, but Macy published them along with the artist's preparatory drawings. See also *Quarto-Millenary; The First 250 Publications and the First 25 Years 1929-1954 of the Limited Editions Club; A Critique; A Conspectus; A Bibliography; Indexes*, New York: The Limited Editions Club, 1959, 21. I am grateful to Henry Adams for pointing out the usefulness of this volume.

3. Benton's *The Adventures of Tom Sawyer* appeared in the 10th Series (November 1938 - September 1940), No. 114; *Huckleberry Finn* in the 13th Series ((November 1941 - October 1942), No. 132; and *Life on the Mississippi* in the 15th Series (January - December 1944), No.158. Curry's *The Prairie* by James Fenimore Cooper was in the 12th Series (November 1940 - October 1941), No.119 and *The Red Badge of Courage* by Stephen Crane in the 15th

Series (January - December 1944), No.155; he also illustrated *The Literary Works of Abraham Lincoln* (1942) and Stephen Vincent Benet's poem, *John Brown's Body* (1948; published after Curry's death) for Macy. Curry hoped to illustrate Willa Cather's *My Antonia*, but Macy could not come to an agreement with her publisher, Houghton Mifflin (Macy to Ferris Greenslet, December 2 and December 4, 1937; microfiche files of the George Macy Companies at the Easton Press, Norwalk, Conn.). Other artists associated with the American Scene movement were Reginald Marsh: *Sister Carrie* by Theodore Dreiser, 10th Series (November 1938 - September 1940), No.110 and others; and Boardman Robinson: *Spoon River Anthology* by Edgar Lee Masters, 13th Series (November 1941 - October 1942), No.134; Macy planned to have Robinson illustrate *Babbitt*, but the arrangements could not be completed.

4. The complete 8th series is: *Le Morte d'Arthur* (No. 83); *Paradise Lost* and *Paradise Regain'd* (No.84); *The Frogs of Aristophanes* (No.85); *The Life of Benevenuto Cellini* (No.86, with an introduction by the critic Thomas Craven, a champion of Grant Wood and other Regionalists); *The Ballad of Reading Gaol* by Oscar Wilde (No.87); *Pinocchio* (No.88); *Main Street* (No.89); *Camille* (No.93; illustrated by Marie Laurencin, one of the few instances of a woman being commissioned for illustrations by the Limited Editions Club).

5. *Quarto-Millenary*, 250.

6. Lewis, Sinclair, *Main Street*, with a new introduction by the author, illustrated by Grant Wood, New York: Limited Editions Club, 1937. *The Perfectionist* is opposite p.42; *Sentimental Yearner* opposite p.82; *The Radical* opposite p.122; *General Practitioner* opposite p.162; *The Good Influence* opposite p.202; *Practical Idealist* opposite p.242; *Booster* opposite p.282 and *Village Slums* opposite p.322. All the drawings were signed in the block letters typically used by Wood for his signature. All include a copyright symbol and are dated 1936 except for *Village Slums*, which is dated 1937, and *General Practitioner* and *Main Street Mansion*, which have no visible date.

7."The Limited Editions Club announces its Eighth Series...." *The Saturday Review of Literature*, vol.XIV, no.25, October 17, 1936, 15.

8. In a letter of 1944, he explained that much of the reason his books were reasonably priced was because he did not have to pay royalties to authors but could concentrate his expense on the physical object of the book itself. Disappointed that the publishers Harcourt, Brace and Company would not waive royalties for an illustrated edition of *Babbitt*, he wrote, "The simple truth is that The Limited Editions Club...[is] engaged in the making of illustrated editions of the classics; and, since these classics are usually in the public domain, we have never made provision in our budgets for royalties upon the texts. It is obvious that we have built our business on the shoulders of dead authors. But this is because the texts we issue in illustrated editions are available to our customers in editions much cheaper than ours; and it is only by lavishing our expenditures upon the artist's fee, the cost of reproducing his illustrations, the special typography and special binding, that we are able to cause our customers to buy our expensive editions." Macy to S. Spencer Scott (Harcourt, Brace and Company), January 10, 1944. Later, Sinclair Lewis stepped in and encouraged his publisher to accommodate Macy: "Mr. Lewis would like to see an illustrated edition of BABBITT, and we should be entirely willing to have you do it on the same basis as you did MAIN STREET. That is, for a fee of $500." S. Spencer Scott to Macy, January 13, 1944. Macy's original offer to Harcourt Brace was $1000.00, double the fee he had paid for permission to publish *Main Street.* Macy to Spencer, November 5, 1943. Much of Macy's correspondence regarding the Limited Editions Club can be found today in the microfiche archives of the Easton Press in Norwalk, Connecticut. My sincere thanks to Mike Hendricks of the Easton Press for making these files available to me. I also greatly appreciate the assistance of the staff at the library of Norwalk Community College; through their facilities I was able to research the microfiche archive.

9. "A Midwest Artist Views 'Main Street,'" St. Louis *Post-Dispatch*, Sunday Magazine, May 23, 1937, A1.

10. Lewis, Sinclair, "A Note on Book Collecting," *Saturday Review*, vol. XII, no.24, October 12, 1935, 17.

11. But even the *Main Street* book wasn't as much of a bargain as the lithographs he produced in editions of 250 for the Associated American Artists: these sold for $5.00.

12. Lewis, Sinclair, "Introduction," *Main Street*, New York: Limited Editions Club, 1937, x.

13. Lewis, "Introduction," ix.

14. Letter from Macy to Boardman Robinson, October 15, 1943. Easton Press microfiche archives.

15. Letter from Lewis to Macy, October 26, 1943. According to a letter from Robinson, he was "not disappointed" after the *Babbitt* project was given up, not only because it freed up more time for him, but more importantly because "I have been dubious about doing Red Lewis justice, too. Far from being friends, he has never forgiven me for a caricature I once did of him. It appeared in the old "Dial", and is now in the Minneapolis museum, his home state. It is a good caricature, but Red can't take what he can dish out." Robinson to Macy, January 22, 1944. In his biography, Mark Schorer gives this account of Robinson's drawing: "Sonya Levien said that in these later years his very ugliness had become a kind of distinction, and a caricature-portrait by Boardman Robinson which had portrayed him with much exaggerated weakness of chin and bulge of brow, rather bears her out." *Sinclair Lewis: An American Life*, New York: McGraw-Hill Book Company, Inc., 1961, 671. Macy must have assumed that Lewis would not be willing to write another introduction to *Babbitt* since, on the same day Lewis wrote him to say he would do it, Macy invited William Allen White, famed editor of the Emporia [Kansas] *Gazette*, to contribute an introduction, for a fee of $100.00. Macy to White, October 26, 1943. All letters in Easton Press microfiche archives.

16. Letter from Macy to Ferris Greenslet (Houghton Mifflin Company), December 2, 1937 and Greenslet to Macy, December 3, 1937. Both letters in Easton Press microfiche archives.

17. Letter from William Kittredge, The Lakeside Press, to Macy, October 27, 1937. Easton Press microfiche archives.

18. Letter from Macy to Kittredge, December 13, 1937. Easton Press microfiche archives. "I don't think the Benton and Curry books should resemble *Main Street.* As you gathered from my letters, I didn't like *Main Street* as much as you did; I didn't like the binding or the type page. And I didn't think we got good value for money; balanced against the sum we paid Lakeside for the job [which was $6000.], I thought we got an unusually cheap binding material and a paper which because it is not a clean paper and does not contain rags, is not an honest paper for us to put into a book to sell at ten dollars."

19. Benton also produced pictures related to John Ford's 1940 movie production of *The Grapes of Wrath*. When the critic and Regionalist supporter Thomas Craven saw the illustrations in the summer of 1940, he wrote to Macy, "Benton has surpassed himself in this job and the final proofs will be rich and stunning and the book abundantly and nobly illustrated." Craven to Macy, July 19, 1940. Macy himself had not been quite so satisfied when, the month earlier, he suggested that Benton infuses the pictures with "more melodrama" and "more pathos" and that he send no more "like the drawing of the flushing of the toilet." Macy to Benton, June 3, 1940. The Easton Press microfiche archives. Benton's always entertaining book on his development as an artist contains accounts of some of his travels: *An Artist in America*, New York: Halcyon House, 1939.

20. "Company History," Limited Editions Club Collection, Harry Ransom Humanities Research Center at the University of Texas at Austin. http:www.hrc.utexas.edu/research/fa/limitededitions.html. For more information on Sidney Shiff and the current Limited Editions Club, see Grossman, especially 36-39.

21. One of the books reissued by the Easton Press is *Main Street* (1965). In this edition, however, the final illustration, *Village Slums*, was left out, perhaps because the drawing could not be traced.

Grant Wood's Main Street Color Plates

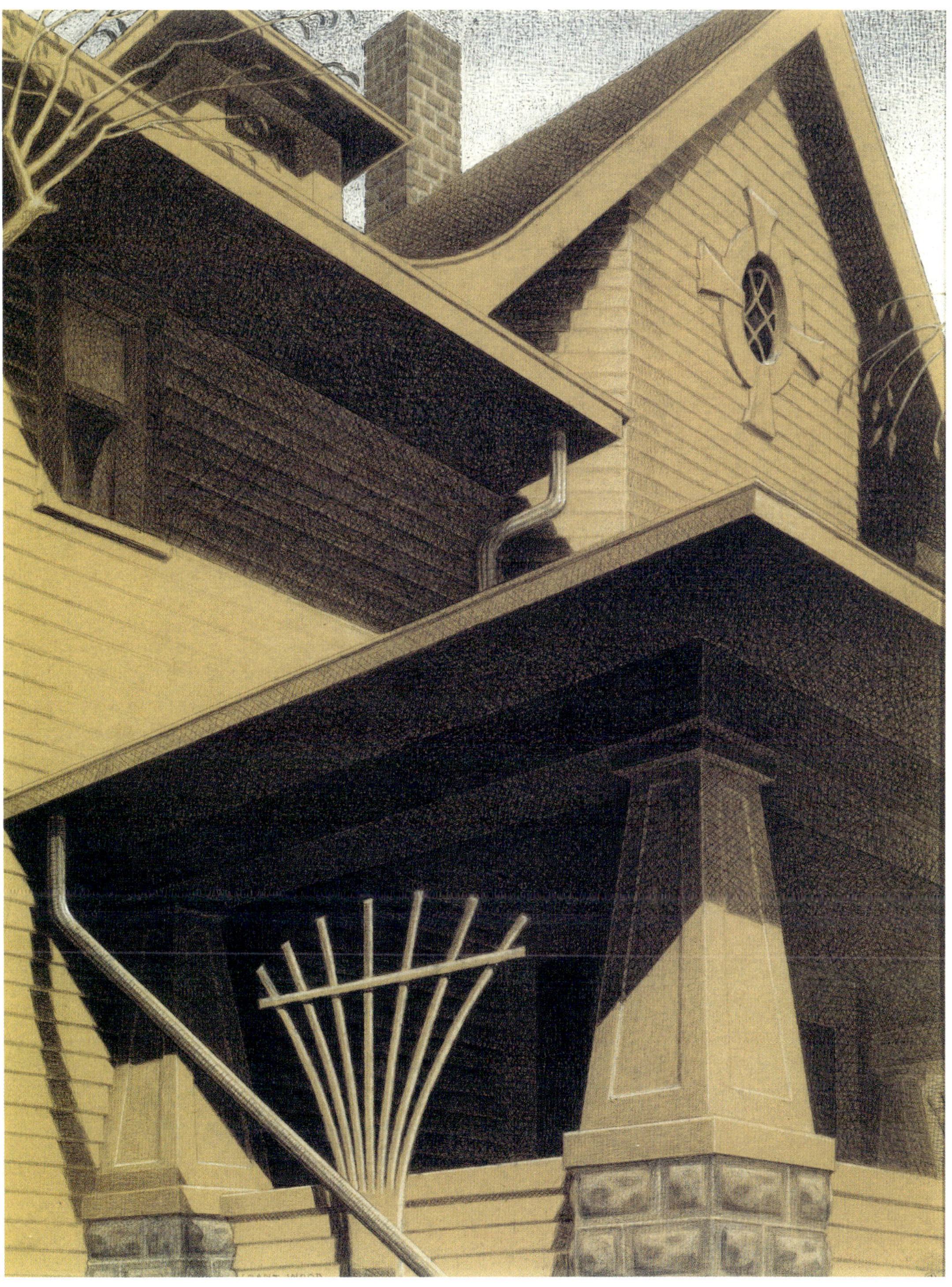

Figure 43 Main Street Mansion

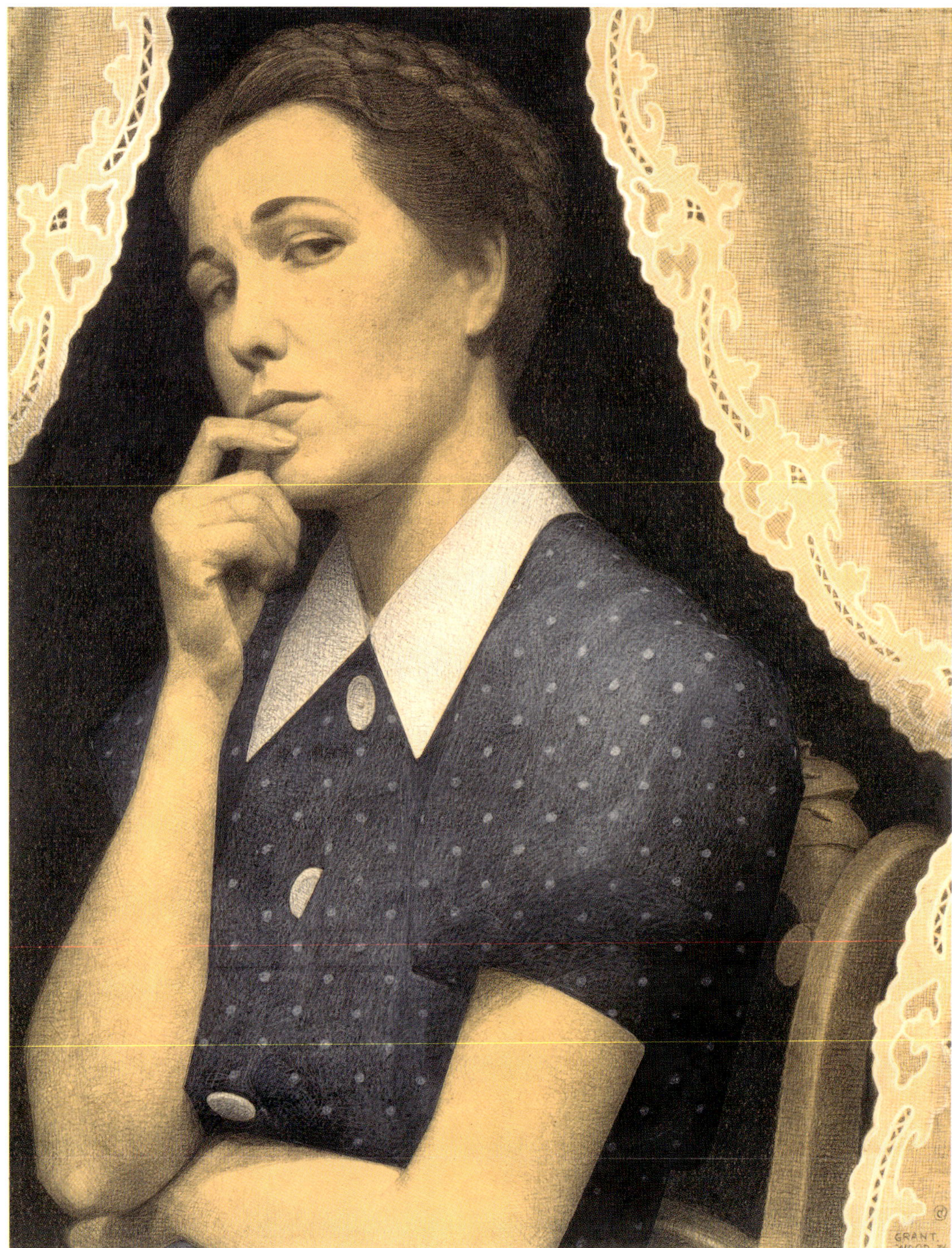

Figure 44 The Perfectionist

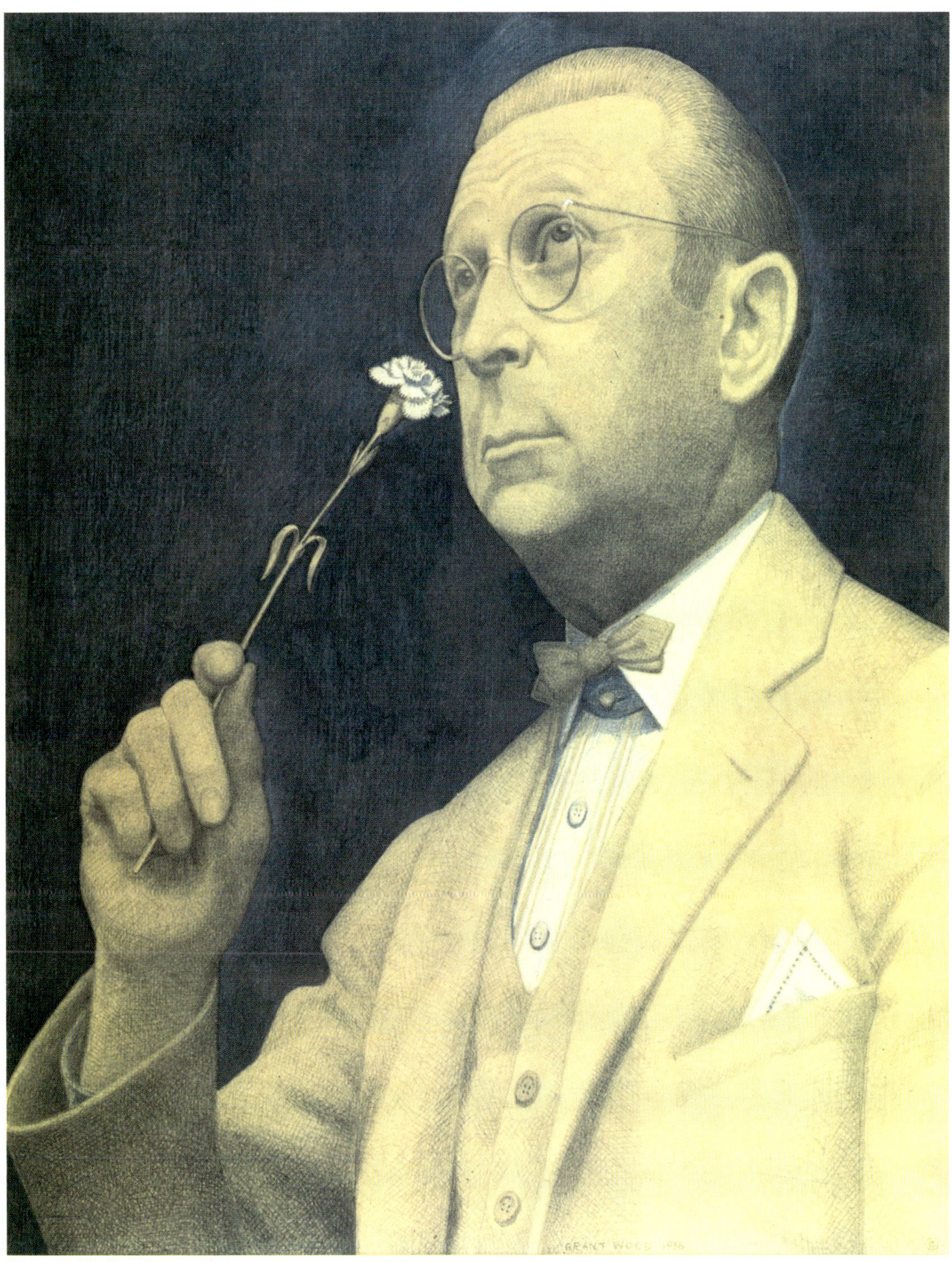

Figure 48 Sentimental Yearner

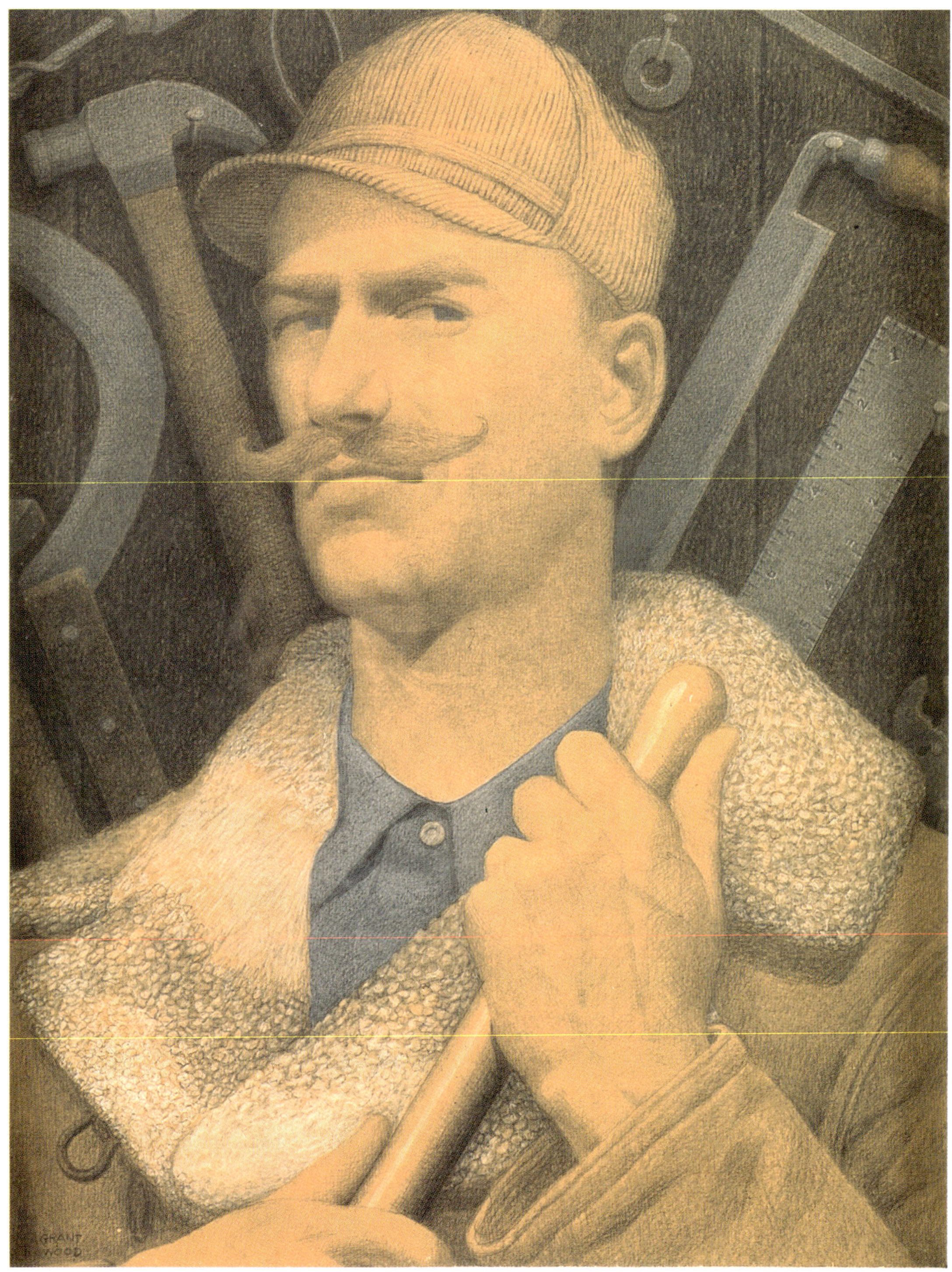

Figure 54 The Radical

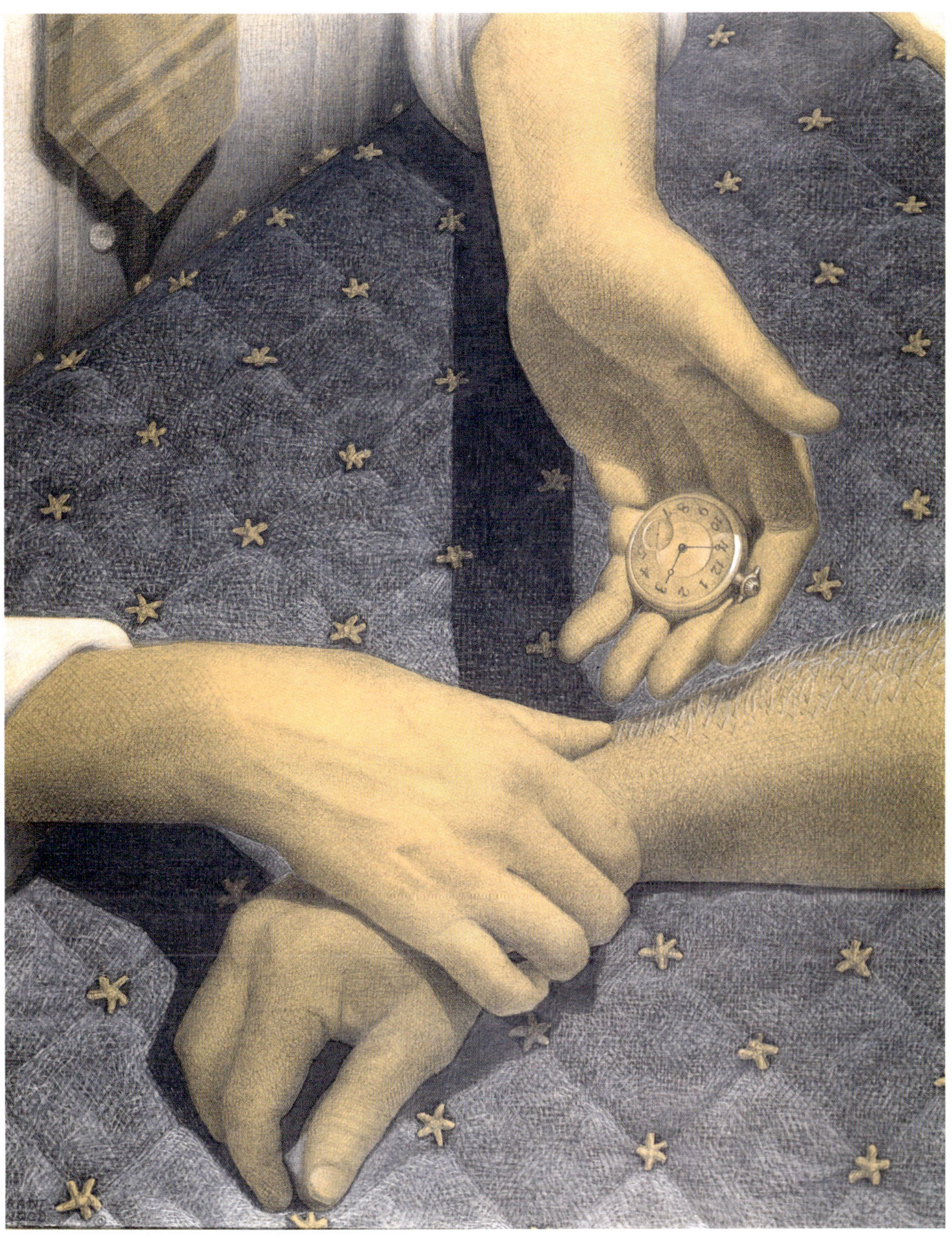

Figure 58 General Practitioner

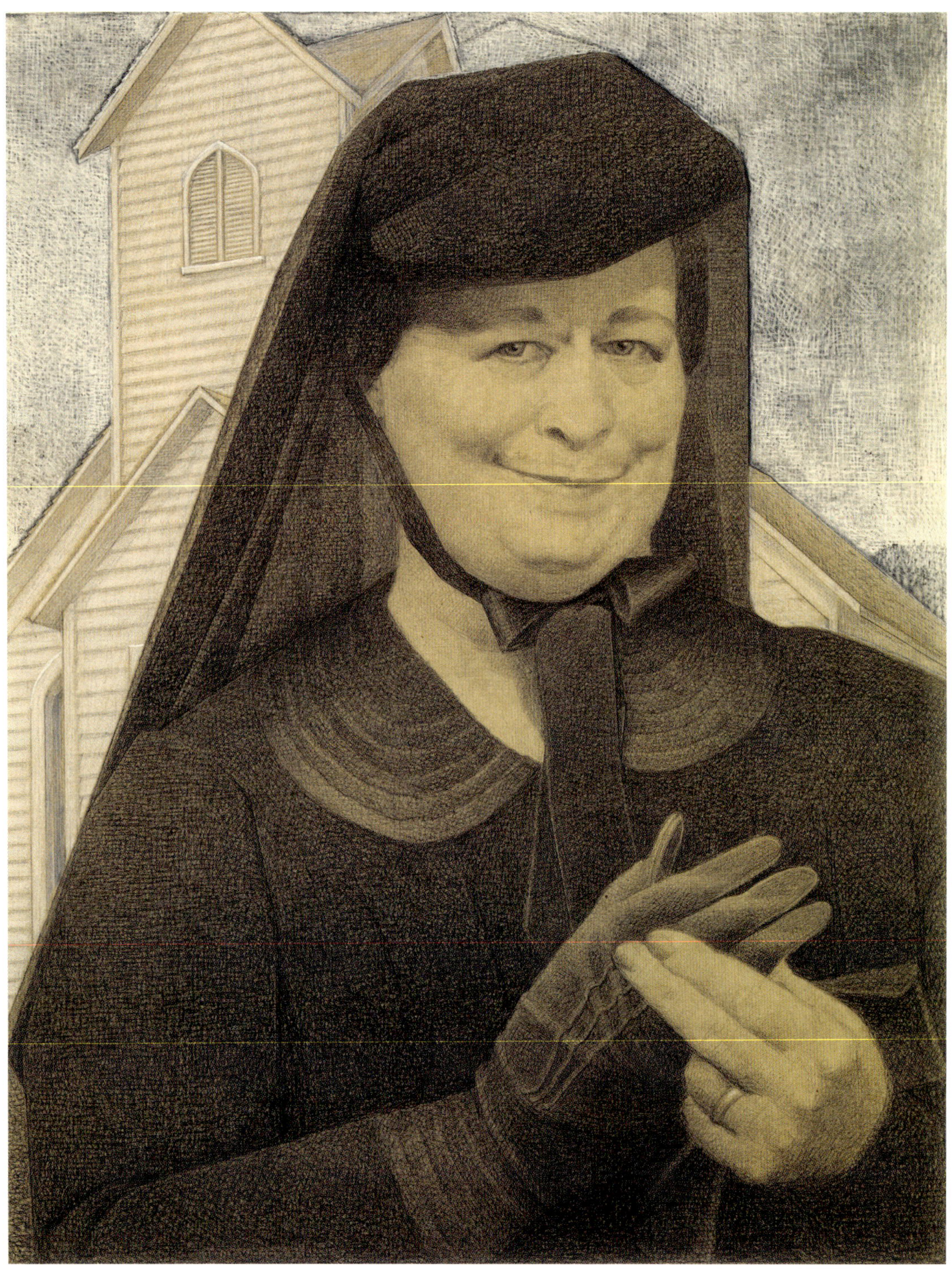

Figure 64 The Good Influence

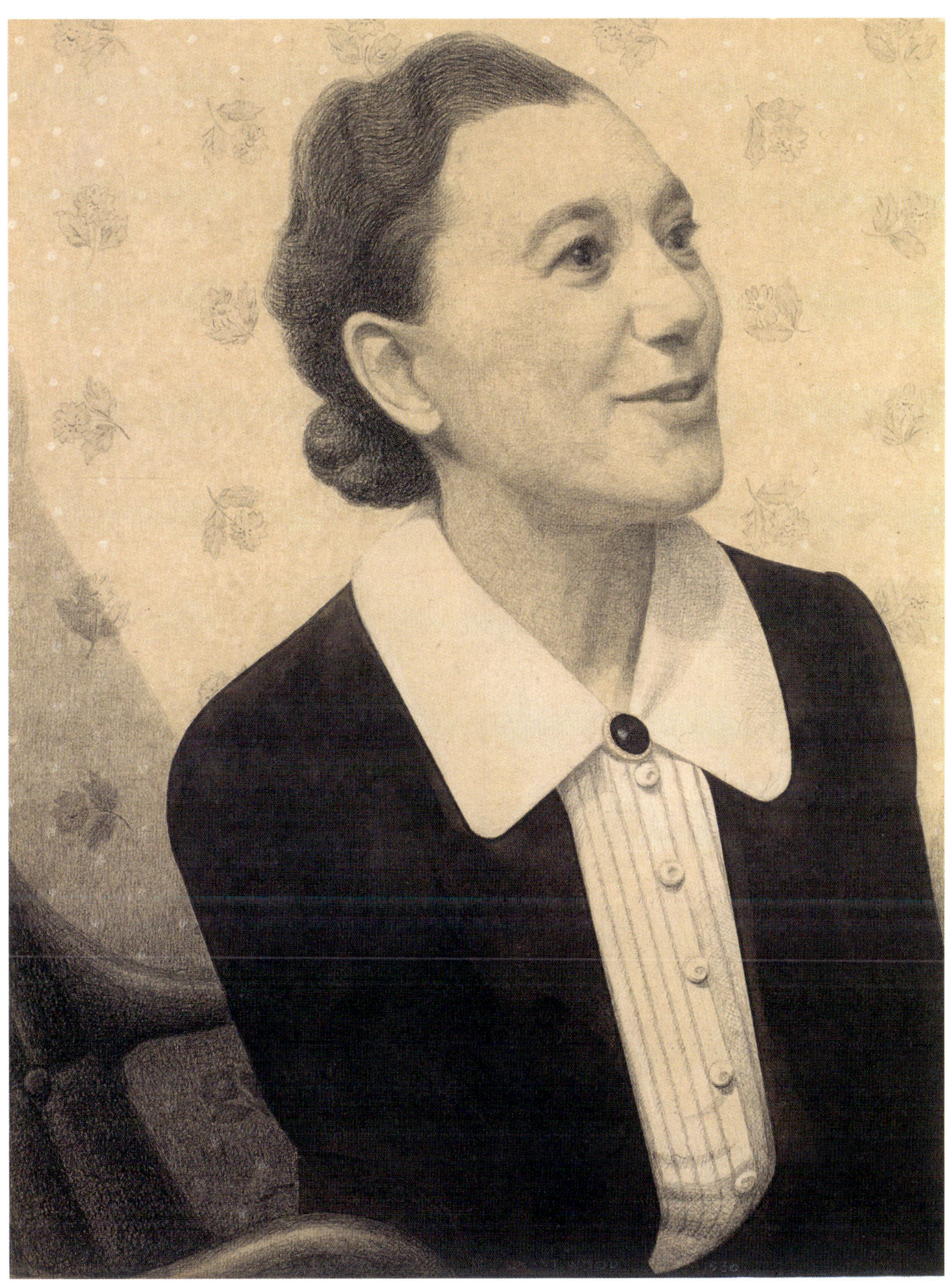

Figure 66 Practical Idealist

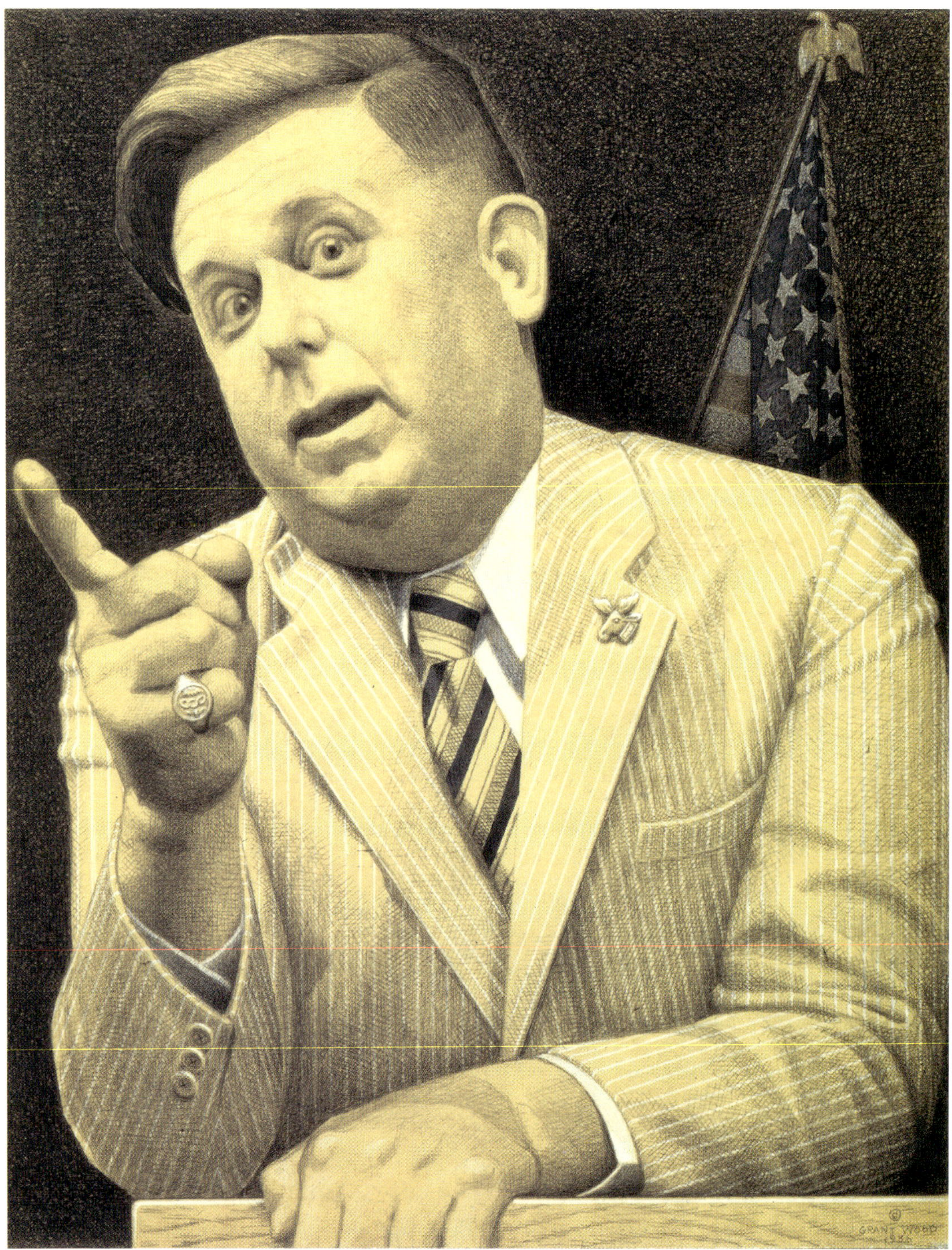

Figure 67 Booster

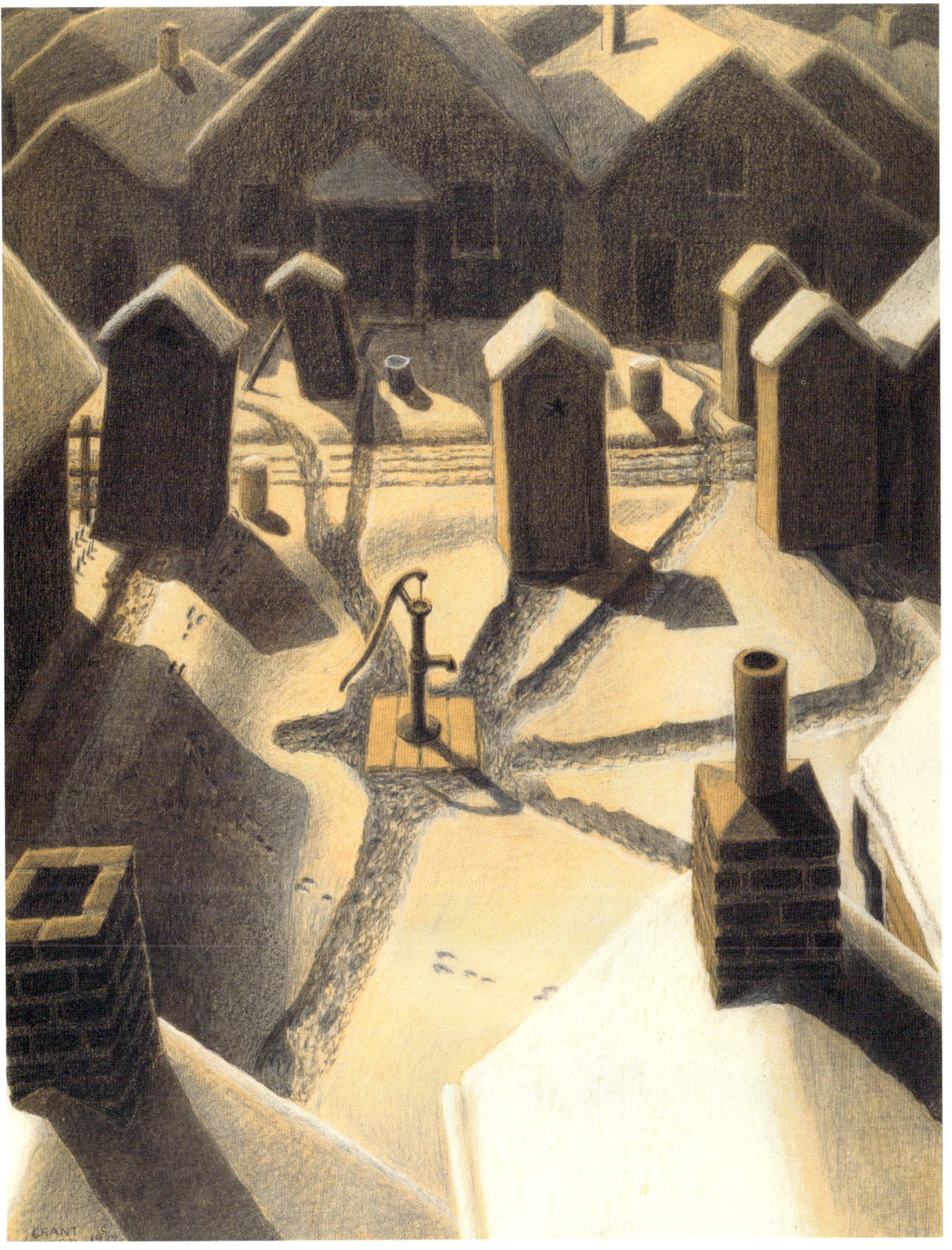

Figure 72 Village Slums

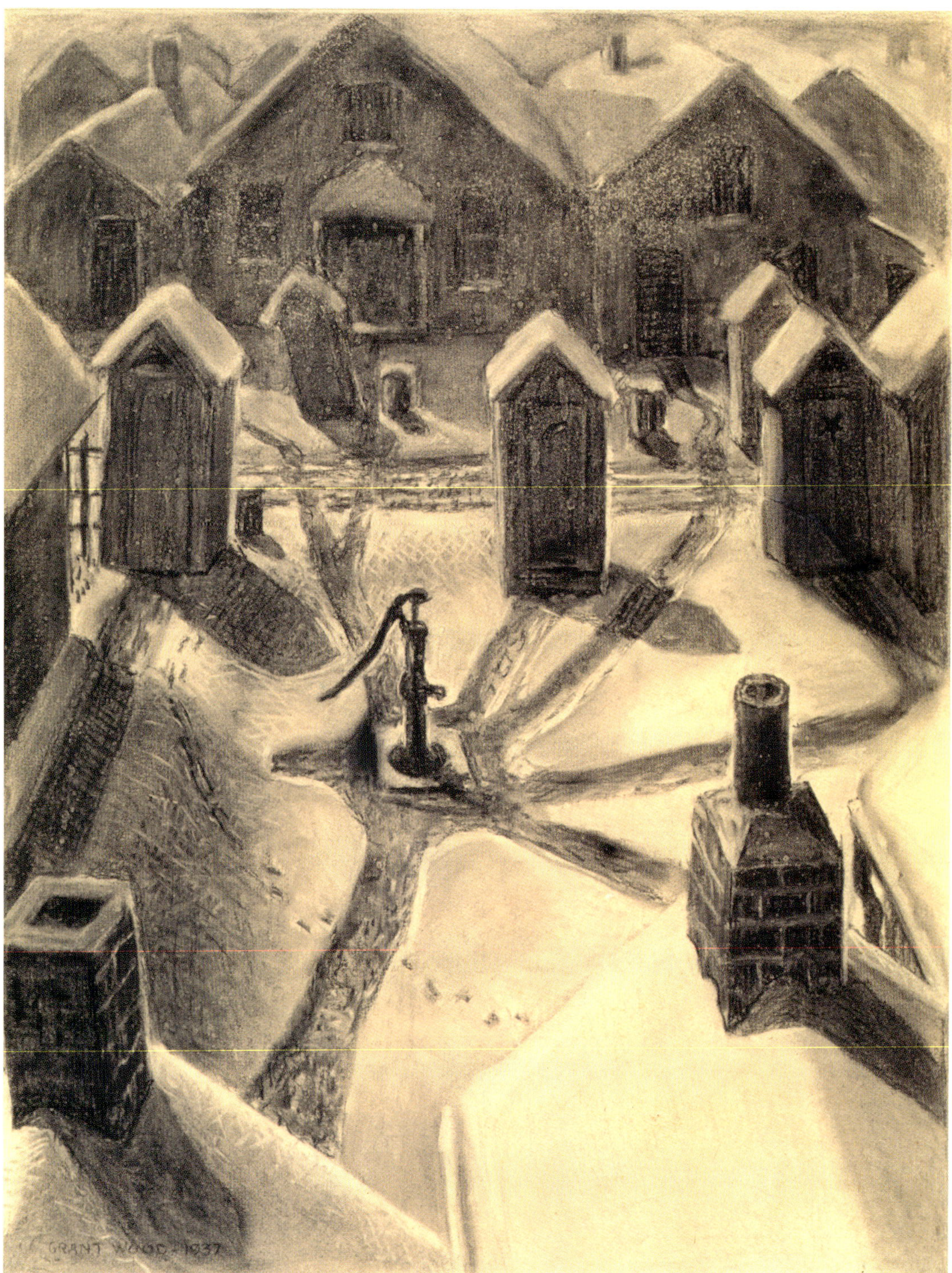

Figure 73 Study for Village Slums

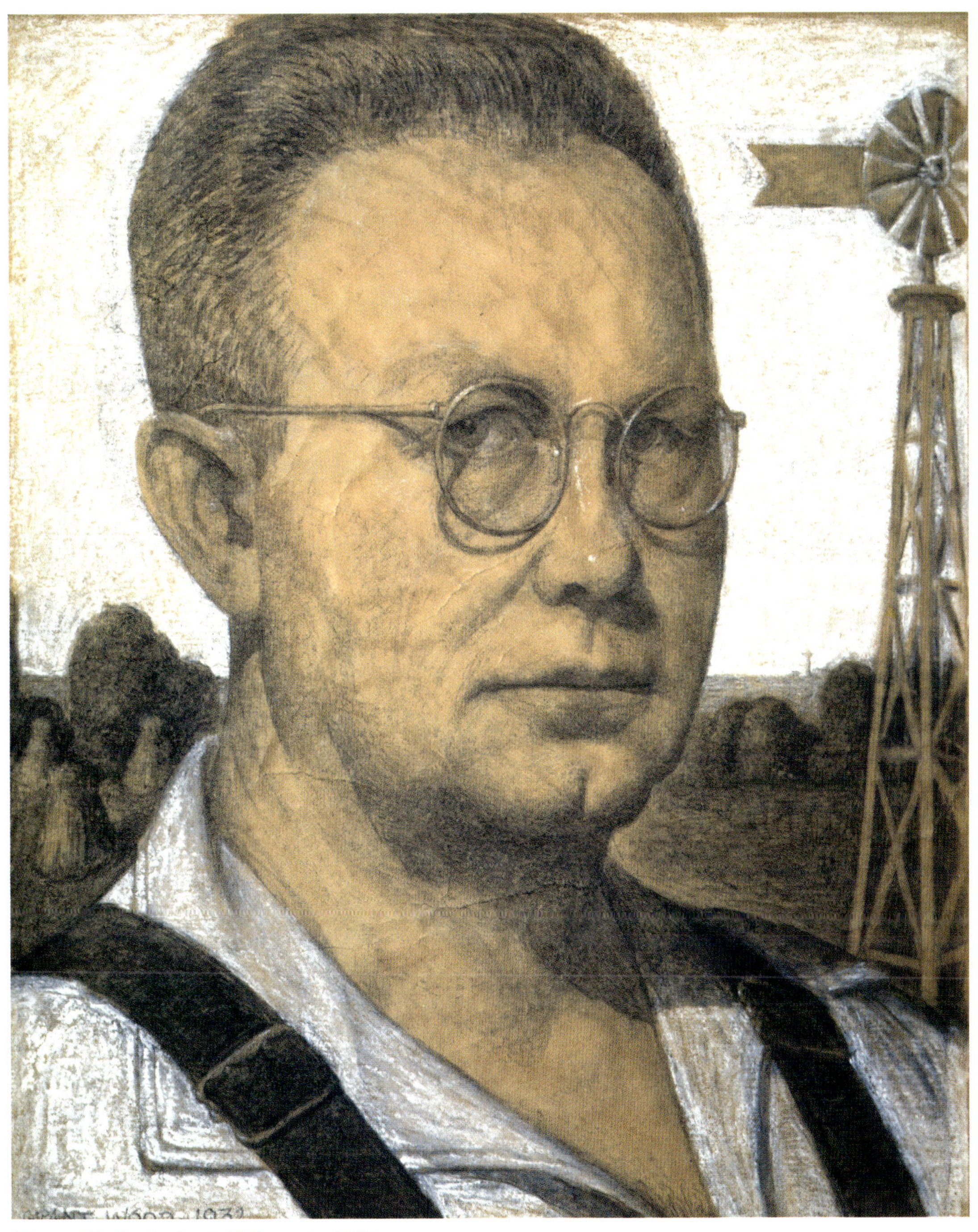

Figure 79 Study for Self-Portrait, 1932

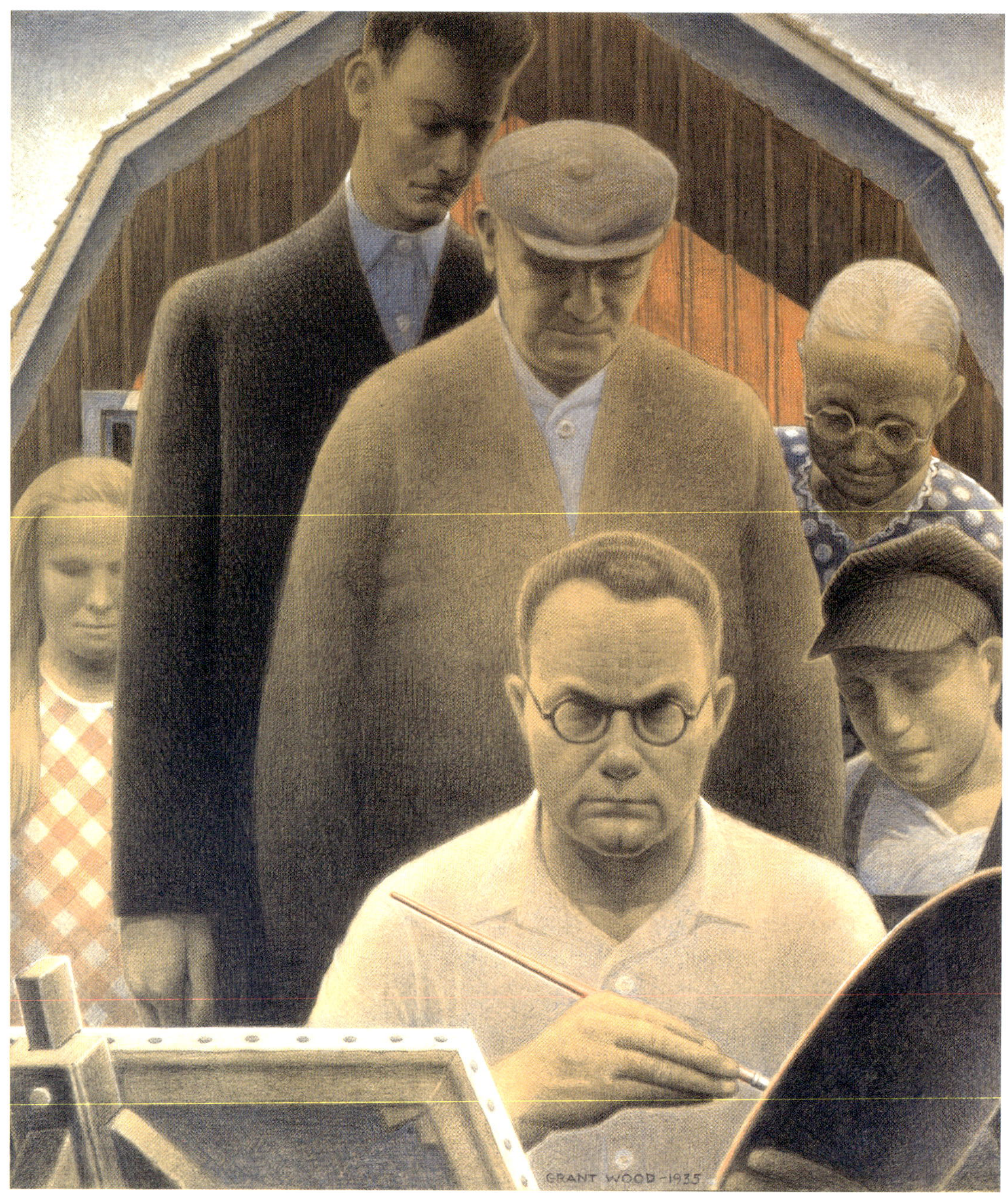

Figure 80 Return from Bohemia, 1935

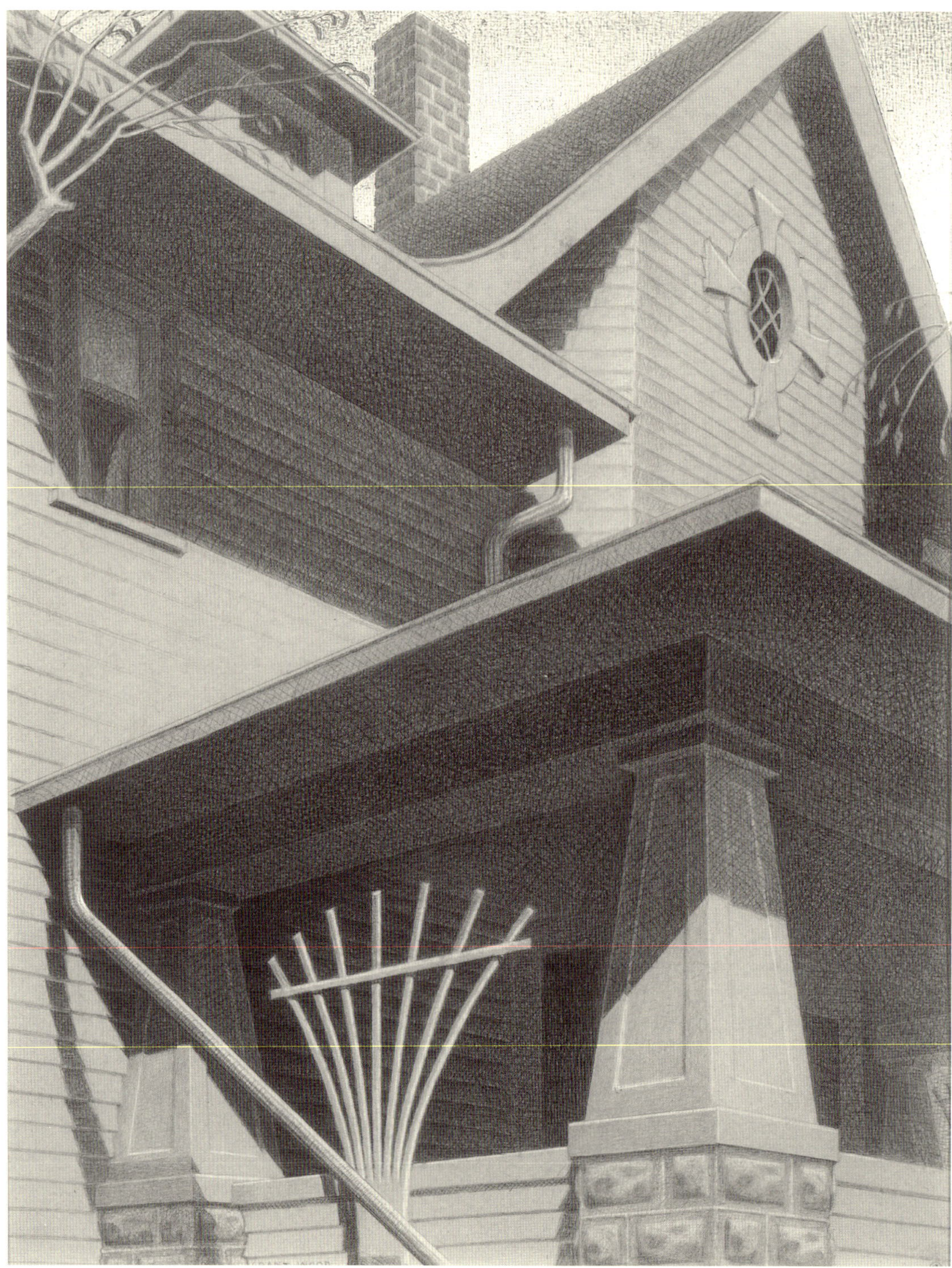

Figure 43 Main Street Mansion

Chapter 6 The *Main Street* Drawings

Main Street Mansion

Whose house is this? Is it Will and Carol Kennicott's house? Or the new house Will promises to build? Is it Sam Clark's new house, which Will plans to surpass when he builds his own? Or, is it a composite of the hundreds of "mansions" Wood had seen along the Main Streets in his own life? This drawing is the most geometric and abstract of the series and the only one without an obvious human presence. Even *Village Slums*, while vacant, shows traces of human activity. Yet, as we examine this structure that seems so obvious on its surface, it begins to exhibit a personality, just as the human subjects do. It is massive and closed, able to withstand the extremes of Midwestern weather while it hides the lives of those inside. When Carol wonders what the villagers really say about her, we can imagine those conversations taking place in such houses. It is well suited to contain Carol's loneliness and emptiness as she waits for acceptance in Gopher Prairie and then, her desolation when she realizes that it will never come. It is also a house able to absorb the bulk of Will Kennicott, often described as a large, thick, physically powerful man, with the endurance to drive through blizzards and perform operations in his patients' kitchens.

In Lewis's novel, architecture is often a metaphor for the conventional lives of its comfort-loving inhabitants, who are absorbed in the most prosaic details of existence. The plainness of Gopher Prairie architecture edges beyond an honest pragmatism into a spirit-crushing gracelessness. With its tone of repressed, constricted lives and its abundant ugliness, we wonder how Edward Hopper or Charles Burchfield would have illustrated the architecture of *Main Street*. In Wood's hands, this architecture holds the dichotomy found in much of his best work. Wood may have tried to reflect the parallax views of the Kennicotts toward Gopher Prairie, introduced when they return from their honeymoon: Will, proud and excited; Carol, appalled and disgusted. "She glanced at the houses; tried not to see what she saw....'This town — O my God! I can't go through with it. This junk-heap!'" Having informed his bride that his house, their house, was old-fashioned "'but nice and roomy, and well-heated; best furnace I could find on the market,'" Kennicott rides beside his new wife as "she held his hand tightly and stared ahead as the car swung round a corner and stopped in the street before a prosaic frame house in a small parched lawn." {23}

Her impression does not improve as she takes a fuller look. "A concrete sidewalk with a 'parking' of grass and mud. A square smug brown house, rather damp. A narrow concrete walk up to it. Sickly yellow leaves in a windrow with dried wings of box-elder seeds and snags of wool from the cottonwoods. A screened porch with pillars of thin painted pine surmounted by scrolls and brackets and bumps of jigsawed wood. No shrubbery to shut off the public gaze. A lugubrious bay-window to the right of the porch. Window curtains of starched cheap lace revealing a pink marble table with a conch shell and a Family Bible." {24} It sounds dreadful, and yet for Will, it was commodious and nurturing, and for the hired girl, Bea Sorensen, it represented an urbane, exotic escape from the farm. Although Wood's interpretation leans towards Carol's perception, it leaves room for less damning views. A firmly grounded structure, it is a refuge and reward for the doctor after he drives home through a deadly snowstorm from a midnight house call to a farmer. The house he returns to certainly does not have the insubstantiality Carol attributes to many she sees in Gopher Prairie: "She thought of the coming of the Northern winter, when the unprotected houses would crouch together in terror of storms galloping out of that wide waste. They were so small and weak, the little brown houses. They were shelters for sparrows, not homes for warm, laughing people." {27} Kennicott's home is not "small and weak" to him, and it is considerably something more than the "brown cube of a house" {55} that Carol sees. For him, it is shelter from a harsh environment, and he is not a "sparrow" but a doctor who goes resolutely about his rounds. And for him, it *is* warm, emotionally because he loves Carol from the root of his being, and literally because of his wintertime diligence. Considering the descriptions of the Minnesota winters and Carol's often muted responses to him, perhaps we can sympathize with Dr. Kennicott's obsession with his furnace.

Judging from Lewis's description of the Kennicott's house, Wood's drawing takes considerable license; it seems to say at least as much about Wood's architectural inclinations as it does about Gopher Prairie's. The house of the novel is hardly a "mansion" and leaves the impression of being a rather modest, creaky structure in not-exactly-prime condition; Kennicott had described it to Carol as "old," {23} "old-fashioned" and "Mid-Victorian" {24} (although Kennicott's grasp of architectural styles is probably not to be relied upon). In fact, the Kennicott house sounds much like the one in which Lewis grew up at Sauk Centre, Minnesota, the small town that is generally considered to be the model for Gopher Prairie. Dating from 1884, the Lewis boyhood home (now on Sinclair Lewis Avenue) is a wooden-frame, two-story house that does indeed have a rather "squarish" effect. The "pillars of thin painted pine surmounted by scrolls and brackets and bumps of jigsawed wood" that are not present in Wood's house are to be found in the Sauk Centre house. It is very near a lake, across which the "galloping" storms of the Northern winter might well have made the house feel like an insubstantial "shelter for sparrows." Wood's "mansion" looks more like the large house that is next door to the Lewis home, a house that has, on one side, an oval-shaped window similar (it lacks the four keystone elements) to the one he drew in

Main Street Mansion. Although there is no evidence that Wood traveled to Lewis's hometown to see its Main Street for himself (or that he was even concerned about faithfulness to the look of the actual place), the similarity between the features of this nearby house and the one invented by Wood for his drawing, *Main Street Mansion*, is intriguing. [1]

Wood seems to have been given (or took) a good deal of latitude in his selection and interpretation of incidents from *Main Street*. Apparently, it was he who gave names to his drawings. So, we wonder at the title *Main Street Mansion*. Is it part of Wood's satire? Is this truly a mansion, or is it only a mansion by Midwestern standards? The scale of his drawing makes the structure seem enormous: its expanse cannot even be contained with the frame. But we cannot be sure of its size. If he had chosen to depict it from the front as seen from the street, it might have been easier to determine its true size. It is the worm's eye view from below and the jutting, powerful angles of the house that make it seem so monumental and overwhelming. In addition, the tenebristic rendering of those sharp, muscular angles imparts almost a Caravaggesque drama to an ordinary dwelling. We cannot tell how big the house actually is or how much it expands beyond the portion we see, so it is impossible to know if the term "mansion" applies to it physically. Is it one compacted corner of something bigger or just an over-dramatized little bungalow from a dreary row of ten others?

Whatever its exact size, the house does have serious substance; it is not just a shack. Obviously, it is two stories, possibly three, and the architecture has some complexity. It is carefully built with neat masonry, shaped mouldings and an oval, cross-paned window above the porch. It may be an odd mix of architectural elements, but it is not entirely uninformed about historic stylizations. The eclecticism of that Baroque-descended oval window and its four keystones coupled with the planar colonial clapboards is not uncommon in American architecture and has produced some fascinating structures. But Wood seems to be laughing a bit at the Midwestern, small town appropriations of architectural styles to which they have little conscious historical connection. The elaborately edged oval window can be seen as Wood's *Main Street* update of the gothic window in the house of *American Gothic.*

One of the themes of Regionalism was the necessity of throwing off European historical styles (and the contemporary modernistic ones as well) to embrace the indigenous architecture of the United States. [2] But until the 1930s, Wood himself revealed a broad — and eclectic — taste in architecture and decoration. [3] From young manhood, he had built his own family's houses and then, with increasing success, those for well-to-do clients in Cedar Rapids. In his design of buildings, interiors and objects, he drew on what must have been in that time and place a sophisticated range of historical knowledge. The Arts and Crafts style was an early design preference for Wood, and his "mansion" partakes of that style as well as related architectural modes such as Mission and the Bungalow style. For his design commissions in the 1920s, he expanded his repertoire to employ features of classical, American colonial, medieval and other styles. Not until about 1932 when he built the Armstrong

House in Cedar Rapids did he throw off the influence of accepted historical forms to really concentrate on the plain, vernacular buildings of pioneer Iowa and the nearby Amana colonies. [4] (To some extent, it could be argued that he never stopped his eclectism. For example, his decoration of the headquarters of The Society for the Prevention of Cruelty to Speakers was designed, however laughingly, in a Victorian mode. [5]) (Figure 16) His Main Street "mansion" might well echo the kind of historical borrowing he had done and for which, with a touch of self-parody and a grin at his own former architectural aspirations, he had some genuine regard. His feelings about this house, as for so many other subjects in his art, appear mixed.

If, however, observed by anyone sympathetic with Carol Kennicott, this house is nothing more than a prison: dark, suffocating and oppressive. Its dark sobriety is not alleviated even by the direct sunlight that falls onto its facade. The unrelenting bleakness of the house arises largely out of two devices. The first is its literal darkness. Shadows are thrown over every opening in the structure, except for the small, useless oval window (and even it is recessed and cross-hatched with pane moldings). Wood emphasizes the roof overhangs and exaggerates the darkened eaves beneath them. Each exaggerated angle creates an area that huddles back into itself and won't come into the open. These angles are so muscular that if seen as abstractions, they constitute a dynamic activity, like the shifting and clashing of geologic strata. One way or the other, the house seems designed to crush all who approach it. But there is no way to enter this house: the low walls and rusticated stone supports of the porch hide most of the doorway. And even if we could see the doorway or access to it, the porch is so forbidding that we might wish to excuse ourselves from making a call. It is not clear in the drawing whether Wood intended this to be the screened porch so common in Gopher Prairie; if so, that might account for some of the obscurity of the entrance, though it does not alleviate the mood of the image.

In most of America, especially the Midwest and the South, the porch was traditionally the most inviting part of the home. It was available to the out-of-doors, but sheltered; it was furnished for comfort and sociability and was associated with leisure, rest and pleasure. Before television, it was where people gathered after supper to chat, put their feet up, sit in the porch swing, look at the stars — hardly anything unpleasant happened on the porch. It was where the family greeted the outside world and where the outside world was invited into the family. [6] Even in *Main Street*, some of the most relaxed and hopeful scenes take place on the porch. But Wood has chosen the porch to exacerbate his heavy effect, not lighten it.

The second device Wood uses to achieve his bleak effect is through the house's relationship to nature. Throughout the novel, the grandeur and beauty of the land gives us the few glimpses beyond the smallness and materialism of Gopher Prairie. Even in its harshness, the landscape is a comfort to the unhappy Carol Kennicott. Will Kennicott is also sensitive to it, although his appreciation centers on hunting and land speculation. In his description of his hometown when Will Kennicott first meets Carol, he calls on the natural setting when he tells her, "'And it's a darn pretty town. Lots of fine maples and box-elders.'" {11} As he woos her and persuades her to come with him to Gopher Prairie, one of the enticements is nature, although an abbreviated remnant of it: "We've been doing a lot with lawns and gardening the past few years, and it's so homey — the big trees—"{14} His boasts about the attractions of Gopher Prairie do not refer to its surrounding landscape. No matter how "pretty" or "homey" Gopher Prairie is, it always suffers in contrast to the vast and various nature that surrounds it, at least in the eyes of Carol (and Sinclair Lewis). Wood's picture expresses how the little mercantile town has reduced that giant landscape to a paltry minimum.

The massive sky of the northern prairies is crowded out of the picture and the giant landscape is ignored. Only two tree branches edge into the composition from the right and the left, their thin foliage suggesting winter or the waning days of autumn. However, even if they were in full leaf and at their best, they probably would not hold their own against this house and all it embodies. Nature is relegated to the periphery in the town of Gopher Prairie and in the consciousness of its inhabitants. Despite being surrounded by farms and defined by the productivity of the land, Gopher Prairie thinks of nature as an addendum. Even the rain that falls on the Main Street mansion is channeled through a network of gutters and drainpipes. The only allowance for nature is intimated by the trellises on either end of the porch where morning glories or sweet peas could be trained to grow in a predetermined pattern. But they are as barren and inhospitable as the house they are intended to adorn. The trellis is like a stiff imitation of a real tree with its rounded top and branches springing from the trunk. The cascading shape of the tree limb on the right (in contrast to the other branch which juts and claws its way into the space) is the reverse of the fountain-like trellis, but it still suggests a source in nature for its shape; the curves in these two forms are among the very few in the picture. Nevertheless, this branch with its faint, tiny leaves is so limp and paltry that nature is again defeated, this time by the raw, skeletal manufactured trellis. What might have been a relief in Wood's angular, sharp-edged composition, the little sprig of a tree limb only reiterates the regimented, unfertile image of the mansion.

Houses were a speciality of Grant Wood's. He had built them and decorated them for years. He had definite ideas about what sort of domestic architecture was right for the Midwest. *Main Street Mansion* is, like much of his work, a compromise between two conflicting approaches. It represents the pretension and spiritual emptiness that Carol finds, but it also expresses the solidity, comfort and triumph over the elements that satisfy Dr. Kennicott. Perhaps the house that Wood portrayed is not any existing house, but the one that Dr. Kennicott keeps promising to build for Carol. They make plans, but because of their disagreements and the disruptions in their marriage, the novel closes before the house is built, if indeed it ever will be. But Lewis leaves us with an idea of what the doctor had in mind.

"'I'm getting to the point where I feel we can afford one — and a corker! I'll show this burg something like a real house! We'll put one over on Sam and Harry! Make folks sit up an' take notice.'

It proved that what he wanted was a house exactly like Sam Clark's, which was exactly like every third new house in every town in the country: a square, yellow stolidity with immaculate clapboards, a broad screened porch, tidy grassplots, and concrete walks; a house resembling the mind of a merchant who votes the party ticket straight and goes to church once a month and owns a good car." {242}

Notes: *Main Street Mansion*

1. My thanks to Roberta Olson, President of the Sinclair Lewis Foundation in Sauk Centre, Minnesota for information on the two houses. The Lewis Boyhood Home is named to the National Historic Landmarks, a division of the National Park Service.

2. One of the most interesting, if not artistically accomplished, depictions of this theme is found on the east wall of the mural cycle, "The Social History of Des Moines," in the Des Moines Public Library. Carried out from 1937 to 1941 under the Federal Art Project of the Works Progress Administration (FAP/WPA), it is the work of a group led by Harry Donald Jones, an Iowa artist who was active in the New Deal art programs in Iowa. He worked with Wood on his Public Work of Art Project (PWAP) in Iowa City in 1934, helping to paint the murals for Iowa State University, and was also part of a team led by Francis Robert White, which painted a controversial mural cycle (now painted over) in the Cedar Rapids Court House under the Treasury Relief Art Project (TRAP). Both of these social/artistic documents merit further study. Jones was also the head of the Federal Art Project in Iowa and a founding member of the Iowa Cooperative Artists.

3. A survey of Wood's work as an architect, builder and decorator is found in Wanda Corn's essay for her exhibition catalogue, *Grant Wood, The Regionalist Vision*, New Haven: Yale University Press, 1983.

4. See Corn, 37-38.

5. For photographs of the decoration of the S.P.C.S. clubroom, see the reproductions in Mott, Frank Luther, "The S.P.C.S.," *The Palimpsest*, vol.XLIII, no.3, March 1962, 113-132; and Corn, figs.65-74. For the decoration of his Iowa City home, see Corn, fig.77; Dennis, James M., *Grant Wood: A Study in American Art and Culture*, Columbia: University of Missouri Press, 1986, fig.145; and Graham, Nan Wood, *My Brother, Grant Wood*, Iowa City: State Historical Society of Iowa, 1993, 128, 134, 161. Perhaps Wood's use of Victorian decor was not completely parody. Since it was the style he used in the Iowa City home upon which he lavished so much attention and expense, possibly he actually liked it, as one writer suggested. "I recall visiting Wood's home and studio in Iowa City not long before he died. I had expected some impression of Iowa culture, filtered through Wood's satiric or sarcastic representation of it. I even looked for hints of parody. To my surprise I found everything in harmony with the land where the tall corn grows. The wallpaper was provincial and the pattern was flowery; the paintings he chose to display were celebratory of the wheat-field and the threshers; the furniture would have been acceptable in any nice farmhouse and appropriate to it. There was no swank, parody, or sneer, and certainly there was none in Wood himself." Davis, Earle, "Grant Wood: He Painted America," *Kansas Quarterly*, vol.4, no.4, Fall 1972, 5-11, 10-11. Wood may have felt that there was genuine worth and beauty in aspects of Victorian or "provincial" design. His primary home decor crime seems to be only that he did not care for modernism.

6. For more on American front porches, see Dolan, Michael, *The American Porch: An Informal History of an Informal Place*, New York: Lyons Press, 2002 and for a shorter appreciation, see Young, Dwight, "Sweet Shelter," *Preservation* (The Magazine for the National Trust for Historic Preservation), July/August 2003 (vol.55, no.4), 76.

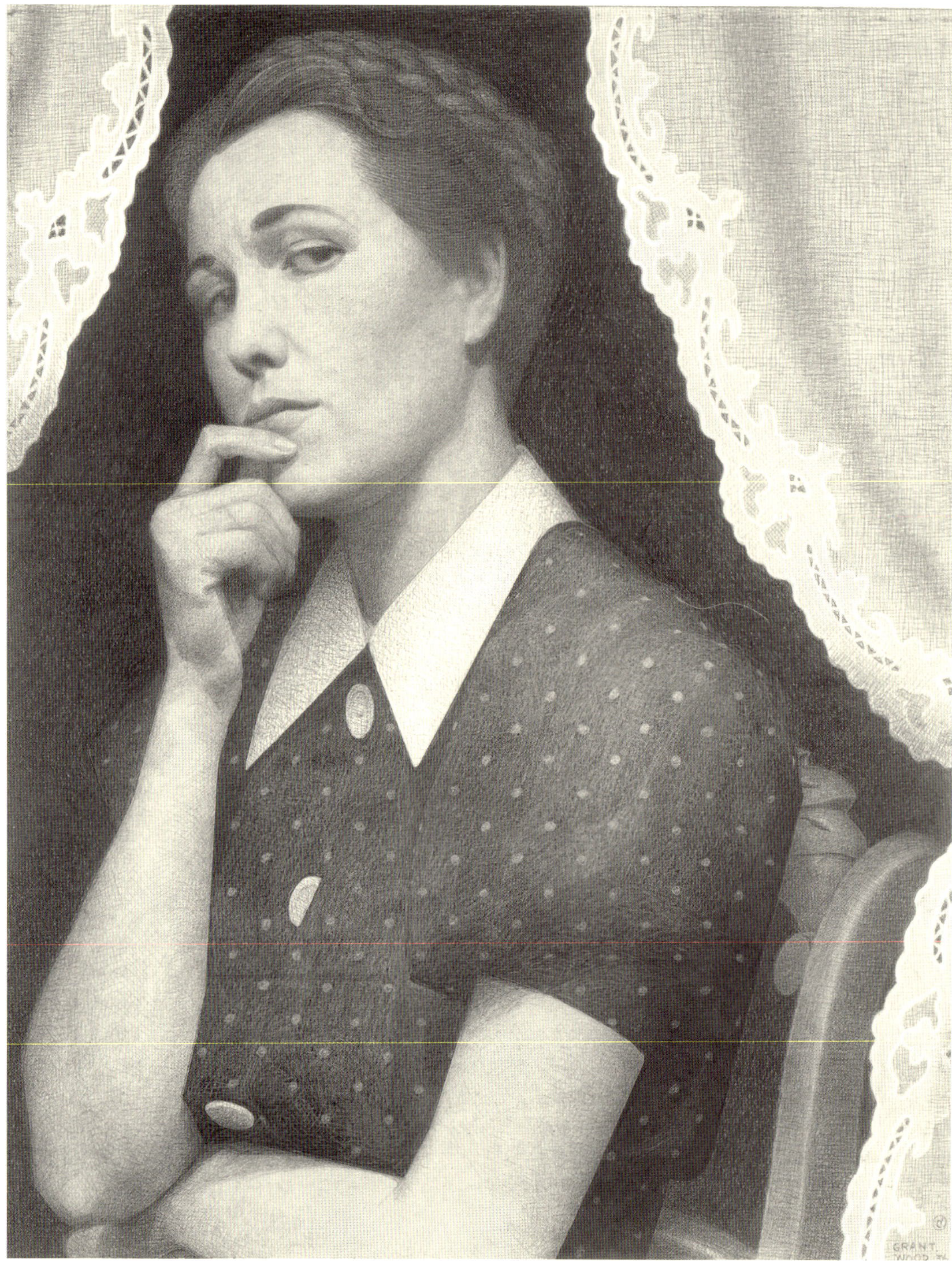

Figure 44 The Perfectionist

The Perfectionist (Carol Kennicott)

Wood's interpretation of Carol Kennicott is, at best, unsympathetic, and at worst, unjust. It can even be accused of being unfaithful to the character that Sinclair Lewis created. Without instruction, many readers of *Main Street* would assume that "The Perfectionist" is not Carol at all, but one of her constantly nosy neighbors, scanning the territory beyond her porch window for diversity or scandal (or excitement) of any kind. She might be one of the ladies of the Jolly Seventeen club whose comfort with themselves and their world cannot be shaken by any self-doubt or new information, women who are always taking the measure of everyone around them — and finding them inadequate. (The Jolly Seventeen is the provincially haughty social club that is the apex of Gopher Prairier society; the other women's club is Thanatopsis, the sort of literary gathering which specializes in studying all of English poetry in a single afternoon meeting.) The portrait captures how the villagers look at (and disapprove of) Carol as much as how she views them. [1] In scene after scene, they barely disguise their resentment and antagonism toward the Doctor's wife, with her citified ideas about how to "improve" them.

Wood's Carol suggests none of the genuine despair Lewis's Carol experiences, her anger at injustice or her confusion and embarrassment as she is continually snubbed and laughed at in Gopher Prairie. This Carol is not the woman who maintains a friendship with her Scandinavian maid, Bea, even after Bea marries the town outcast, Miles Bjornstam. When no one else in the little town would condescend to socialize with the immigrant couple, Carol visited them often and allowed her son and theirs to be playmates. Certainly this person in the drawing is not the courageous, devoted woman who cared for Bea and her little son, Olaf, through a horrendous illness until their deaths. When the high-spirited young schoolteacher, Fern Mullins, is run out of town by vicious gossip, it is Carol who visits her in her dingy hotel refuge, then personally begs each schoolboard member to listen to the truth. In both action and spirit, Carol shows almost heroic resistance to pettiness and ignorance, but there is no hint of that kind of strength of character in Wood's drawing.

Wood's picture of Carol seems to reflect Dr. Will Kennicott's frustrations with his wife more than the multidimensional character Sinclair Lewis portrayed. Perhaps this is not surprising since, judging by *General Practitioner*, the artist appears to have had a high opinion of the doctor, suggesting no failings of his character, but only his stolid devotion to duty. Kennicott has a certain devotion to his marriage as well, tolerating Carol's funny ideas, her periodic escapes from Gopher Prairie and even a two-year separation near the end of the book. But on several occasions in the book, Dr. Kennicott describes his wife in a way that could be the source of Wood's pictorial interpretation. In an early quarrel, the doctor calls her "so damn high and mighty about people" {138}, then observes, "You *know* you feel superior to folks....What's the reason you're so superior? Why can't you take folks as they are?" {141} "Perfectionist" is not among the accusations he aims at his wife but it is certainly implied. In one of their most accusatory encounters, Kennicott is truly angry and mocks Carol's aspirations to "improve" their community. "I've got to hand it to you. You're consistent, all right. I'd of thought that...you'd get over this high-art stuff, but you hang right on....My, we're just going to change everything, aren't we? Going to tell fellows that have been making movies for ten years how to direct 'em; and tell architects how to build towns; and make the magazines publish nothing but a lot of highbrow stories about old maids, and about wives that don't know what they want. Oh, we're a terror!...Come on now, Carrie; come out of it; wake up!"{161} The self-delusion that her husband assigns to Carol is echoed in Wood's characterization as she looks out with appraising and ungenerous calculation. Not revealed is the honesty that she often applies to herself (frequently in conversations with Kennicott), most bluntly near the end of the story when the estranged couple meet in Washington and she admits to him, "I know it must have been pretty tiresome to have to live with anybody as perfect as I was." {356} Here, as elsewhere, she seems fully capable of recognizing her failings, and she consistently takes seriously all accusations against her, even if she cannot ultimately accept them. Never in the novel is Carol directly referred to as a "perfectionist." The townspeople do not regard her so much a perfectionist (what would there be to perfect in their town?) as a snob. Aside from the times when she applies it to herself, [2] the term "perfection" is directed toward Carol only by the "practical idealist," Vida Sherwin, the patient reformer. When Carol, discouraged by Gopher Prairie, announces that "the trouble is spiritual, and no League or Party can enact a preference for gardens rather than dumping grounds," Vida retorts, "In other words, all you want is perfection?" Carol's reply: "Yes! Why not?" {219}

Among the strongest qualities embodied in Wood's *Perfectionist* is one that Kennicott voices to himself and, occasionally to Carol: her coldness. {322} While Lewis makes it clear that Kennicott refers partly to her lack of sexual passion for him, he also means her overall demeanor, which is conveyed by Wood's drawing. The light comes entirely from outside the picture; there is no suggestion of a light source inside the frame and we see her only because we look from the lighted outside world into a darkened inhospitable house with no hint of warmth or welcome. Although *Sentimental Yearner* has a plain background too, the carnation-sniffing gentleman has a shaft of light that beams into the composition. But *The Perfectionist* emerges from complete darkness. Sitting in a carved chair of dainty proportions, she wears a prim dress with puffy sleeves and a sharp, stiff collar. The style of her clothing seems plain and too dowdy for a woman who dresses in "frocks" of textures and colors not commonly found along Main Street. The polka dots of her blouse are a favored pattern in Wood's painting (the apron worn by the woman in *American Gothic* is a variation on polka-dots), and usually suggests a simple, folk-like design associated with unpretentious Midwestern farmwomen. Her dress has the kind of mail order catalogue hominess that the fashion-conscious Carol would have avoided. She was more sophisticated in her dress (the other ladies would have probably said "extravagant") than this prissy, unadventurous style suggests. In addition, it is hard to imagine this woman being cautioned by her husband, as Carol is, against immodesty — to not show her knees "too plain." {64}) The starched, fancy curtains that scallop around her have a precise lace edging that looks machine made; in their fussiness and falseness perhaps they are intended to suggest Carol's erratic ideas about class and what constitutes refinement. [3] These characterizations, along with other details that imply a fastidious personality: the unwrinkled clothing and the sleek, tucked-in hairdo, are nearly comforting and human compared with her composed, self-possessed and cold-hearted stare. If this is the woman to whom Dr. Kennicott declares, "You've my soul!" we can only feel sorry for him.

Two small incidents in *Main Street*, both related to Carol's flirtation with Erik Valborg, the young tailor/aesthete, may have suggested elements of *The Perfectionist*. Early in their acquaintance, she encounters Eric while on a walk with her young son along the railroad tracks. As she instructs her child to say how-do-you-do, Valborg fusses about a detail in the boy's clothing. "'Oh, dear me, he's got a button unbuttoned,' worried Erik, kneeling. Carol frowned, but then noted the strength with which he swung the baby in the air." The half-undone button in the blouse of Wood's figure is often taken as the artist's joke on "The Perfectionist" — not so perfect after all. But it is an odd choice. Again, it seems stubbornly contrary to Lewis's character. In fact, the author makes it clear that Valborg's notice and correction of the button is off putting to Carol, who is established in the novel as a liberal, even indulgent, mother. His fussiness would have compromised her attraction to him if he had not immediately counteracted it with a gesture of physical strength. In the second incident, Carol sends Valborg out of her house after he has arrived uninvited on an evening when the doctor is out. He had insisted on being taken upstairs to see the Kennicott's sleeping child, Hugh, and to glimpse her private room before kissing her and declaring his love. As Carol stands at her window wondering if she should go after Valborg and "get this threshed out," {301} she realizes that she has been observed from Main Street. "He was not to be seen. But Mrs. Westlake was. She was walking past, and in the light from the corner arc lamp, she quickly inspected the porch, the windows. Carol dropped the curtain, stood with movement and reflection paralyzed." {302} For his drawing, Wood used the half-done button, the curtain, and the woman's placement at the window to establish her criticizing temperament. But in the novel, these same elements are used to imply a liberal though repressed woman, not the self-assured snob of *The Perfectionist*. In *Main Street*, Carol often looks out of her window, but usually in despair.

Why did Wood portray her so unsympathetically and why did Lewis not dispute the interpretation? We might have expected that the artist would identify with Carol's struggles and her depression instead of depicting her as a self-satisfied critic. There may be two primary reasons, one personal, and one philosophical. From his personal experience, Wood had not constantly suffered the same kind of rejection that Carol did. Admittedly, Cedar Rapids was larger than Gopher Prairie, but it was still very much a Midwestern town, and a fairly conservative one. Yet, there Wood had found both moral and artistic support. His paintings were purchased, he was welcomed among the upper crust and, thanks to a local family, the Turners, he was given a place to live and work along with a small stipend. There must have been many Cedar Rapids citizens who didn't like art and didn't consider Wood as anyone they wanted to associate with, yet he was able to find a comfortable niche and to receive recognition for his talents. Years before his fame with *American Gothic*, he had a home among these Midwesterners and, though he made hopeful forays into Chicago and even Europe, he always found himself back in Cedar Rapids. He lived in small towns nearly all of his life and apparently never seriously considered moving away from them permanently, even after he became famous. [4]

Yet, we know from his behavior in the 1920s, expressed mainly through his trips to Europe, that Wood had been dissatisfied with his surroundings — a memory that might have disposed him to some sympathy for Carol. [5] To what extent those feelings persisted into the 1930s can't be known exactly. His self-portraits certainly do not suggest complete peace of mind about his situation. But three factors of his life in the 1930s might have mitigated the emotions of the 1920s, leading to greater personal contentment. First, he became famous — without having to leave home. The world had come to him. Second, he traveled throughout the country giving lectures and attending exhibitions, so that restlessness and desire for new places was abated somewhat and home, in fact, had more appeal. And third, by 1935, Wood was the self-appointed spokesman for Regionalism; to suggest that he might be happier and more fulfilled elsewhere would have seemed personally dishonest. When he moved to Iowa City in 1935 to become a professor in the Art Department at the University of Iowa, his support in the Midwest grew (at least for a time). As pointed out earlier, he was regarded as an important figure in that academic world. A Midwestern home, then, had proven to possess personal benefits for Wood that he was disinclined to betray by showing any sympathy with Carol Kennicott's discontent.

In addition to personal considerations, a philosophical one is also present. Wood had made a career out of insisting that the Midwest was a good place for art — not just for him personally, but for any honest artist. He always stipulated that regionalism meant not merely Midwestern Regionalism, but the "genuine" use of material from whatever region an artist knew best. He never wanted to be considered provincial by championing his own region to the detriment of others; he was happy to see regionalism blossom throughout the country. Yet, he was a Midwesterner and he might have argued that this region was the origin and main focus of the movement. He could not, and would not, have argued that the desire to separate from Europe and develop our own distinctively American art came exclusively from the Midwest. But he certainly could argue that the effort to create a specific program with its own schools and its own agenda did come from the Midwest, specifically from Iowa and, more specifically, from him. His establishment of the Stone City Colony and Art School in 1932 was an early example of that effort. When he set up the Public Works of Art Project in the Art Department at the University of Iowa and staffed it primarily with young artists/disciples who had attended Stone City, it constituted another "official" act as the leader of the Regionalist movement. Wood was clearly the philosophical leader and the conscience of the Regionalist movement. Significantly, it was Wood who persuaded and encouraged both Thomas Hart Benton and John Steuart Curry to leave the East and return to their roots.

With these factors in mind, Wood might have felt it would be hypocritical to positively present a character that constantly fantasizes about abandoning the Midwest for a more adventurous, rewarding life. Wood might have observed that Carol is herself a Midwesterner, born in Mankato and educated in Minneapolis. She had traveled little before her marriage and was even uncomfortable among the "Bohemians" in Chicago, where she spent a year doing graduate library work ("She was shocked by the free manners which she had for years desired." {8}). Although she is critical of Gopher Prairie, she is often timid and uncertain outside of it, as on the trip to Minneapolis to see four plays {169-175} and then when she escapes Gopher Prairie to live in Washington. One of the interesting things about her character is the extent to which she is herself completely a Midwesterner, although a more sophisticated one, a description that could also apply to Grant Wood. In the end, she settles into Gopher Prairie, recognizing that it is where she will live out the rest of her life. If Wood felt any sense of identification with her struggle, he did not infuse it into the drawing.

Wood's interpretation may also be tied to uneasiness with Carol's discontent with her traditional domestic role. She does not reject that role entirely, but she finds housecleaning a drudgery, cooks very little (the Kennicott's employ a maid-cook most of the time) and is generally bored with the day-to-day details of housekeeping. Though her love for her little son is genuine, she is occasionally openly grumpy about having to look after him and even leaves him for an extended West Coast vacation with her husband. She certainly does not hesitate to separate the child from his father when she decides to abandon Gopher Prairie for Washington. Wood did depict women who worked outside the home (such as his sister, Nan, and the *Main Street* character, Vida Sherwin), but Carol Kennicott is the only character in his *oeuvre* who does not seem to define herself primarily (and contentedly) through her role in the home (or in traditional female duties). Neither his mother nor his sister seems to have expressed any conflict about their traditional female stations in life. Even his contentious wife, Sara, seemed to glory in her role as hostess of the Wood home. Considering the times, his personal experiences, and his shyness around women, perhaps it is not surprising that he tended to see women traditionally.

One of Wood's major early commissions (1922) was *The Adoration of the Home*, a large

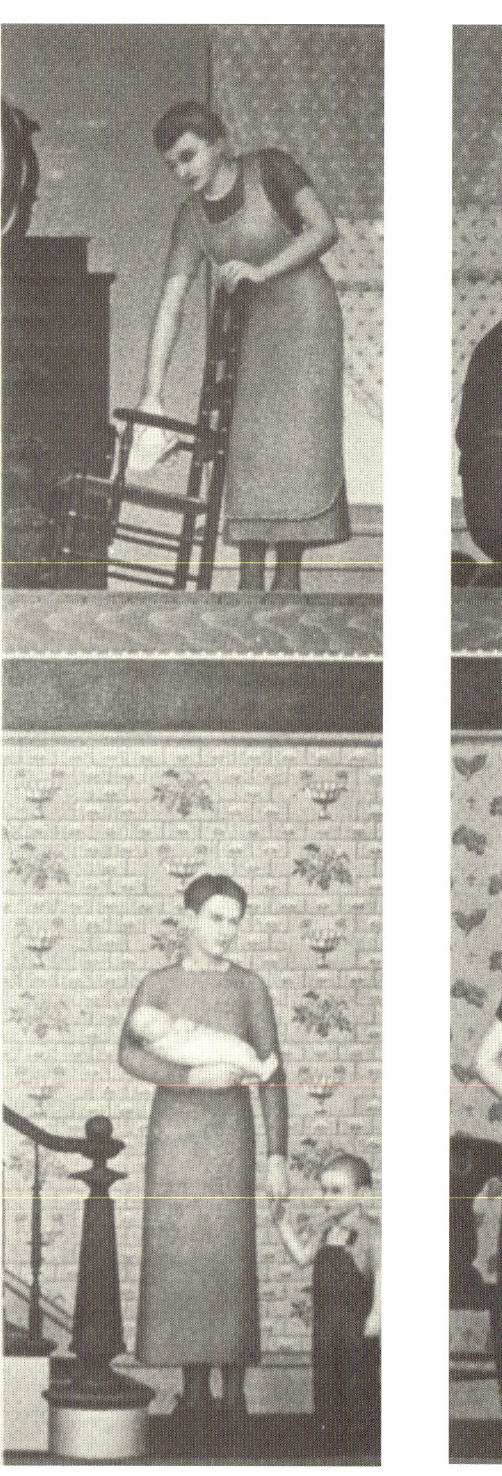

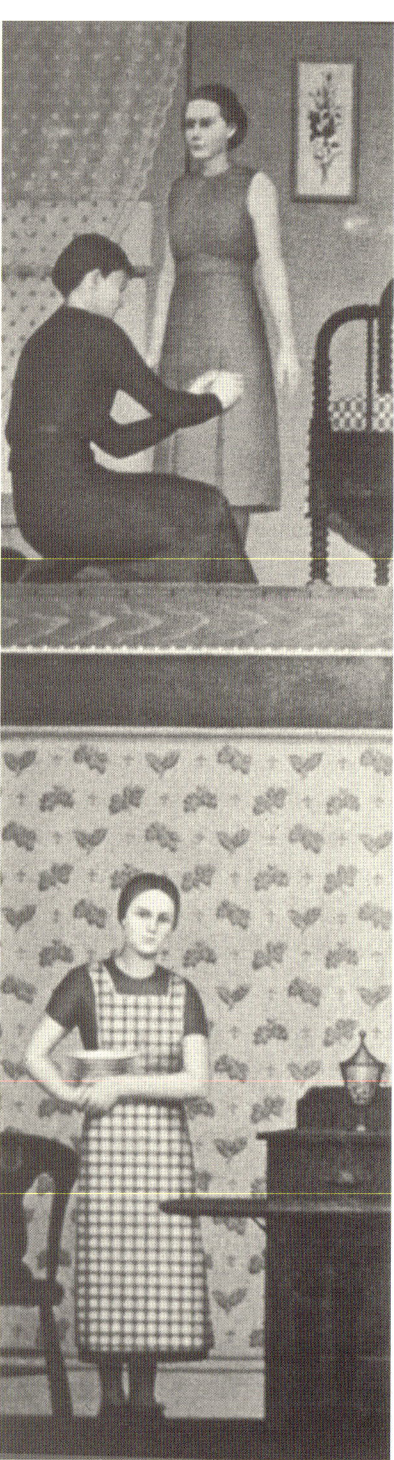

Figure 45 Home Economics *(detail of* Where Tillage Begins, Other Arts Follow*),*
1935. Parks Library, Iowa State University

painting that glorified the Midwestern home and all the occupations and pursuits that guaranteed its prosperity and harmony. At the center of the painting, as at the heart of society, he placed women engaged in traditional roles (men were also shown in their time-honored roles, such as farmers and mechanics). Commissioned by a Cedar Rapids real estate company, it is not known what Wood's exact instructions were or if he himself provided the title for his painting. But he certainly would have devised the imagery and infused it with its honorific tone. Over a decade later, when he designed the PWAP murals for the Iowa State University Library, Wood again showed women in traditional occupations exclusively: housecleaning, garment making, cooking, and child bearing and rearing. (Figure 45) Of course, these depictions reflect (perhaps at the request of the school) the courses of study in the College of Home Economics, which was then the major of most women students. Although women were allowed in the schools of Agriculture and Engineering (the other colleges depicted in the murals), female enrollment was low, as might be expected during these times. (Ironically, men were not allowed to enroll in Home Economics classes, a situation that prevailed until after World War II when men were permitted into Christian Petersen's sculpture class, a part of the Applied Arts curriculum.) [6] The tasks of the women of the library mural were the same that had engaged women for centuries, with little obvious updating of their status in the twentieth century, even in the setting of higher education. [7] It is possible that Wood was uncomfortable about or felt ill-equipped to convey Carol's boredom with her traditional role — her unabashed feminism — whether he philosophically sympathized with it or not. Perhaps the suspicion that permeates her portrait reflects Wood's personal suspicions (or outright dislike) of chronically unhappy women.

Carol's primary adversary among the women of *Main Street* is not Mrs. Bogart (*The Good Influence*) or even the ladies of the Thanatopsis Club and the Jolly Seventeen. The person who criticizes her most unsparingly is her friend, Vida Sherwin, the high school teacher and *Practical Idealist*. By the novel's end, Sherwin has been revealed to be as thoroughly false and narrow as anyone in town. Her ill will toward Carol is masked by her solicitousness and by her willingness to advise Carol — for her own good, of course! — of all the ways in which Gopher Prairie dislikes and ridicules her. Sherwin's discontent runs as deep as Carol's and is more pathological — and, of necessity, more hidden. The ease with which her secret unhappiness is erased after marriage is a measure of its shallowness and immaturity. Carol's complaints are at least based on observed reality. Yet, Wood's most favorable characterization in the *Main Street* series is bestowed on Sherwin and not on Carol, with her larger, more informed view of culture.

He must have expected that his two drawings would be compared and mentally placed side by side (or actually hung near each other in an exhibition). (Figure 46-47) When they are, the compositions imply the lack of true friendship between the two. In one juxtaposition, the two women face opposite directions, with their chairs back-to-back. If placed in the other relationship — turned in the direction of each other — there is no sense of

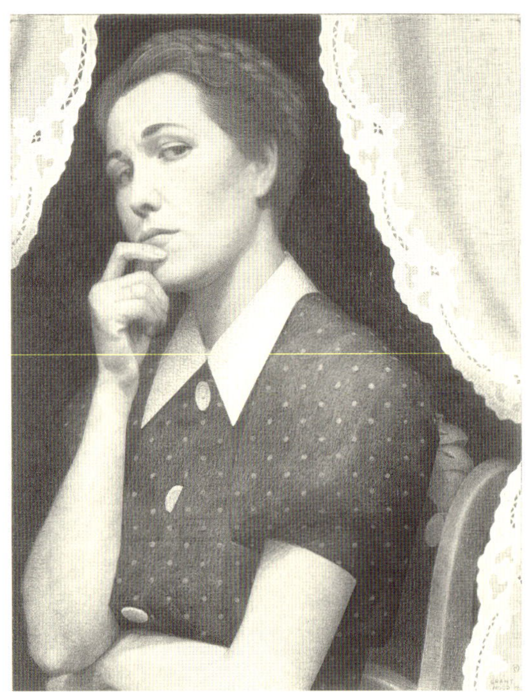
Figure 46 The Perfectionist

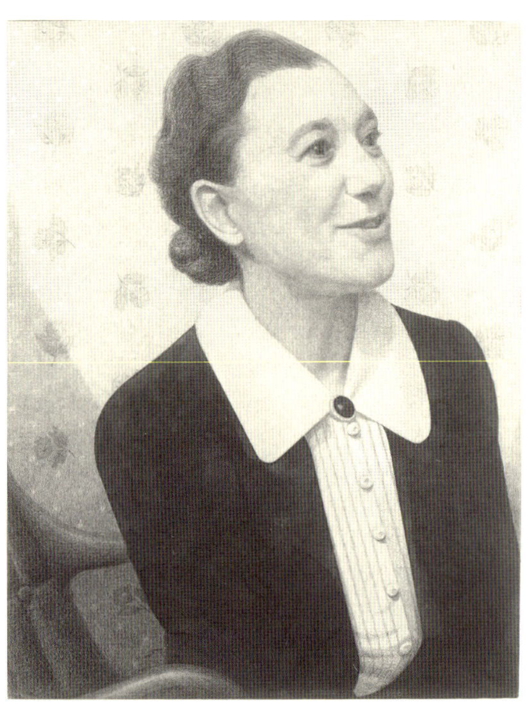
Figure 47 Practical Idealist

communication or acknowledgment between them. In fact, the two women seem to shun each other and to deliberately disconnect. Sherwin's gaze misses and moves beyond Carol. Carol's is directed towards us, the viewers, as if she is trying to decide how to improve us — or if it is even worth her effort. Placed in any relationship to *Practical Idealist*, *The Perfectionist* comes off poorly, and we wonder again why Wood's portrayal of her is so unredeeming.

In her 1983 catalogue for the Wood retrospective, Wanda Corn provides the most plausible explanation. "Involved in a difficult marriage when he created these illustrations, Wood may have over-sympathized with the doctor, who suffers a young, energetic wife constantly urging him and the townsfolk to better themselves." [8] Wood's marriage in March of 1935 to Sara Sherman Maxon was welcomed by few of his friends. Though a native Iowan, Maxon had developed for herself a worldlier persona that may have led her to look down on local culture. As a singer of art songs and light opera, her career had given her a genuine acquaintance with the world beyond the Midwest. Shortly after the marriage, the couple moved from Cedar Rapids to Iowa City where they embarked on a more lavish, high profile lifestyle than Wood had ever concocted for himself alone. Wood left behind friends in Cedar Rapids who, in their later comments on the marriage, suggested that tensions between Wood and Maxon emerged early and were exacerbated by Wood's financial ineptitude. Without direct accusations, some observers seemed to regard his wife as ambitious, aiming for a starrier social status for herself and her famous husband.

At the same time, there is evidence of the benefits she brought to the marriage. Maxon reportedly was kind to Wood's mother, who was in poor health during their courtship and died soon after the marriage. [9] Wood had lived with his mother much of his adult life and it is possible that the prospect of being alone prompted him to overcome his shyness toward women. After the marriage, Maxon managed the household and took charge of some business affairs and correspondence. Guests found her an attentive hostess, and the Wood home in Iowa City became a social hub. Finally, she provided Wood with a family which, according to one writer, he genuinely cared for. [10] Her son by an earlier marriage, Dr. Arthur Sherman Maxon, moved with his wife and young child to Iowa City where they all lived in the Wood home. Dr. Maxon, a dentist, served as the model for one of the *Main Street* drawings, *The Radical*.

The model for Carol Kennicott was the least firmly identified person in the literature on the *Main Street* drawings. All of the other portraits had been convincingly assigned to specific individuals in Wood's acquaintance, but no such information emerged about this most important model. The only known reference occurred in an unidentified newspaper clipping in the Nan Wood Graham Scrapbooks: "Carol is a version of his daughter." [11] Wood, of course, did not have a daughter, but he did have a daughter-in-law at this time. In her 1993 book, *My Brother, Grant Wood*, the artist's sister, Nan Wood Graham, also identified Dr. Maxon's wife (whose name was Dorothy) as the model. [12] According to a Cedar Rapids friend who visited the Woods in Iowa City, Dr. Maxon's wife was "dark and attractive and appeared to be competent, and a generally nice person. [13] "Dark" and "attractive" do describe the woman in Wood's drawing. If she was indeed a "nice person" and someone of whom Wood was fond, he might have employed discretion by not naming her as his model for such an unflattering portrayal. Or perhaps the lack of identification was at Dorothy Maxon's request.

Notes: *The Perfectionist*

1. There are numerous examples throughout the book of the town's critical stance toward Carol Kennicott: the garage conversation between Cy Bogart and a friend, overheard by Carol {84-85}; several disastrous club meetings, including her first at the Jolly Seventeen {70-75} and Vida Sherwin's subsequent revelation about the town's opinion of Carol. {76-79}

2. After this conversation with Vida Sherwin, Lewis writes of Carol that "she laid her dreams of perfection aside," as if she had acquiesced in Vida's opinion of her.

3. It is odd that Wood would choose these kinds of curtains since they are more easily associated with the house that Carol inherits from Will Kennicott's mother than something Carol herself would select. Her first reaction to the house — which appalls her — includes her notice of its curtains that seem to act as an introduction to an oppressive "Mid-Victorian" interior: "Window curtains of starched cheap lace revealing a pink marble table with a conch shell and a family Bible." 64.

4. For discussions of Wood's situation in Cedar Rapids during the 1910s and 1920s, see Dennis, *Grant Wood: A Study in Art and Culture* and Corn, *The Regionalist Vision.* For informal accounts of these years, see Brown, Hazel E., *Grant Wood and Marvin Cone: Artists of an Era*, Ames: Iowa State University Press, 1972 and Graham, Nan Wood, *My Brother, Grant Wood*, Iowa City: State Historical Society of Iowa, 1993. Darrell Garwood's *Artist in Iowa: A Life of Grant Wood* (New York: W.W. Norton and Company, Inc., 1944) is a biography of the artist, but it has usually not been regarded as a reliable source of facts. Graham in particular felt that his book contained numerous misrepresentations.

5. There are other suggestions that he was not entirely content with Cedar Rapids just the way it was. During the 1920s, he was often an instigator of drama groups, art activities and parties, especially costume parties. In fact, his social agenda during those years sounds a bit like what Carol Kennicott was trying to do in Gopher Prairie. But unlike Carol, Wood found a much better reception than she did. When he suggested changes in, for example, the decoration of some of the finer homes of the city, he was listened to. He was partially successful in creating a kind of Parisian Latin Quarter where a few "Bohemian" ideas might circulate. The Wapsipinicon River was not as favorable a shore for that sort of thing as the Seine and sometimes, when we read of those days in Wood's life, we imagine him as a one-man avant-garde crusade, American heartland version. Yet, even if he did not transform Cedar Rapids, his failures were not as dismal nor as public as Carol Kennicott's. At some point in his life, he seems to have resolved some of his discontent and become invested in Cedar Rapids in a way Carol never did in her town.

6. Throughout his career at Iowa State University, Christian Petersen was part of the Home Economics faculty in the Applied Arts department. For a discussion of the gradual integration of enrollment in his sculpture classes, see Bliss, Patricia L., *Christian Petersen Remembered*, Ames: Iowa State University Press, 1986, 126-129.

7. While it is easy to condemn these murals today for perpetuating stereotypes of women, it is also possible to judge them more generously. The fact that the higher education of women is acknowledged at all in these murals

is not something to take for granted. Although the Home Economics panels are painted on a narrower wall and are thus smaller than the Agriculture and Engineering murals, they occupy as prominent a place. Approaching up the staircase from the first floor (where *Breaking the Prairie Sod* is placed), the viewer encounters the Home Economics paintings first; only on the landing do the Agriculture and Engineering murals come into view. Home Economics and the pursuits of women are just as important to society as are the occupations of men, the mural seems to assert. Also, the women are treated with seriousness, as if to express respect for the inherent dignity of their labor. Finally, the mural implies the modern, scientific ideas that were being applied to the home and the activities within it. Modern theories of child development, advanced information about nutrition, new concepts of hygiene and public health — these were the kinds of studies required of the Iowa State coeds. They were not just being taught how to dust a chair, make gravy or diaper a baby; their curriculum embraced the "science" of making a home more efficient, safe and productive. My thanks to Matthew DeLay for the suggestion of Wood's discomfort with the feminist aspects of Carol Kennicott's character.

8. Corn, 114.

9. The most extensive comments on the Wood marriage occur in Hazel Brown's *Grant Wood and Marvin Cone: Artists of an Era* and Nan Wood Graham's *My Brother, Grant Wood*. Brown transcribes reports and letters of Cedar Rapids friends, adding her own observations, but the materials she uses cannot always be found today and so cannot be depended upon in a scholarly way. Her book makes no pretense of being anything other than a personal reminiscence that includes her own judgments. Neither she nor Graham consistently document their sources so that their comments must be considered with qualifications. Neither writer has a favorable opinion of the marriage or of Maxon. Brown probably accurately reflects the feelings of many in Cedar Rapids about Maxon and her marriage with their favorite son. Much of Brown's reporting is probably correct in its spirit, but it is colored by her personal disapproval of both Maxon and the marriage. In regard to Maxon's behavior toward Hattie Weaver Wood, the artist's elderly mother, Brown is more charitable. See Brown, 79-85, 90-94; Graham, 127-128, 133-134, 149-152 and Garwood, 187-190, 213-215 217-221.

10. The writer was Bruce McKay and his account of a visit to the Wood household is included in Brown, 92.

11. Selby, John, "Grant Wood Denies He's Art Prophet," unidentified newspaper clipping, NWG Scrapbook No.2, 45.

12. Graham, 139.

13. The account of the visit is by Bruce McKay and is quoted in Brown, 91-92. McKay was an old friend with whom Wood had built and restored several houses. No photographs of Dorothy Maxon have been found.

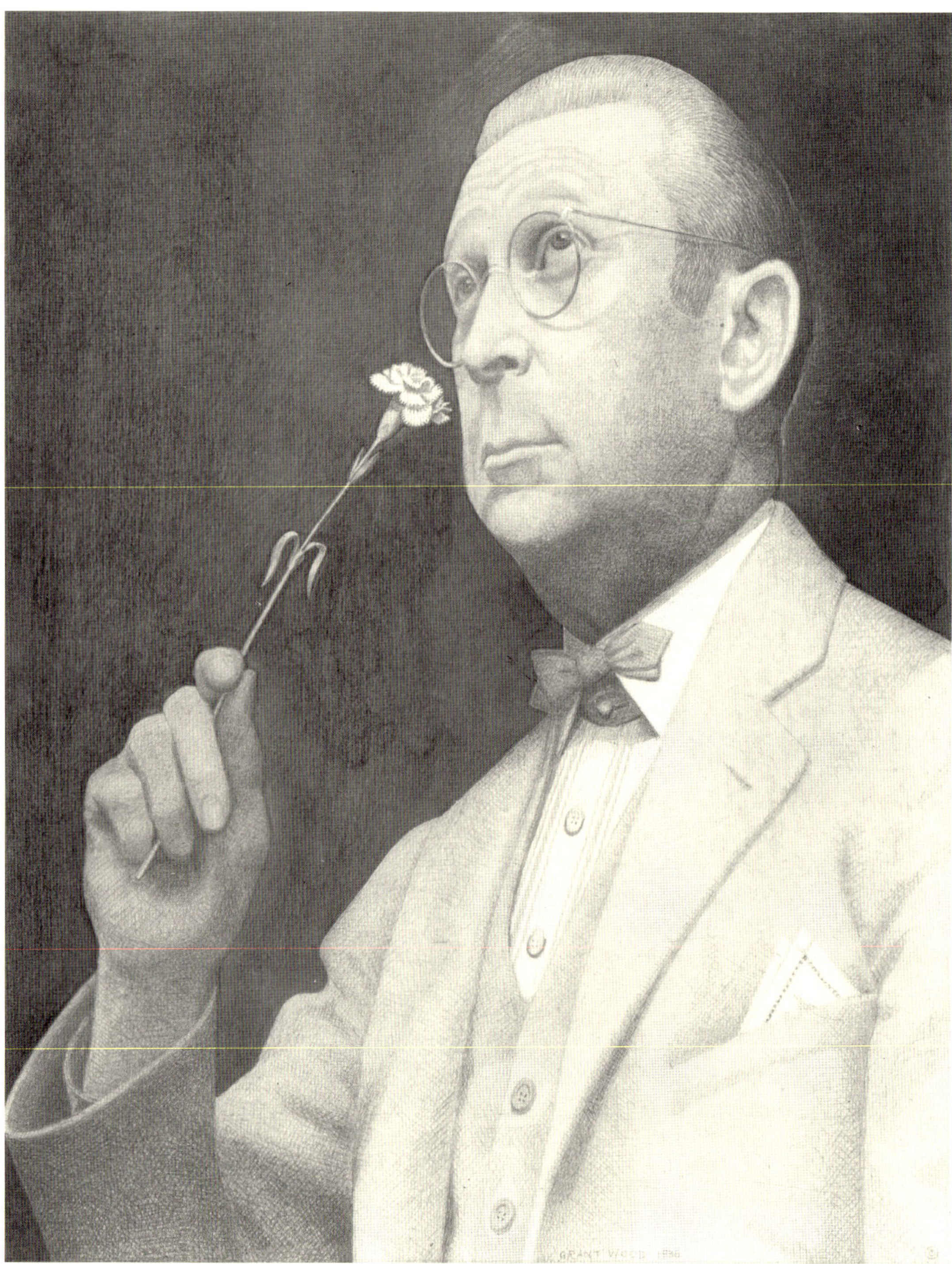

Figure 48 Sentimental Yearner

Sentimental Yearner (Raymond P. Wutherspoon "Raymie")

Raymond P. Wutherspoon (usually known by the diminutive "Raymie") is one of three male characters in *Main Street* who does not entirely fit the Main Street definition of Real Men, as exemplified by Dr. Will Kennicott and his friends. Wutherspoon is the solicitous salesman of ladies' shoes and purveyor of "gent's furnishings" at the local Bon Ton Store. In this less-than-manly triumvirate, he is joined by Erik Valborg, farm boy-turned-tailor referred to by the town as "Elizabeth" and by the wilted and lonely lawyer, Guy Pollock. Toward Valborg and Pollock, Carol Kennicott feels an attraction that is clearly returned by each of them (though she is never unfaithful to her husband). Regarded by the town as nothing more than a "Swede tailor,"{266} Erik is the more serious romantic prospect; their liaison is ended only when Dr. Kennicott puts a stop to it and discretely forces the young man out of town. Carol nevertheless maintains a certain longing for him until nearly the end of the novel. As for Guy Pollock, his own cowardice and inertia drain him of any sexual allure by the sixteenth chapter, less than halfway through the book. After that point, he is as inconsequential for Carol as he is for the rest of Gopher Prairie. Though it is understandable why he might be identified as the "sentimental yearner," the descriptions in the novel seem better fitted to Raymond P. Wutherspoon. In addition, there is at least one contemporary source that identifies the drawing as Wutherspoon. [1] Carol is not remotely attracted to Wutherspoon, and indeed, it is one of the novel's most surprising and delightful plot twists when someone is. The December-December marriage of Vida Sherwin and her Raymie (or "Ray" as she calls him after they marry) works a fascinating change in both characters, but especially in Raymond. Wood, however, hardly acknowledges the changed Raymond Wutherspoon; the figure in the drawing is certainly the pre-marriage, pre-soldier, pre-Major, and pre-war hero Raymie.

Wood's drawing was inspired by incidents in the first half of the book that portray Raymie as a gentle, but ineffective, aspirer to the finer things in life. At first, Carol hopes that he will be her ally in literary and dramatic efforts to improve and lift the cultural horizons of the town, but she soon realizes that Raymie's tastes are the most provincial incarnations of those pursuits. His personality is sketched in an early scene: surrounded by men (including Dr. Kennicott, whispering to Carol something about "gentleman hen") who ridicule him at every turn, he welcomes Carol to Gopher Prairie. He assures her that "'there are a great many bright cultured people here'" (including "'Miss Sherwin of the high school...such a pleasing, bright girl'"). He admits "'lots of folks try to jolly me for trying to get up shows and so on. I tell them they have more artistic gifts than they know.'"{47-48} But the "artistic gifts" he refers to are those of local bands of hobbyist musicians and by "culture," he means the "dandy" shows and recitations provided by itinerant entertainers.

He informs Carol that he does like to read, but prefers movies over books because books "'are not so thoroughly safeguarded by intelligent censors as the movies are.'" [2] With books, he worries, one risks running into accounts of bad behavior: "'I'm not narrow, but I must say I don't see any use in this deliberately dragging in immorality. Life itself is so full of temptations that in literature one wants only that which is pure and uplifting.'" {48-9} He proudly announces that he has had a novel by Balzac pulled off the library shelves. [3] (The French novelist Honoré de Balzac had already been dead for over sixty years by the time Raymie took offense and spared Gopher Prairie his low, Gallic morality.) Pure and uplifting: that is Raymie's credo and the state of mind and heart that Wood depicts in his drawing, along with his own commentary that this silly yearner is not to be taken seriously. We surmise that Wood agrees with Carol and the rest of the town who find Raymie insubstantial and ineffectual, a minor player in the competitive game of life.

Lewis's descriptions of Raymie's appearance are reflected in the drawing. A "professional bachelor," he had a "pale, long, spectacled face and sandy pompadour hair,"{47} with pale and watery eyes "like those of a dog waiting to be let in out of the cold."{48} Before their courtship, Vida Sherwin saw him as "a thin man with spectacles, mournful drawn-out face, and colorless stiff hair," but afterwards she observed that "his jaw was square, that his long hands moved quickly and were bleached in a refined manner, and that his trusting eyes indicated that he had "'led a clean life.'"{209} We recognize him also from one of the alterations made by his wife in his former appearance: "She persuaded him not to wear the small bow ties which made him look like an elongated Sunday School scholar."{210} [4] Wood offers no hint of the warrior who would later emerge, as Lewis does when Raymie first appears. Fed up at last with the men insulting him in front of Carol, the otherwise unfailingly civil gentleman "bared his teeth like a belligerent mouse," and growled, "'You make me tired!'"{49}

The main inspiration for the drawing is derived from the description of Raymie at Carol's first party in which she, the Perfectionist, labels him the Sentimental Yearner. (The scene also gives an early hint at the eventual pairing of Vida and Raymie.) Determined to liven up the social scene, Carol confides to Vida that she will have none of the "stunts" that pass for entertainment in Gopher Prairie, to which the schoolteacher replies:

> "That's good. I tell you: why not have Raymond Wutherspoon sing?"
>
> "Raymie? Why, my dear, he's the most sentimental yearner in town!"
>
> "See here, child! Your opinions on house-decorating are sound, but your opinions of people are rotten! Raymie does wag his tail. But the poor dear — Longing for what he calls 'self-expression' and no training in anything except selling shoes. But he can sing. And some day when he gets away from [his employer's] patronage and ridicule, he'll do something fine."
>
> ....While Raymie blushed and admitted, "Oh, they don't want to hear

> me," he was clearing his throat, pulling his clean handkerchief farther out of his breast pocket, and thrusting his fingers between the buttons of his vest....[Carol] wanted to laugh at the gratified importance in Raymie's half-shut eyes; she wanted to weep over the meek ambitiousness which clouded like an aura his pale face, flap ears and sandy pompadour." {61}

After three songs, even Vida Sherwin, "that trusting admirer of all that was or conceivably could be the good, the true and the beautiful," had to admit that perhaps Raymie couldn't sing all that well, but both women agreed that he had "so much *feeling*" in his performance.{62}

This "feeling" is often referred to in the novel as "yearning," and it is sporadically applied to characters other than Raymie, including Carol who cautions herself not to become a yearner who sidesteps real life.{131} To yearn is to have a feeling of longing or desiring, usually for something that is impractical or out of reach. What one yearns for is something that one despairs of ever getting. Thus, if the yearning is made public, the yearner may be criticized as unrealistic, too steeped in daydreams, or simply ridiculous. The Gopher Prairians consider Raymie such a yearner that he is a well-worn topic of conversation in that regard. When Carol invites Vida Sherwin and Guy Pollock to dinner hoping for some intellectual conversation, she finds that the party gets no further than "a controversy regarding Raymie Wutherspoon's yearnings."{122} We can imagine them basing their comments on encounters like Carol's at the Bon Ton in which he "tiptoed up to her, his long sallow face bobbing, and...besought" her to try on a pair of slippers he had "set aside" just for her. After the sale, he mourned, "'I'm not a salesman at all! I just like elegant things. All this is so inartistic.'"{97}

Before his romantic rebirth in marriage and his baptism in trench warfare, Raymie reveals that he has one small but genuine talent. Carol Kennicott goads a few Gopher Prairians into presenting a play, which she directs. After first protecting the town from "irreligious ideas" and "immoral writers"{177} in the choice of a play, Raymie shows himself to be a "surprisingly good" actor, especially compared to Guy Pollock, "who pulled his soft mustache, looked self-conscious and turned [his role] into a limp dummy. But Raymie, as the villain, had no repressions. The tilt of his head was full of character; his drawl was admirably vicious."{181} The Raymie of Lewis's novel presented opportunities for Wood to shade the character of his *Sentimental Yearner*, but he focused on those qualities which made him more of a type than an individual. In addition, the pre-war and pre-husband portion of Raymie was more susceptible to satire, a more fruitful subject for the artist.

In addition to his fastidious clothes, appropriate for a salesman of gent's furnishings, and his halo-like eyeglasses, Raymie has two props: the carnation and the shaft of light that beams across his "sandy pompadour." Lewis does not mention Raymie sniffing flowers, giving flowers or associating himself with flowers. The carnation is supplied by Grant

Wood, with possibly two ideas in mind: first, integrating the use of symbolic objects — or attributes — as the Old Masters had, and second, construing a well known iconographic symbol into a personal comment on the masculinity of his subject. As part of his admiration for Flemish and German late Medieval-Early Renaissance painting, Wood noticed the role of flowers and integrated them as symbols into his own artistic vocabulary. In one of his earliest paintings in his post-Munich style, he had placed a common Iowa wildflower in the hand of the child, Susan Angevine Shaffer. His famous picture of his mother, *Woman with Plants*, does not include a blossom, but it does depict plants (a geranium and a begonia) that do produce flowers in Midwestern gardens and houses. Though normally non-flowering, the sansevieria (snake plant or mother-in-law's tongue) held by his mother is a symbol of her love of gardening and the hardiness of Midwestern pioneers. In one of his murals for Iowa State University, *Breaking the Prairie Sod* [see Figure 28], he strewed a catalogue of native plants and flowers, all with the detailed accuracy of a fifteenth century northern European painting (and entirely appropriate for a college of scientific agriculture). The multitude of flowers there, like a *mille fleur* tapestry, symbolizes the plenitude of nature and, in this case, the natural beauty of the virgin prairie being sacrificed to the plow.

He may also have been aware of the use of flowers in paintings by contemporary German artists, especially Christian Schad and Otto Dix. In his early (1912) *Self-Portrait* (Figure 49), the young Otto Dix depicted himself holding a carefully painted pink carnation, as had medieval sitters, but in his twentieth century update, Dix seems to be making the painful point of his lack of both love and religion. Dix included a single flower in many of his paintings of the 1920s and 1930s, usually to make a caustic comment on deterioration of some sort. [5] In Schad's work, too, the flower is a constant although it is usually a cultivated, somewhat exotic kind symbolizing an ironic separation from nature. Like Wood, these artists were influenced by late Medieval Northern European painting, although they turned it to different effects in their painting. [6]

A carnation is a symbol of love in the European paintings Wood studied. If it is red, it symbolizes pure love and if it is pink, it symbolizes marriage, and is often carried by a bride. In fact, pink is so commonly associated with carnations that they are often referred to as "pinks." Carnations or pinks (*Dianthus carophyllus*) were a staple of the late Medieval gardens that were sometimes shown in the backgrounds of paintings Wood would have seen. Much of our information about gardens of this period comes from these paintings (and manuscript illustrations) in which a lady is shown amidst the plantings. [7] In addition, Wood might have been familiar with carnations or pinks because they were a feature of late Victorian gardens known as "cottage gardens" of the sort that his mother and his Midwestern neighbors cultivated. [8] Wood, like everyone else, would have associated gardens in general and carnations in particular with women and things that appeal to women. Love is traditionally evoked by the carnation, but in Raymie's hands, it is that moping distant cousin of medieval courtly love: sentimentality. [9]

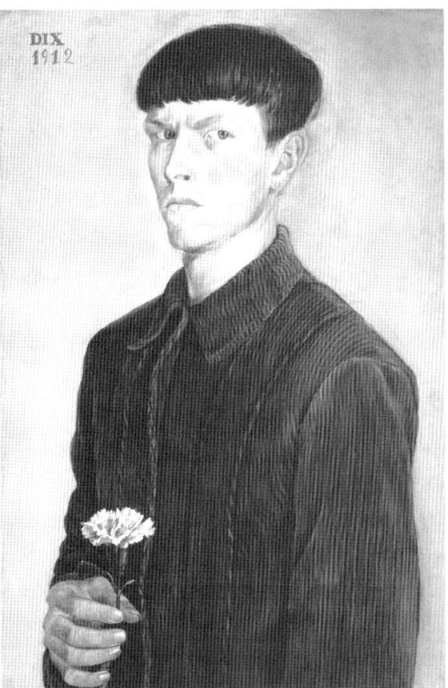

Figure 49 Otto Dix. Self-Portrait, *1912*

Raymie's swooning sniff of the carnation goes beyond just a common cultural association. We do not have the impression that he intends to hand it over to Vida or any other woman. Hc has it because he enjoys it — he, himself, whether a woman is involved or not. Raymie's masculinity is jokingly questioned throughout the novel until he marries and goes to war. He is characterized as not only a yearner, but also a *sentimental* yearner: both concepts popularly associated with women. Both yearning and sentimentality are states of mind, not forms of action. Raymie acts on very little until his marriage (and his sexual activation); this lack of action and physicality is part of what causes Gopher Prairie to make slurs (wrongly, as it turns out) against his masculinity. His well-cut but fussy clothes, his excruciatingly well-groomed hair, his rolling uplifted eyes, and that deadly carnation condemn Raymie to the slightly suspicious ranks of manhood, at least among the shallow gossips of Gopher Prairie. As we study the details of Wood's characterization, we wonder if he did not share their opinion of unproven men like Raymie. Although he is not blatantly cruel, Wood seems to join in the "jollying" of Raymond Wutherspoon by placing a pink carnation in his hand (something Lewis did not do in the novel).

The drawing *Sentimental Yearner* is the plainest and least elaborate in the series, particularly in its background. Here, we see only a beatifying beam of light. It is a modest showering of radiance, but it is enough to convince us of Wood's mockery of his subject. It encircles and shines out beyond the back of Raymie's head, bathing his face (especially the upturned eyes) in its glow. It originates somewhere above the sitter's head, but Wood treats it as he does all the other accessories in the picture: as an affectation. We suspect it may reflect Raymie's opinion of himself as a practitioner and safe-guarder of virtue. But we can be certain that it expresses Wood's opinion of people like Raymie, with his silly notions of art, morality, and the relationship between them. This faux-saint would petrify true art by his timidity and his prejudice, as illustrated in his statement to the town drama group. "'It seems to me that a play that doesn't leave a nice taste in the mouth and that hasn't any message is nothing but — nothing but —Well, whatever it may be, it isn't art.'"{177}

In at least two places in the novel, Lewis suggests a light shining around Raymie, and these may have influenced Wood's conception. In responding to a literary question from Carol, Lewis tells us that Raymie "shone at her like a dim blue March moon, and sighed."{48} Later, when he sings at Carol's party, he exudes an "aura" of earnestness that she finds laughable.{61} Wood may have also used the light to parody Raymie's religiosity. Practically the first thing he relates about himself is that he sings in the Episcopal choir {48} and, until he leaves for the war, he is a constant sentinel against immorality posing as "art." After she becomes his wife, Vida Sherwin prizes what she calls his "spiritual nobility"{212} and declares, "'Do you know, I've always thought that Ray would have made a wonderful rector. He has what I call an essentially religious soul. My! He'd have read the service beautifully!'"{216} This is the sort of remark that would set up any character as a target for parody — and Wood rose to the challenge. The artist's most pointed comments about religion are lavished on *The Good Influence*. Still, Wood reminds us that, while it is not as outrightly damaging as Mrs. Bogart's religion, Raymie's paltry version is not always harmless. Whether it is self-generated or imposed by the artist or both, the mock-heavenly ray of light is one of Wood's most comic and most damning devices.

Sentimental Yearner has often been identified as the well-read lawyer and "poetic bachelor,"{54} Guy Pollock. But both the novel and the drawing present evidence that Guy Pollock is not the subject of Wood's characterization. Ground down by what he calls "the Village Virus," Pollock is gradually revealed as less a victim of the small town than of his own laziness and lack of ambition. He is not pathetic because he is not self-deluded nor is he ever ridiculed as Raymie Wutherspoon is. Any man with the self-awareness (however negative and overstated) to refer to his life as "the biography of a living dead man"{127} cannot be regarded as silly, sentimental or inconsequential, as is the figure in Wood's drawing. But the main argument against identifying Guy Pollock as the sentimental yearner is the sexual tension that exists between him and Carol Kennicott. The earliest clear state-

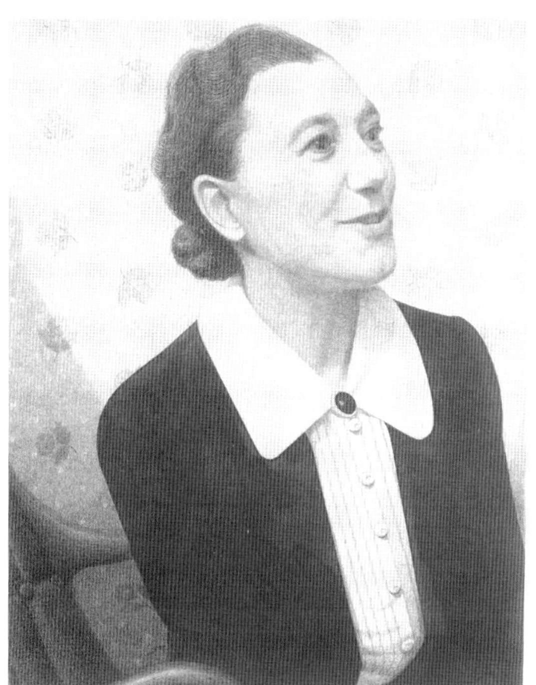

Figure 50 Practical Idealist

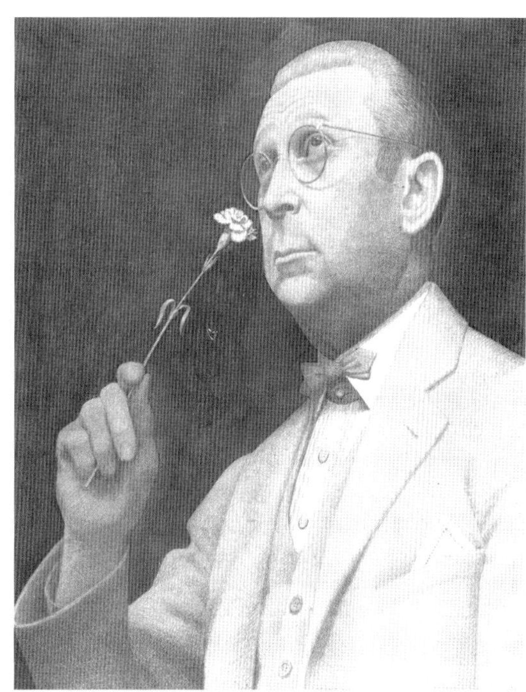

Figure 51 Sentimental Yearner

ment of it occurs at her first party when, as she walks down the stairs in an alluring costume, she is aware of the "hunger" of two men who stare at her: her husband and Guy Pollock.{62} When she visits Pollock in his apartment (by mistake), their mutual attraction is obvious, though held in check. For some time afterwards, she entertains bookish fantasies about Pollock while he looks at her "as though he had a right to."{147} But finally, his faintheartedness and "love of dead elegances"{164} disappoints her and he vanishes from her emotional life. Though the figure in Wood's drawing might embody a love of dead elegances, he could hardly inspire fantasizing from Carol.

An additional argument for the identification of *Sentimental Yearner* as Raymond Wutherspoon is its artistic and narrative effect on the overall series. Although the subtitle of *Main Street* is "The Story of Carol Kennicott," it could also be called the story of a marriage. Of all the characters in the novel, the two essentials are the husband and wife, Carol and Will. If *Sentimental Yearner* is Raymie, it elaborates the comment on marriage by creating a pendant with the portrait of Vida, thus encouraging a comparison of the two couples. (Figures 50-51) Wood's concentration on Raymie's pre-marriage persona is understandable since he is much less vividly described afterwards; in fact, he is given no dialogue and we have little idea of his feelings. We are told only of what he does. Still, readers of the novel would know him as the husband of Vida and recall that, after he took his soldier's uniform off, part of his mystique evaporated and Carol could note that, in the end, "he was Raymie." {336} With that in mind, the choice of these two characters encourages us to muse on the kind of marriage created between Raymie and Vida, on their happiness with each other and their contentment in Gopher Prairie, especially when compared with the contentiousness of the Kennicott alliance. Because Wood himself was recently married (and, it seems, already unhappy), he might have been especially sensitive to the marriages portrayed in Lewis's novel and interested in inserting his own commentary.

In another way, *Sentimental Yearner* (Raymie) can be seen as a narrative pendant to *Practical Idealist* (Vida Sherwin) in that they represent apparently opposite ways of dealing with the world (one active, one inactive). Yet, in these two pictures, they have more in common than we might at first suspect (and that may be implied by Wood's compositions, as discussed below). Both would like to change the world, or perhaps more accurately: *improve* the world, but neither is seriously discontented nor angry. They are not pessimists. Neither of them is violently mistreated by the world they hope to alter just a little. Perhaps they are overlooked or they have to tolerate some "jollying" (as the jokers of Gopher Prairie say), but no one perceives them as a threat, and rightly so. Together, far from working at cross-purposes, Raymie and Vida can be seen as constituting an effective, balanced force. The idealist and the yearner; practicality and sentiment: divergent inclinations blended — not sacrificed — into a partnership of satisfaction. Vida tells Raymie to "talk deep" {211} and joins him in standing up to his employer. Raymie takes Vida out of the boarding house and into the sanctity of her own home, then provides her with a war-hero. We may surmise from this couple that marriage need not be a contest or an instrument of repression. As he studied the novel for insights to use for his drawings and reflected on his own life, Wood might have been interested in counteracting the stress of the Kennicott relationship as well as mitigating that in his own.

Finally, an argument for Raymond Wutherspoon as *Sentimental Yearner* is the artistic pendant it provides for *Practical Idealist*. In the series of drawings, these are the only two portraits that do not acknowledge the viewer. Both look off to the side and both lift their eyes (though admittedly Raymie's are a little less focused). Both figures arise out of a corner of the composition and a clear shaft of angled light illuminates both. A decorative object (a brooch and a bow tie) is placed at the throat of both sitters. Pendants are intended to be hung side by side, though we do not know what relationship Wood preferred for these two drawings, or if he even imagined them exhibited together; their sequence as illustrations to the book cannot set up visual comparisons. If hung together, they would again create a balance in that they could either look toward each other or split our gaze and direct it equilaterally in opposite ways. They cannot be said to actually look at each other (Raymie's gaze is too self-absorbed and internalized), but their poses are turned so that compositionally their association is implied.

The model for *Sentimental Yearner* was Charles Leo Sanders, a professor of journalism at the University of Iowa. [10] Along with Wood and Frank Luther Mott (the model for *Booster*), Sanders was one of the originators of the Society for the Prevention of Cruelty to Speakers. [11] After graduating from the University of Missouri, he had worked at several newspapers and colleges, primarily in advertising, before joining the staff of the journalism school in 1930 with a specialty in radio. [12] He earned his Master of Arts degree from the university in 1933, then was appointed to the faculty where he taught principles and practices of advertising and radio news until he left in 1943 to head the Des Moines Office of Price Information for the federal government during World War II . From 1934 to 1943, he was director of the news service of WSUI, the university's radio station. [13] Photographs in *The Hawkeye*, the yearbook of the University of Iowa, show him in group pictures as advisor for the journalism fraternity, Sigma Delta Chi, and a men's social fraternity, Phi Delta Theta. [14] (Figure 52 –53) From these, it is clear that Wood changed the proportions of Sanders's face from rounded to a more elongated shape, probably to elicit a "yearning" attitude and to follow the description given in the novel. It seems Wood focused on Sanders's large, slightly bulging eyes and his full head of hair. The lower half of the face in the drawing, with its thin lips, disappearing chin and fleshy jowls does not correspond well with Sanders's appearance in these photographs. As a member of the Society for the Prevention of Cruelty to Speakers, with its practice of photographing its members and guests in quaint, mock-Victorian costume, Sanders likely enjoyed his chance to play a role in satirizing the "sentimental yearner."

Notes: *Sentimental Yearner*

1. "A Midwest Artist Views 'Main Street,'" St. Louis *Post-Dispatch*, Sunday Magazine, May 23, 1937, A1.

2. The time period of the novel is about 1911 to 1919 when movies were silent. There are many references throughout the novel to the movies and their importance in the lives of the townspeople. It was during this decade that films passed from being novelties to a major form of mass communication and entertainment. The movie theater as a community fixture and a new form of architecture gained increasing importance. It was also a time when the artistic potential of film began to be realized. In fact, one of the Kennicotts' quarrels is instigated by Carol's disappointment in the artistry of a movie they have just seen. Notable films that would have appeared on Main Street during the novel's time period are *Birth of a Nation* (1915) and *Intolerance* (1916), both by D.W. Griffth, the Keystone Kops series and *The Tramp* (1915) with Charlie Chaplin. Other important movie stars were Mary Pickford, Douglas Fairbanks, Jr. and William S. Hart. For the dust jacket of the first edition of *Main Street*, Sinclair Lewis was specific about wanting to include in the illustration a movie marquee. One of the changes he requested was that the figure of Carol Kennicott not block out the marquee of the "Rosebud Movie." Pastore, Stephen E., *Sinclair Lewis: A Descriptive Bibliography*, New Haven: Yalebooks, 1997, 92.

3. Did this incident (and others in *Main Street*) influence Meredith Willson in his musical and movie, *The Music Man*? (Broadway production, 1957) With River City, Iowa loosely based on his hometown Mason City, Iowa, Willson spoofs the little town's provincialism and silly worry about "trouble right here in River City." One indication of rampant modern immorality is the fact that Marian the Librarian had allowed a book by the French (French!) realist novelist Honoré de Balzac (1799-1850) to sully the purity of the River City library. The song in which the town ladies warn Professor Hill about Marian ("Of course I shouldn't tell you this, but she advocates dirty books") is sung against a background chorus of "Pick-a-little, talk-a-little, cheep, cheep, cheep." See note 4 for the entry on *The Good Influence*. The musical takes place about the same time (c.1912) as *Main Street* when Balzac had been dead for half a century and his novels, as modern literature, were already pretty dusty. But in Gopher Prairie and River City, "Oh, we got trouble! Yes, we got trouble!" Willson, Meredith, "Ya Got Trouble" and "Pick-a-little, talk-a-little," *The Music Man*, New York: Frank Music Corporation and Meredith Willson Music, 1986.

4. After her marriage, Vida rephrases that description of his Sunday School demeanor and speaks of "Ray's spiritual nobility." {212}

5. For discussion of Dix's painting, see Karcher, Eva, *Otto Dix*, Cologne: Taschen, 2002. The *Self-Portrait with Carnation* is today in the collection of the Detroit Institute of Arts. Other examples of Dix's integration of flowers are *Girl with Rose* (1923), 106; *Lovers with Nasturtium* [sic](1930), 179; *Portrait of the Painter Hans Theo Richter and His Wife Gisela* (1933), 182; and *Mother and Eva* (1935), 185.

6. For Christian Schad, see *Christian Schad and the Neue Sachlichkeit*, ed. by Jill Lloyd and Michael Peppiatt, Neue Galerie New York, 2003. For examples of his use of flowers, see *Self-Portrait* (1927), 145; *The Poet Ludwig Baumer* (1927); and *Sonja* (1928).

7. Sometimes the lady is a Medieval woman, sometimes she is the Holy Virgin or the Madonna. See Landsberg, Sylvia, *The Medieval Garden*, London: Thames and Hudson, no publication date given; especially the illustrations throughout.

8. Strong, Roy, *Small Period Gardens*, New York: Rizzoli, no publication date given, 130-133.

9. The carnation as a symbol of feminizing and sentimentality is perhaps echoed in a popular song written after Wood's and Lewis's career: *A White Sport Coat and a Pink Carnation*. In the song, a young man dresses in pink and white to please a woman then finds that he's all dressed up with no place to go.

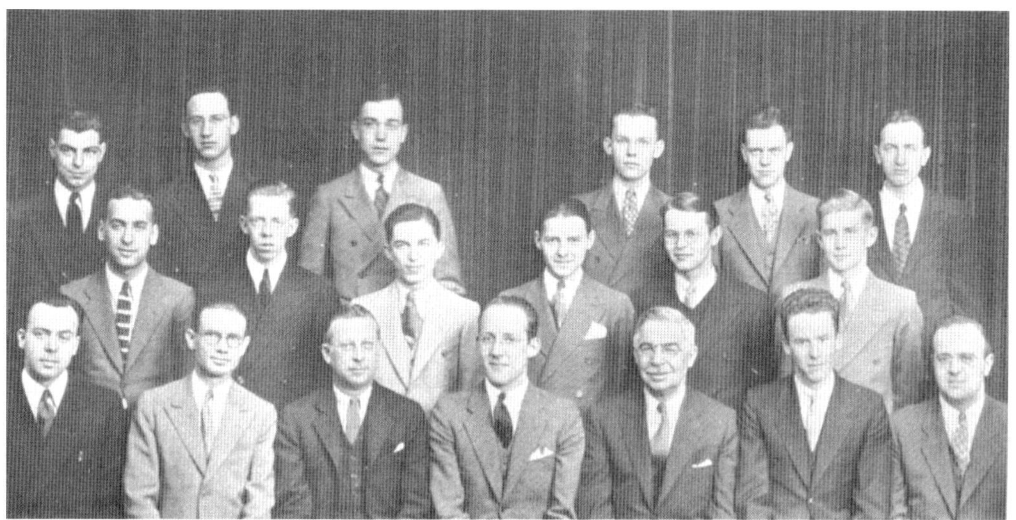

Figure 52 Charles L. Sanders (bottom row, third from left). The Hawkeye, *1936*

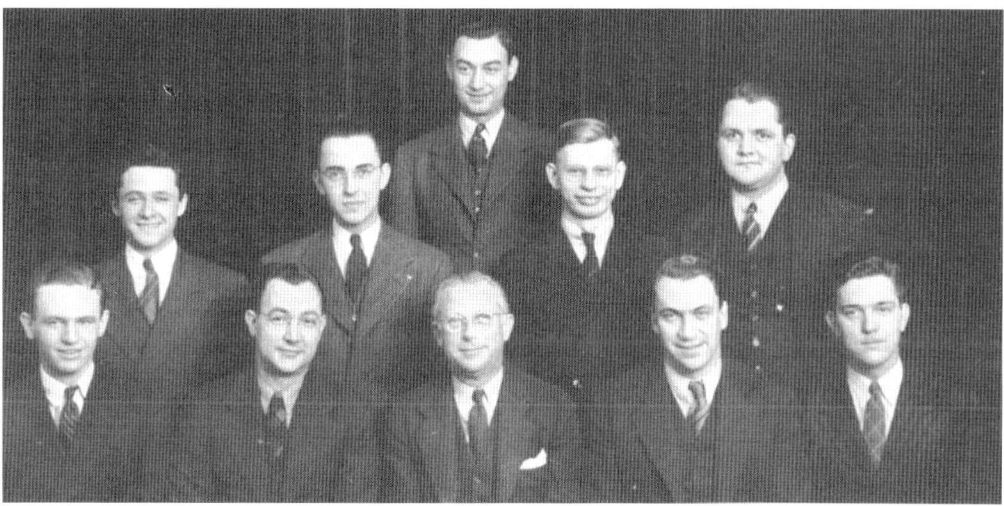

Figure 53 Charles L. Sanders (bottom row, third from left). The Hawkeye, *1941*

10. The identification, "supplied by Edwin Green," occurs in a memo in the faculty files and is also found a newspaper article about Sanders's departure from the University of Iowa: "Prof. Sanders is also one of several local people who served as a model for Grant Wood's illustrations for *Main Street*." "Prof. C.L. Sanders Takes Leave; Joins OPA in Des Moines," unidentified newspaper clipping, June 26, 1943, Faculty file, Special Collections, University of Iowa Library.

11. "Prof. C.L. Sanders Takes Leave."

12. After graduation from the University of Missouri, Sanders worked at the St. Joseph (Missouri) *News Press*, the Vernon (Texas) *Record* as advertising manager, the Amarillo *Daily Tribune* as assistant advertising manager, at the College of St. Thomas in St. Paul, Minnesota in charge of publications and publicity, at the Portland Cement Association in Chicago in charge of advertising and publications and at Creighton University. "Prof. C.L. Sanders Takes Leave." The article does not give the dates of his employment and may not be entirely reliable.

13. Employment card file, Special Collections. Sanders's career according to this source: M.A. 1933 University of Iowa; 1930-35, Associate, Journalism; 1935-43, Assistant Professor, Journalism; 1944-45, Leave of absence for government service. He died June 1, 1967 in Portland, Oregon. Also in Special Collections is one publication by Sanders: *A project in 'organized' publicity using radio as the medium*, 1934.

14. In *The Hawkeye* of those years, individual faculty members were not photographed; only deans and, occasionally, heads of departments had individual pictures. In two of the group photographs, Frank Luther Mott, head of the Journalism school, is found along with Sanders (1935 and 1939). Photographs of Sanders in *The Hawkeye*: 1934, p.380; 1935, p.351; 1936, p.55; 1938, pp.47, 216; 1939, p.37; 1940, p.132; 1941, p.224; 1942, p.256; 1943, p.241. These photographs were located through the use of the index in each volume, which are not always complete; it is possible that there are other photographs of Sanders in the yearbooks.

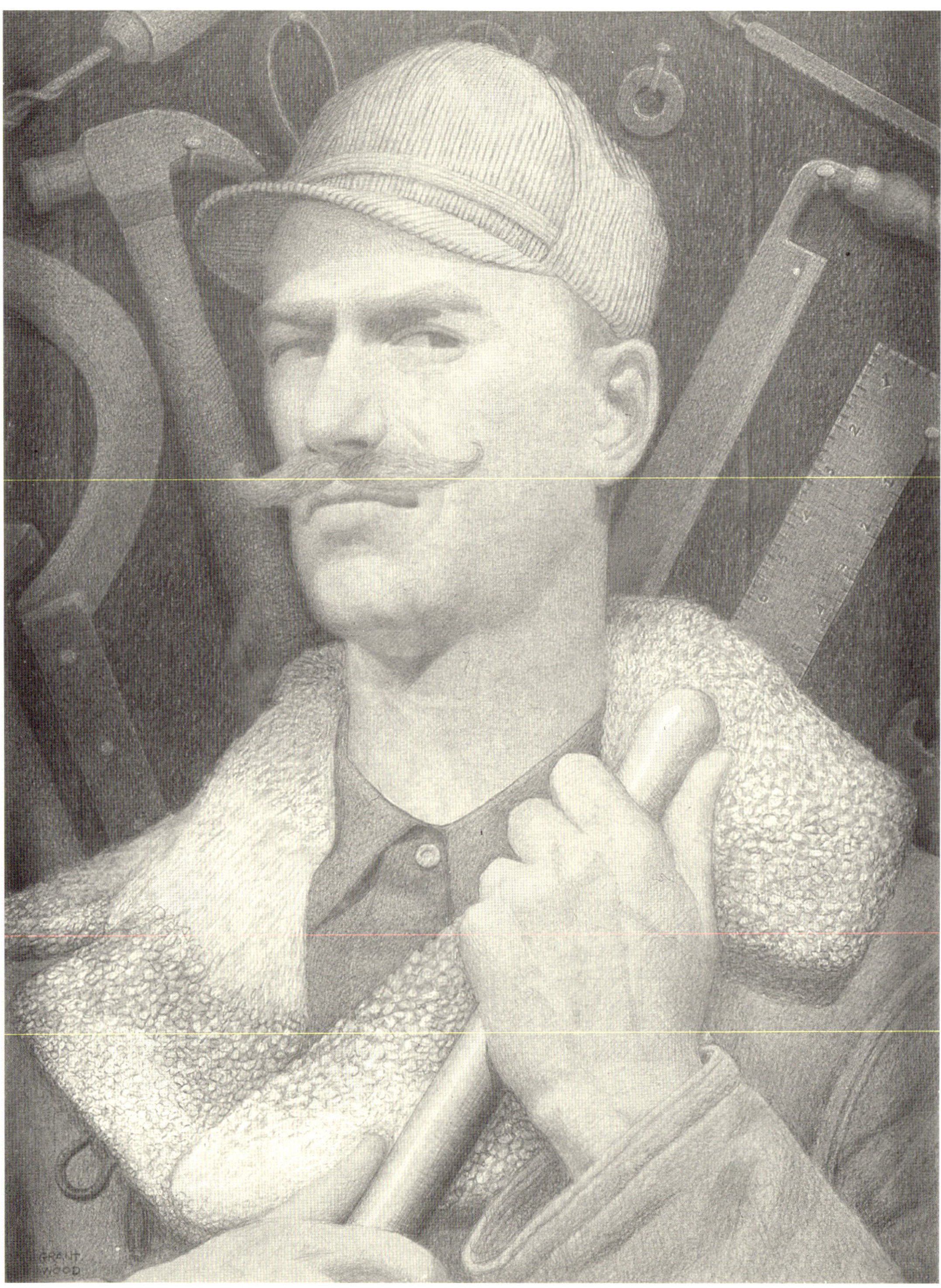

Figure 54 The Radical

The Radical (Miles Bjornstam "The Red Swede")

Miles Bjornstam (The Red Swede) is the saddest figure in *Main Street*. Most of the other major figures are essentially content with their lives except Carol Kennicott, and even she finds some resolution by the end of the novel. When Bjornstam takes the train from Gopher Prairie and passes out of the novel, we see only grief, desolation, and bitterness before him. There seems little left in his life to bring him happiness or even peace of mind. His sins against the little community seem insufficient to justify his great loss, and the town's behavior to him after the death of his wife and child are cruel retribution, even by Gopher Prairie standards. Little in Wood's drawing, however, suggests sympathy for the tragedy in this man's life. In fact, the artist seems to agree with the town's opinion of the "Red Swede." He doesn't look like a very reasonable character and, if he has trouble, he probably brought it on himself.

Part of the lack of dimension in this character may arise from Wood's determination to work with types rather than individuals. If one is a "type," any additional layers of personality are submerged under the dominance of a single trait. Yet, varied readings are possible in other *Main Street* portraits such as *The Good Influence*, *Booster*, and even *Practical Idealist* and *Sentimental Yearner*. If not completely positive, the characterizations at least have innocuous or comic overtones. The other two portraits, *The Radical* and *The Perfectionist,* seem wholeheartedly negative. In both of the drawings, these two malcontents look out askance at the world, their eyes hooded and their mouths contemptuous. In *The Radical*, the narrowed eyes in the sidelong glance and the slight sneer around the mouth discourage any interpretation other than an anti-social, misanthropic outcast — a suspicious, cantankerous "calamity-howler" who would have the irreverence to proclaim, "'The dollar sign has chased the crucifix clean off the map.'" He's the town crackpot — without the charm. Wood presents only the antagonistic, irritating face of the "Red Swede," as the town calls him, and we can feel the uneasiness that he stirs in the satisfied citizens. He represents powerless workers, immigrants, and the poor who were beginning to agitate for justice and opportunity in America and throughout the world in the new twentieth century. Miles Bjornstam may be an essentially harmless individual, but the ideas he openly espoused truly threatened the status quo — and Gopher Prairie didn't like it. The town likes to "razz" the Red Swede, but beneath the surface of their ridicule, they take him seriously. Wood's drawing suggests both the derision and the discomfort he inspires. He does not like them, and they certainly do not like him — and neither side attempts to hide their feelings.

According to the 1975 pioneering study of Grant Wood by James Dennis, Wood had an earlier concept of *The Radical* that was much more sympathetic. Dennis wrote, "Though initially moved by the pathos surrounding Bjornstam, the most convincingly tragic character of the book, Wood finally decided to discard his first compassionate treatment of the handyman, in which raised brows and untrimmed mustache endowed the face with a melancholy, timid aspect. In the published version he satirized instead the banker's eye view of the opinionated atheist-anarchist as the slightly insane bad man of the town." [1] This earlier drawing is today unlocated; it was owned at one time by Wood's sister, Nan Wood Graham, who donated it to a local art association from which it was sold. [2] Why Wood changed his concept to such a grim one is not known, but *The Radical*, along with *The Perfectionist*, is one of the most unredeeming characterizations in his portraiture.

If the element of humor is removed from Wood's art, does it lose its capacity to study the human character? Is the power of much of his imagery, including the human face, based in his abilities as a satirist (despite his detestation of the term)? When he removes the element of light-hearted ridicule, does his characterization go flat? Though both of these negative drawings (*The Radical* and *The Perfectionist*) have elements of intrigue, they don't provoke as much speculation about the subjects' lives and personality as do the others. Why are they unhappy and critical? Wood does not explore this question. Perhaps he does not because this kind of analysis was not his goal; he made it clear that his interest was in types, not in specific individuals. And besides, these two people were unhappy in an environment that Wood had spent much of his career celebrating. Both Carol Kennicott and Miles Bjornstam were outcasts in a place that believed itself to be as free and accommodating as any on earth. Wood might have appreciated the hyperbole of Carol's comment to the Practical Idealist reformer, Vida Sherwin, about the people of her little town, but he was disinclined to share the basic sentiment, "'And you want to 'reform' people like that when dynamite is so cheap?'" Such outbursts pair the doctor's wife and the radical through their lack of appreciation for Main Street. Bjornstam, asked by Carol whether she should worry if the townspeople thought her "affected," replied, "'Kick 'em in the face! Say, if I were a sea-gull, and all over silver, think I'd care what a pack of dirty seals thought about my flying?'"{96}

In Miles Bjornstam, Wood had a challenging character who changes over the course of the story. As did Raymond Wutherspoon, Bjornstam marries, creating for himself a new life and revealing unsuspected aspects of his personality. In Raymie's case, marriage makes him more assertive and tough, in Bjornstam's more compliant and vulnerable. As he did with Raymie, Wood depicts Miles in the earlier, pre-marriage part of his life and personality. Introduced as the "town handyman," Lewis describes Bjornstam as "a tall, thick, red-mustached bachelor, opinionated atheist, general-store arguer, cynical Santa Claus. Children loved him, and he sneaked away from work to tell them improbable stories of sea-faring and horse-trading and bears. The children's parents either laughed at him or hated him. He was the one democrat in town. He called both [rich and poor] by their first names. He was known as "The Red Swede," and considered slightly insane."{66} When encountered in the slums by Carol Kennicott, Bjornstam is further detailed by Lewis: "Before a tar-paper shack...a man in rough brown dogskin coat and black plush cap with lappets was watching her. His square face was confident, his foxy mustache was picaresque."{93}

As they talk during Carol's visit to the slums, it becomes clear that Bjornstam has no illusions about himself, his status in the town, or his success in changing the society of which he is so critical. "'I'm what they call a pariah, I guess.'" (When asked later what he means by that, he replies, "'I'm poor, and yet I don't decently envy the rich.'") "'I'm the town badman, Mrs. Kennicott: town atheist, and I suppose I must be an anarchist, too. Everybody who doesn't love the bankers and the Grand Old Republican Party is an anarchist....[I'm] half Yank and half Swede. Usually known as 'that damn lazy big-mouthed calamity-howler that ain't satisfied with the way we run things.'...I'm just a bookworm. Probably too much reading for the amount of digestion I've got. Probably half-baked. I'm going to get in 'half-baked' first, and beat you to it, because it's dead sure to be handed to a radical that wears jeans!'"{94} Except for Dr. Kennicott, who refers to himself as a general practitioner, Bjornstam is the only character in the *Main Street* drawings who identifies himself by the name Wood gave to his drawing.

Radicals and anarchists were feared in American political life of the early twentieth century. When Carol mentions, however timidly, some of the "radical" ideas of the time, such as industrial unions or the rights of women, she is greeted with a negativity that borders on hysteria. [3] Both she and Bjornstam are barely tolerated politically in Gopher Prairie, she because of her social position, he because of his usefulness. Bjornstam is taken more seriously than she, partly because he is a man, but largely because he is so open and unapologetic about his beliefs, so "big-mouthed" and confrontational. The label "anarchist" was a damning one at that time and guaranteed a precarious place in society, especially in those as rigidly controlled as Midwestern small towns. Anarchy (the lack of any government at all) had many adherents around the turn of the century and into the period of the first World War (when the novel takes place), and anarchists were responsible for generating unrest and for a number of violent acts. Mainstream America was so horrified by their ideas and their activities, by anything perceived to be "radical," that almost any measure that promised to keep these agitators in check was sanctioned. For example, late in the novel, the Gopher Prairie elders (including Dr. Kennicott) heartily approve when they learn that a mob in a neighboring village had run an organizer for a farmers' union out of town. [4]

In addition to his politics, Bjornstam is "half Swede" and identifies himself with the immigrant population; he marries Carol's "Svenska" maid. Radical ideas, anarchy, Socialism — all of these things were frequently associated with immigrants who were perceived as not fully American. Even after the death of Bjornstam's wife and child, Gopher Prairie despises the Red Swede for his political beliefs: no one comes to his family's funeral and, after he has gone, Dr. Kennicott relates the general opinion: "'Don't know but what the citizens' committee ought to have forced him to be patriotic — let on like they could send him to jail if he didn't volunteer and come through for [war] bonds and the Y.M.C.A. They've worked that stunt fine with all these German farmers.'"{264}

In the 1930s, there remained similar mistrust of certain political types, but in the disastrous economy of the Depression, many ideas that had been "radical" in the period of the novel had gained currency. The fear of the working class was not as hysterical as in earlier decades and, in fact, workers were becoming enshrined as heroic American types by many artists. One of the prominent themes in New Deal art for post offices, courthouses, and schools was the American worker: strong, monumental, the salt of the earth and the foundation of American civilization. Wood, however, did not participate in this new elevation of workers. The subject of his apotheosis was not the industrial or manufacturing laborer: it was the farmer. Both his writings and his paintings reverenced the farmer and his contribution to civilization. In the mid-1920s, Wood had carried out a series of paintings showing workers at the Cherry-Burrell factory in Cedar Rapids, but these had more to do with admiration of the success of local business than with an examination of workers' lives. The men shown in these paintings express no discontent or sense of exploitation, but instead exhibit their craftsmanship and pride in their occupations. [5]

If Wood was not known to sympathize with workers' rights or similar ideas, Sinclair Lewis had been active in such causes since college days, when he worked as a janitor at Upton Sinclair's utopian socialist colony. Significantly, around the time Wood was drawing the illustrations for *Main Street*, Lewis was experiencing a burst of notoriety for *It Can't Happen Here* (1935), a play that warned about fascism in America. Lewis was associated in various ways with liberal, even some radical, causes, and he used his literary reputation to advance his political values. Wood, as pointed out earlier, made no overt political announcements through his art and had no standing as a political figure or commentator. Nevertheless, the author and the artist seem to have had a high regard for each other, and Lewis reportedly liked the illustrations Wood made for his story. In the novel, Bjornstam is an admirable and honest, if unkempt, fellow who falls into tragedy largely because of his politics. Wood might have used the drawing to comment on the town's cruel and inexcusable behavior to Bjornstam and his family or to address the societal injustices that victimized the Red Swede. Even the most condemnatory reading of Lewis's novel would have allowed a more sympathetic portrait than *The Radical*. The reasons for Wood's harsh portrayal remain elusive.

Though it might over-personalize Wood's characterizations, the possibility that he associated these portraits with the people who modeled for them cannot be completely eliminated. His son-in-law (whose mother Wood was on the verge of divorcing) modeled for *The Radical* and his daughter-in-law modeled for *The Perfectionist*, the two most unpleasant personalities in the *Main Street* series. (Figures 55-56) Neither Dr. Maxon nor his wife, Dorothy, were actually blood relations of Wood's. They had come with a marriage that was quickly souring, and they crowded into a household of increasing tensions. Having recently

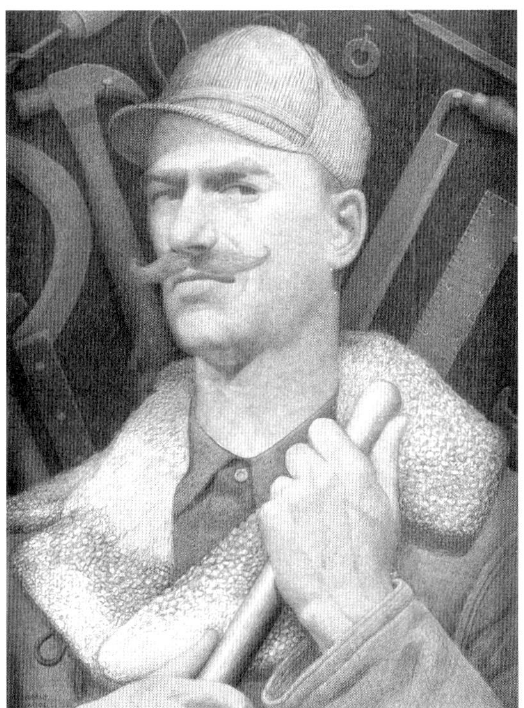

Figure 55 The Radical

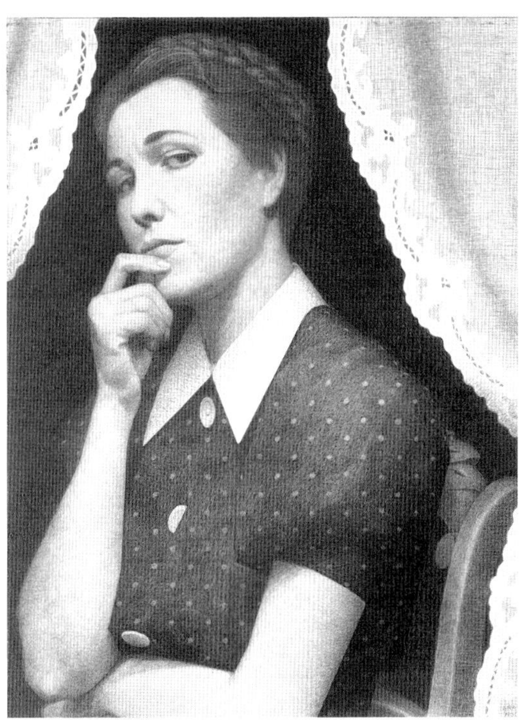

Figure 56 The Perfectionist

lost his mother to death and his sister to marriage and a move to California, Wood may have been disoriented and resentful about the changed tenor of his familial situation. Although there is reason to believe that Wood's relationship with Dr. and Mrs. Maxon was cordial, the artist may have been wrestling with some unacknowledged, unresolved feelings. The fact that a study for *The Radical* was much more sympathetic than the finished drawing arouses suspicions that his deteriorating home life may be reflected in the evolution of the portrait. When Wood's preparatory studies for these drawings are rediscovered, they will surely provide insight into his artistic and emotional process for these portraits.

As mentioned earlier, Bjornstam, Raymond Wutherspoon, and Will Kennicott are all married late in life. Kennicott's changes are subtle and emotional (his genuine love for his difficult wife), Wutherspoon's come from outside himself (Vida's promptings and the war), but Bjornstam's are more fundamental and self-generated. After his marriage to "plump radiant" {50} Bea Sorenson (friend and former maid to Carol Kennicott), he put aside his antagonism toward Gopher Prairie and tried to make a place of comfort and good regard for his wife and, later, their son, Olaf. "Miles had turned respectable. He had renounced his criticisms of state and society; he had given up roving as horse-trader...; he had gone to work as engineer in [the] planing-mill; he was to be seen upon the streets endeavoring to be neighborly with suspicious men whom he had taunted for years."{187} But the citizens of Gopher Prairie were unforgiving and, except for visits from Carol, the family was ignored by the town.

The extension of the town's disdain to his wife, to whom he was devoted, angered Bjornstam, but he labored on in Gopher Prairie, enlarging their house, starting a dairy (and prospering) and aspiring to have his wife join the Jolly Seventeen women's club and his son sent East to college. Despite the radical changes in the radical Red Swede, the town's enmity is permanent, and his loss is the consequence of his former behavior. As his wife and child sicken with typhoid fever, he traces the illness to the "bum water" they have been using. "'We used to get our water at Oscar Eklund's place,...but Oscar kept dinging at me, 'Sure, you socialists are great on divvying up other folks' money — and water!' I offered to pay Oscar but he refused — he'd rather have the chance to kid me. So I starts getting water down...in the hollow there, and I don't believe it's real good. Figuring to dig my own well this fall.'"{260} Dr. Kennicott, who is not called earlier because Bea "'thinks the doc doesn't like us,'" treats the mother and child, and Carol nurses them from morning to midnight for a week, but they die agonizingly after hours of delirium. Nevertheless, the town's lack of charity continues, as the gossip grows more vicious with each retelling. While Carol rests at home, exhausted and unable to attend the funeral, she is certain that someone in Gopher Prairie will try to comfort Miles. But as she looks out her window at the funeral procession, she sees there is only the Red Swede. A member of the little town's upper crust later tells her, "'Too bad about this Bea, that was your hired girl. But I don't waste any sympathy on that man of hers. Everybody says he drank too much, and treated his family awful, and that's how they got sick.'"{262}

After the death of his family, Bjornstam sells his dairy and leaves town, saying goodbye only to Carol, who observes "he did not walk with his former spring. His shoulders seemed old."{263} Wood's drawing seems to be based on the earlier Miles Bjornstam, not the bereaved husband and father. It is possible to read in the portrait the anger that flashed at three women (including Vida Sherwin) who finally visited in the last days of his wife's illness only to be cursed and told, "'You're too late. You can't do nothing now.'"{261} The narrowed eyes with the close drawn eyebrows hovering over them like storm clouds contain the capacity for that kind of rebuff. But after this point in the novel, Lewis describes a man without strength, confidence, or resolution. The sneering, disdainful mouth in the drawing suggests a man who is confident in his convictions, the sort of man who would not hesitate to refuse to work for the town banker and then proudly relate the incident. "'Thinking it all over, I don't like your application for a loan. Take it to another bank, only there ain't any,' I says, and I walks off on him." {96} Such an action, rude and scornful but full of certainty, would not be possible in a man brought so low as Miles Bjornstam had been by the end of the novel.

As in the other portraits, Wood uses props and the background to elaborate on his subjects. Bjornstam's rough workman's clothes are the ones he wears when, as winter approaches, he is "commissioner general" of Gopher Prairie, rushing "from house to house till after bedtime....Icicles from burst water-pipes hung along the skirt of his brown dogskin overcoat; his plush cap, which he never took off in the house, was a pulp of ice and coal-dust; his red hands were cracked to rawness; he chewed the stub of a cigar."{66} The tool handle that he holds, the hands in which he holds them, and the array of tools behind him all bespeak his competence in every sort of construction, repair, or anything that requires dexterity, skill, and strength. Even the disapproving Gopher Prairians could agree: "Bjornstam could do anything with his hands."{66}

The fascination he holds for children extends to young Hugh, son of Dr. and Mrs. Kennicott and playmate of the beautiful, graceful Olaf. To the Kennicott child, "the Red Swede was the most heroic and powerful person in the world." Among the attractions of "Uncle Miles" were all the tools that the delighted Hugh was allowed to touch. "The tools! In his office Father had tools fascinating in their shininess and curious shapes but...they distinctly were not for boys to touch...But Uncle Miles, who was a person altogether superior to Father, let you handle all his kit except the saws. There was a hammer with a silver head; there was a metal thing like a big L...And there were nails, very different and clever...." Tools, arranged around him like the rays of a workman's halo, form the background for Bjornstam's portrait. Next to the hammer is a sickle, a kind of harvesting tool. The juxtaposition of the two tools would have been instantly understandable to anyone from the 1930s and probably through the 1980s. The hammer and sickle were the symbols of communism, the Soviet Union, and everything that threatened capitalism and, many felt, America itself. A sickle is never mentioned in the novel as being used or owned by Bjornstam, so we may assume that Wood used it as his own commentary on the Red Swede's political inclinations. It is clear by their nickname for him — the *Red* Swede — that the townspeople associate him with communists, revolutionaries, Bolsheviks, and other dangerous sorts who had overthrown the Russian czar and set up the Soviet Union. Wood's props acknowledge the danger Gopher Prairie felt from this radical, and most Americans would have immediately understood the artist's implication. [6]

The model for *The Radical* was Dr. Arthur Sherman Maxon, (Figure 57) Wood's stepson. After Sara Sherman Maxon married Wood, her son, then about twenty-seven years old, moved with his wife and child to Iowa City where he joined the orthodontia staff of the school of dentistry. He had graduated from the University of Minnesota School of Dentistry in 1931 and practiced privately in Minnesota before beginning a Master of Science degree at the University of Iowa in 1936 (he received his M.S. in 1938). During his years there, he taught in various capacities in the dentistry school until World War II broke out, and he enlisted in the Army as a 1st Lieutenant. By April of 1942, just five months after the bombing at Pearl Harbor, Maxon was on active duty as a dental instructor in a military hospital in Denver. [7] He is mentioned in both Brown and Garwood as a person with whom Wood had good relations [8] and a Cedar Rapids friend who visited the Woods described him as a "tall, studious young man" for whose young family Wood seemed to have affection. [9] The University of Iowa yearbook of 1939, *The Hawkeye*, shows Dr. Maxon in a group photograph of the dental fraternity, Delta Sigma Delta, as a slim, mustached man who projects nothing of the sneering critical attitude portrayed in Wood's drawing. [10]

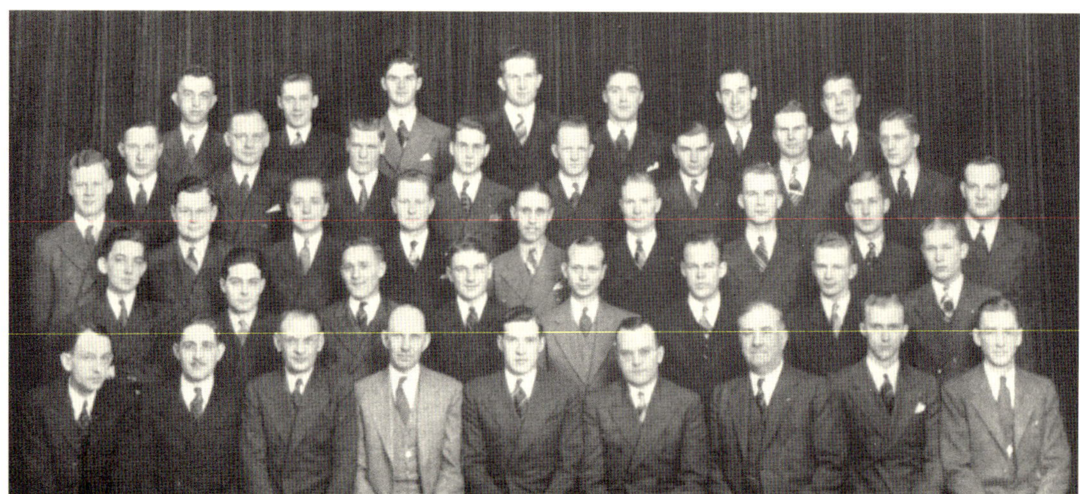

Figure 57 Dr. Arthur Sherman Maxon (bottom row, first from right). The Hawkeye, *1939*

Notes: *The Radical*

1. Dennis, James M., *Grant Wood: A Study in American Art and Culture*, Columbia: University of Missouri Press, 1986, 122.

2. Nan Wood Graham gives this account of the two drawings: "I had *The Radical*, and obviously there were two, because a Beverly Hills art dealer showed me another. He said he was having difficulty selling it because people with no knowledge of farm tools thought the sickle in the drawing was a communist symbol. The drawing he had was slightly different from mine, and it was the version used in the book. Both were done on brown wrapping paper with black, white and blue pencil, chalk, and India ink. I donated my drawing of *The Radical* to the Riverside Art Association when they exhibited my collection of Grant's early works, and it was purchased by an anonymous buyer." Graham, *My Brother, Grant Wood*, Iowa City: State Historical Society of Iowa, 1993, 140. The dealer's drawing is the one in the current exhibition; the other, presumably earlier one, described by Dennis and owned by Graham remains unlocated. In a 1962 newspaper photograph, Graham is shown with two drawings, *The Radical* and *Brush of the Medieval Monk*. Porter, Bill, "No detail was too small for artist Grant Wood; Exhibit here next week," Riverside [California] *Daily Enterprise*, October 20, 1962. NWG Scrapbook No.11, 90.

3. When Carol bluntly tells Guy Pollock of her beliefs in feminism and equality, she sees him visibly wince, and he exclaims, "'See here, my dear, I certainly hope you don't class yourself with a lot of trouble-making labor-leaders! Democracy is all right theoretically,...but...'"{163}

4. The most notorious aspect of this attitude was the "Red Scare" of 1918-1920 when the civil rights of anyone suspected of sympathies with the "Reds" were compromised. "Reds" was a generalized term that applied to socialists, anarchists, communists, or nearly anyone who didn't, as Bjornstam put it, "'like the way we run things.'" Legislation aimed at immigrants and dissidents included the Espionage Act of 1917, the Sedition Act of 1918, and the Immigration Act of 1920. The Attorney General of the United States, A. Mitchell Palmer, instigated what were known as the "Palmer Raids," directed against those perceived as dangerous to the United States. In particular, the "Reds" of the Red Scare referred to communist revolutionaries who had overthrown the Russian czar in 1917 and who would soon create the Soviet Union. When Percy Bresnahan, a Gopher Prairie native who had made good in the East and had contacts in the government, visits his hometown, he is asked by Carol about the Russian Revolution. Her husband, embarrassed that she has brought up this topic, asks, "'Is there much to it, Perce?'" and Bresnahan answers: "'There is not!...Carol, honey, I'm surprised to find you talking like a New York Russian Jew, or one of these long-hairs! I can tell you...as a matter of fact the Czar will be back in power before the end of the year....He'll show these damn agitators, lazy beggars hunting for a soft berth...where they get off!'"

5. Both characters, Carol Kennicott and Miles Bjornstam, might be assumed to support movements that sought to create a fairer economic and political situation for farmers. Carol, in particular, shows sensitivity to the plight of farmers when she suggests to her husband that the town merchants are "parasites" on the farmers, at the same time they look down on them.{46} Wood is not known to have supported, or even acknowledged, the protests of farmers during the Depression.

6. There is another instance of an Iowa artist using Soviet symbolism in his work. Harry Donald Jones was the chief painter on "The Social History of Des Moines," a Federal Art Project/Works Progress Administration (FAP/WPA) mural in the Des Moines Public Library. In the scene showing the Louisiana Purchase, he depicts a contemporary-looking farmer in overalls handing gold to a figure in Napoleonic costume. The farmer holds a curved sickle in his hand, positioned so that it is next to a red star on a glove, a juxtaposition that was read by some as a reference to (and sympathy with?) communism and the Soviet Union. Jones explained that the star was simply the decoration on every pair of gloves from the Red Star brand and he was just being accurate, but few observers

then or since have regarded the positioning of the red star and the sickle as incidental.

7. Dr. Maxon's appointments at the University of Iowa were: 1936-1937: Resident Assistant in Orthodontia; 1937-1938: Assistant Demonstrator, Operative/Clinical and Operative Dentistry, Dental Analysis; 1938-1941: Demonstrator, Dentistry and Dental Analysis. He was born April 2, 1909 in Chicago. Faculty files, Special Collections, University of Iowa Library.

8. Brown, 91-92; Garwood, 203.

9. Brown, 92. The description occurs in Brown's recording of a letter or manuscript from Bruce McKay.

10. *The Hawkeye*, 1939, 87. Little is known of Dr. Maxon's personality or his reasons for leaving his dental practice to bring his young family to join the Wood household. Few traces of his family have been found after he left Iowa City.

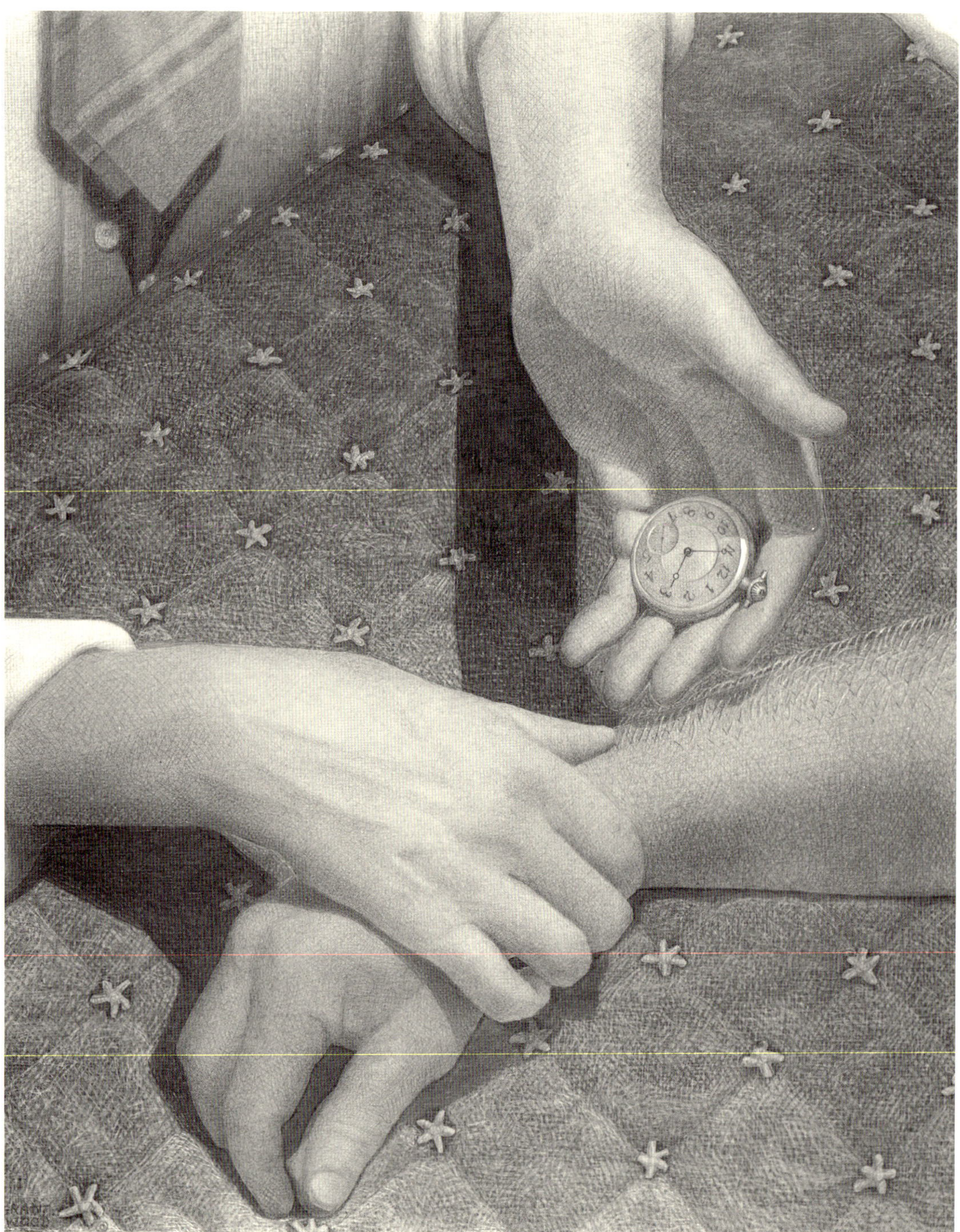

Figure 58 General Practitioner

General Practitioner

Grant Wood's *General Practitioner* is the only *Main Street* drawing that is not a portrait. In every other case, Wood found a model to represent the American "types" he discerned in the characters of *Main Street,* but for Dr. Will Kennicott, he depicted only his hands at work. Kennicott was a physician and surgeon who had trained at the University of Minnesota in Minneapolis, then chose to practice in the little town of Gopher Prairie. His office was in town, but he was what is called a "country doctor" because he practiced much of his medicine on the distant farms for which he was constantly on call. In emergencies, country people were not always brought into town; the doctor went to them. *General Practitioner* depicts one of those house calls, with the doctor taking the pulse of a felled, weakened farmer whose arm rests on a homemade quilt. The feeble light shining from above evokes the oil or kerosene lamps used in pre-electric farmhouses by which the doctor often had to examine, and sometimes operate on, his patients. The watch reads 2:55 and the light comes from directly overhead (as it would not in a daytime interior), so we assume this is a nighttime emergency. The novel relates many times when Dr. Kennicott is called out in the middle of the night and must make his way to a farm and then return home in beastly, sometimes dangerous, weather. In one incident, Dr. Kennicott and Carol, who has accompanied him, are on their way home after amputating a farmer's arm on the kitchen table. When a blizzard suddenly overcomes them, they barely make it to a barn. Carol suggests they run for the farmhouse, to which the doctor replies against the din of the storm outside, "'Not yet. Might never find it. Might get lost ten feet away from it.'"{157}

In medical matters (as in all else), Kennicott is dependable and matter-of-fact about his heroic, routine, life saving. This combination of heroism and humility is recognized by his wife and genuinely admired. Some of the novel's most generous assessments of the doctor take place in the mind and the conversations of Carol. In one account of a typical incident, Carol gains perspective about her husband: "Late at night, a step on the wooden porch...the storm door opened...the buzz of the electric bell. Kennicott muttering 'Gol darn it,' but patiently creeping out of bed, remembering to draw the covers up to keep her warm, feeling for slippers and bathrobe, clumping downstairs." After dressing, he writes down his destination, then goes out, "hungry, chilly, unprotesting" and, on returning, tends to the furnace so the house would be warm. As his wife awakens, she tells him, "'Seems just a few minutes ago that you started out!'" "'I've been away four hours,'" he replies, "'I've operated on a woman for appendicitis, in a Dutch kitchen. Came awful close to losing her, too, but I pulled her through all right. Close squeak. Barney says he shot ten rabbits last Sunday.' She marveled that in what was to her but a night-blurred moment, he should have been in a distant place, have taken charge of a strange house, have slashed a woman, saved a life."{143} The character of Dr. Kennicott was based in part on Sinclair Lewis's father, who had also been a doctor in a small Minnesota town.

General Practitioner is a self-assigned title: it is exactly the term Dr. Kennicott uses to describe himself. However, when he applies it to himself, it is not in a prideful way — in fact, just the opposite. He uses it in almost a disparaging way to suggest that his knowledge and ambitions are greater than one might assume. In one of his quarrels with his discontent wife, he tells her, "'You never think of me as having ambitions, just as much as you have!'" When she replies, "'I think of you as being perfectly satisfied,'" he pushes on. "'Well,'" he informs her, "'I'm not, not by a long shot! I don't want to be a plug general practitioner all my life....If you think for one moment I want to be stuck in this burg all my life, and not have a chance to travel and see the different points of interest and all that, then you simply don't get me. I want to have a squint at the world, much's you do. Only, I'm practical about it.'"{142} As he often does in his conflicts with his wife, the doctor defends himself vigorously and yet, it is clear that he takes her condescending opinions seriously

In a second instance, he again refers to himself as a general practitioner in a defensive way, hoping to persuade his listener that, in fact, he is a good deal more than just that. His listener in this case is the wife of one of his friends, the stingy, bullying town druggist, Dave Dyer. Maud Dyer's agenda for her visit to the doctor is even more complex than the neurosis from which she thinks she suffers. Although she is a Christian Scientist, Maud comes to Dr. Kennicott complaining of a vague ache in her back, but he declines to examine her, admonishing, "'To be honest,...I think your troubles are mostly imaginary.'" At that, she accuses him of not being up on all the latest scientific ideas as are the "'new nerve-specialists'" who "'claim that lots of 'imaginary' ailments...are what they call psychoses, and they order a change in a woman's way of living so she can get on a higher plane —'" He interrupts her. Dr. Kennicott will not tolerate any suggestion that he is not current with the latest medical thinking. And indeed, throughout the novel, he reads medical journals, goes to Minneapolis and the Mayo Clinic for consultations and is clearly the most competent, well-informed doctor in the area. When World War I breaks out and all the doctors in town want to join the Army, they get together and decide that the one professional the town cannot relinquish to the war effort is Dr. Kennicott. He is chosen to stay home and keep the community healthy and, though disappointed, he does so. The accusation that he is just some local, out-of-touch physician must be corrected without hesitation. "'Whoa-up! Wait now....Why, Good Lord, Maud, I could talk about neuroses and psychoses and inhibitions and repressions and complexes just as well as any damn specialist, if I got paid for it, if I was in the city and had the nerve to charge the fees that those fellows do.'" However, there is a clear-eyed combination of his own integrity and the town's familiarity with him that prevents such a diagnosis. "'But you know me — I'm your neighbor — you see me mowing the lawn — you figure I'm just a plug general practitioner. If I said, 'Go to New York,' Dave and you would laugh your heads off and say, 'Look at the airs Will is putting on.'...As a matter of fact,'" he admits, "'you're right. You have a perfectly well-developed case of repression of sex instinct, and it raises the old Ned with your body. [1] What you need is to get away from Dave and travel, yes, and go to every dog-gone kind of New Thought and... Hooptedoodle meeting you can find....But how can I advise it?'" Being a "plug general practitioner" means that Kennicott also knows his clientele and its limitations. If he were to recommend such a thing, he tells the medically and morally ambiguous Mrs. Dyer, her husband "'would be up here taking my hide off. I'm willing to be family physician and priest and lawyer and plumber and wet-nurse, but I draw the line at making Dave loosen up on money.'" He may know better than to separate Dave Dyer from what he most treasures — his money — but that very evening, Dr. Kennicott, the "plug general practitioner," embarks on an affair with Mrs. Dave Dyer.

This character flaw is not acknowledged in Wood's "portrait" of the doctor nor are any of his other failings. Instead, Wood complies with Kennicott's central self-concept as a healer. Is it possible he is the one character Wood felt he could not capture in traditional portraiture, whether of the head only or the entire figure? It is not known why, exactly, the artist concentrated on the doctor's hands and avoided the face and figure. Perhaps he was aware of a sculpture by one of the Iowa artists with whom he had worked on the PWAP at the University of Iowa in 1934. Around the same time (c.1936) that Wood was drawing his illustrations for *Main Street*, Christian Petersen (1885-1961), by then sculptor-in-residence at Iowa State College in Ames (now called Iowa State University), was working on a sculpture of a sturdy man carrying a medical case, entitled *Country Doctor*. (Figure 59) Dressed in a winter coat, a hat with fur flaps and a muffler whose ends blow off to the side in the wind, he is striding forward through nasty weather, perhaps a blizzard. The body and features of this figure resemble those of Dr. Kennicott and the honorific tone of the sculpture is in harmony with that doctor's dedication to his patients. Petersen probably did not take his inspiration directly from the novel (the work apparently was based on actual doctors who had treated the Petersen family) [2] although his explanation of his purpose in creating the work sounds as if he knew it well. [3] If Wood had been aware of the sculpture (as he easily could have been),[4] he may have wanted to avoid any comparisons. There is reason to believe that Wood and Petersen were not on the best of terms, so any hint of an association between the two images of a country doctor would have been most unwelcome on the part of both artists.

Wood's decision to focus on the doctor's hands may have been inspired by several descriptions of them in the novel. Carol, who prizes fashion, is engaged in one of her critical assessments of her husband's appearance when she observes his hands. "She noted that his nails were jagged and ill-shaped from his habit of cutting them with a pocket-knife and despising a nail-file as effeminate and urban. That they were invariably clean, that his were the scoured hands of the surgeon, made his stubborn untidiness the more jarring. They were wise hands, kind hands, but they were not the hands of love." The farmers saved from death and misery may not have agreed with her assessment that they were "not the

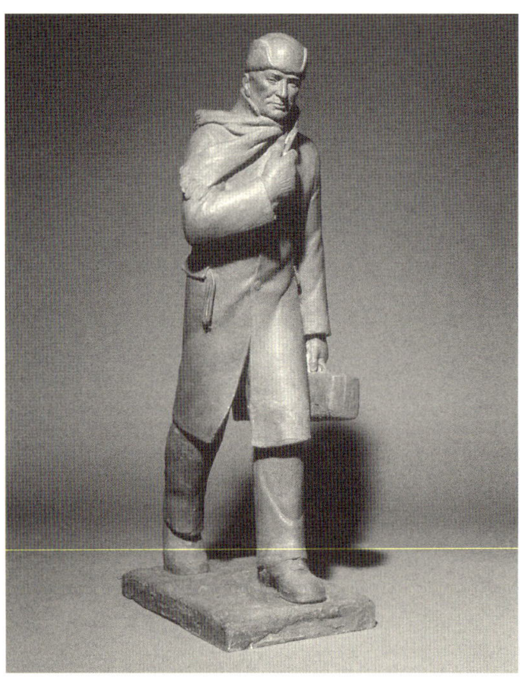

Figure 59 Christian Petersen. Country Doctor, *1936*

hands of love" nor would the artist. But she grows more charitable after gaining some perspective during their separation late in the story. "She looked down at his hands, and the fact that his nails were as ill-treated as ever touched her."{354} Dr. Kennicott is often described as thick, solid, bulky, and physically powerful. At their introduction, his future wife noticed when they shook hands that "his hand was strong; the palm soft, but the back weathered, showing golden hairs against firm red skin."{10} These descriptions do not exactly match the long, slender, rather graceful hands shown in the illustration. They and the doctor's forearms both appear hairless although the tops of the forearms are darkened slightly. The hands in the drawing might be judged skilled-looking and sensitive, but they don't easily suggest the hardened, "thick" hands of the rough-edged country doctor.[5] This description actually applies more successfully to the farmer whose forearm is bristly with short, thick hairs drawn in precise, staccato marks with both white and black crayon. In addition, there is clearly dirt under the thumbnail of the rugged hand. The farmer's hand, dirty and work-worn, shows that Wood could have coarsened the appearance of Dr.

Kennicott's hands, had he chosen to. The only feature of the drawing that does suggest his thick physical character is the bulge of his stomach against the edge of the bed.

One of the most affecting scenes in *Main Street* uses Dr. Kennicott's hands as a revealing accessory to its narrative and to its emotional tone. It may have inspired Wood to tell Dr. Kennicott's story through an image of him at work, using his hands not just to make a living but also to make life itself possible. Having acknowledged his wife's rejection of him and sent away a potential lover, he asks, "'Carrie, do you understand my work?'" He continues his appeal, trying to explain himself and his feelings to her. "He leaned forward, thick capable hands on thick sturdy thighs, mature and slow, yet beseeching, 'No matter if you are cold, I like you better than anybody in the world....You're all the things that I see in a sunset when I'm driving in from the country, the things I like but can't make poetry of. Do you realize what my job is? I go round twenty-four hour a day, in mud and blizzard, trying my damnedest to heal everybody, rich or poor....And I can stand the cold and the bumpy roads and the lonely rides at night. All I need is to have you here at home to welcome me. I don't expect you to be passionate...but I do expect you to appreciate my work. I bring babies into the world, and save lives, and make cranky husbands stop being mean to their wives.'"{323} He finishes his plea to maintain his marriage by asking, "'Oh, honey, am I so bad? Can't you like me at all?'" Carol shows her acceptance as "she snatched up his hand...and kissed it."

Wood's "portrait" of Dr. Kennicott is not just a picture of his hands; it is a symbol of a useful life, lived stoically with endurance and purpose. The scene described above may have aroused Wood's sympathy for the character. An unpretentious man, the doctor does not aspire to a life of eminence and, though he is clearly intelligent, he does not wish to be an intellectual. Perhaps more than any other character in the book (except possibly Vida Sherwin, the "practical idealist") Kennicott represents the best qualities of the Midwesterner, the sort of figure who was both inspiration and (Wood hoped) audience for the artist's Regionalism. The "high-brow" cultured wife, the aimless tailor/aesthete (Erik Valborg), the "lover of dead elegances" (Guy Pollock), and the sentimental yearner (Raymond Wutherspoon) all come off as inferior to the earthy, yet noble physician. Considering the reception Wood had received from some of the art establishment, it is possible he preferred an audience of Dr. Kennicotts to one of Carol Kennicotts.

Aside from the novel itself, one other possible influence might have been at work. In the January 4, 1936 issue of *The Saturday Review of Literature*, a photograph of hands appeared in Christopher Morley's column, "The Bowling Green." [6] The photograph, by Samuel Kravitt, was entitled "Censorship" and was used as an illustration for Morley's article on the recent arrest of a New York bookseller for selling an obscene book. (Figure 60) Dark in tonality, the photograph focuses on a pair of hands, one folded over the other, as they rest on a book. Though the hands here are at rest in contrast to Kennicott's working hands, the idea that a composition based on hands alone could have an emotional impact

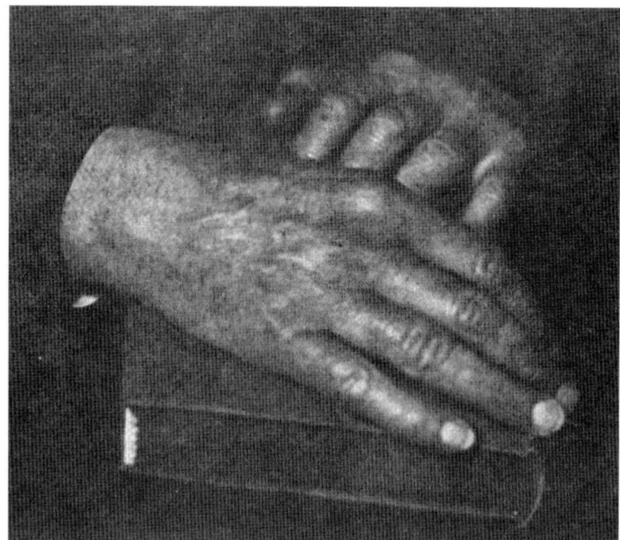

Figure 60 Samuel Kravitt. Censorship, *c.1936.*

may have been suggested to Wood by this photograph. Morley, a contributing editor of the magazine, had been one of Wood's most enduring and supportive figures in the literary world. He had visited at the University of Iowa in spring of 1934 [7] and Wood spent time with him during his visits to New York. On the occasion of the artist's 1936 Ferargil Gallery exhibition, Morley recorded in his column of February 1, "Grant Wood, the Iowa painter was in town the other day, looking about to see what sort of fresh and modern and forward-peering ideas we alert Easterners are having in the arts. We gave him an example of New York's creative originality that sent him home to Iowa with joy and excitement." [8] It turns out that the esteemed New York creation was a banal Long Island Railway poster, appropriate for making Morley's point that the Midwest was at least as vital in the arts as the East. At this time, Wood had received his commission for the *Main Street* drawings and may have been making some arrangements related to it during his New York trip. The photograph of hands appeared in the issue of *The Saturday Review* three weeks earlier (January 4, 1936) than the notice of Wood's contact with Morley, and Wood had been mentioned in Morley's column two weeks before that. [9] In addition, the cover of the April 4 issue of *Saturday Review* was the work of one of Wood's students, Richard Gates, and the magazine credited Wood with bringing the young artist to their attention.[10] The magazine also was alert to currents in Midwestern literature and other forms of culture, noting, for example, the establishment of *American Prefaces*, a literary magazine at the University of Iowa, to which Wood contributed an article for its first issue in 1935. [11] Such regular notices strongly suggest that Wood was a regular reader of *The Saturday Review* and would have certainly seen a photograph in the middle of his friend Morley's column.

The composition of the drawing relates in its structure to *Village Slums* and in its coloration to *The Perfectionist*, and both associations add to Wood's interpretation of the character of Dr. Will Kennicott. Like *Village Slums*, *General Practitioner* has a radiating composition that focuses on a strong central feature. In *Village Slums*, it is the communal pump and in *General Practitioner*, it is the juncture of the doctor's hands with that of his patient. The positions of the doctor's arms, especially the left one, in relation to his torso is not entirely sensible, anatomically. Wood understood human anatomy and could draw it accurately, as other works attest. It is possible that he was not as exacting in this drawing as he could have been, but it seems more likely that he deliberately took license with anatomical correctness in order to adjust the composition to other concerns. The abstract demands of the picture probably took precedence, as they often have with other artists, over exactitude.

Both compositions imply a coming together, a sense of contact and, especially in *General Practitioner*, a literal tactile sensation. All the other drawings exhibit subjects in isolation, but these two are communal images. They are also the only two in which the artist takes a downward view which, when coupled with the central focus, creates the effect of a vortex with its broad end at the edges and its point funneling to the composition's center. Although it is placed off center, the round watch held in the doctor's hand echoes the rounded shape of the pump base and the circle of trampled snow immediately surrounding the platform. A concentration of forces and an interlinked situation are the communal implications of both compositions. At the same time, both have grids that stabilize the dynamic linear patterns of conjoined hands and spoke-like paths. *Village Slums* displays horizontals and verticals in the architecture, especially in the outhouses and the two prominent chimneys in the foreground. In *General Practitioner*, the grid is even clearer and much more regularized in the neat squares of the quilt stitching and ties. The star-like ties reiterate the radiating pattern at the same time that they vivify the grid of the quilt.

Integrating complicated compositions of both grid and radiating patterns, Wood's drawings evoke the complexity and interdependence of community life. It is no surprise that he would find it appropriate to use these kinds of compositions for these two drawings since Dr. Kennicott is the only figure in the novel that is equally comfortable and equally well regarded in both upper crust society and the slums. The rough hand on the plain, homely quilt clearly refers to his ministering to the sick and injured among the rural poor and the working class inhabitants on the wrong side of the tracks. Of all the characters in *Main Street*, he is the only one who would be welcome in any home from the Main Street "mansions" to the Swede Hollow shacks.

In coloration, *General Practitioner* is a pendant for *The Perfectionist*, the portrait of Dr. Kennicott's wife, Carol. The gesture of the arms and the patterns also contribute to the affiliation of these drawings of husband and wife. Both pictures possess a muted, nuanced light that is neither simple nor garish; both are dominated coloristically by the bluish tonality found in the quilt and in Carol's dress. These specific areas have a depth that imparts a rich, almost glowing quality to the pictures. In both cases, no actual blue pigment is present, but a judicious and complex layering of black ink with black and white crayon creates that effect. In the quilt of *General Practitioner*, no paper surface shows through, suggesting a solid layer of ink such as Wood used in sections of *Practical Idealist* and *The Good Influence*. Thousands of small white marks made upon an ink base constitute the image of the quilt and then, through the various levels at which light can strike and then be reflected off the waxy surfaces, it takes on a muted, but distinctly blue tone. Throughout the drawing, white crayon is laid on in separate marks (which are sometimes so sharp and textured that they read as brushed-on gouache) and sometimes the white is formed into a smooth, thin waxy layer that nuances the color. Around each star-shaped quilt tie is a line of black that intensifies it and differentiates it from the background. Similarly, Wood uses a fairly thick black line on the bottom edge of the farmer's arm, the top edge of the doctor's right hand, and the lower edge of his left to clarify these shapes against the bluish quilt background. [12] He uses a white line along the top of the doctor's left, watching-holding hand to achieve the same purpose. In contrast to several other *Main Street* drawings, no lines remain visible to indicate the composition was squared for transfer.

All of the *Main Street* drawings except *Practical Idealist* include one or both of the sitter's hands and use them to convey Wood's interpretation of their character. The hands and arms of Will and Carol Kennicott show the husband and wife carrying out their different occupations: Carol, making critical judgments, and Will, ministering to a patient. (Figures 61-62) The doctor's hands are busy, well employed and useful. His wife's are idle and self-referential. Dr. Will, we may assume, is so absorbed in the selfless pursuit of medicine that it is acceptable to sacrifice his head and facial features in presenting his "portrait." Both drawings use a polka-dot pattern that was a constant in Wood's designs, but dots in *The Perfectionist* appear on a fussy, puffy dress and in *General Practitioner* they emerge from the ties on the plain but dignified homemade quilt. In subtle and obvious ways, Wood shows how deeply he preferred the earthy, utilitarian doctor to the petty cultural snobbery he attributed to the doctor's wife.

General Practitioner is the only *Main Street* drawing known to have been translated into a lithograph, known as *Family Doctor*. Wood was much involved with lithography in the last five years of his life, partly because of his need to ease his financial difficulties. He entered into a relationship with Associated American Artists, headquartered in New York, which commissioned and distributed his lithographs in editions of 250. [13] *Family Doctor*, (Figure 63) however, was an entirely commercial project, commissioned by Abbott Labora-

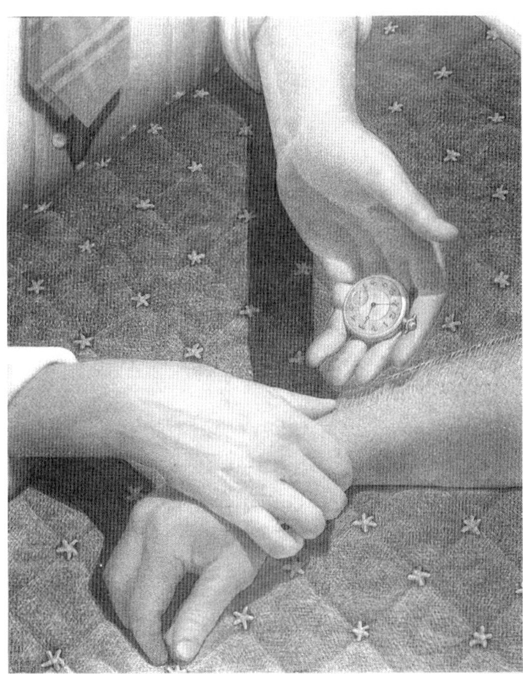

Figure 61 General Practitioner

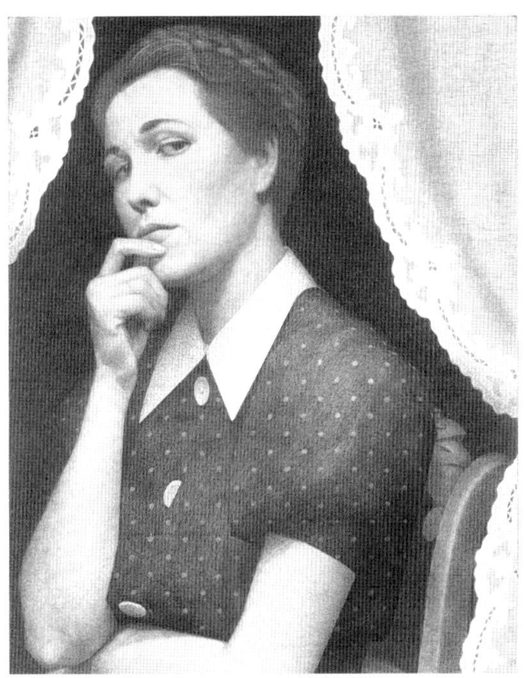

Figure 62 The Perfectionist

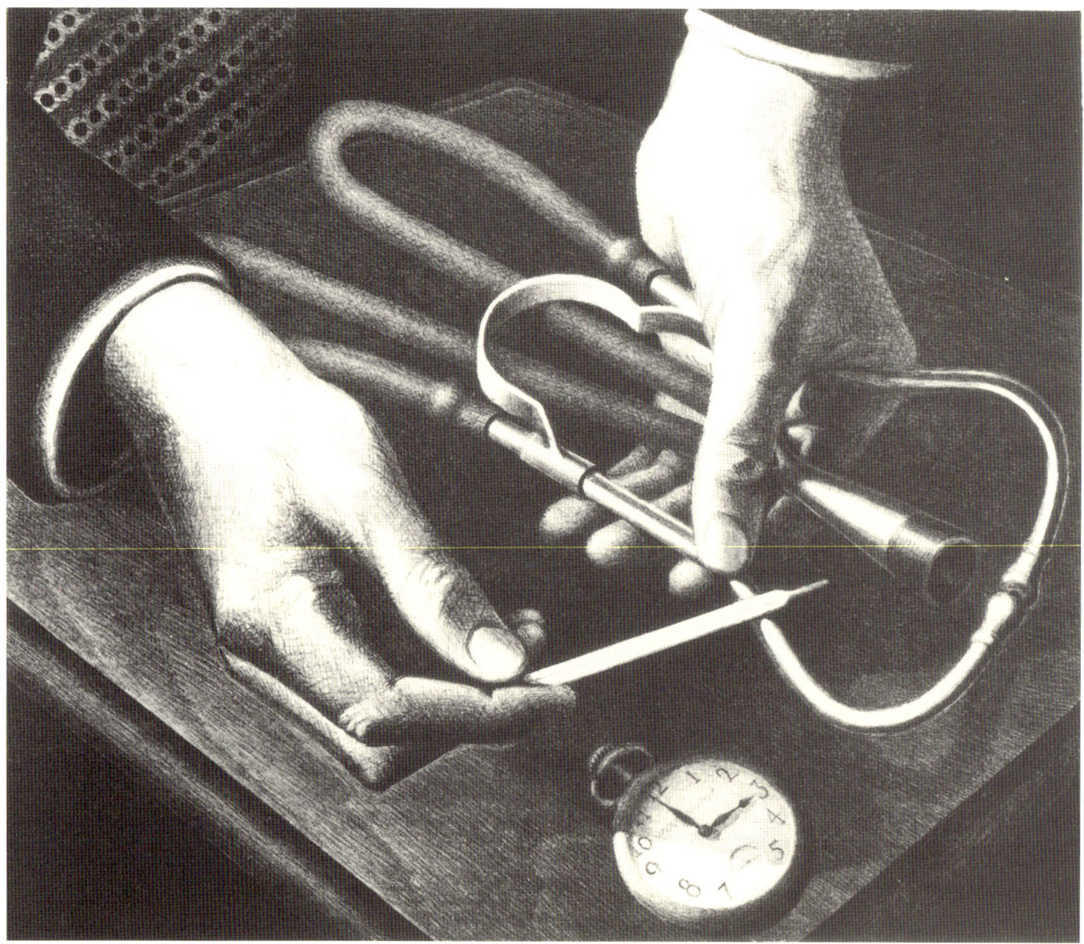

Figure 63 Family Doctor, *1941 (lithograph)*

tories of Chicago for distribution to doctors (from an edition of 250). It was his last print and among his last works of art completed before his death in February of 1942. Though there are differences between the two pictures, as will be noted, the fact that this lithograph is so similar to the *Main Street* drawing may suggest Wood's feelings of pressure and preoccupation near the end of his life. He was growing increasingly aware of the criticism of his style and subject matter, and he was eager to extricate himself from financial difficulties. These two factors, along with his poor health, may explain why he did not develop a new composition for the Abbott Laboratories commission, but adapted an older one. The wishes of the patron may have also been involved.

Despite the obvious similarities in the two compositions, the lithographed image does not seem to portray a country doctor called to a rustic farmhouse. In the *Main Street* drawing, *General Practitioner*, the doctor's coat is off, his shirtsleeves are rolled up, and his slightly too short tie has a sharply defined stripe. The later image implies a more sophisticated, citified, or even academic situation: the doctor wears his dark suit coat while neat cuffs emerge exactly the correct amount from the coat. His tie is a more subtle pattern and seems more generously cut. Perhaps most tellingly, no patient is in the picture, though it is implied by the activity of holding the thermometer in a position where it can be read by the doctor. The lithograph has a less immediate sense of the "human touch," and the physician is not shown literally at the patient's bedside. Only the doctor's hands are depicted, not his patient's, as they hold two medical devices (a thermometer and a stethoscope) in addition to a watch similar to the one Dr. Kennicott uses (his has an additional circle at the bottom for measuring seconds). The watch here reads five minutes later (3:00) than the timepiece in the drawing (2:55) and is perhaps Wood's lightly comical reference to the fact that this image was done later than the *Main Street* one. The surface against which they are depicted is not a simple square-patterned quilt but a tabletop with a molded edge. This doctor's hands are a little less elegant than those Wood drew for Dr. Kennicott, but they appear equally immaculate and competent. This composition is less adventurous and abstract, with a simpler diagonal orientation, but again Wood seems to place greater value on the design than on anatomical accuracy. The doctor's arms would have to be strangely attached to his shoulders to maneuver themselves into this position, especially the one holding the stethoscope. The model for the drawing and the lithograph has long been acknowledged as Dr A.W. Bennett of the University of Iowa Hospitals, who attended Wood during his final illness. [14]

Notes: *General Practitioner*

1. "Raising the old Ned" is an expression meaning "raising the devil" or having a bad effect on Mrs. Dyer's body.

2. *Country Doctor* (Michels, 178) may have been a tribute to Dr. A.I. Haugen of Ames, Iowa, whose emergency surgery saved the life of Petersen's wife in 1935. Bliss, Patricia Lounsbury, *Christian Petersen Remembered*, Ames: Iowa State University Press, 1986, 105. That same year, 1936, Petersen also sculpted *The Surgeon* (Michels, 190) for Dr. Charles Ryan of Des Moines who had also cared for the Petersens. Due to his extremely low college salary, Petersen would have had a difficult time paying for the care, especially the surgeries, provided by these doctors, if he could pay them at all. His gratitude may have been similar to that of the farmers who could pay Dr. Kennicott only when their crops came in, if they ever did. The Michels numbers are from the catalogue raisonné of Petersen's work: Michels, Dana L., DeLong, Lea Rosson and Pohlman, Lynette in DeLong, *Christian Petersen, Sculptor*, Ames: Iowa State University Press, 2000.

3. Petersen wrote about his sculpture: "The sculptor must place in a single figure all of the self sacrifice, kindly good will, and dependable patience, gentle gruffness, and shrewdness of insight into human nature which have made the American country doctor an institution as well known, as greatly respected, and as highly esteemed as any other institution on earth....No matter what the weather, the time, no matter how fatigued they may be, they are always at beck and call, and they can be depended upon to arrive in time. For he is not a specialist; his work is more varied and all-inclusive, than any other on earth....I have tried to call up in the imagination...the untiring dependability, the confidence, the universality and all the rest of the characteristics which make up that great institution...the country doctor." Manuscript in Christian Petersen Papers, Special Collections, Parks Library of Iowa State University. See Bliss, 105-106. Petersen's wife, Charlotte, was knowledgeable about a wide range of literature, and she would have certainly been familiar with Sinclair Lewis's books. The literary associations found in her husband's work (the inscription from James Whitcomb Riley for *The Marriage Ring*, for example) probably originated with her, and it is possible she acquainted him with the character of the country doctor in *Main Street*. Charlotte Petersen was a founder and the first reader of The Book Club on WOI, the radio station of Iowa State University.

4. Petersen had the habit of making numerous sketches and models, often long before he executed his sculpture, and this one may have had its genesis during his Iowa City days (January - August, 1934) when he was working with Wood in the Public Works of Art Project (PWAP). Although the only mural paintings finally installed by Wood's PWAP were those at Iowa State University, the Project was working on plans for other murals which Petersen's concept of a country doctor would have fit. *The History of Dairying* began as a PWAP commission but was assumed by Iowa State College when the government program ended in mid-1934.

5. A pair of hands that more closely corresponds to those of Dr. Kennicott as described by Lewis is found once again in the work of Christian Petersen. In 1936-1937, he produced an over life-size figure of a veterinarian holding a sick puppy (Michels, 196). These thick hands, highly competent but also gentle, evoke the spirit of the general practitioner. The sculpture is a symbol of the College of Veterinary Medicine at Iowa State University and has come to be a symbol for the veterinarian profession.

6. Morley, Christopher, "The Bowling Green," *The Saturday Review of Literature*, January 4, 1936, 13. My thanks to Mrs. Samuel Kravitt for discussing her husband's work and facilitating the reproduction of Kravitt's photograph, "Censorship." Mrs. Kravitt has provided the following information about her husband: "A professional photographer and filmmaker, Samuel Kravitt had a hobby of photographing the hands of people in various professions. The hands in this photograph belonged to Professor Chauncy B. Tinker, Curator of Rare Books at Yale's Sterling

Memorial Library. The original title of the photo, Keeper of Rare Books, was changed by Kravitt's friend, Christopher Morley, to illustrate his essay on the subject of censorship. Kravitt's series on the Shakers of Hancock and Mt. Lebanon has been exhibited in Connecticut, New York, and Massachusetts. As an official photographer for the New York World's Fair Corporation, he documented the construction of the Fair from 1937-1939. After making the transition to filmmaking, he earned numerous awards for his documentaries in the fields of news, fashion, and surgery. One repository of his work is in Yale's Sterling Library. Additional selections from his archive are intended for the Library of Congress, Wolfsonian Museum and the New Haven Colony Historical Society."

My thanks also to the Candace Perich Gallery in Katonah, New York for help in locating the family of Samuel Kravitt.

7. Mott, "The S.P.C.S.," *The Palimpsest* 43, March 1962, 120.

8.Morley, February 1, 1936, 11-12. Sometimes Morley's column was a short essay; at other times it was a series of smaller notes, observations, and reports such as this one about Wood's visit to New York.

9. Morley, December 14, 1935, 11. "We are also saying thank you [sic] to such artists as Chaucer and Jerome Kern and Grant Wood."

10. *Saturday Review*, April 4, 1936, cover. See p. 35, n.19.

11. "We Should Like to Know," *Saturday Review*, November 23, 1935, 8. "A new weekly magazine called *American Prefaces* has been launched from the University of Iowa under the pilotage of Wilbur Schramm and Norman Foerster. Its avowed purpose is to be a voice for the younger writers of America, especially, one supposes, of mid-America." vol.XIII, no.4, November 23, 1935, 8. Wood continued to make comparisons between writing and painting as late as the summer of 1941. "'Painting is much like writing,' said Grant Wood, Iowa's noted artist, as he paused in his work for a moment to speak of his companion pictures *Spring in Town* and *Spring in the Country*, now being completed in his improvised studio on the north shore of Clear Lake. 'One writes best out of his own experiences and so does one paint best. I do not choose Iowa landscapes because I think them more beautiful than any others but because I am more familiar with the scenes of Iowa. Why should I attempt to paint pictures of some distant land where I may have been but once when the hills and slopes of Iowa are a part of my very life?'" "Grant Wood Says Painting, Writing Are Much Alike," Mason City *Globe-Gazette* July 1, 1941. NWG Scrapbook No.4, 34.

12. These distinct lines appear to be drawn with charcoal; they have more of an effect of light absorbing rather than light reflecting, as would be the case with a wax medium such as crayon.

13. For a listing of his lithographs for A.A.A. and other good discussions of this aspect of Wood's career, see Worthen, Amy N., *Thomas Hart Benton, John Steuart Curry, Grant Wood: Lithographs*, Des Moines: Iowa Arts Council, 1978.

14. In *My Brother, Grant Wood*, Nan Wood Graham included a recollection by the wife of Dr. Bennett. "Grant Wood gave our family both [*Main Street* and *Family Doctor*] originals, along with four others....Dr. Bennett always said how generous Grant Wood was to everyone. While he was a patient at the University Hospital, he gave a signed lithograph to every janitor, nurse, orderly, and doctor." Iowa City: State Historical Society of Iowa, 1993, 143. Mrs. Bennett's recollection of Wood's generosity may seem exaggerated today, although it is certainly accurate that Wood did give away some of his work. It is not possible at present to verify the claim that the original *Main Street* drawing of *General Practitioner* was owned by the Bennett family.

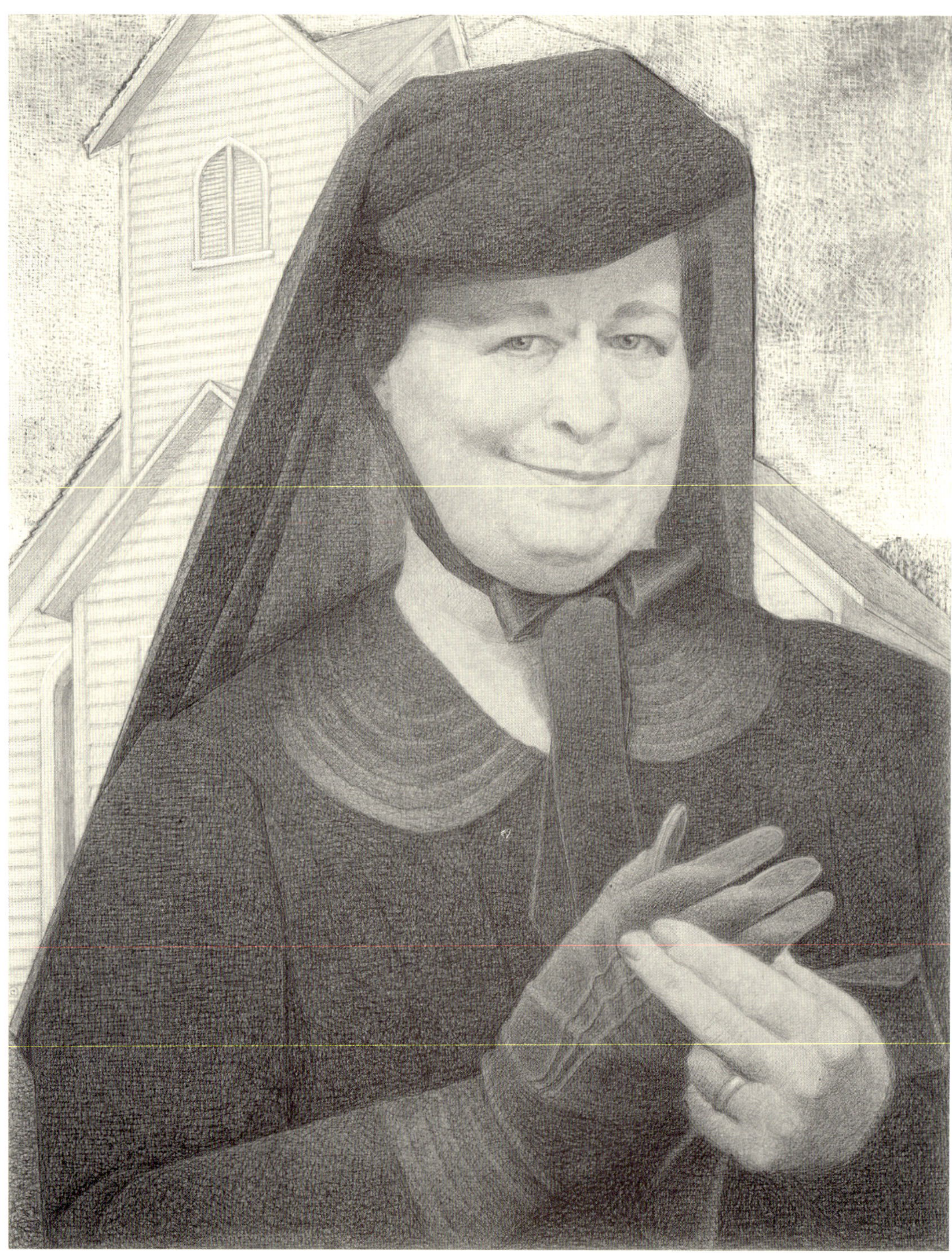

Figure 64 The Good Influence

The Good Influence (Mrs. Bogart)

Most of the people Grant Wood draws in *Main Street* are benign. We might not seek out their company, but they do not seem truly injurious. Even the radical, surrounded by all his tools, would do no more than give us a good argument. Until we come to *The Good Influence*. Here is a person to fear. Despite her sickly sweet smile, we recognize her quickly from our own experience as one who can do great harm and take pride in doing it. The novel makes it clear that Mrs. Bogart's brand of religion can be very dangerous. She presents herself as secure in her personal knowledge of God's will and His plan for the human race, or at least the Gopher Prairie section of it. She takes a good deal of responsibility for implementing God's dictums as she goes about her condemnatory business in her little town. Sinclair Lewis portrays many of the denizens of Gopher Prairie as small-minded, ignorant, and callous, but Mrs. Bogart is lethal. While most of the villagers just indulge in backbiting and gossip, Mrs. Bogart actually damages a person: namely, the schoolteacher, Fern Mullins. Because of her false charges and her bullying of the school board, the spirited young woman is fired and is shamed out of town. If the harm to the young woman is not permanent, it will certainly influence her life for a long time. Even without reading the novel, most of us can easily suspect from Wood's drawing how good "The Good Influence" is.

Wood's title for Mrs. Bogart is also the label Lewis uses when he introduces her as the Kennicott's neighbor who "kept an eye on the house"(needless to say, without being asked to). The novelist describes her as "a widow, and a Prominent Baptist, and a Good Influence. She had so painfully reared three sons to be Christian gentlemen that one of them had become an Omaha bartender, one a professor of Greek, and one, Cyrus N. Bogart, a boy of fourteen who was still at home, the most brazen member of the toughest gang in Boytown."{56} This Cyrus is a reprehensible, useless young man whose petty thuggery is unrelenting throughout the story. Like his mother, young Cyrus causes genuine harm while completely evading any sense of responsibility or moral culpability. In one instance at the outbreak of World War I, he beats up (without consequence and with the tacit support of Gopher Prairie) the son of a German farmer, a boy who later is killed trying to rescue a fellow American soldier during a battle in a French forest. (Cyrus spent the Great War in Gopher Prairie.) In the incident with his high school teacher, Fern Mullins, Cyrus accuses her of getting them both drunk and then making advances to him (it was actually the other way around). Ma Bogart's campaign to defend the perfidious morality of her young hoodlum results in the expulsion of the teacher from her first job. Ma Bogart's twisted enforcement of private and public morality, though some citizens disagree with her, is tolerated and sanctioned in Gopher Prairie.

Aside from tales such as these, the novel gave Wood some specific features for his interpretation of the Good Influence as she appeared during a visit to Carol. Prefacing her remarks with "'Don't you think it's awful, the way folks talk in this town?'" she leans in toward Carol to disgorge a stream of gossip, giving her listener a clear view of her face. "Her large face, with its disturbing collection of moles and lone black hairs, wrinkled cunningly. She showed her decayed teeth in a reproving smile." And then she is off, sanctimoniously ravaging everyone in town she suspects of enjoying themselves, often beginning with "'Well, I don't like to say it, but...'" or "'Heaven knows I never want to start trouble, but....'"{150}

Wood knew her type and had already lampooned it in his art. Curiously, both he and Sinclair Lewis compared Ma Bogart to a hen. "Mrs. Bogart was not the acid type of Good Influence. She was the soft, damp, fat, sighing, indigestive, clinging, melancholy, depressingly hopeful kind. There are in every large chicken-yard a number of old and indignant hens who resemble Mrs. Bogart, and when they are served at Sunday noon dinner, as fricasseed chicken with thick dumplings, they keep up the resemblance." {56} A few chapters later, when she tries to finagle the confession of an indiscretion from Carol, Lewis continues the analogy. "She had a hen-like, crumb-pecking, diligent appearance. Her smile was too innocent. The pecking started instantly." {293} Old biddies of this sort were also a subject in Wood's art, such as *Victorian Survival* (1931).

According to his autobiography, *Return to Bohemia*, chickens were Wood's favorite animals when he was a child growing up on a farm near Anamosa. He especially liked the Plymouth Rock chickens that he found "friendly and communicative."[1] Darrell Garwood's anecdotal biography includes a story about the artist, at three years of age, telling his mother that the semi-circular lines he was drawing were chickens; she deduced that he was drawing the feather pattern of her Plymouth Rock hens, which he would later paint. [2] Chickens appeared in some of the landscapes from his early career, but it was in 1931 that a chicken played a major role in one of his paintings. In *Appraisal*, a Plymouth Rock chicken separates the country woman from the city woman and is probably the reason for their meeting. (Figure 13) A fur-wrapped city woman with a beaded purse has come to the farm to buy a chicken, probably for the Sunday noon dinner of which Lewis spoke. While she is appraising the prospective main dish, she is in turn being appraised by the farm woman whose steady eyes and composed demeanor suggest a discrete disdain. Wood seems to share the country woman's dubiousness about the city woman. The chicken in this picture is a rooster, not a hen, and Wood does not give it quite the same damning gaze he later gives to the female chickens in *Adolescence*. But the silent exchange between the two women is intense enough to set the stage.

In 1940, Wood finished a painting based on a 1933 drawing that had been exhibited in his first one-man show in New York at the Ferargil Galleries in 1935, not long before he began his *Main Street* commission. The drawing was owned by the president of R.R. Donnelly and Sons Company, whose Lakeside Press would publish the new edition of *Main Street.* [3]

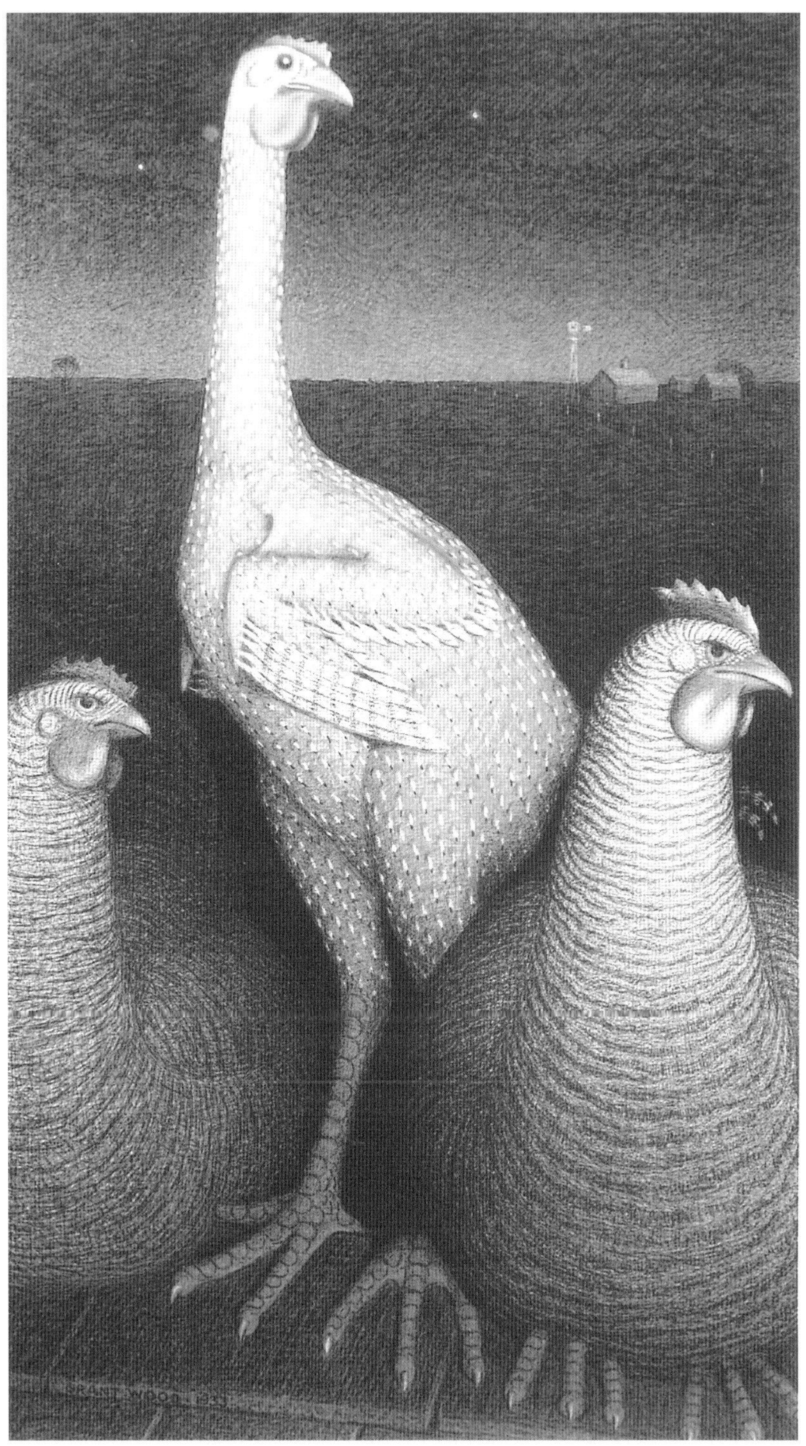

Figure 65 Adolescence, *1933*

Titled *Adolescence*, (Figure 65) it depicts a spindly young featherless chicken between two fat hens, all looking sharply off to one side so that we have a full view of the eyes on the right sides of their heads. The eye of the young chicken is round, as if it were taking in as much of the world as it could, innocently and without judgment. The narrowed eyes of the hens, however, capture the same malevolent expression we see in Mrs. Bogart. Their purpose seems less to protect the youngster than to repress it and to act as enforcers of the old order, vigilant against the impulses of youth. [4]

In *The Good Influence*, the smile is self-satisfied and forced but it betrays nothing more than veniality. It is the eyes that are more troubling. A 1938 article intimates that Wood expressed the hypocrisy of the character by treating the two parts of the face as separate forms. The writer recommended that to understand the drawing, we should "cover up the mouth and look at the eyes; the eyes are hard, cold, unsmiling," [5] Wood's approach in developing the *Main Street* face was likely similar to what he had done for the book jacket of *Passion Spins the Plot* in 1934. He had asked Florence Sprague, a teacher of sculpture at Drake University and at the Stone City Art Colony, to fashion two different portrait heads, one showing an innocent girl, the other showing that same girl after a life of dissipation. He shaved off part of each head, put them together to form a single sculpture, then based his drawing on the composite form. [6] Other observers did not see the duplicity nor regard Mrs. Bogart quite so harshly. There was the impression that Wood was just poking gentle fun at the self-righteous, but harmless, townswoman. In at least two cases, the gossip of Gopher Prairie is even dubbed "benevolent." According to a Chicago critic of 1936, "One can almost see on the artist's face a tenderly wicked smile, as he painted the wedding ring on the finger of the benevolent lady. You feel that temptation has never brushed her, even with a light finger, and that forgiveness of sins is no doubt her favorite pastime." [7]

In his 1944 biography, Darrell Garwood wrote charitably about the drawing (or had sympathy for the model?). "If you knew the people who posed for [Wood], it was sometimes difficult to see in them the types they were considered to represent." His statement might suggest that in the sense of being an artistic synthesis of the personality of a fictitional character, the ideas of the artist, and the actual looks of a real person, the drawings constitute a success for the artist; he achieved his goal of creating types rather than individuals. In describing *The Good Influence* specifically, Garwood related an anecdote about Wood's method of composing Mrs. Bogart's face that, if accurate, would relate it to the book jacket illustration for *Passion Spins the Plot*. In both cases, the artist scrutinized two different aspects of his subjects, the blended them into a single image. "The drawing that attracted the most attention [among the *Main Street* series] was *The Good Influence*, the model for which was Mrs. Mollie Green, hostess at Iowa City's leading hotel. Grant drew her once with a solemn, brooding expression, and once with a benevolent smile. Then he put them together, using the eyes of the first drawing with the smile of the second — a device that Leonardo is supposed to have found useful. The result was a benevolent expression, but with a startling quality, too — a suggestion of suffering behind the serene exterior." [8] Although the illustration is not usually read this way, it possesses enough depth to encompass this interpretation.

As in his other *Main Street* drawings, Wood used architecture, objects and clothing to augment his portraits. Mrs. Bogart poses in front of her beloved Baptist church, her angles and overall shape echoing those of the building. Surely she would consider the church to be the foundation of the community and herself as a fine example of correct behavior. The church is the wood-framed clapboard type that is found in a number of Wood's compositions, notably in *The Midnight Ride of Paul Revere* of 1931. This little church with its truncated tower is a poor relation of the high steepled one that dominates the New England landscape, but both share the same general design. [9] Aside from those he painted in Europe (which were more tourist sights than defining forces in the community), churches are often found in Wood's depictions of small towns. Though they are sometimes relegated to the edges or backgrounds of the composition, their presence suggests the pervasive influence they exert, especially in small towns. For example, *Stone City*, one of his first paintings in his mature style, has a large white building whose one gothic window identifies it as a church. A church of similar proportions as the one in *The Good Influence* crowns the wholesome *Spring in Town* (1941) and a thin steeple in the background blesses *American Gothic. Arbor Day* (1932), with its country schoolhouse (whose architecture has ecclesiastical overtones), pinpoints a distant town by its tiny church steeple. [10] By placing Mrs. Bogart in front of the church, Wood may be implying that the church authorizes her damning judgments. But is Mrs. Bogart's supposed moral authority bestowed by the church? Or is that authority something that, in her self-righteousness, she usurps? Is Wood contrasting true morality (the architectural monument of the church) with the petty, punishing moralizing in which Mrs. Bogart indulges herself? There is no evidence to suggest that Wood himself was a religious person, but he obviously understood religion's importance in the character of the Midwest, and of America.

Just as clothes are a theme that runs through the novel, Wood used costume to convey subtleties about his figures. Lewis describes carefully how his characters are dressed, using clothing at times to insinuate aspects of their personality. In the case of Carol Kennicott, shallowness and self-indulgence is implied when in the midst of her rebellion, confusion, and intellectual frustrations, she often thinks about clothes. Clothing was also important in Wood's art as well, and he used it as effective symbolism in much of his painting. It figures in one of his most famous statements about how, on his 'return from Bohemia," he discovered beauty in the rickrack on farm women's aprons. The painting which presages *The Good Influence*, *Appraisal*, was briefly entitled *Clothing* to express Wood's emphasis on the symbolism of costume.

Mrs. Bogart's clothes are black and sober, proper for a permanent widow, but they do not impart to her the introspection, reserve or even dignity that we might expect. [11] Within the confines of the color black, Wood created a variety of textures and lights: the diaphanous veil, the shiny stitched collar and the soft, light-catching leather gloves. [12] Even Mrs. Bogart is not immune to the appeal of clothing: she allows herself a few restrained notes of finery, with her satiny bonnet ribbon and her kid leather gloves. [13] Wood's drawing of the coarse old woman suggests that he set himself the challenge of portraying her oily, false spirituality, even down to her accessories. The gloves, for instance, are featured in Lewis's detailed description of Widow Bogart's worst deed, and Wood obviously understood their role. After ordering her boarder, the young school teacher, Fern Mullins, out of her house, the widow soon emerges, "poking at her bonnet." After making her rounds through town, "Sister Bogart," as Will Kennicott greets her, "charged into the living-room, waving the most unctuous of black kid gloves." After she gives her account of Miss Mullins' crimes against decency (some of which have to do with the way she dresses), Lewis concludes, "The gutter comedy turned into high tragedy, with Nemesis in black kid gloves." Nemesis was the Greek goddess of vengeance and the word has come into our vocabulary as a term for one who seeks retribution for real or imagined crimes. The black kid gloves make one more appearance, but this time with a different effect. The Good Influence has advanced her arguments until finally even Dr. Will is sated and exclaims, "'Oh, for God's sake quit it!'" His and Carol's lack of outrage dampens Ma Bogart enough to set up one of the few times when she arouses some sympathy. She defends her worthless son, but Carol fires back that his corruption originated in "your sinless town" well before Miss Mullins's arrival. "Mrs. Bogart did not rage in return. Suddenly she was hopeless. Her head drooped. She patted her black kid gloves, picked at a thread of her faded brown skirt, and sighed, 'He's a good boy, and awful affectionate if you treat him right.'" Her abashment lasts for just a moment, however, and then she charges on in her crusade to rid the town of Carol's only friend.

There are two rings shown in the *Main Street* drawings. One is the Odd Fellows ring worn on Honest Jim Blausser's little finger in *Booster* and the other is the wedding ring worn by Mrs. Bogart. Today, there are few rules to govern when a widow may remove her ring, but in the past, it was assumed that a woman would be in mourning for at least a year after her husband's death. Calculating from the age of her teenage son, Cy, we may assume at least that Mr. Bogart was still alive fifteen years ago. Though we do not know the exact date of Mr. Bogart's demise, we have the distinct impression that Mrs. Bogart has worn her ring since then and will continue to dress in widow's black indefinitely into the future. Today and in the past as well, the removal of the wedding ring is a signal that a woman will receive suitors. If we speak with less gentility, it means she is sexually available, which Mrs. Bogart decidedly is not. The one feature of her personality that Lewis lampoons most mercilessly is her sexual repression and the way it colors her perceptions. As he notes after describing one of her gossip sessions, "There was, it seemed, no person in town who was not living a life of shame except Mrs. Bogart, and naturally she resented it." {150}

Notes: *The Good Influence*

1. Rinard, Park, *Return from Bohemia; A Painter's Story, Part I*, Thesis for Master of Arts in the Department of English, State University of Iowa (University of Iowa), August, 1939, Special Collections, University of Iowa Library. "Of all the creatures on the farm, I liked our Plymouth Rock chickens the best. Our white turkeys were shy and aloof. And the guinea fowl, so smooth they looked actually metallic, were too cynical and distrustful to appeal to a child. But the Plymouth Rocks were friendly and communicative. Often when I sat on the back step with a cookie, the chickens came up and shared it with me, clucking appreciatively as they pecked between my fingers." 11. Later on, Wood remembers a cholera outbreak among the farm animals; he didn't mind so much the hogs dying, but he would have minded if "our Plymouth Rocks" had died. 82-85.

2. Garwood, Darrell, 17.

3. "Wood Works," *Time*, April 22, 1935, 56. The article included the reaction Benton had to this "most newsworthy" feature of the Ferargil exhibition. "Recently Artist Wood's good friend and competitor, Thomas Benton, saw it, grew hugely excited, wrote Grant Wood that if he did not make a painting of it at once, Benton would do a picture on the same subject. *Adolescence* will probably be Wood's next painting." In fact, the painting was not completed until 1940.

4. Dennis discussed the young chicken as a male, a rooster, and attributes his featherless state to having been pecked (by the hens, we assume) down to his pinfeathers (120-121) while Corn sees it as a female, perhaps in a "featherless adolescent state." (124) According to *Time* magazine (April 22, 1935, 56), the drawing "showed a gaunt, pin-feathered Plymouth Rock cockerel rising in the faint light of early dawn between his plump parents for his first lusty crow." *Return from Bohemia* includes a story about the farm-boy Wood's responsibility in which he shows concern for the young chickens as they pass through exactly this stage. "The Plymouth Rocks were not only my favorite pets; now that I had the chore of feeding them and gathering their eggs, they were also my responsibility. I had watched them hatch and grow up and when they had been in the featherless adolescent stage, I had even gone so far as to rub mutton tallow on their wings to relieve a sun-burn." 82-5. Also in *Return from Bohemia* is Wood's memory of finally escaping from church after a long service, but being "wedged in between two elderly ladies who were engaged in a lively whispering conversation. 'Wasn't it awful today?' said one lady making a grimace as if she had tasted alum. 'Shameful!' hissed the other.'" They were discussing a form of singing that had been performed in the church service by a person who had been to Europe. One of Wood's fellow artists on the PWAP, John Bloom, painted a scene very much like the one described by Wood; *After Church* (1934) is Bloom's memory of trying to race out of St. Joseph's in DeWitt, Iowa, his way impeded by two plump ladies standing in the doorway. According to Hazel Brown in *Grant Wood and Marvin Cone, Artists of an Era*, the model for the farm woman in *Appraisal* was Edward Rowan and the city woman's features are those of her business partner, Mary Lackersteen. 71-70. The idea of identifying these gossiping old biddies with hens is also seen later on in Meredith Willson's *The Music Man* (1957), a musical and movie set in fictional River City, Iowa around the same time as *Main Street*. As the ladies of River City warn Professor Harold Hill about the local librarian (who advocates dirty books like the novels of Balzac), it is sung with a chorus of "Pick-a-little, talk-a-little, cheep, cheep, cheep" and, in the movie, scenes of hens are interspersed with shots of the River City ladies with their elaborately feathered hats. Willson's story has several elements in common with the story in *Main Street*. See note 3 in the entry on *Sentimental Yearner*. Willson, Meredith, "Pick-a-little, talk-a-little, cheep, cheep, cheep," *The Music Man*, New York: Frank Music Corp. and Meredith Willson Music, 1986.

5. S.A.N., "The Happy, Busy Toiler In Overalls Who Is Grant Wood, The Iowa Artist;" Kansas City *Times*, February 14, 1938.

6. "Artist, Sculptor Use Their Imaginations for Design," Des Moines *Register*, January 28, 1934 and "How Grant Wood Made a Book Cover," St. Louis *Post-Dispatch*, January 28, 1934. Both clippings appear in NWG Scrapbook No. 1, 111.

7. Pynchon, Adeline Lobdell, "Dinner Table Art," *Chicago Journal of Commerce and Law; LaSalle Street Journal*, March 20, 1936; NWG Scrapbook No.1, 61.

8. Garwood, 203-204. Dennis reaffirmed the identify of the model in his 1973 interview with George D. Stoddard, a former Dean at the University of Iowa. (240, n.24).

9. Wood's design of this part of the church may be faulty. Pentimenti in the area above the black hat shows reworking that suggests he may have changed the shape of the upper boundary of the hat or he may have had a line from the side gable extended a little farther. The perspective of the tower is confusing enough to make it impossible to say for certain if he imagined a very narrow steeple arising from its center. Perhaps he intended it to accommodate a steeple as thin as the one in the background of *American Gothic*.

10. The most common architectural forms found in Depression era paintings of the Midwest, whether of the town or the country, are the church steeple, the windmill and the silo. Most of the windmills are now gone, but still today, as one drives through the region, the clearest indicators of a town in the distance are the steeple and the silo. Though many small towns are now nearly deserted, they often contain magnificent churches, inevitably with majestic steeples, that testify to their former vitality.

11. A 1922 watercolor by Otto Dix, *The Widow*, also depicts a woman dressed in black clothing, black lace gloves, and a hat with a diaphanous black veil, standing in front of a church. She holds a stem of white lilies, usually a symbol of purity, but in a typically cynical element, Dix depicts her lifting her skirt enough to reveal a lace edging and part of her leg. Lewis is unmistakable in his commentary on Ma Bogart's sexual repression and envy, but Wood (typical of him), restrains himself from making such an obvious (and perhaps he would say, coarse) comment. For Wood, the prominence of her wedding ring, waiting to be covered or revealed by the black glove, is sufficient to instigate speculation about the widow's subconscious life. Dix's watercolor is reproduced in Karcher, Eva, *Otto Dix; 1891 - 1969*, Cologne: Taschen, 2002, 88. Among Wood's possessions bequeathed by his sister to the Davenport Museum of Art is his mother's mourning veil. (Inventory number M.65.197). This veil may have provided some visual reference for Wood as he was drawing the Widow Bogart's veil.

12. Although Ad Reinhardt would be horrified by any link between himself and the Regionalists, Wood's drawing provides some small sense of the depth, luminosity and range within the color black that Reinhardt would explore in the 1950s.

13. Wood's concentration on these black gloves raises the question of whether he knew the 1881 series of etchings entitled *The Glove* by German artist Max Klinger (1857-1920). Considered a forerunner for surrealism, this group of ten prints fantasizes about the adventures of a lady's black glove.

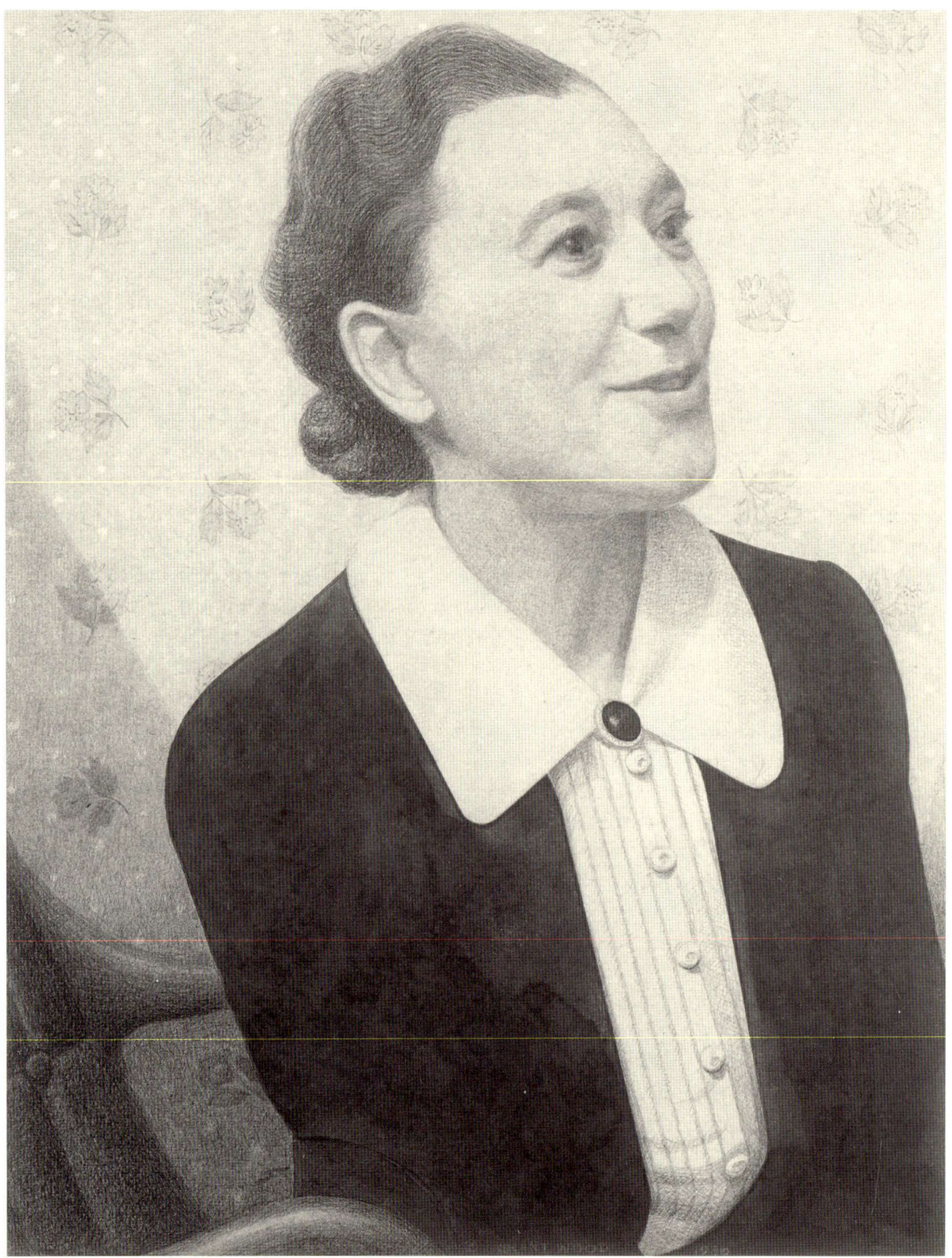

Figure 66 Practical Idealist

Practical Idealist (Vida Sherwin)

Wood chose to illustrate three women from *Main Street*: the heroine, Carol Kennicott; the town gossip, Mrs. Bogart; and the school teacher, Vida Sherwin. Of these three, Sherwin is the most appealing and the one Wood most admired. She is not critical and supercilious, like Carol; she is not narrow and mean spirited, like Mrs. Bogart. She strikes us as unpretentious and not given to dishonesty or depression. The term "practical idealist" is not found in the novel, but was apparently Wood's invention. The word "practical" is implied when Vida describes her own approach to life and when she and Raymond Wutherspoon compare themselves to Carol Kennicott who, they agree, is not at all practical {208} "Idealist" is not applied to Vida, but is implied to be a more appropriate description of Carol (Vida goes even further and calls her an "impossibilist"{220}) Vida's practicality is posed against Carol's preposterous aspirations for the town — fantasies for which Vida has little patience. For example, in one encounter, Miss Vida Sherwin refuses to see the advantage of Venice over Gopher Prairie as she retorts to Carol in her common sense way, "'I imagine gondolas are kind of nice to ride in, but we've got better bathrooms!'" {219}

"Miss Sherwin of the high school"{48} teaches English, French, and Latin, organizes and encourages the debate team, and chaperons dances. But she is not just a school teacher; she is the town's reformer and mediator, keeping peace among its factions. She balances between being the confidant of the discontented Carol Kennicott and the intimate of the ladies' clubs whom Carol irritates. She dislikes Carol almost as much as the other women do, but her feelings are tempered by her innate charity and determined self-improvement. At times, Vida stops the clubwomen from "pecking" Carol, but she also informs the Gopher Prairie misfit of the town's criticism of her, which is deeply distressing to Carol. Wood's drawing does not show the character complexity that is developed in the novel. In fact, his *Practical Idealist* seems incapable of the shades in the personality of Lewis's Vida Sherwin. As in the case of *Sentimental Yearner*, Wood depicts the pre-marriage Vida, before the release of her energy into the aggrandizement of her husband and the minutiae of domestic life. This is Vida when all her passions are invested in the town's betterment, not in her personal life.

The artist concentrates on her energy, her optimism, and her dogged warmth for the little town and its possibilities for improvement. His characterization comes largely from Lewis's description when she calls to introduce herself to the new bride. "Despite Vida Sherwin's lively blue eyes, if you had looked at her in detail you would have found her face slightly lined, and not so much sallow as with the bloom rubbed off; you would have found her chest flat, and her fingers rough from needle and chalk and penholder; her blouse and plain cloth skirts undistinguished; and her hat worn too far back, betraying a dry forehead.

But you never did look at Vida Sherwin in detail. You couldn't. Her electric activity veiled her. She was as energetic as a chipmunk. Her fingers fluttered; her sympathy came out in spurts; she sat on the edge of a chair in eagerness to be near her auditor, to send her enthusiasms and optimism across." {52} This last image is precisely the one Wood used in his drawing. She is indeed perched on chair's edge (she sits so far forward we can barely see the back of the chair), ready, focused, and positive.

Wood's task here went beyond pose and likeness; he needed to capture the vibrancy of her temperament, to give the impression of her energy and her activity. It wasn't the sort of thing he had been noted for in his earlier art. Stasis dominated most of his compositions, and his portraiture showed reserved, self-controlled subjects, such as his picture of his mother in *Woman with Plants* (1930). Facial expressions found in his paintings are seldom animated or unselfconscious — or even pleasant. In the *Main Street* group, Sherwin is one of only two figures who do not look directly out at the viewer (the other is *Sentimental Yearner*) and the only one who does not seem completely self-involved. She is outward directed, and we imagine that her conversation is not about herself but on some altruistic topic. Spontaneity and vividness are not sensations we associate with Wood, but those are exactly the qualities that marked the character of Vida Sherwin. His success in conveying them in this drawing is one measure of the seriousness he brought to this commission.

Wood's art overall has a deliberate, stately quality and, even when forms are shown moving, it is a measured sort of motion, like plodding through a plowed field. He often depicted humans and animals in motion, but they usually have a stilled, if not actually wooden, quality. The drawings that he had created just before the *Main Street* drawings, those for the children's book, *Farm on the Hill*, show creatures in many activities, but they are full of angles and hard shapes that do not mimic physical movement. Like these designs, much of the movement in Wood's art has a ritualized tone that quiets any sense of impulse or spontaneity. His compositions are rhythmical, but not full of dynamic motion, [1] even when they depict forceful efforts, like the figure chopping down a tree with an axe in *Breaking the Prairie Sod.*

Wood's shaping of his portrait of Sherwin did not involve broad movements or sweeping gestures; it was more a matter of conveying a kind of vibration. Her humming vitality and her energetic hopefulness were the dominating qualities of her personality, and Wood seems to have challenged himself to convey that solely through less obvious means. *Practical Idealist* is the only *Main Street* drawing in which the sitter does not make some telling gesture or hold some symbolic object; in fact, she is the only one whose hands are not visible at all. They seem to be tucked into her lap (and probably clasped together) as if she is trying to contain her enthusiasm. As Wanda Corn noted in her 1983 catalogue, hands and eyes are primary elements for conveying narrative and drama in these drawings, [2] but here Wood denied himself one of those pictorial options. The minute depiction of facial expression and her compact, alert body wedged into a corner of the picture are the devices

Wood employs. In addition, his rendering of the tense muscles of the neck and the slight sagging of the muscles and skin of the lower face combine to suggest her distinctive blend of innocence and experience. She sits forward in her chair, flowers and dots popping in the wallpaper behind her, ready to engage us in her entirely reasonable plans for the improvement of Gopher Prairie.

Did Wood identify with Vida Sherwin? Despite his sudden fame and the controversies of his life and his art, he was not a revolutionary or even a rabble-rouser. When he lived in Cedar Rapids and tried to make it a Midwestern Mecca for the fine arts, he did so in a way that endeared him to the community, not alienated him from it. He took the same incremental approach to raising the cultural standards of the community that Miss Sherwin did. [3] Like her, he had been a school teacher, and it was with the young minds of his students that he began to raise the communal sights toward what he called the Imagination Isles of creativity. Like Sherwin, he was regarded in the town as a genial, unchallenging personality of unfailing good humor, a guise that masked his ambition and his impatience with intolerance and provincialism. Wood might not have been as pleased with his town as Sherwin was with hers (He probably would not have said, as she did, "'It's the spirit that gives me hope. It's sound. Wholesome'"{53}), but he might have had some sympathy with statements like, "'Oh, I do hope I'm not a sentimentalist. But I can't see any use in this high-art stuff that doesn't encourage us day-laborers to plod on.'"{53} Such a pronouncement might have fitted well with his Regionalist philosophy and his rejection of European modernism.

Wood may have also reflected upon the change that occurred in the lives of both him and his subject in middle age. After living their entire adult lives as a bachelor and spinster respectively, both the real and fictional persons embarked on marriage. Sherwin allowed herself to fall in love with Raymie Wutherspoon, a man described early in the book as a "gentleman hen," and became passionately devoted to him. This relationship causes both of these blunted individuals to blossom and to gain new respect in the community. Raymie even goes off to service in World War I and returns a hero. Both are transformed by their marriage (Lewis hints broadly about their sexual satisfaction in it), and life is richer and more meaningful. Vida Sherwin was about 39 when she married; Wood was 44. With little support from his friends, in March of 1935, he entered into marriage with a singer, Sara Maxon; four years later, the marriage ended in a costly, but welcome, divorce. Aside from this outcome, there is anecdotal evidence that the marriage held tensions from the beginning, including the most acrimonious sort: financial trouble. [4] It is possible that Wood's unhappy marriage caused him to admire the character whose marriage solved problems, not created them. He may also have felt some affinity with Sherwin when she, who usually presented such a rosy face to the world, cried out to Carol, "'What do you know about the thoughts in hearts? You just play at reforming the world. You don't know what it means to suffer.'" {304}

The model for the practical idealist was Norma Agnes Englert (1898-1976), a librarian in the College of Engineering, [5] about whom little else is known. Much of the brown paper in the upper half of this drawing is left uncovered as part of the wallpaper pattern. The flowers on the wallpaper are lightly sketched without the detail that we often associated with Wood's work, and the pattern appears to be of the same vintage as the wallpapers in the childcare and cooking panels of the Home Economics murals in the library at Iowa State University (1934). [6] Perhaps this kind of wallpaper, so popular in middle class Midwestern homes, suggests Sherwin's essential contentment within that millieu and her eventual domesticity. Much more vivid in the drawing are the white dots interspersed regularly among the flowers. In contrast to the retiring effect of the flowers, these dots stand out; creating a staccato effect that is perhaps intended to mimic the energy and vivacity of Vida Sherwin. When the drawing was reproduced in the 1937 *Main Street* book, the dots were much stronger than they have appeared in subsequent reproductions. Wood also used dots in the blouse of *The Perfectionist*, but in that drawing, the starkness of the white is tempered by the underlying layers of crayon. [7] The face of the *Practical Idealist* is shown in a three-quarter view that suggests movement of the head: not the stasis of the full frontal nor the rigidity of a profile. By putting the head in this position, Wood emphasizes the lift of the chin and the outward direction of the subject's gaze, so that we sense at once her engagement with someone outside the frame. The face is so animated and the background so fragmented that the nearly solid black of the jacket acts as a weight and a balance in the composition. Leaning diagonally into the picture (another device to suggest dynamism), the wedge of her upper body and the generalized arrow shape of her blouse front and collar direct us to the dark, intense eyes (echoed by her black dot of a brooch) and the graying hair.

Wood's choice of clothing is more stylish than that described by Lewis. In the novel, her style is serviceable, even drab: "Her blouse and plain cloth shirts [were] undistinguished."{52} The meticulous buttons and sharp pleats of her blouse paired with the black jacket and the deep black brooch against the bleached white collar, though admittedly "plain," do not strike us as "undistinguished." Wood creates a costume with a sense of ageless style, an accomplishment we must attribute more to Wood than to the *Main Street* character. Later in the novel, just before her marriage to Raymond Wutherspoon, Lewis describes Vida Sherwin once more, supplying details that Wood did not include in his drawing, but that obviously affected his interpretation. "She was small and active and sallow; her yellow hair was faded, and looked dry; her blue silk blouses and modest lace collars and high black shoes and sailor hats were as literal and uncharming as a schoolroom desk; but her eyes determined her appearance, revealed her as a personage and a force, indicated her faith in the goodness and purpose of everything. They were blue, and they were never still; they expressed amusement, pity, enthusiasm. If she had been seen in sleep, with the wrinkles beside her eyes stilled and the creased lids hiding the radiant irises, she would have lost her potency."{204}

This "potency" is what Wood conveys in his most sympathetic *Main Street* interpretation. In contrast to the other portraits (except the symbolic portrait of Dr.Kennicott), this one is overwhelmingly positive. What is there to criticize or dismiss in this confident, congenial personality? In every other portrait there is something to dislike, suspect or ridicule. Wood's Vida is not the small time reformer who is comfortable in her provincial little town, but a person of hope, enthusiasm and pragmatism — someone who could succeed in Gopher Prairie, or anywhere else.

Notes: *Practical Idealist*

1. "Dynamic" is used here as an adjective in the sense of expressing strong, forceful motion of a form. In terms of artistic theory, however, Wood was a thorough believer in the use of dynamic symmetry to organize compositions. Developed by the American art educator, Jay Hambidge, dynamic symmetry is a system for devising and ordering compositions using a strict division of space (based on thirds) so that a two-dimensional design achieves a mathematical (or geometric) balance. Wood taught his students how to apply it in their work, as Elizabeth Catlett, who did graduate work under Wood, explained in a 1984 interview, quoted in Dennis, James, "Grant Wood's Native-Born Modernism," in Roberts, Brady, *Grant Wood: An American Master Revealed* Daveport (Iowa) Museum of Art, 1995, 63, n.44. Dynamic symmetry lines can be seen clearly in many of Wood's drawings, even in reproduction, for example, in the sketch for *Grandma Mending* (1936), one of the illustrations for *Farm on the Hill*. (University of Iowa Museum of Art, reproduced in Dennis, plate 186) Two lines extending from the handkerchief in *Sentimental Yearner* are probably dynamic symmetry lines. Dynamic symmetry was commonly used by American artists in the 1920s and 1930s and is an aspect of American painting that merits more study and understanding.

2. Corn, Wanda, *Grant Wood: The Regionalist Vision*, New Haven: Yale University Press, 1983, 114.

3. Though not regarded as scholarly or reliable in matters of exact facts, Hazel Brown's reminiscence, *Grant Wood and Marvin Cone; Artists of an Era*, does convey a sense of how Wood was regarded in the Cedar Rapids community of the 1920s when he was teaching school, decorating local homes and living in the Turner Alley studio.

4. There are many indications of their financial stress, one of which is a letter handwritten by Sara Maxon Wood at the direction of her husband to his New York dealer, Maynard Walker, on December 26, 1935. The letter is about conditions and requirements for the sale of Wood's art, along with the explanation that there was "a good stiff bill to meet" for renovations of the old house the couple had bought in Iowa City. AAA, Maynard Walker files, reel 2025, frames 992-995.

5. Employee card at Special Collections, University of Iowa Libraries. According to this file, Englert was a stenographer and librarian 1919-1922, then a librarian and clerk 1922-1927 in the College of Applied Science. From 1927 to 1928, she was librarian and clerk in the College of Engineering. After that, there is no record of her employment. She was born February 19, 1898 and died September 27, 1976. No photographs of Englert have been found. Though "Vida" is an unusual name today and may also have been during Wood's lifetime, he did know a woman in Cedar Rapids named Vida, who was married to his childhood friend, Paul Hanson. It is not known to what extent, if any at all, Wood incorporated this Vida's looks or personality into his characterization.

6. Wood used wallpaper patterns in several other works, including *Dinner for Threshers* (1934) and *Portrait of Sally Stamats* (1927). Wallpapers were used in his own interior designs; he did not always follow the Modern

requirement for plain, monochromatic walls. For more on his interior design, see Corn, 23-25. Photographs of his Iowa City home also show the use of wallpaper. The neatly planted rows in *Stone City* (1930) and *Appraisal* (1931) mimic wallpaper and have a similar effect in the composition.

7. Dot patterns are found in many of Wood's works, including *Boy Milking a Cow* (1932), *Farmer with Pigs* (1932), *Portrait of Nan* (1933), the housekeeping and sewing panels of the Home Economics murals in the library at Iowa State University, *Return from Bohemia* (1935, both versions: Curtis Galleries and Davenport Museum of Art), and the dot-like pattern in the apron of *American Gothic* (1930).

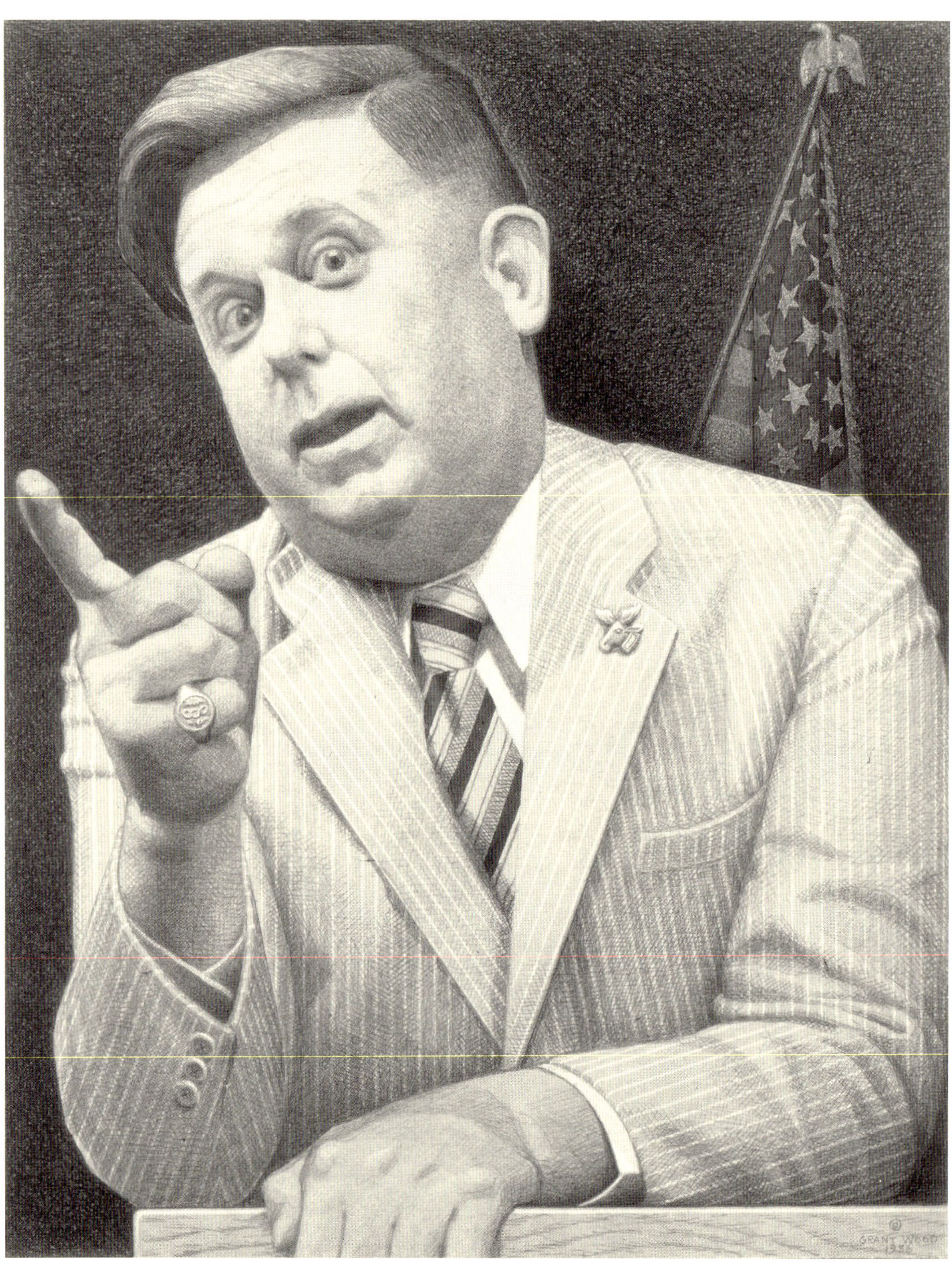

Figure 67 Booster

Booster
(James "Honest Jim" Blausser)

Why did Wood choose the booster, James Blausser, for one of his illustrations? Blausser is a minor character introduced near the end of the book whose appearance and then disappearance from Gopher Prairie take up only a few pages. Why did Wood overlook more influential characters, like Sam Clark, Champ Perry, Juanita Haydock or Maud Dyer? How could he pass up the chance to have fun with Uncle Whittier or Aunt Bessie? Did he think about the contrast he could create between Ma Bogart's boy, Cy, the town bully, and his earlier study of his young assistant, Arnold Pyle, in *Arnold Comes of Age* (1931)? Why would he choose Blausser over Erik Valborg, the young Swedish farm boy who makes his living as a Gopher Prairie tailor while he dreams of designing women's clothes in New York? His bookishness and interest in style lead the Real Men of Gopher Prairie to dub him "Elizabeth," and in such a humiliating guise, he is introduced to Carol. But Carol finds that she and Valborg share the conviction of being misplaced in the small Midwestern town, and they nearly drift into an affair until village gossip prods Dr. Kennicott to put a stop to it. Why would Wood not have felt some identification with this artistic young man trapped in provincial society by poverty? He bypassed more important figures to portray Blausser, an outsider who comes to Gopher Prairie, tells it what it wants to hear, is paid, heeded, and embraced — and then found blameless when nothing much comes of his boosting.

Wood's drawing shows Blausser in his quintessential mode: addressing the local club of businessmen ("boosting," as Dr. Kennicott would say or, if it were someone he agreed with less, "gassing"). He leans over a podium that seems too small to contain him and grips its edge with one hand while the other points in accompaniment to one of his exhortations. In back of "Honest Jim" Blausser, as he liked to be called, is the American flag, which would today still be displayed in the lodges and meeting rooms of civic and commercial organizations. But in light of the Kennicotts' confused arguments about boosters and patriotism, the flag is more than just an accurate prop in the background. It represents the "Red-Blooded Americanism" that Blausser uses to promote his commercial prospects, but that can be subverted to less benign causes, as it was in the novel.

He wears a suit coat that is well made and whose stripes match perfectly (at the breast pocket and the shoulder seam), suggesting a person who takes some care in choosing his wardrobe (as we know Dr. Kennicott does not). The stripes of the jacket are a little too vivid to be called pinstripes so that when paired with a boldly striped tie, the ensemble is, to say the least, striking. It may give the impression that the wearer is something of a bumpkin, as apparently it did to the writer of a Cedar Rapids newspaper article. Comparing the booster's attire with that of the model, a prominent University of Iowa professor and administrator, the writer commented, "We never have seen you in a suit just like this one, Professor Mott, but one can imagine that Mr. Wood would see to it that the 'Booster'...wore a suit of that kind." [1] Again, Wood's visual decisions can be read more than one way. Actually, combining stripes in two articles of men's clothing is not incorrect, but they must be carefully selected in order to coordinate and not clash, and they must be worn with a white shirt, as Blausser does. [2] It is easy to mishandle these two patterns, but it seems Blausser has the sartorial sophistication to make these kinds of choices (although in Wood's hands, there is just enough edginess to make us wonder). This, as well as the cut of the suit, suggests that Blausser is perhaps not as much of a "good old boy" as he pretends. In his speech to the Commercial Club, Blausser admits to Gopher Prairie that he has been to London ("nothing but a bunch of fog and out-of-date buildings that no live American burg would stand for one minute" {338}) and seems familiar with New York and the East (referred to as Yahooville-on-the-Hudson). His personal background is glossed over, except when it serves his purposes, and Gopher Prairie appears disinclined to investigate his credentials. Despite the technical correctness of his attire, there remains something a little flashy and ersatz about this booster. His hair is brushed over boyishly, and he looks well fed and prosperous. [3] His wrists are thick, his arms seem to bulge against his sleeves, his face is fleshy and his jowls are well developed. Sinclair Lewis often describes Dr. Kennicott and his friends as having a similar appearance.

In addition to his clothing and the flag, *Booster* contains two other symbols through which Wood shades the interpretation of this character. On the little finger of the hand [4] that points in emphasis of his speech, Blausser wears a ring of the International Order of Odd Fellows and in his lapel is the insignia of the Moose Lodge. Both of these are organizations exclusively of men in local chapters who meet at regular intervals for fellowship and other reasons, notably for making business contacts. Both are national (even international), yet they are often associated with the Midwest, perhaps partly through the portrayal of fraternal organizations in writings by and about Midwesterners (such as Lewis's *Main Street* and *Babbitt*). In Lewis's novel, several such groups are found in Gopher Prairie: the Knights of Pythias, the Maccabees, the Woodmen, the Beavers, and the Masons [5]. The Odd Fellows appear through their meeting hall in which dances are held, including the twice-a-year dances of the Jolly Seventeen, the women's social club of Gopher Prairie {86, 136}; the Moose Lodge is never mentioned. Why did Wood choose these two particular fraternities for his illustration? Partly perhaps because they both have unusual names that some consider rather comical; their names and their association with the Midwest might have appealed to Wood's sense of humor. But as a small town Midwesterner — and a person quite unapologetic about his Midwestern background — Wood must have known the serious nature of these groups and may have used them to convey a layer of meaning about Honest Jim.

Both the Odd Fellows and the Moose are associated with philosophies and charitable acts that seem out of place in Blausser's exploitative character. Founded in England in the eighteenth century, the Odd Fellows were so named because they were devoted to helping the poor and unfortunate; anyone who put the welfare of others above their own was considered then an "odd fellow." [6] According to their tradition, the Odd Fellows' missions of mercy implied a criticism of the ruler's competence, leading them occasionally into conflict with the authorities so that they met in secret and adopted passwords among each other. In America, the Independent Order of Odd Fellows was established in Baltimore in 1819 and set about helping orphans, factory workers, farmers and others in need of assistance. The ring that Blausser wears has the three interlocked links that symbolize the Odd Fellows' creed of Friendship, Love and Truth. In regard to the link of Truth, the Odd Fellows ritual expands to caution its members against coldness in expounding Truth: "Truth combined with our sublime meaning of tolerance teaches us the compassion needed in [all] our dealings." Had Blausser forgotten this oath when he advocated his philosophy of chasing dissidents out of town ("scategory," he called it). Wood's detailing of the ring is so precise that we can even make out two other symbols on either side of the ring. One is the "all-seeing eye...of Omnipotence" which, according to I.O.O.F. ritual for the Third Degree, "illustrates that sleepless goodness which looks down in mercy upon our frailties." The other symbol is the skull and cross-bones, intended to remind the Odd Fellows "of the consuming process of nature" and of their obligation to honor their dead. [7] None of these symbols, which Wood defines so readably in his picture, denote minor concepts or virtues and, if he took the care to include them as he did, is he not counting on the knowledge of at least some in his audience to understand their meaning? And, would he not use that understanding to make a sly, but pointed comment about the shallowness of this "booster"? If Wood also knew that their Order's objective was "To Improve and Elevate the Character of Mankind," he might have been complying with Lewis's depiction of small town narrowness and false charity by using the Odd Fellows insignia in association with a character who was not at all "elevated" nor the least charitable.

The lapel pin signifies membership in the Moose Lodge and is typical of those worn in the 1910s. [8] The Moose lodge was founded in Louisville in 1888 with the partial purpose of assisting working men and their families, as they did in the recession of 1893 when they provided benefits to unemployed members. (By 1912, they had paid out $1,500,000 to needy Moose brothers.) It was a fairly small organization until the membership expanded dramatically from around 80,000 in 1910 to over half a million in 1915, about the same time that *Main Street* takes place. Headquartered in Illinois, the Moose continued its charitable activities throughout the Midwest and elsewhere in part by establishing homes for orphans and the elderly. [9] Wood took some liberties with the design of the pin, notably by lessening the detail of the antlers and emphasizing the ear of the animal. But he faithfully copied the letters P A P, the initials for the Moose motto: "Purity, Aid, Progress." This motto, along with that of the Odd Fellows, and the history in both organizations of the inclusion of working class men and charitable activities suggests a shallowness, if not a duplicity, in Blausser's appropriations of their insignia. His sort of "progress" is not related to Progressivism or to any sympathy with workers, farmers or the poor. In fact, these are exactly the sort that he marginalizes, ridicules and portrays as a threat to the red-blooded prosperity of real Americans. How is Wood's use of these fraternal orders' insignias to be read? Is he simply reflecting the popular (and perhaps to some extent justified) perception of these organizations? Does he see them as bastions of small town economic opportunism and greediness; as promoters of preposterous claims of civic distinction; as fraternal enclaves of a phony elite? Or, does he deliberately choose two organizations whose widely known purpose was charity and friendship toward the poor, the unemployed, the sick and the unfortunate? By introducing these two lodges (of the many he could have chosen) into his depiction, does he throw Honest Jim's falseness into a sharp, unmistakable profile that would have been recognizable to the thousands of ordinary Midwesterners who were Moose or Odd Fellows members or had been aided by their efforts? Or, on the other hand, if the audience for Wood's work is in the East where, one assumes, such organizations have a lower community profile and are associated with small town Midwesterners, then perhaps Wood is counting on the presumptions and clichés about his home region to give a reliable (if erring) humor to his *Booster*.

In the novel, James Blausser blows into town near the end of World War I when wheat prices are booming and land speculation could bring large, quick profits, as they did for Dr. Kennicott who in three months made four times more money than he earned being a doctor. [10] Blausser was embraced by Gopher Prairie, as Carol never was, even though he begins immediately advocating changes more superfluous (and expensive) than anything Carol or Vida Sherwin had ever proposed. [11] Portrayed as being not very smart, he had other qualities more valued in that commercial culture: he was shrewd and congenial, a deadly combination for any unsuspecting burgher. "Mr. Blausser was known as a Hustler," {337} we are told, but the folks of Gopher Prairie meant it as a compliment. Wood's drawing conveys the good impression Honest Jim made, despite his rough edges. When Carol "spoke ill" of him, Will defended him. "Maybe he is kind of a roughneck but you got to hand it to him; he's got more git-up-and-git than any fellow that ever hit this burg....Hear what he said to old Ezra? Chucked him in the ribs [Blausser is always touching someone, including the aloof Carol] and said, 'Say, boy, what do you want to go to Denver for? Wait'll I get time and I'll move the mountains here. Any mountain will be tickled to death to locate here once we get the White Way in!'" The White Way was one of Blausser's triumphs, the sort of thing that, if Carol had suggested it, would have been cause for hilarity. A "fashion in the Middlewest," it was an installation of "ornamented posts with clusters of high-powered electric lights along two or three blocks on Main Street." {339} A worthy enough idea, but it is not hard to imagine that Honest Jim received a kickback for this civic advance, as he likely did for bringing to town the "shy factory" which lasted a year before going broke. As we look at Wood's drawing, we can see why Gopher Prairians might feel he was one of their own (albeit with a little more hustle) and not suspect that he had anything in mind but good will and solid profits. He may be a shyster, the drawing says, but he is so good-natured about it, how can you really dislike him? Perhaps that duality is what attracted Wood to Honest Jim. Certainly it demonstrates that Wood well understood our American propensity for embracing shady characters if only they are pleasant enough.

Despite his brief appearance, Blausser is a provocative figure, seen in opposite ways by Dr. Kennicott and his wife. In fact, it is his success in affecting Gopher Prairie that makes Carol finally decide to leave. "She could not sit applauding Honest Jim Blausser. Kennicott had begged her, in courtship days, to convert the town to beauty. If it was now as beautiful as Mr. Blausser...said, then her work was over, and she could go."{340} Her lack of appreciation for him as well as her "failure to glow over the boosting"{341} pushes the doctor to exasperation. "'By golly, I've done all I could, and now I expect you to play the game. Here you been complaining for years about us being so poky, and now when Blausser comes along and does stir up excitement and beautify the town like you've always wanted somebody to, why, you say he's a roughneck, and won't jump on the bandwagon.'"{431} The quarrel in which she informs Dr. Kennicott that she will leave him is provoked because of her sympathy for those parts of society that do not "jump on the bandwagon" but who persist in being discontent.

The stage for this particular disagreement was set in the speech Blausser had given to the Commercial Club, an event Wood seems to depict in his drawing. Addressing an audience of Gopher Prairians (we can almost see them nodding their heads in approval) the booster trumpeted the uselessness of "knockers" which led him to glorify patriotism which led him to castigate political dissidents, the Farmers' Nonpartisan League to be exact. "'Way I figger it, you folks are just patriotic enough so that you ain't going to stand for any guy sneering and knocking his own town, no matter how much of a smart Aleck he is — and just on the side I want to add that this Farmers' Nonpartisan League and the whole bunch of socialists are right in the same category, or, as the fellow says, in the same scategory, meaning This Way Out, Exit, Beat It While the Going's Good, This Means You, for all knockers of prosperity and the rights of property!'"{338} Not long afterwards, an organizer for the National Nonpartisan League was indeed run out of a nearby town by a mob of local businessmen, an action which Kennicott and his friends approved of, except that "they ought to have lynched him!"{341}

When Will and Carol face off about the incident, they construe it into a conflict about patriotism and pro-German sympathies in the midst of World War I and from there to her feelings about Gopher Prairie. Kennicott listens to Carol move from politics to her disdain for his town until he finally explodes, "'That'll be about all from you! I've stood for your sneering at this town, and saying how ugly and dull it is....I've even stood for your ridiculing our Watch Gopher Prairie Grow campaign. But...I'm not going to stand my own wife being seditious.'"{342} She connects their argument to Blausser and everything he stands for. "'Will!...Am I pro-German if I fail to throb to Honest Jim Blausser?'" {343} Several of Wood's characterizations, such as this one of the booster and *Practical Idealist*, are not as harsh as Lewis's. As we look at his rendering of an amiable, wide-eyed, small town businessman, more comical than sinister, it is a bit hard to see a man whose half-baked political utterances could affect public opinion or end a marriage.

Wood may have wanted to emphasize the pivotal role Blausser plays in the Kennicotts' marital psychology, or he may have wanted a chance to comment on the other Lewis creation who symbolized the Midwest more than Carol Kennicott and anyone in *Main Street*: Babbitt. *Main Street*'s Blausser is something of a rehearsal for the major character of *Babbitt*, the novel Lewis published two years later in 1922. Like *Main Street*, it was a best seller and its title and the name of its main character filtered into American vocabulary as a symbol of mindless boosting, misplaced provincial pride and everything else ridiculous about the Midwest. While the Babbitt of Lewis's novel is not as one-dimensional as Blausser, he came to represent the "booboisie" of an utterly provincial region. Not surprisingly, Wood had little patience for outsiders' condescension toward the Midwest and had no intention of furthering its more uncharitable images. His own parodies were at least semi-comical and even *Daughters of Revolution* failed to project the meanness Lewis placed in some of his characters. As recently as 1932, Wood had declared that he would not deal with overdone, "heavily derided" subjects like Babbitt. [12] But the commission to illustrate a Sinclair Lewis novel might have been just too tempting.

The model for *Booster* was Frank Luther Mott (1886-1964), professor, writer, compatriot of Wood's in the artistic/literary life at the University of Iowa and self-described "eager beaver." (Figure 68) [13] Born in What Cheer, Iowa, he worked at a variety of journalistic endeavors, including a brief stint as editor of a family-owned newspaper in El Reno, Oklahoma. He joined the University of Iowa's English faculty in 1921 as a teacher of American literature and short story writing; in 1925 he and John T. Frederick founded an esteemed literary journal, *The Midland*, which focused, of course, on the Midwest. In 1925, Mott was appointed head of the journalism school where he was a colleague of another *Main Street* model, Charles Leo Sanders *(Sentimental Yearner)*. Mott's academic specialty was magazines, and two volumes of his four-volume study, *The History of American Magazines*, won the Pulitzer Prize in 1938. In 1942, the year of Wood's death, Mott left to become the dean of the University of Missouri School of Journalism. [14]

Mott was also a founder of a series of independent organizations that invited speakers on a wide range of cultural topics to visit the University of Iowa. The first, started in the late 1920s by Mott and Frederick, was called the Saturday Luncheon Club. In his 1962 autobiography, Mott recalled that the club's goal was to set up "a kind of friendly communion with some of the leading American writers of the time if we could get them to come out to Iowa City." These visits were to be informal and conversational, with small gatherings.

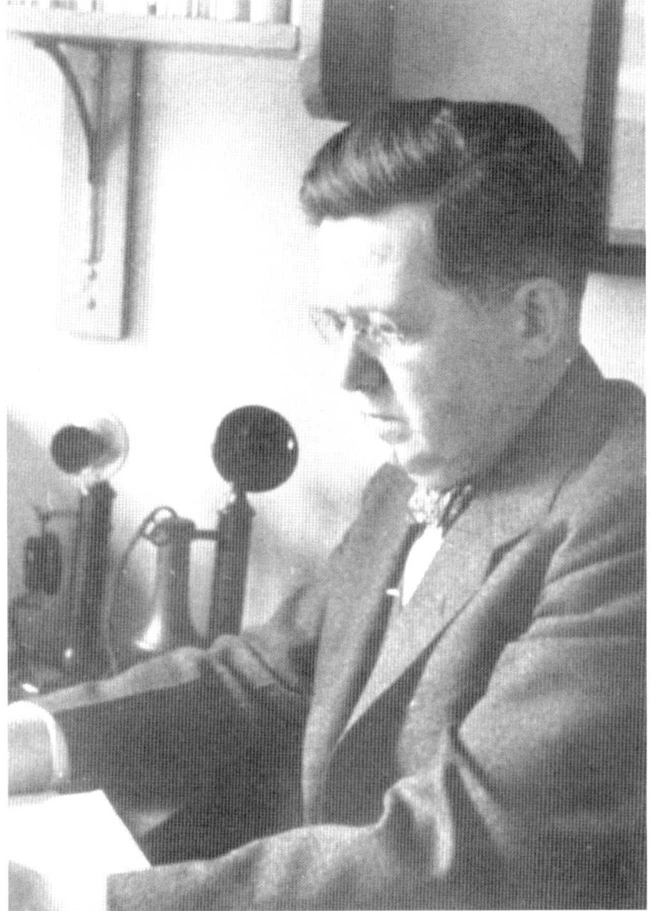

Figure 68 Frank Luther Mott. The Hawkeye, *1939*

Sherwood Anderson, e.e. cummings, Robert Frost and Carl Sandburg were among those who accepted their invitations. This luncheon club changed into the Times Club in 1933, then in 1934, with Wood integrated into the University's cultural set, found its own meeting place. Located above the nearby Smitty's Cafe, their clubroom was decorated by Wood in what he described as "'the worst style of the late Victorian period.'" [15] As an addenda to their club, the members instituted the Society for the Prevention of Cruelty to Speakers (S.P.C.S.), whose primary function was hospitality for their famous guests, such as Thomas

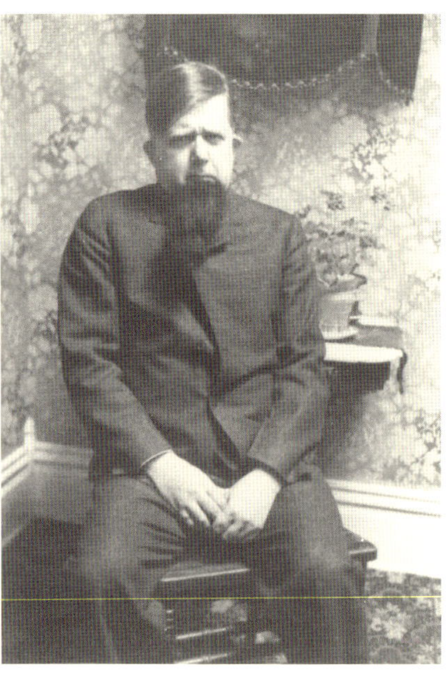

Figure 69 Frank Luther Mott at the Society for the Prevention of Cruelty to Speakers, c.1934

Hart Benton (Figure 17), Stephen Vincent Benet, MacKinlay Kantor (Figure 19), and Christopher Morley (Figure 15) of *The Saturday Review of Literature*. Among the Society's practices was photographing their guests in horrible, mock-Victorian costumes with equally fun-loving props and poses. A photograph of Mott (Figure 69) shows him playing a pre-*Booster* role. With slicked-down hair and long goatee (obviously false), he is sitting stiffly and trying to achieve a proper Victorian scowl, and failing. Clearly, he is enjoying the joke and will soon relax into laughter. If Wood really was investing *Booster* with his commentary on Midwestern clichés and *Babbitt*, the choice of Mott as a model for the drawing is appropriate; Mott had already proven adept in these sorts of parodies through his role in the satires of the S.P.C.S. Possibly it was Mott who wrote the tongue-in-cheek questionnaire the S.P.C.S. sent out to speakers which included the inquiry, "Do you wish to Rotarianize, Kiwanisize, Lionize, or otherwise yield to the importunities of service clubs or similar groups while in our midst? We're just asking you." [16] The *Main Street* drawings may have given both Wood and Mott the chance to exercise their sense of fun by saying "yes" to that question.

Wood may have asked Mott to pose for a *Main Street* illustration because there is a character named Mott in the novel. Like the real-life Mott, the character uses all three of

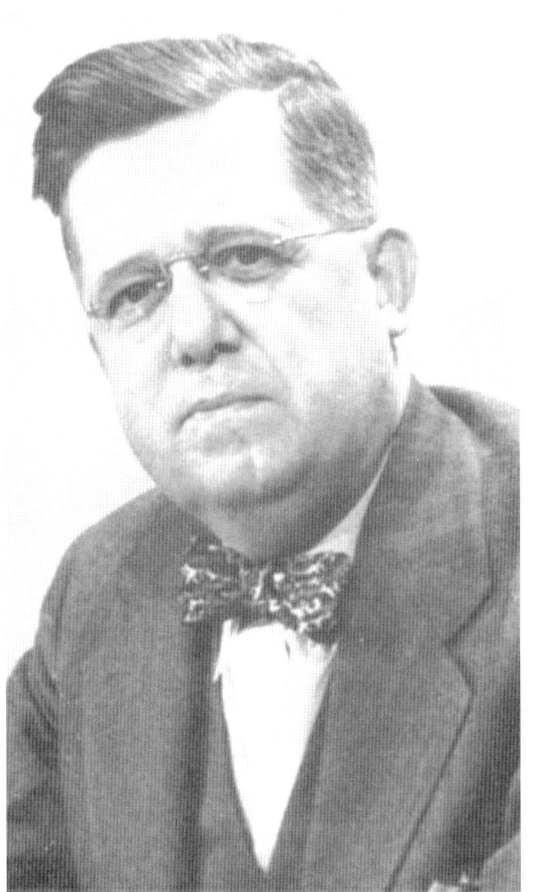

Figure 70 Frank Luther Mott. The Hawkeye, *1941*

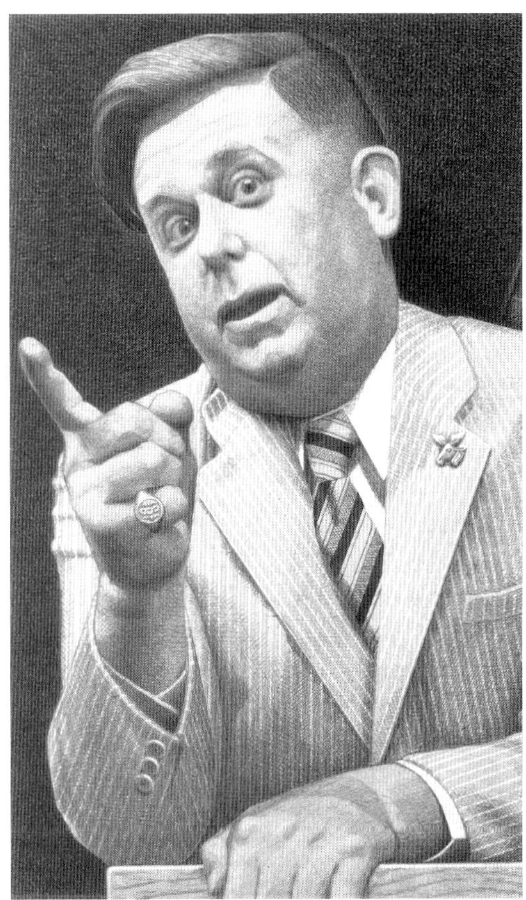

Figure 71 Booster

his names (George Edwin Mott) and he was an educator. As superintendent of the local high school, he was known around Gopher Prairie as "professor" and was considered the repository and arbiter of all matters "educational." But Carol soon discovers that he is no more progressive than his neighbors when she asks his opinion of "'the new educational systems [such as] modern kindergarten methods.'" He replies, "'Oh. Those. Most of these would-be reformers are simply notoriety-seekers. I believe in manual training, but Latin and mathematics always will be the backbone of sound Americanism, no matter what these faddists advocate — heaven knows what they do want — knitting, I suppose, and classes in wiggling the ears!'"{35} The real-life Mott was the head of a school where advertising, radio and all sorts of new media were taught — exactly the sort of educator ("would-be reformers," "notoriety-seekers," "these faddists") the Gopher Prairie Mott found irrelevant. Both Wood and his friend Mott (the real one) would have seen the comedy in the similarity of their names and the use of the journalist's features for the bombastic Honest Jim. (Figures 70-71)

The humor was acknowledged in an article that appeared in the Cedar Rapids newspaper soon after the special edition book was published. Apparently Wood had not named his model, but the community, including students and former students such as the article writer, were enjoying their recognition of one of themselves. "Over here in Cedar Rapids they are saying it is you, Dr. Frank Luther Mott, who struck the humorous pose for this picture, and those of us who studied journalism under your instruction at the University of Iowa insist that if it isn't you — then who is it?....It is a beautifully bound and illustrated volume in which you, Professor (or somebody that looks like you) appears, and all the illustrations by Mr. Wood are equally fascinating. Printed on paper of distinction, set in exquisite type, 'Main Street' merits your appearance (pardon, if we are wrong), in a Grant Wood illustrated edition. You have a place among other fine illustrations....Tell us, Dr. Mott, is it really you?" [17] If Mott, as much a Midwesterner as Wood, minded lending his face to one of the most ubiquitous, lampooned and unsympathetic icons of American provincialism, there is no record of it.

Notes: *Booster*

1. Montz, Wanda, "'Booster' — By Grant Wood; From Special Edition Of 'Main Street,'" Cedar Rapids *Gazette*, May 9, 1937.

2. My thanks to Iowa's premier clothier, Bill Reichardt, for his help in assessing and interpreting the men's clothing worn here and in *Sentimental Yearner*. The stripe in this jacket would be termed a "chalk" stripe.

3. Many people (including Midwesterners) perceive that Midwesterners tend to look "well-fed." For example, in Iowa today, there are frequent local jokes about the large numbers of overweight attendees at the yearly State Fair. Phil Stong, a contemporary of Grant Wood's and the author of the novel (and later, musical) *State Fair* took the issue more seriously, according to a 1940 article. "Iowans are not leaders in the arts, Stong says, because we are too well fed. 'A plague of health has cursed us, artistically,' he says. He thinks it possible that Grant Wood is one of the

greatest painters who ever lived; 'aside from that there is nothing much in the arts of Iowa that is likely to prove immortal, at this time.'" Montz, Wanda, "Stong's 'Hawkeyes' Scratches Iowa's Surface Here And There," Des Moines *Register*, August 18, 1940. According to this article, Wood's painting *Stone City* was reproduced on the jacket of Stong's new book. NWG Scrapbook No.2, p51C. A few years earlier, during a 1934 Midwestern trip, Christopher Morley, columnist for *The Saturday Review of Literature*, made a similar observation. "Literature's only enemy in the midland empire is those enormous meals of hot biscuit and chicken gravy. It is difficult, with such generous eating, to preserve the divine discontent which is the germ of writing. But let's forget literature for a moment and at the Montrose Coffee Shop in Cedar Rapids (where Grant Wood's murals are) try the Iowa Corn-fed Sirloin Steak." "Interpolation," *Saturday Review*, vol.XI, no. 19, November 24, 1934, 311.

4. In common American parlance today, this might be referred to as a "pinky" ring worn on the "pinky" finger. A ring worn on the "pinky" is usually not a ring of substance or significance but is simply a decorative accessory. A ring that was truly to be taken seriously, a wedding ring, for example, would seldom be designed for or worn on the pinky finger.

5. Several of these are the lodges whose signs are seen on the second story of Howland and Gould's Grocery when Carol makes her first survey of Gopher Prairie {28}. The ring on Blausser's hand has been identified as a Masonic ring, and Wood had had earlier associations with the Masons: in the mid-1920s, he produced a painting for the local Masonic chapter in Cedar Rapids. At her introduction to Dr. Kennicott's friends, just as they step off the train from their honeymoon, Carol has the impression "that all the men had coarse voices, large damp hands, toothbrush mustaches, bald spots and Masonic watch-charms."{22} Perhaps because of his own connections with the Masons, Wood did not wish to carry forward any characterizations of them that might seem negative. The Shriners are not mentioned in *Main Street*, but in 1939, Wood made a lithograph, *Shrine Quartet*, which would have meshed with Lewis's portrayal of Midwestern fraternal organizations.

6. I would like to thank Kathy Green of the Grand Lodge Office of the Des Moines Odd Fellows chapter for supplying materials on their history and symbols, including the clipping "The Odd Fellows History Corner: The Story of the Odd Fellows" by George E. Hill in the *Montana Odd Fellow* (3), a copy of the membership application which explains symbols and goals, and "Definition of Oddfellowship," *The Hawkeye Odd Fellow*. April 2003.

7. The F (Friendship) ring is white ("the strongest bond of fraternity that teaches goodwill and harmony"); the L (Love) ring is blue ("the basis for all life's ambitions, service to others and family"); and the T (Truth) ring is red ("the standard by which we value people and the foundation for our society"). Membership application. My thanks again to Ms. Green for providing excerpts from the Degree of Truth and the Third Degree in Odd Fellows ritual.

8. See the advertisement by Lehman Jewelry Company (Pittsburgh, Pennsylvania) for "Moose Buttons" in *Call of the Moose*, vol.3, no.11, May 1912, 19. Some Moose pins place the moose head within a circle. My thanks to the head of Moose Charities, Robert Zaininger, for providing this source.

9. The history and purpose of the Moose is derived from materials provided by and telephone conversation with Robert Zaininger, for whose help I am grateful.

10. Lewis could not have known when he wrote his novel in 1920 that the wartime high prices for grain and the land speculation would prompt the farming of marginal land to increase wheat profits. This kind of land could not support the forced agricultural production for long and, when in the 1930s it was exhausted from over-plowing and dried out from drought, much of the land blew away. In the Southern Plains, these conditions were so severe and long lasting that it was dubbed "the Dust Bowl." After World War I when demand declined and prices crashed,

farmers experienced an economic depression that prophesied the Great Depression of the 1930s.

11. My thanks to Matthew DeLay for his observation that Blausser achieved change quickly whereas Carol struggled for years. Her suggestions were rarely accepted or even listened seriously to and, in addition, she was resented for making them in the first place.

12. "Grant Wood's New Picture Causes Talk," Omaha *World-Herald*, November 33, 1932. NWG Scrapbook No. 1, 81.

13. Mott, Frank Luther, "The S.P.C.S.," *The Palimpsest*, vol. XLIII, no.3, March 1962, 113-132, 126. This same article was included in Mott's autobiography, *Time Enough: Essays in Autobiography*, Chapel Hill: University of North Carolina Press, 1962, Chapter 9, 132-145. His reminiscences of *The Midland* and the University of Iowa in the 1920s are in Chapter 8, 123-131.

14. The outlines of Mott's career and photographs of him may be found in the Special Collections of the University of Iowa Library and in two histories of the University: Persons, Stow, *The University of Iowa in the Twentieth Century*, Iowa City: University of Iowa Press, 1990 and in Gerber, John C., *A Pictorial History of the University of Iowa*, Iowa City: University of Iowa Press, 1988. In addition, the university yearbook, *The Hawkeye*, provides a number of photographs of Mott.

15. Mott, "The S.P.C.S.," 122.

16. Mott, 129. Perhaps it is notable that Wood and Mott did not include in this comical questionnaire any reference to the Odd Fellows or the Moose Lodge, whose insignias Wood drew in his portrait of James Blausser.

17. Montz, Cedar Rapids *Gazette*, May 9, 1937.

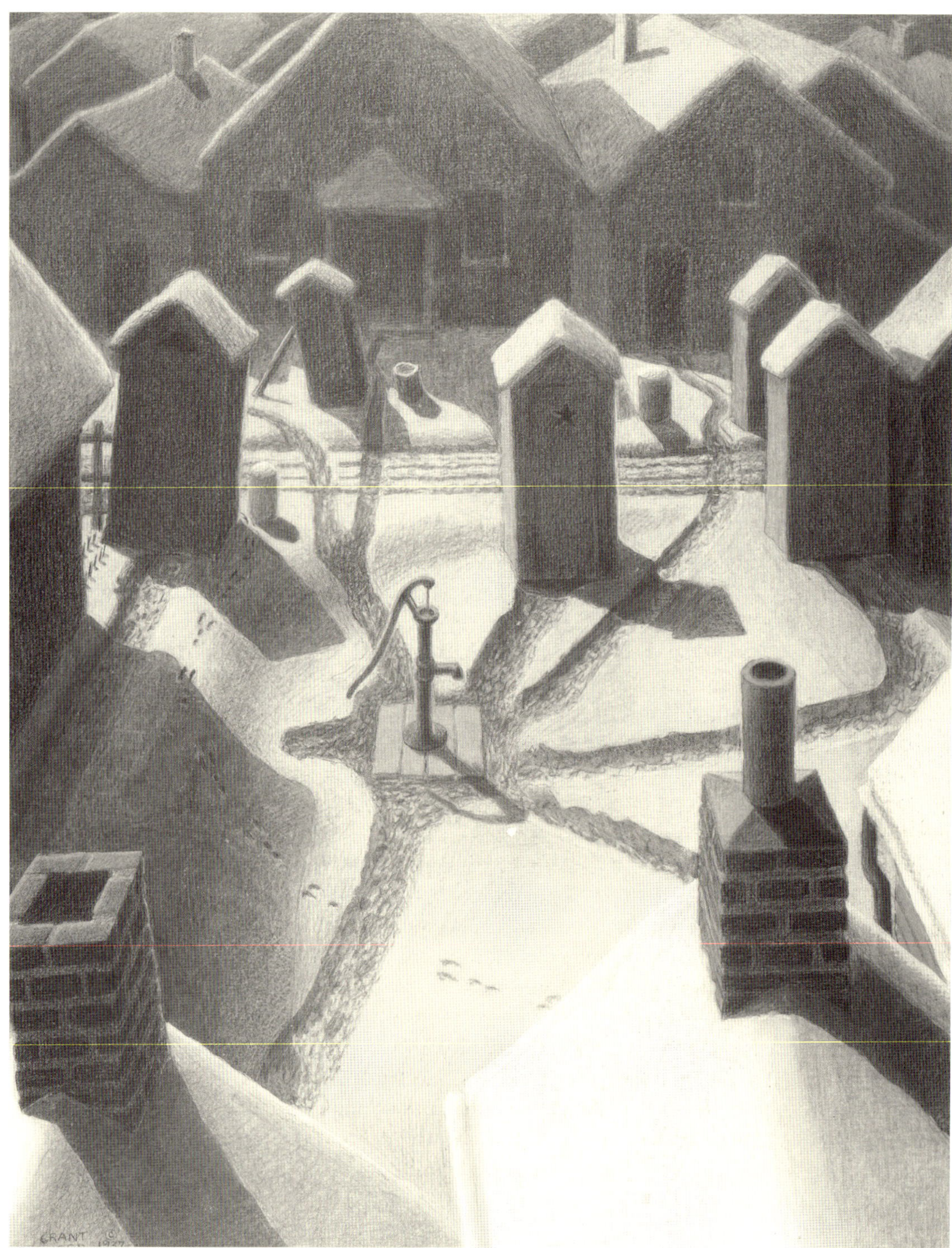

Figure 72 Village Slums

Village Slums

Architecture formed the beginning and the end of Wood's series of drawings for *Main Street*: *Main Street Mansion* is the frontispiece and *Village Slums* concludes the illustrations. We do not know for certain why the drawings were arranged as they were in the book, but in this case we assume *Village Slums* actually was the last drawing produced since it arrived three months later than the eight others. [1] It may have been simple procrastination, or it is also possible that *Village Slums* was not originally planned as part of the series or, in fact, that the idea of using architecture as a subject had not emerged until near the end of Wood's work. Having drawn *Main Street Mansion*, Wood may then have had to think a while about what an appropriate pendant image would be. This drawing has the distinction of being the only one of the series for which a sketch is currently known. (Figure 73) As mentioned earlier, there are surely other sketches and preparatory studies related to *Main Street* which remain unlocated. Wood gave this sketch (it is the same size as the finished drawings) to Park Rinard and inscribed it "Village Slums; an illustration for 'Main Street' Dedicated (though curiously inappropriate) to Park Rinard." [2] Why was it "curiously inappropriate" other than the obvious fact that Rinard was not, and presumably never would be, a slum dweller? Perhaps it reflected a joke shared between the two men. In any case, these two drawings provide an opportunity to observe something of Wood's creative process.

The *Main Street* series begins with *Main Street Mansion*, the face that Main Street presents to the world and an exemplar of the fine homes of which Gopher Prairians liked to boast. *Village Slums* (at the end of the book) is the other side of the civic coin and one for which the Main Street Mansioners have no sympathy and accept no responsibility. This part of town is invisible to most citizens and, in the novel, only Carol and her husband the doctor (and he only professionally) take much notice of it. It is home primarily to immigrants, especially the Scandinavians whom the Gopher Prairie elite refer to as "Scandahoofian clodhoppers"{73} and "Svenskas."{72}) The immigrant groups at the edge of town are further marginalized by Gopher Prairie's attitude toward them: they are ridiculed, disparaged, and poorly paid. [3] Dr. Kennicott alone voices the belief that these people will, in the next generation, take their place in a prosperous, homogenized America. The village slum, "Swede Hollow," is the first stop for the newcomers such as those seen by Carol on her walk through this part of town. "A family of recently arrived Finns were camped in an abandoned stable. A man of eighty was picking up lumps of coal along the railroad."{92} It is also the abode of any one who has not negotiated the American ladder of success or of others, like Miles Bjornstam, who have chosen to remain outside the system. Gopher Prairie prides itself on what it regards as its perfect democracy and abundant opportunity; if people find themselves in these slums, it is, they reason, their own fault. It is certainly not anything the town

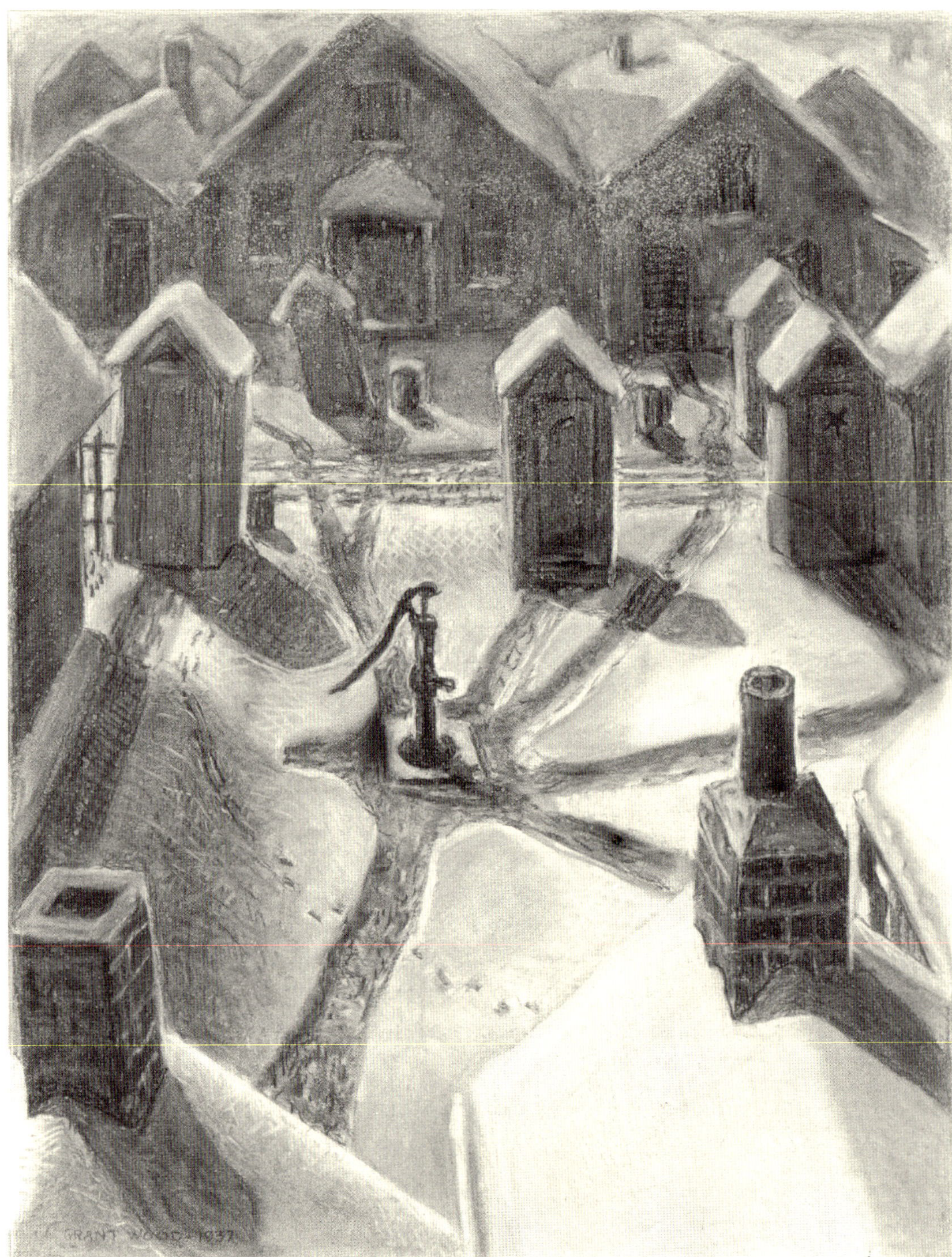

Figure 73 Study for Village Slums

should try to remedy; the slum dwellers have made their own choices. As Dr. Will Kennicott declares, "'This is an independent town....Everybody's free here to do what he wants.'"{80}

Of the subjects illustrated by Wood, this one is the least described in the book. Lewis did provide a description of the slum, but Wood's image seems to be largely his own invention. Perhaps it is based on something he saw in Cedar Rapids, Iowa City, or another small town. The focus of Wood's composition is a hand-operated water pump in the center of a common area with the snow immediately surrounding it tramped down by dozens of boots. Six major snow-packed paths radiate out like the spokes of a wheel, leading between the single water source and the numerous houses and outhouses (an outhouse, or a privy, is an outdoor toilet). Though not derived strictly from the novel, Wood's picture does capture some of the poverty and grimness of the slum as described when Carol, wife of a well-to-doctor, views the scene. Feeling lonely and isolated, she has ventured out of her "creepy" house for a walk, even though it is thirty degrees below zero.

> She circled the outskirts of the town and viewed the slum of 'Swede Hollow.' Wherever as many as three houses are gathered there will be a slum of at least one house. In Gopher Prairie, [it was] boasted, 'you don't get any of this poverty that you find in cities — always plenty of work — no need of charity — man got to be blame shiftless if he don't get ahead.' But now that the summer mask of leaves and grass was gone, Carol discovered misery and dead hope. In a shack of thin boards covered with tar-paper she saw the washerwoman, Mrs. Steinhof, working in gray steam. Outside, her six-year-old boy chopped wood. He had a torn jacket, muffler of a blue like skimmed milk. His hands were covered with red mittens through which protruded his chapped raw knuckles. He halted to blow on them, to cry disinterestedly. {92}

As Carol prepares to return to her warm, comfortable home, she encounters Miles Bjornstam, the town radical or "calamity-howler," who offers his own assessment of Swede Hollow: "'Fine mess. No sewage, no street cleaning and the Lutheran minister and the priest represent the arts and sciences.'"{93} All true: the slum is a mess, and some of the lives within it are hopeless. And, as Miles will discover, tragedy lurks in the conditions he so off-handedly describes.

But the Gopher Prairie citizens have no worry about that. As far as they are concerned, they have been far more generous than these people deserve. The ladies of the Thanatopsis Club [4] are mystified and then offended when Carol suggests that the club sponsor some programs to assist the poor: "direction in washing babies and making pleasing stews, possibly a municipal fund for home-building." What is worse, she asks that they think of these things not as charity, but as "a chance for self-help." Led by the wife of a local minister, they explain to her how misguided she is in such impulses. "'Wherever genuine poverty is encountered, it is not only *noblesse oblige* but a joy to fulfil our duty to the less fortunate ones....The Bible has laid it down for our guidance. 'The poor ye have with ye always,' which indicates that there never can be anything to these so-called scientific schemes for abolishing charity, never!....Besides, if these shiftless folks realize they're getting charity, and not something to which they have a right, they're so much more grateful.'"{115} "'Besides,'" adds the wife of the town banker, "'There isn't any real poverty here. Take that Mrs. Steinhof you speak of:...I must have sent her ten dollars worth [of washing] in the past year alone!'" These poor people are fakers and freeloaders and, the banker's wife continues, when her husband forecloses on their mortgages, it's "'the only way to make them respect the law.'"{115} When Carol then suggests that for the old clothes they give to the poor they might "'mend them first and make them as presentable as we can,'"{116} the Thanatopsis ladies have stood all they can stand. "'Heavens and earth, they have more time than we have!'" said the banker's wife. "'They ought to be mighty good and grateful to get anything, no matter what shape it's in. I know I'm not going to sit and sew for that lazy Mrs. Vopni, with all I've got to do!' ...They were glaring at Carol. She reflected that Mrs. Vopni, whose husband had been killed by a train, had ten children."{116}

In his drawing, Wood gives us no glimpses of Mrs. Steinhof, Mrs. Vopni or anyone else in "Swede Hollow." In fact, by not including any human beings, he evades the chance to make a clear political or social comment. Yet, as in the other *Main Street* drawings (and much of his art), Wood's imagery cannot be regarded as neutral. His commentary is subtle, not direct, with multiple possibilities of interpretation. This lack of directness, in fact, empowers his art when it relieves his images of specific time and situation. It makes his art intriguing to viewers beyond Wood's time and place and, just as importantly for the *Main Street* series, to those who know nothing about the novel. If the slum he portrays is not a Midwestern Hell's Kitchen, it is still a dreary place. Lives of drudgery are suggested by the dark sameness of all the houses that stretch without variety beyond the frame of the drawing, especially along the upper edge. The houses are dark, partly because it is a nighttime scene, but also because they actually would have been lit very poorly, perhaps only by oil lamps. Electric lights in homes and on streets were not consistently available in American communities of the early twentieth century, and it would not be unusual for neighborhoods like this one to have no electricity at all, even in the 1930s. Honest Jim Blausser might have been able to convince Gopher Prairie to pay for a White Way of electric lamps on Main Street, but the boosting would not have extended so far as to provide such civic amenities to Swede Hollow. [5] Wood's village slum is lit only by the moon.

The presence of the outhouses and the pump indicates there is no indoor plumbing and no running water, as was often the case in poorer sections of America in the early twentieth century. [6] For all of the houses shown and likely many others, there is only one source of water. Obviously, to deal with common human needs, the slum dwellers must endure not only a lack of privacy but also considerable discomfort (especially if we think of the weather when Carol visits the slum: it's thirty degrees below zero). Having to go outside for access to a bathroom and a water source might well provoke or prolong an illness. On a farm in the country, these conditions are inconveniences and discomforts. But in town, with this many people crowded together, the lack of sanitation facilities and clean water can be dangerous. As we regard the communal pump, used round the clock, all year long, we recall the cause of death for Miles Bjornstam's young family. Seen in this light, the proximity of the privies in this shacktown isn't so charming and half-comical any more.

We cannot be sure, however, that Wood saw this slum in such damning terms. Perhaps he saw it as a distinct little community, just not as well off as the rest of the town. He inserted no suffering widows or child laborers, but provided only a setting. It is possible that he saw some good in this place: at least it is a neighborhood and not the singular isolation of *Main Street Mansion*. The tramped down paths suggest that people congregate and have more frequent, less pretentious contact than do the merchants and professionals of Main Street. Another element suggests that his view is not completely negative. The footprints in the snow are all massed together and confined to the paths, except for the rabbit footprints that curve across the lower left quadrant of the picture. Are these rabbit tracks evidence of the trivializing illustrator that some critics thought Wood to be, or does it represent a confident, substantial artist/intellectual sure enough of himself to risk putting this anecdotal element into his composition? Is this incident in the drawing just a whimsical, sentimental touch or a metaphor of the endurance required by the slum dwellers? Is it the artist's comment on a grim existence that, in Wood's hands, still has an overlay of charm? Might this be an example of a failure to avoid the dreaded sentimentality (as described in his writing about Mark Twain)? It may be difficult at first to see bunny tracks in the snow as anything but an idle detail, but there is reason to believe Wood imbued them with a more weighty idea. Rabbit footprints are a major part of the story in two other works: his 1937 lithograph, *January* (Figure 74) (the same year *Main Street* was published) and, more substantially, in the 1940 oil painting, also entitled *January*. By the tracks in the snow, we know that the rabbit, active even in the dead of winter, has hopped into a corn shock for shelter where he is now safe, sheltered, and hidden. In a letter about *January*, Wood described his sense of the underground life that pulsed within the Iowa land: "Here in Iowa, winters are severe, Heaven knows, but even at the height of winter, one does not get the feeling of utter bleakness and desolation....it is a land of plenty...which seems to rest, rather than suffer, under the cold. In light of this, it seemed to me that nothing caught the spirit of an Iowan winter more aptly than the familiar scene of a field of corn shocks partly covered with snow. The rabbit tracks, leading into the snug shelter of the shock...are a piece of symbolism with which I had some fun." [7]

Outhouses, like rabbit tracks, are usually a visual punch line to a joke everybody gets, and putting them into a serious work of art takes a considerable risk. The prominence of

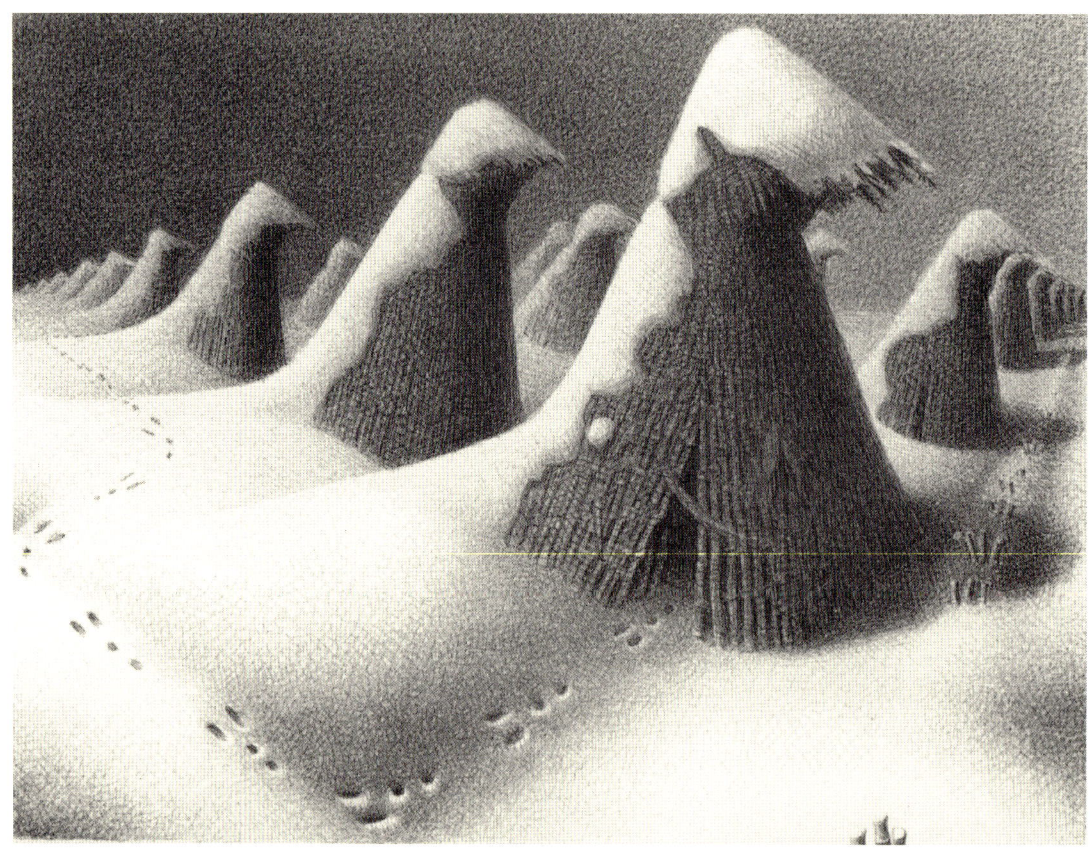

Figure 74 January, *1937, lithograph*

the outhouses in this composition may suggest a down-to-earth realism on Wood's part or might be an example of slightly irreverent humor. Outhouses are funny, especially if you don't have to use them. Across the street (or perhaps it is an alley; we do not know for sure), one of the privies is about to fall over and is propped up by a board. Assuming it is not tilted solely for compositional purposes, is this an example of the ramshackle accommodations of poverty or a joke waiting to happen? Should we laugh? Such a quandary is typical of the double-edged situations in Wood's art, and part of what keeps it intriguing.

Wood's idea of the slums may have been more in sympathy with the Ash Can School's than with Upton Sinclair's. Sinclair's novel *The Jungle* described horrendous slums and deadly working conditions for the poor in the Midwest of the early twentieth century. [8] Around the same time, Robert Henri, George Luks and other Ash Can School painters saw vitality and a shared humanity in these same urban, largely immigrant underclasses. Paintings like George Luks's *The Spielers* looked at these hearty people as poor only in material things, not in spirit. John Sloan's *Backyards, Greenwich Village* depicted a slum neighborhood in the snow, just as Wood's *Village Slums* does, but in both cases, they are not really desolate or hopeless. They may not be crowded with people, but a sense of life infuses both scenes. A British art magazine admired Wood's ability to transform a "sordid" place through his art. "Grant Wood's very expressive drawing of *Village Slums* tells dramatically one of the many tragic tales of discomfort which such conditions impose. He has made something beautiful out of the snow and moonlight which shroud a sordid subject." [9]

Wood was not a social realist nor is he known to have ever made a public political statement. There are reasons to believe he was a Democrat (his participation in liberal New Deal programs like the PWAP, for example), but politics seems to have interested him little. It has long been noted that his art fails to acknowledge the Great Depression of the 1930s, despite the fact that Iowa, like the rest of the country, was devastated by the economic catastrophe. Much of the rural population was driven into poverty by low agricultural prices and the loss of their farms, but Wood never reflected that in his work. [10] Instead, most of his art exudes contentment and confidence, celebrating a peaceful, prosperous way of life and hardworking, ordinary people. He occasionally makes fun of certain types of people, but he is not savage about it, and the worst fate of his targets is ridicule. His own life was not always easy, and his personal affairs were often in disarray, but he did not take despair or ruin as subjects for his art. In choosing the small town slums of Gopher Prairie as one of his illustrations, Wood could have unleashed a tirade against the injustice, poverty, avarice, cruelty and outright crime that characterized human events in the 1930s. Swede Hollow could have been a microcosm of all that was wrong with the world, but Wood declined to see hopelessness. Even in a darkened world, the moonlight still shines on the snow.

The overall effect of *Village Slums* is that of community, albeit one with deprivations. All of the other drawings, except one, focus on a single subject, either a person or, in *Main Street Mansion*, a house. Though they are intended largely as character types, the people of the drawings are nevertheless distinct individuals whom one could recognize (as their models *were* recognized). There can be no such recognition in the abandoned anonymity of *Village Slums* nor in the drawing with which it has the most affinities, both as narrative and as composition: *General Practitioner*. (Figures 75-76) Two people are involved in the "story" of *General Practitioner*, but neither are rendered as recognizable individuals; we see only their hands and arms and a bit of the torso of the doctor. As Corn and Dennis have both pointed out, the character with which Wood had the most sympathy is Dr. Will Kennicott. He is one of the few Gopher Prairie citizens who actually does any good and who has the most consistent, intimate contact with all of the community. He is the doctor for everyone from the banker's wife to the immigrant farmer. The novel often details the difficulties of attending to the ill or injured on the farms surrounding the town, which the doctor unfailing does, sometimes at the risk of his own life. He does not hesitate to go among the sick at every level of society, as he does for the wife (formerly the immigrant maid in his own household) and child of Miles Bjornstam. He is integrated into the fabric of the town's life in a way that his wife and his friends are not. Wood's compositions for the two drawings reinforce the association between them. Both *General Practitioner* and *Village Slums* are drawn from a downward angle, in contrast to *Main Street Mansion* and all the other images in which we look upward. Both compositions have elements that radiate outward like the spokes of a wheel and both have areas of emptiness. At the same time, both have subtle grid-like elements in the horizontal/vertical design of the huddled slum houses and the even pattern of the bed quilt. Finally, both drawings are set at night, with the light falling at a high overhead angle.

By placing *Village Slums* as the last illustration after using *Main Street Mansion* as its frontispiece, the special edition encourages a comparison of these two scenes. (Figures 77-78) The drawings represent not just architectural polarities, but societal ones as well, expressed partly through compositional devices. The overall conclusion of such a comparison is the singular individuality of the massive house against the community of the multiple dwellings. As discussed above, *Village Slums* can be read as an image of community. The ignoble commonality of the water pump and the compromised privacy of the outhouses, though not desirable, do create an increased awareness of one's fellow humans; though not always pleasant, community is unavoidable. In terms of visual perspective, the downward angle of the view intimates a gathering or collecting of forces, not a dispersal, and Wood's emphasis is less on the houses than on the gathering place at the pump. In contrast to this composition, the forceful upward thrust, sharp angles, and darkened entrance of *Main Street Mansion* do not invite us in. But the house is nevertheless a testament to success and to the material comfort a person can gain. It also represents the status that each individual craves whether in Gopher Prairie or Paris. It is a formidable structure that can symbolize stability, protection and a differentiation not possible in the crowded sameness of a slum. Such buildings can even inspire awe, as Bea Sorenson, the Scandinavian farm girl, was awed on her first walk through Gopher Prairie. Had she survived, her husband, the radical Miles

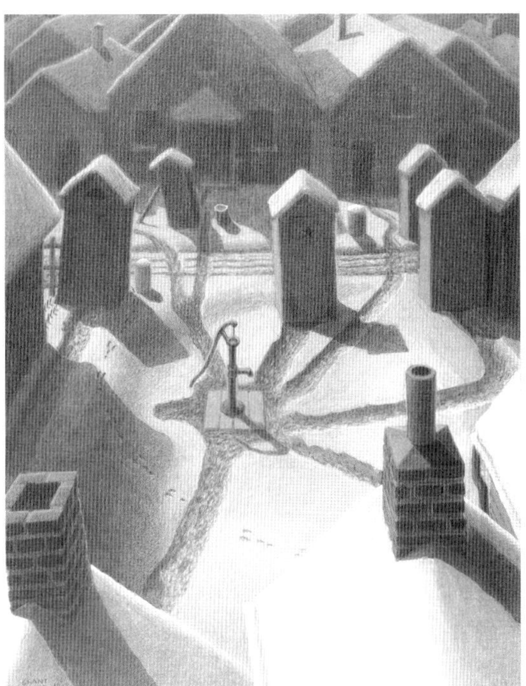

Figure 75 Village Slums

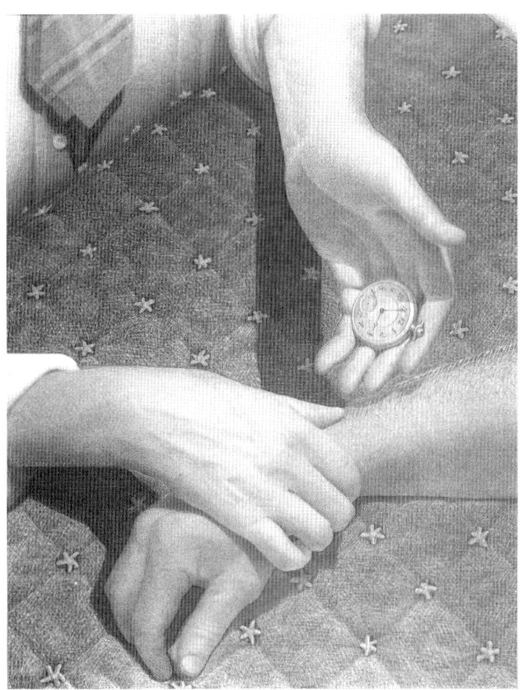

Figure 76 General Practitioner

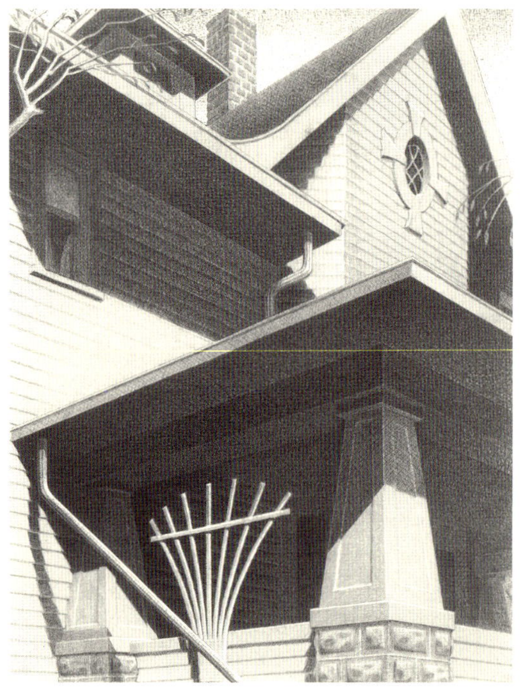
Figure 77 Main Street Mansion

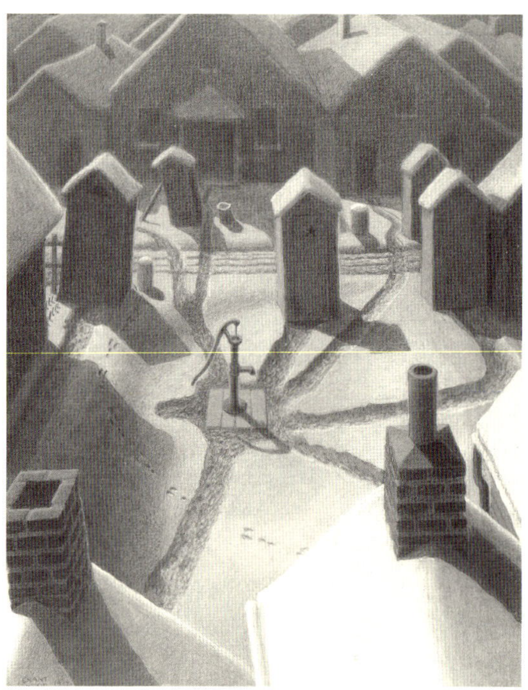
Figure 78 Village Slums

Bjornstam, would have aspired to put her in such a house and to send their son to a prestigious school in the East.

With its sharp upward angle, its filling of the frame, and its overall sense of authority (even if it is just the little town of Gopher Prairie), the imposing Main Street house suggests an absolutism that contrasts with the egalitarian composition of *Village Slums*. Its wheel-like design with the "spokes" of community paths suggests a societal structure of greater openness and mobility than that represented by *Main Street Mansion*. As pointed out earlier, Wood's view of the slums has more in common with the Ash Can School of the 1910s and 1920s than with 1930s Social Realism. His picture has little in common with other Depression era images of similar subjects, such as those by Reginald Marsh, Alexander Brook or Farm Security Administration documentary photographers (Dorothea Lange, Walker Evans, and Jack Delano, for example). *Village Slums*, for all its material deprivations, does represent a democracy in which the Finns must share with the Swedes and the Norwegians must mingle with the Yankees. No one person or group is better (or worse) than the next, and equality — even if it is equal poverty — is a constant. Wood's picture, with its radiating composition, does not suggest a sinkhole of unrelenting, futile struggle, but a neighborhood. Like the rest of his work, this picture is without complete despair or hopelessness. Opportunity is not abundant in Wood's slums, but it is not entirely lacking either, suggesting an agreement with both Dr. Kennicott and Bjornstam when, in several instances in the novel, they express confidence about the future success of the next generation. If everyone in Wood's slum lives in the same depressed conditions, at least everyone has the same incentive for rising in society — and there's nowhere to go but up.[11]

For decades, *Village Slums* was unlocated and was not included in exhibitions or studies of Wood's art. There is no record of it in the literature after 1937. When George Macy's edition of *Main Street* was reprinted by the Easton Press in 1965, *Village Slums* was no longer among the illustrations. Although there were very clear differences between the Rinard sketch and the reproduction in Macy's original edition, the Rinard sketch had replaced the finished drawing in exhibitions and publications; it was the only known image of *Village Slums*. Recently, however, Wood's final drawing of *Village Slums* has emerged to join the other *Main Street* drawings, making it possible to reunite the entire series.[12] It shares with all the drawings an intricate, detailed complexity of technique. Like the others, it is richly colored by layers of marks that create depth and a mysterious sense of light. Carried out on brown kraft paper, Wood again uses that middle tone to move into darks and lights that, without pigment other than black and white, achieve a remarkable and evocative chromatic range.

The Smithsonian sketch shows both the exactness of Wood's compositional planning and the flexibility that he left for himself as he moved toward the final version. The rabbit tracks are one example of this process. As expected, these elements do not possess the tonal richness of the finished drawing and are broadly drawn without the detailing and clarity found elsewhere in his work. The paths rendered so precisely that we can almost perceive individual footprints in the book illustration and the drawing are, in the sketch, broad marks made with a piece, not a pencil, of charcoal or may actually be brushed. The rabbit tracks that are clear in the finished drawing are so broadly indicated in the Smithsonian sketch that they cannot be identified as rabbit tracks at all and, in fact, could be human footprints.

Charcoal, not crayon, is the primary medium, along with a few incidences of a silvery graphite and areas that seem to be a wash of some sort. Chalk is also listed among the media. The condition of the sketch is an issue in its appearance today, including an area of apparent damage. A crescent-shaped gouge arcing across the bottom front of the outhouse on the extreme right appears to be filled in with graphite. In addition, graphite is placed in various sections along the edges of the drawing, particularly at the upper right and along the left edge almost as if it were an attempt to "fill in" the edges. These graphite marks have the effect of additions to the original, and it is not clear if they are the work of the artist or someone else. The support of the Smithsonian *Village Slums* is not the brown kraft paper of the other drawings, but paperboard. Its yellow-brown color thus is largely the result of the inherent instability of this material that has created discoloration and deterioration. A broad stain runs along the upper right margin (not seen when the drawing is in its frame) and it retains a slightly soiled appearance.

The upper area of the sketch where the rooftops recede is shadowy and faintly drawn, with some sections covered by a wash that appears water splashed or finely bubbled. Especially well noted on the facade of the houses is a grainy texture in which the paper surface can be seen and which seems to have been created either by lifting out the medium with something absorbent or by a drying process. The paper surface does not appear to have been revealed through loss of the medium (it is not clear what exactly the medium is in these areas) although there is reason to believe exposure to high light levels may have faded and deteriorated the overall image. Using many broad, spontaneous-looking marks, the artist has rendered the forms here with dozens of short, layered marks that build up form in the nine finished drawings. Some crosshatching is present, but it is executed with thick lines, fairly few in number, and is created, apparently, by lifting out pigment with an eraser or possibly a stump. It seems, then, that this sketch represents Wood's finalizing of decisions about the composition and is only a brief rehearsal for the intricacy of the marks found in the finished drawing. The sketch is signed in Wood's characteristic block letters, but, unlike other *Main Street* drawings, this one does not contain the copyright sign unfailingly placed in his other major works. He was scrupulous about copyright by this time in his career, so it is clear that this work was not intended for publication (or sale, at least for the foreseeable future).

Wood was exacting about the matting and framing of his pieces and *Main Street* was no different, especially since these were the first drawings he planned to present as finished works, intended to "stand on their own feet as individual pictures." [13] As discussed earlier, he wanted to reconsider the framing of the entire series after a portion of them had been framed "hurriedly" in order to get them into an exhibition at the Art Institute of Chicago. He planned to bring all of the drawings back to Iowa City and check them before pricing them and releasing them to his dealer. [14] *Village Slums* is the only drawing that appears to retain the artist's original matting and framing. In addition to his signature, date and copyright symbol (at the lower left of the picture), Wood also inscribed along the upper edge of the brown paper on the back of the matte: "'Village Slums' / an illustration for Main Street / by / Grant Wood"; (he then added another signature and copyright symbol). On the lower edge of the matte, where it could easily be seen, he block-lettered the title, "VILLAGE SLUMS."

Notes: *Village Slums*

1. Dennis, James M., *Grant Wood: A Study in Art and Culture*, Columbia: University of Missouri Press, 1986, 239, n.21. This drawing is the only one of the *Main Street* series with a copyright date of 1937 inscribed on it.

2. The sketch remained in Rinard's collection until it was given to the Smithsonian American Art Museum in 1991. During those years, the drawing often hung in the Iowa congressional offices in Washington D.C., where Rinard worked in several capacities.

3. One of Carol Kennicott's first offenses against the women of Gopher Prairie was the fact that she paid her maid $6.00 a week. "They gasped....'Don't you think it's hard on the rest of us when you pay so much?'" {73}

4. "Thanatopsis" is a meditation on death; it is also the title of a well-known poem by the nineteenth century American poet, William Cullen Bryant.

5. Many areas of the country, especially in rural sections, did not have electricity until well into the 1940s. The New Deal agency, Rural Electrification Administration (REA), made a major change in rural America, not only because of improvements in farming itself, but in the everyday comfort of life on the farm.

6. The musical, *Oklahoma*, a hit on Broadway during World War II and based on the novel *Green Grow the Lilacs* by Lynn Riggs, includes the song *Everythin's Up To Date in Kansas City* in which the Oklahoma cowboys sing their astonishment at the modern advances they've seen in Kansas City: "With every sort of comfort ev'ry house is all complete; You c'n walk to privies in the rain and never wet your feet!" *Oklahoma!* Music by Richard Rodgers, book and lyrics by Oscar Hammerstein II, New York: Williamson Music, Inc., 1943. (The musical was first performed March 31, 1943.) The period of this play is just a little earlier (c.1907) than *Main Street*, but both stories occur when small town America was adapting to modernity. Lynn Riggs was one of the regional writers Wood praised in *Revolt Against the City*.

7. Letter from Grant Wood to King Vidor, April 26, 1941. Quoted in Dennis, *Grant Wood*, 202. In the Smithsonian sketch, these tracks that angle off beyond the paths tracked down by the slum dwellers cannot, in fact, be identified as rabbit tracks. Though placed in the sketch's composition where they would appear in the final drawing, they are very broadly drawn, looking more like human footprints than those of an animal. Possibly Wood decided to make them into identifiable rabbit tracks later in his drawing process.

8. Upton Sinclair, author of *The Jungle*, met Sinclair Lewis as a college student when he worked as a janitor at Sinclair's utopian colony in upstate New York. The two men, because of the similarity in their names, were often confused by the public.

9. "Grant Wood: Brilliant Painter of the Mid-Western Scene," *The London Studio*, February 1938, 88-93; reproduced on 91; NWG Scrapbook No. 4, 4.

10. Some of the Iowa artists who had worked with him at Stone City or in the PWAP, such as John Bloom, Helen Henrichsen and Harry Donald Jones, did integrate Depression subject matter into their work.

11. Wood's undespairing interpretation of the slums and his democratizing composition may also recall his earlier faith in cooperative movements. Such ideas were important, especially in the first half of the 1930s around the time Wood was organizing his own cooperative project at the University of Iowa under the Public Works of Art Project. In another example (and one Wood knew about), a group of Iowa artists had banded together in 1933 to form the Iowa Cooperative Artists (sometimes known as the Iowa Cooperative Mural Painters) with the partial purpose of soliciting mural projects from the New Deal art agencies. In this goal, they had some success, largely through the efforts of Edward Rowan who had been a former director of the Little Gallery in Cedar Rapids and had gone to Washington to help set up and then administer New Deal art projects in 1933. A group of four Iowa artists, led by Francis Robert White, received the commission through the Treasury Relief Art Project for a large mural cycle on the four walls of the Federal Court House in Cedar Rapids. (The murals have been painted over, but can be studied from old photographs.) Wood was not part of the Iowa Cooperative Artists, but he knew all of the members and, judging from his comments praising cooperative methods, agreed with their goals. By 1935, however, there seems to have been a break between Wood and some of the other Iowa artists, and after that time, he seldom commented on cooperative movements. The rift is most clearly indicated by his refusal to accept leadership (or even participate) in any New Deal programs after the PWAP ended, a decision that was provoked by a letter of protest sent by some of his PWAP artists to Washington complaining about his control of the Project and the lack of individual opportunities for painting. Even though he was estranged from some artists in Iowa and no longer wished to be involved himself in cooperative art projects, the theoretical concept of cooperative endeavors may have still been acceptable to him.

12. I am greatful to Roger Howlett of the Childs Gallery for contacting me about the final drawing for *Village Slums* and informing me of its provenance and to Joann Moser of the Smithsonian American Art Museum for informing the gallery about my reasearch. I am especially grateful to the late Vance Jordan, Carol Irish and Kendall Scully of Vance Jordan Fine Arts for further cooperation in researching the drawing and for contributing it to the exhibition.

13. Letter from Wood to Maynard Walker, October 21, 1935. AAA, Maynard Walker files, reel 2025, frame 987.

14. To his dealer in New York, Wood wrote from Iowa City, "Framing and matting of these drawings had to be done hurriedly at Donnelleys, and I am not very well satisfied with the results. As the unframed drawings have to be returned here to be framed and matted, anyway, I am having the ones at the Art Institute returned here too for checking. I want to see them all together and satisfactorily framed before giving you my ideas on prices for them." Wood to Walker, March 11, 1937. AAA, Maynard Walker files, reel 2025, from 1005.

Judging from the time and effort he expended on his *Main Street* drawings, Wood must have hoped that they would be looked at as seriously as his paintings had been. Taken together, the series encapsulated his philosophy (with all its conflicts) as well as any other single work of art and, in addition, it showcased his abilities as a draftsman in a way no other work had done. It was not common at that time for American artists to offer a series of drawings as an achievement equal to a painting or a sculpture, but Wood was clear that the *Main Street* illustrations were to be seen as finished, independent, and significant works of art. The drawings were not as well received as he had hoped; they did not sell as a nine-part unit, and the individual drawings were dispersed in a piecemeal fashion. As pointed out earlier, they were not highly regarded for many years, and several of them disappeared from sight for a time. Reunited, the series can now be newly assessed not only as works of art, but as an expression of Wood's ideas and feelings about *Main Street*, the novel, and about the Midwestern Main Street that he carried in his intellect and his heart.

When Grant Wood drew his version of *Main Street*, it was well over a decade since the novel had been published in 1920 and, despite his admiration for the novel and Sinclair Lewis, he could not completely identify with Lewis's dislike of the small Midwestern town of Gopher Prairie. Though Wood had his conflicts about those kinds of places too, he had embraced his roots and become an advocate for their way of life. Faced with the prospects of illustrating a book whose premise he disagreed with in many regards, he took the artistic risk of creating his own Main Street. In an assertion of his authority as an artist, backed perhaps by his own literary instincts, he chose his subjects and then interpreted them according to his own feelings and convictions. He tended to depict the characters as Gopher Prairie saw them, sidestepping the criticisms that Lewis had integrated into his text. Those people whom the town had valued were the same ones that Wood valued: Dr. Kennicott *(General Practitioner)*, for example. Those they had found ineffectual and a little silly, Wood gently ridiculed: Raymond Wutherspoon *(Sentimental Yearner)*. If Gopher Prairie liked Honest Jim Blausser *(Booster)* even if he was an opportunistic blowhard, Wood presented him in his most hopeful, persuasive guise. And those that the villagers disliked were the ones Wood treated more harshly. Despite the nuances of their characters and the frustrations in their lives (things that Wood could have certainly understood), he treated Carol Kennicott *(The Perfectionist)* and the Red Swede *(The Radical)* in his illustrations the same way Gopher Prairie did in the story. In the end, his *Main Street* drawings seem to place Wood on Gopher Prairie's side.

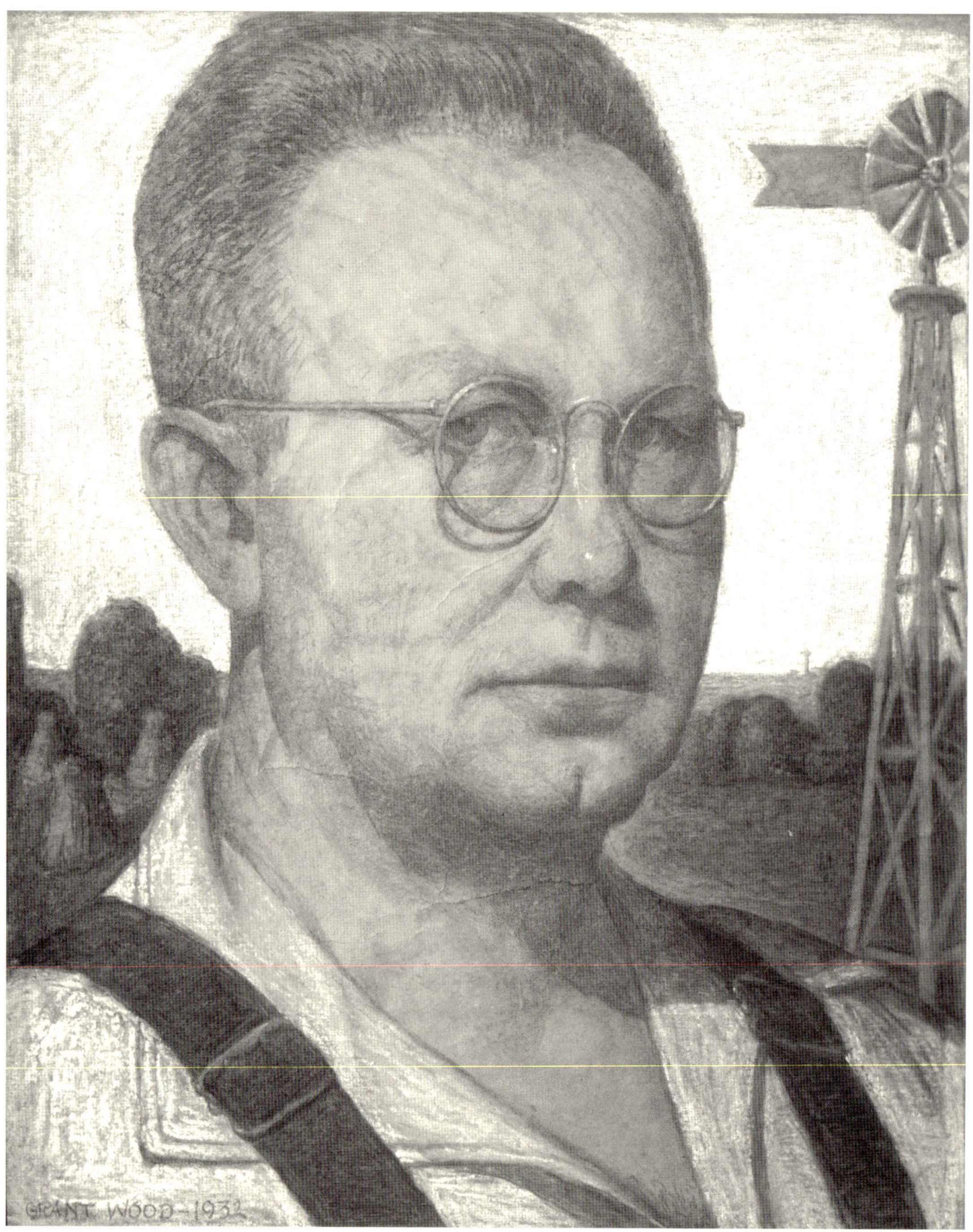

Figure 79 Study for Self-Portrait, *1932*

Chapter 7
Self-Portraits as Midwesterner

Six of the nine *Main Street* illustrations are portraits, and portraiture was an important part of Wood's art, a genre for which he displayed a distinct ability. Even when his portraits are intended to represent a type or a character in a narrative, as in *Main Street* or *American Gothic*, Wood depicts the subject in a way that encourages us to speculate on the person shown. As we have seen, much can be derived from clothing, objects, poses, and other factors in his portraits; nearly everything is something the artist can use to teach us about this specific individual and about human nature. As the *Main Street* portraits have shown, the artist is not restricted to only the facial features in his "story" of the person he is portraying. If his own self-portraits are viewed as the *Main Street* drawings have been, what can we learn about Grant Wood?

Wood created two major self-portraits, and both exist in more than one version. The *Study for Self-Portrait* (Figure 79) is a drawing in chalk and pencil from 1932, created for a competition sponsored by the Iowa Federation of Women's Clubs. [1] He portrays himself as the quintessential Iowan: dressed in overalls, lush landscape in the background, windmill, and most of all, a sober expression befitting a hardworking, salt-of-the-earth son of Iowa. [2] It is similar to the unsmiling visage of the *American Gothic* woman, for whom his sister modeled. He is serious about himself, and he intends that he shall be taken seriously by anyone who sees him. Just because he is a Midwesterner — a citizen of the heartland cornfields — does not mean he will allow himself to be taken for any less substantial a person. He is as grounded and steadfast as the land around him, glaring out at us as if daring someone to call him a hick.

Around this time, Wood was formulating his Regionalist philosophy and adjusting to the fame that washed over him only two years previously as a result of *American Gothic*. He had already endured condescending commentary about his art, and even those who wrote of him sympathetically seemed to regard him as an oddity. An artist from Iowa who not only failed to regret his Midwestern parentage, but who was actually pleased about it? This *was* unusual, and Sinclair Lewis, Sherwood Anderson, Edgar Lee Masters, and a host of other writers had not prepared the artistic and intellectual world for Wood's defiance. He was the first visual artist of Iowa to have a national reputation and one of the very few artists well known outside his region (and outside the United States) who willingly lived in the Midwest. Not until he persuaded Benton and Curry to join him did he have any rivals for national attention. In 1932, however, he scarcely knew these other two artists who were both still on the East Coast, and he alone was carrying the Regionalist banner on his overalled shoulders. Because it was drawn for an Iowa competition, he may have wished his portrait to appeal to his audience (and the jury). On the other hand, he was certainly aware that anything from his hand might well receive national exposure, and therefore the drawing might have presented an opportunity to "take his stand" as an unapologetic Midwesterner, declaring himself to any doubters. He wasn't a farmer, but he would don a costume that, as far as anyone outside the Midwest was concerned (especially those from the East), was shorthand for "I'm from the country," with all that that implied: hard work, long hours, fortitude, and endurance, but also lack of sophistication, backwardness, and zero cultural awareness. [3] Flaunting the false assumptions of the urban and Eastern critics, it is almost as if Wood is admitting he is a hay seed and asking, "So?" Overalls are not known to have been a constant in his wardrobe until the early 1930s, so his adoption of farmer apparel can surely be seen as a symbolic message to the world that "hay seeds" were about to have their day.

The other major symbol in *Study for Self-Portrait* is the windmill. Windmills were ubiquitous in rural and small town America, and artists of the 1930s frequently used them to confirm the rural setting of their paintings. Alexandre Hogue, Joe Jones, William Palmer, and other artists known for their scenes of the countryside (often a countryside devastated by environmental and economic disasters) placed windmills in their compositions with regularity. Wood's windmill is here for much the same reason: to locate his environment. But for him, it goes further than just background, as Wanda Corn asserted, "The windmill stands to one side of his head, like a billboard advertising the artist's allegiance to the Midwestern rural landscape. In Wood's other paintings of country life...the windmill is less obvious, but it is *always* there....Like a watchful eye, making sure that all is in order, it was the artist's covert signature." [4] In the hands of an artist like Alexandre Hogue, the windmill is part of the social comment on the ruination and desertion of the land, and we can sense the artist's distress or even anger over that situation. Typically, Wood hasn't any anger in that regard. For him, the windmill is a reminder of a stable, comfortable, worthwhile way of life. It represents his well-known nostalgia for an idealized rural past and an America that is ingenious and resourceful. His Midwestern windmills are like the anchors that were carved in the stone doorways of Waubeek, the little Iowa village settled by New Englanders: they were objects that held fast a culture and a heritage that, in the worst days of the Depression, seemed to be drifting.

Later on, Wood developed his drawing into an oil painting (Figure 36). He kept the windmill, but took out the trees so that the landscape behind him became less typical of eastern Iowa, but the composition gained in clarity and focus. More importantly, he eliminated the overall straps and presented himself in a dark shirt of the sort he more commonly wore. [5] He felt that the straps were "compositionally awkward and drew attention away from his face." [6] Aside from the effect on the composition, his changed attire neutralized the interpretation of the Regionalist artist and made his Midwestern identification less aggressive and doctrinaire. The painted self-portrait remained in Wood's possession until his death and is generally regarded as unfinished. The lower section was never resolved, and Wood obviously intended to keep working on it. Along with his signature and the date, he added the work "sketch."

Wood's second self-portrait, *Return from Bohemia* is a more complicated image. Again, he produced two versions (the exhibition drawing is from the collection of the Curtis Galleries; the other is owned by the Davenport Museum of Art), but in this case, they are nearly identical and it is not known which was produced first or why there are two of them. Neither are preparatory studies, but are, like the *Main Street* drawings, independent works of art. *Return from Bohemia*, as both drawings are titled, was the image Wood planned as the primary "illustration" for his autobiography of the same name. This book, as already discussed, was never completed, and only the first section, covering Wood's childhood, was written. It is believed that it is primarily the work of Wood's secretary and friend, Park Rinard (who submitted it as his Masters' thesis at the University of Iowa), but the exact proportion of authorship is not actually known. In *Study for Self-Portrait*, the artist's relationship to society is implied by his facial expression and his surroundings; here, it is explicated far more specifically. Wood's comment on the image comes from early in his mature career, not long after he had rejected European modernism and had achieved fame with *American Gothic*. For the Cedar Rapids newspaper, Wood announced his plan for his self-portrait. "The background will be the usual loafing by-standers who find time to watch an artist sketching faces with contempt, scorn and an I-know-I-could-do-it-better look." [7]

Where had Wood encountered such a situation? In Cedar Rapids? Was it an experience he had had since childhood, sketching around his home? Had it happened while he was teaching art in the public schools or when he painted murals for hotels around the state? Most of his paintings before 1930 were outdoor scenes where "loafing bystanders" could have had access to him while he was sketching or painting. Almost all of his European work was also of outdoor scenes that he had surely sketched or painted in public. This statement about "bystanders" is one of the most antagonistic of his career. Does it perhaps relate to the controversy surrounding his stained glass windows for the Veterans Memorial Building, the only known instance in which Wood came into direct and open conflict with his patronage? As already suggested, Wood seemed to have a high level of acceptance in Cedar Rapids and was well enough supported by the community that he could make his living as an artist-decorator. The mortuary owner, David Turner, even provided a home and studio for Wood. As a young man, he had sought to make his way out of Cedar Rapids (sojourns in Minneapolis, Chicago and Europe), but by the 1930s, he seems to have recon-

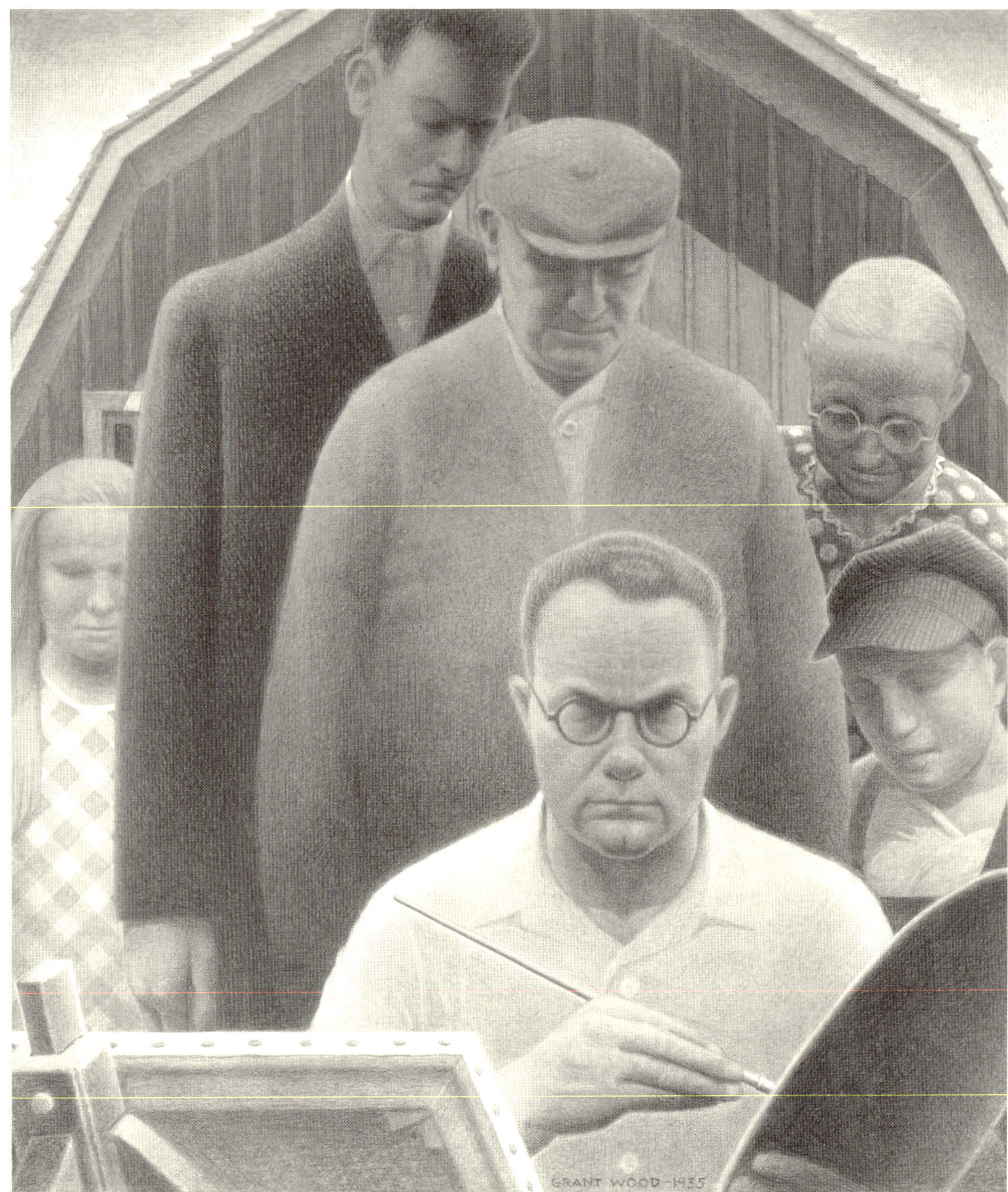

Figure 80 Return from Bohemia, *1935*

ciled those feelings and formed an attachment to his native home.

Throughout his career, Wood occasionally expressed exasperation with the public's reception of his art (notably *American Gothic* and *Dinner for Threshers*), and anyone who spent much time with him realized he was neither a rube nor an innocent. Yet, in a knowing sort of way, he sometimes promoted the perception of himself as a provincial *savant*. In some of his public pronouncements, Wood took a lighthearted approach. He even seemed at times to tailor his remarks to the catchy comment that would read well in a headline as when, for instance, he talked about his best ideas coming to him when he milked a cow. But his congeniality only went so far, as became increasingly apparent as his career went on.

The critic, Thomas Craven, is often thought of as a chauvinistic supporter of Regionalism who saw America's artistic salvation in the work of Benton, Curry and Wood. Yet his commentary on Wood included some of the most frank — and not always flattering — assessments of the artist. In 1935, as Wood was consolidating his position as a heartland Regionalist and was the subject of a considerable amount of inflated publicity, Craven presented a balanced account of the artist. "Wood has been presented as a Horatio Alger hero. He is nothing of the sort. It is true that he discovered his original self somewhat suddenly after years of trial and error, but his bland smile and cherubic face are misleading. He is one of the most deliberate, calculating and intelligent men in the business of art, and of living. He is a born craftsman, a schemer and a worker, an odd compound of small-town shrewdness and amiability, of Rotarian good-fellowship and genius of a rare order — a genius for making pictures and making friends. If he had failed in his major aspirations, I do not think he would have died of grief; he is too capable and level-headed to mope over unattainable desires." [8] In a 1937 biographical article, he discussed that aspect of Wood's career that was probably the source for *Return from Bohemia*: his feelings during the 1920s when he was struggling to become an artist. Admitting that Wood was "at home among his own people, at one with them in their moral code and daily behavior," Craven nevertheless affirmed the difficulty of being an artist (and an ambitious one) in the midst of his hometown community. Frustrated by poverty, Wood had to put off trips to Europe until he could save enough money. Then, having gone to Europe to develop not only skill, but confidence in himself as an artist, he returned home to face the reality of hometown opinion. "At home he was not regarded as an artist — he was no different from anyone else — just a good-natured fellow with a knack for drawing and using his hands. Thus he was moved to revolt against his people....Influenced by Mencken, who at that time was hilariously drubbing the yokels of the Bible Belt and the cornhuskers of the Middle West, Wood revolted against the Babbittry of his people, their arrogance and the indifference to the refinements of the spirit." [9] The rest of Craven's account reports how Wood overcame those feelings, found beauty in his surroundings, and developed into an honest and accomplished artist. But those feelings from his early days were ingrained into his personality, it seems, and from time to time, they resurfaced.

In his drawing, Wood places himself in the center foreground; obviously the drawing is about him, even though there are five other people in the picture. He is doing something while the others are idle, as befits "bystanders" who watch while other people take action and accept risks. In his comment about their "contempt," Wood seemed to credit them with at least some low-level engagement. In his drawing, however, they hardly seem aware of him: in fact, they look like they are asleep. (Surely they are not praying.) Their faces hold very little expression; they are not responding to the artist at all. Only the elderly woman registers anything on her face, and it is nothing more than a benign smile that could suggest blandness, pleasant incomprehension, or senility. They all look in his direction, but their eyes seem closed. They "seem" closed, but even of this we cannot be sure since the eyes look incomplete. It would be tempting to propose that the drawing is unfinished but both drawings have this same, undetailed property. It cannot be accidental, or else Wood was at an artistic impasse unparalleled in his career. In a drawing as detailed and deliberate as this, the rendering of the eyes must be intentional. Why has Wood depicted his viewers in this way? One conclusion to be drawn is that for Wood, these fellow citizens not only do not "see" him, they are *incapable* of seeing him, of understanding him and his art. He has placed himself in their midst; he has accepted his native culture. He is not in some dark Parisian garret or an ivory tower; he is right there in the open, in front of a barn. There is no beret or Bohemian beard or flamboyant clothing or any other clichéd accoutrement to suggest an artist who separates himself from his fellows and embraces alienation. Yet, they still do not respond. In the history of artists' self-portraits, this image is among the most despairing.

Wood's treatment of his own eyes is also inconclusive. Partly obscured by his glasses, it is not clear where exactly he is looking, but his head is up and his hands are active. A brush in one hand and his palette in the other, his canvas is clearly in place in front of him; he is working. [10] His solemn features, along with his veiled eyes, signal his absorption in his mission as an artist. The lift of his head and the slight indication of his open eyes suggest some acknowledgment of us, the current spectators, but it is not a welcoming attitude. As in the *Study for Self-Portrait*, Wood makes no pretense of neighborliness. His vision is directed not toward us, but into himself. It is as if, in this instance, he is following the instruction of the German Romantic painter Caspar David Friedrich, who advised artists to "shut your corporeal eye" so that they could concentrate on and draw strength from their inner vision. [11] As pointed out earlier, this drawing is not really about the people in back of him or the people in front of him; it is about Wood, himself. With his back to the others and his compromised notice of us, he underscores his realization of his aloneness.

According to James Dennis, the stout behatted man directly behind Wood is David Turner, his Cedar Rapids patron. [12] The younger man behind him has a build and facial features that could be based on those of Edward Rowan, who had come to Cedar Rapids to run the Little Gallery and then gone to Washington in 1933 to help administer the New

Deal art programs. Rowan had been instrumental in obtaining mural commissions for Iowa artists and had been especially lavish in his praise of Wood's direction of the Public Works of Art Project in Iowa City. It was probably to Rowan that some artists on the Project had sent a letter of protest about Wood's control of the Project, leading to Wood's refusal to participate further in the government programs and initiating a break between him and some Iowa artists. [13] If Wood held any resentment about Rowan's role in this situation, it may have been motivation to include him among those who fail to appreciate the artist. The elderly woman bears some slight resemblance to Wood's mother, but it is unlikely he would have commented unfavorably about her since their devotion to each other was well known. Rather, the woman has a generic appearance that relates more to the dull trio in *Daughters of Revolution*. As for the boy and girl, they exhibit little personality or distinction in appearance. Children are often symbols for the future and the hope of coming generations, but if that is the case here, Wood is again expressing despair. [14]

It has already been often noted that Wood was not very hard on most of the citizens of *Main Street*. The ones with whom he had the least sympathy (Carol Kennicott and Miles Bjornstam) were the ones who were most critical of Main Street, the very ones who embodied the situation of Wood himself. He had battled the isolation and lack of opportunity, income, and appreciation that haunted the Midlands, all the things that ground down the aspirations of the Carol Kennicotts, the Miles Bjornstams, the Erik Valborgs and the Fern Mullins's. He should have well understood the feelings of those who wanted more art, more theater, more literature, more justice, more honest laughter, more surprise, more of anything that was different from the everlasting monotony and self-satisfaction of the American provinces. One of the puzzles of his *Main Street* series is why he seemed bent on mitigating the harsh characterizations of Lewis's characters. [15] As happens so frequently in studies of the artist, we can discover no clear answer but can only acknowledge the conflicts of Wood's artistic, intellectual and emotional life. The tension that was never resolved continues to inhabit his work and keep it vital. This lack of resolution is a central reason why the *Main Street* drawings cannot be judged simply as illustrations in which Wood recounted a story that had already been told. He knew the Gopher Prairies of the Midwest, and his intellectual and artistic passion required that he tell his own version of the story.

Notes: Self-Portraits as Midwesterner

1. Corn, Wanda, *Grant Wood: The Regionalist Vision*, New Haven: Yale University Press, 1983, 112. When Wood exhibited the drawing in the 1936 Whitney Biennial, it was described in a review as "more formal than most of the drawings,...a quaint testimony of artistic salvation as well as an interesting picture." "Caricature and Decoration," New York *Herald Tribune*, January 19, 1936. NWG Scrapbook No.1, 46. It was also shown at the Maynard Walker Gallery in 1937. A review by E.A. Jewell in a September 12, 1937 article in the New York *Sun Times* reproduced the drawing; AAA, Maynard Walker Gallery files, reel N697, frame 61. In 1938, it was in an exhibition in Hollywood, California: *5 Foremost Americans. The Print Rooms. Hollywood Opening Exhibition of Paintings from the Walker Galleries, New York*, March 14-April 2, 1938; the drawing was #56 in the catalogue. A

review appeared in the March 20, 1938 Los Angeles *Times*, "American Sceners at Their Best." AAA, Walker files, reel N697, frame 68.

2. As in the *Main Street* drawings, this self-portrait has affinities with the famous musical about Iowans, *The Music Man*, by Mason City native, Meredith Willson. As we face down Wood's insistent stare, once again, song lyrics come to mind. In their grumpy self-assessment early in the musical, the Iowans sing, "And we're so by God stubborn, we could stand touching noses for a week at a time and never see eye to eye." The next line of the lyric adds a sentiment that might well apply to Wood's characterization of himself: "You really ought to give Iowa a try, provided you are contrary." Willson, Meredith, "Iowa Stubborn," *The Music Man*, New York: Frank Music Corporation and Meredith Willson Music, 1986.

3. 1932 is generally thought of as the low point of the Great Depression. When the American public, especially in urban areas, encountered men in overalls, it was often in photographs and newsreels showing the horrendous poverty in which much of the rural population lived. Wood's self-portrait, like his other work, does not suggest poverty of the sort that American farmers were experiencing. The land of the portrait is productive and peaceful, as he remembered it from his childhood. Though he is stern, he is not suffering deprivations, or at least not obviously so. Life on the farm may not be fancy, according to the drawing, but it does not leave one destitute. Material poverty is not a factor in the life of Wood's farmers, but he *is* utilizing the frequent assumption that cultural poverty is the lot of the Midwesterner.

4. Corn, 126.

5. He did sometimes wear overalls, but the photographs taken of him in that costume often have the air of publicity about them. The most famous ones are those by the Cedar Rapids photographer, John Barry, who brought his camera out to Stone City to record the visit of John Steuart Curry to the summer art colony in 1933. Curry, who hadn't yet completely renewed his Midwestern roots but was still living in the East, obligingly put on overalls too. The photographs served as a representation of the two artists' solidarity in the Regionalist cause.

6. Corn, 126.

7. Taylor, Adeline, "First to Spurn All Foreign Influences, Adopt American Viewpoint," Cedar Rapids *Gazette*, January 25, 1931.

8. Craven, Thomas, "Home-Grown Art," *Country Gentleman*, November 1935, 18+, 72; AAA, Maynard Walker Gallery files, reel 2424.

9. Craven, Thomas, "Grant Wood," *Scribner's Magazine*, vol. CI, no.6, June 1937, 16-22, 19.

10. Wood's image of his canvas, seen from the back, with prominent nails attaching the canvas to the frame is similar to the iconographic use of the nail-studded frame found in the late paintings of Philip Guston. Nail marks are also seen in other objects in Guston's paintings, such as shoe soles and horseshoes. In 1941, when Wood was on a leave of absence and would soon fall ill (he died in February of 1942), Guston began teaching at the University of Iowa. If he saw this or any of Wood's works, Guston did not comment upon it, but it is possible that they were available for his viewing.

11. Friedrich, Caspar David, "Thoughts on Art," in *From the Classicists to the Impressionists: Art and Architecture in the Nineteenth Century*, Vol. III of *A Documentary History of Art*, selected and edited by Elizabeth Gilmore Holt, Garden City, New York: Anchor Books, 1966, 85.

12. Dennis, James M., *Grant Wood: A Study in Art and Culture*, Columbia: University of Missouri Press, 1986, 152.

13. See DeLong, Lea Rosson and Narber, Gregg R., *New Deal Mural Projects in Iowa*, Des Moines: Bankers Life Company, 1982, 10.

14. One well-known example of the child as a symbol of the future is in Gustave Courbet's *The Artist's Studio*, 1854-1855.

15. Shortly after *Main Street* was published, Lewis wrote to Carl Van Doren that there were characters in his novel that he had positive feelings about. "In Main Street, I certainly do love all of the following people, none of whom could be classed as anything but 'dull' (using your own sense of dull as meaning lacking in conscious intelligence): Bea, Champ and Mrs. Perry, Sam and Mrs. Clark, Will Kennicott's mother and almost all of the farmer patients. And I love Carol who is dull about all the male world that interests Kennicott. And Guy Pollock who is of only a slight and dilletantish[sic] intelligence." Letter from Lewis to Van Doren, October 25, 1921. Carl Van Doren Papers, Department of Rare Books and Special Collections, Princeton University Library, Box 17, Fs. 6- 8.

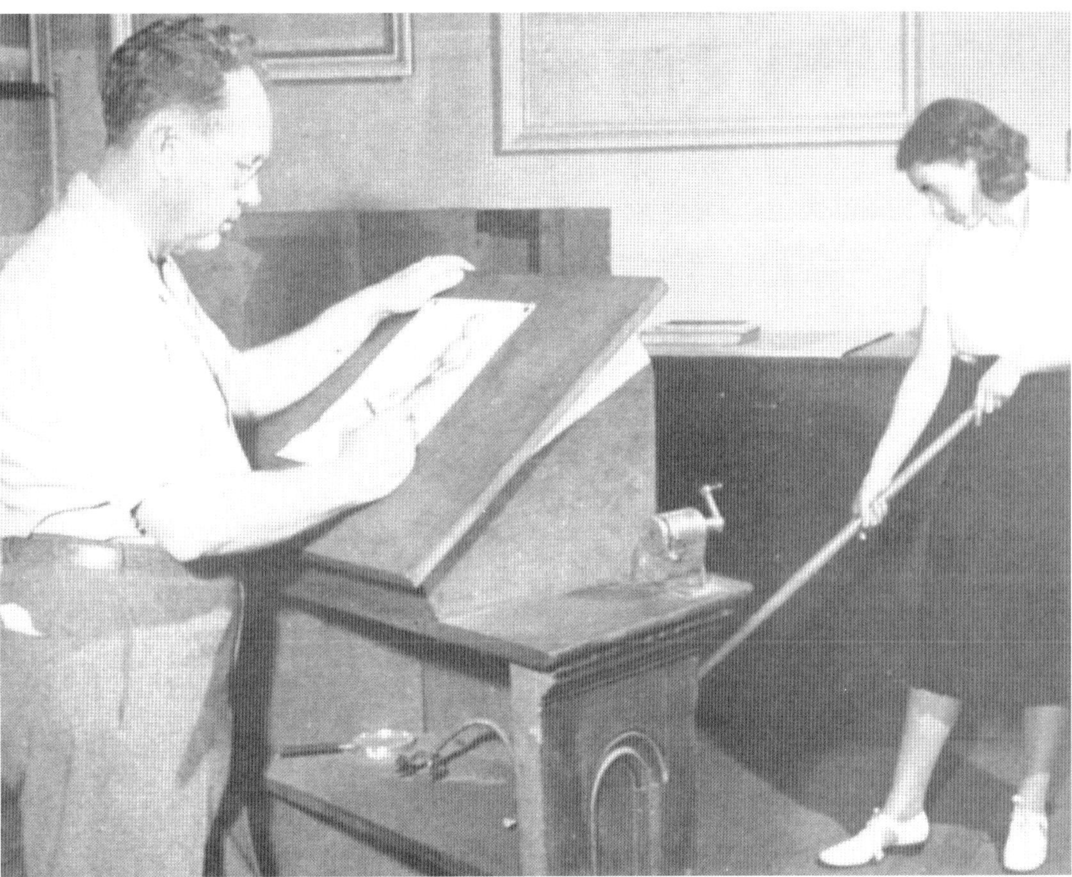

Figure 81 Wood drawing a study for Spring in the Country, *c. 1940-1941.*

Chapter 8 The Structure of Grant Wood's Illustrations to "Main Street"[1]

Main Street tells the story of Carol Milford, a girl of ideals and intelligence, but no special talent, who, after graduating from college in Minneapolis, marries a well-meaning but philistine physician, Will Kennicott, who brings her to his home in Gopher Prairie. She arrives eager to reform and improve village life, but discovers that her neighbors are smug, unimaginative, and resistant to change. Her attempts to beautify the place, to create a dramatic association, to bring about social reform, or to find romance, all fall flat. Eventually she flees the town and settles in Washington D.C., but is still unable to create an interesting or useful life. Two years later, Will Kennicott arrives to fetch her home, and while she feels no love, she dutifully returns to the petty life of Gopher Prairie.

Grant Wood followed the basic structure of the book, but significantly altered the roles of several of the characters. In the book, for example, the radical, Miles Bjornstam is a sympathetic and tragic figure, who suffers from the bigotry of the town. Grant Wood pictures him as the very stereotype that Lewis satirizes—as the villain of a melodrama, even equipped with a wicked-looking mustache. Perhaps most significantly, Wood inverts the role of the two principal characters, Carol and Will Kennicott. In Lewis's book, while he sometimes satirizes Carol's naïve efforts, her character is fundamentally sympathetic. Compared to her busy-body neighbors, she seems idealistic and vulnerable. Grant Wood, however, fundamentally changed this picture. His image of Carol is that of an over-critical snoop, peering out the window to spy on her neighbors, while ignoring her own faults. Conversely, in the book, Dr. Kennicott is insensitive and politically reactionary. Grant Wood, however, pictures him in a purely beneficent role, healing a patient. Alone of the figure drawings, we do not see his face, which gives him a generic, even God-like character. All we see are his hands, taking the pulse of a burly farmer.

In addition, Wood sometimes made curious choices of characters to depict. He omits some of the major characters in the book, such as Guy Pollock, the educated lawyer who has succumbed to "the village virus," or Erik Valborg, Carol's love interest. On the other hand, he includes characters such as Jim Blausser, who make only a brief appearance in the novel.

In short, while he clearly read the book closely, Wood created illustrations that sometimes run at cross purposes to the text. Two factors may account for this. One is that Wood was interested in creating images that would balance with each other, according to an internal logic of their own. The other is that he was projecting feelings from his own personal life and troubled marriage.

One senses that Wood's drawings took on a life of their own, which drew them away from the text. Whether consciously or unconsciously, he organized his drawings to create contrasts with each other, and to exemplify opposite qualities—what a structuralist would characterize as "binary oppositions."

There are nine illustrations. I think Wood conceived them as a series of three triptychs, although the clarity of his conception was obscured in the published edition, which unfortunately scrambled their order. Essentially they deal with the world of women, the world of men, and the world of Gopher Prairie.

The first triptych is centered around Carol Kennicott, the heroine of the story, who is flanked on either side by good and bad women:

The Practical Idealist (Vida Sherwin)
The Perfectionist (Carol Kennicott)
The Good Influence (Mrs. Bogart).

Carol, *The Perfectionist*, represents a figure caught between good and evil, who wants to improve the town but is too naively idealistic to do so. Vida Sherwin, while outwardly homely, represents the town's most positive force. Mrs. Bogart, ironically christened "The Good Influence," is the town busybody, who, behind a façade of Christian holiness, stirs up trouble.

Wood's drawing of Carol Kennicott, *The Perfectionist,* does not suggest the complexity of Carol's character in Sinclair Lewis's account. Instead, Wood focused on a single aspect of it, her discontent with life in a small town, and her critical view of her neighbors.

Wood showed Carol Kennicott standing beside a window, looking out on the town of Gopher Prairie with a mixture of worry and disdain. A contemporary reviewer noted that "it is significant that she is shut away from the sordidness of the town by lace curtains." [2] In short, Wood portrays Carol as a busy-body, rather than as the victim of busy-bodies. As is often the case in Wood's work, however, his satire has a double edge. While Carol is peering out at her neighbors, we are simultaneously peering in at her and are sizing her up in a similarly obnoxious fashion.

The term *Perfectionist* is never actually applied to Carol in the novel, although in one scene Vida Sherwin complains to her that "all you want is perfection" and Carol replies, "Yes! Why not?" [3] In addition, towards the end of the novel, Carol declares apologetically to her husband, "I know it must have been pretty tiresome to have to live with anybody as perfect as I was."[4] In fact, like many of us, Carol seems to have been more skillful in detecting faults in others than in recognizing her own. The errant button in Wood's drawing, a humorous touch, indicates that her perfectionist gaze is directed to everything except herself.[5]

Vida Sherwin, the schoolteacher and reformer, is *The Practical Idealist.* Though physically homely, her glowing energy is captivating. Lewis writes:

"She was small and active and sallow; her yellow hair was was faded and looked dry; her blue silk blouses and modest lace collars and high black shoes and sailor hats were as literal and uncharming as a schoolroom desk; but her eyes determined her appearance, revealed her as a personage and a force, indicated her faith in the goodness and purpose of everything. They were blue, and they were never still; they expressed amusement, pity, enthusiasm. If she had been seen in sleep, with the wrinkles beside her eyes still, and the creased lids hiding the radiant irises, she would have lost her potency."[6]

Wood did not follow this quite literally—for example, the figure's hair is dark rather than blond. But he wonderfully captured the essence of Lewis's description—that of a figure of ordinary appearance who is lit up by an inner radiance. As if to ensure that he would not distract from the radiance of the face, Wood did not include her hands—the only time in the series that he did not.

Wood balanced this benign figure with a wicked one, *The Good Influence*—a phrase that comes directly from the text and is used ironically. Mrs. Bogart is the town gossip and busy body, and the mother of the town bully. Interestingly, however, Wood tempered the severity of Lewis's satire. Lewis's description of Mrs. Bogart is grotesque. Her face is covered with moles and long black hairs, and her teeth are decayed.[7] Wood, however, omitted these grotesque features and focused on the central feature of Mrs. Bogart's character, her insincerity. As a contemporary journalist noted:

"When you look at the portrait of *The Good Influence*, the smiling woman, you know perfectly well that the smile is the smile of a hypocrite.... After he explains it, is all very simple: but he had to find out how to do it. The mouth smiles benignly. But cover up the mouth and look at the eyes; the eyes are hard, cold, unsmiling."[8]

According to Garwood, Wood combined two drawings to create the effect:

"Grant drew her once with a solemn, brooding expression, and once with a benevolent smile. Then he put them together, using the eyes of the first drawing with the smile of the second—a device that Leonardo is supposed to have found useful."[9]

The result is ambiguous. Garwood states that Wood created "a benevolent expression, but with a startling quality, too—a suggestion of suffering behind the serene exterior."[10] Others have read the expression as hypocritical and treacherous.

The men also form a triptych, but with interesting differences from the triptych of women.

The Sentimental Yearner (Raymie Wutherspoon)
Booster (Jim Blausser)
The Radical (Miles Bjornstam)

The center of this triptych, like that of the women, is devoted to a misguided town improver, Jim Blausser, *The Booster*. Blausser is flanked by good and bad men. Filling the role of "goodness" is the *The Sentimental Yearner*, Raymie Wutherspoon — a prissy idealist. Filling the role of "badness" is *The Radical*, Miles Bjornstam – the town badman, pariah, atheist, and political anarchist.

Jim Blausser, *The Booster*, serves as a humorous foil to Carol Kennicott. They are both town "improvers," but whereas Carol is high-minded, Blausser is vulgar and crass, an example of what H. L. Mencken termed the "Booboisie." He wants to transform Main Street into a "White Way" with electric lights, and to build a new factory in town. But like Carol, Blausser's schemes come to nothing. The factory he started folds after a year, and he abruptly leaves Gopher Prairie toward the conclusion of the novel.

Why did Wood choose to make a drawing of Blausser, who plays a minor role in the novel? The best explanation seems to be that Blausser was a tentative sketch of what became Lewis's best-known character, George F. Babbitt, the subject of his next novel. A gallery of Sinclair Lewis characters would have seemed incomplete without such a booster type.

Blausser's crassness contrasts with the idealism of *The Sentimental Yearner,* who is essentially a good, if ineffective, character. Wood's most recent biographers, James Dennis and Wanda Corn, have both misidentified this figure, assuming he is Guy Pollock.[11] In fact, as Lea Rosson DeLong has persuasively argued, he is Raymie Wutherspoon, another frustrated aesthete. The title of Wood's drawing is directly lifted from a passage in the novel, which refers to Wutherspoon. Vida Sherwin states: "Raymie? Why, my dear he's the most sentimental yearner in town."[12] In addition, somewhat later, a group of characters gossip about Raymie Wutherspoon's "yearnings."[13] What is more, Wood's drawing does not correspond with Lewis's description of Pollock, who has a mustache. But it closely follows Lewis's description of Wutherspoon, who has "pale face, flap ears and sandy pompadour" and likes to wear "small bow ties which made him look like an elongated Sunday School teacher."[14] That Wood intended to portray Wutherspoon is confirmed by an early article on the series, which makes this identification.[15]

Throughout most of the novel, Wutherspoon is a ridiculously effeminate figure, though he redeems himself at the end by marrying Vida Sherwin and distinguishing himself as a soldier.[16] The carnation in Wutherspoon's hand thus carries a double meaning, for while it suggests his lack of manliness, it also alludes to his romance with Vida Sherwin.

Wood contrasted Wutherspoon's sweetness and idealism with the slightly sinister qualities of *The Radical*, a representation of Miles Bjornstam. From the physical standpoint, Wood stayed close to Lewis's description.

"Before a tar-paper shack… a man in rough brown dogskin coat and black plush cap with lappets was watching her. His square face was confident, his fox mustache picaresque."[17]

Wood faithfully followed this passage, including coat, cap, and foxy mustache. Lewis also mentioned that Bjornstam had a large collection of tools, which fascinated the village children, and consequently, Wood placed Bjornstam against a background of tools.[18]

From the standpoint of characterization, however, Wood diverged from Lewis's presentation. In the book, Bjornstam is a sympathetic and tragic figure. Wood, however, presents him as the villain of a melodrama, much as he is pictured by the "good citizens" of Gopher Prairie. As Bjornstam confesses to Carol Kennicott:

"I'm what they call a pariah, I guess. I'm the town badman, Mrs. Kennnicott: town atheist, and I suppose I must be an anarchist too. Everybody who doesn't love the bankers and the Grand Old Republican Party is an anarchist…. Usually known as 'that damn lazy big-mouthed calamity howler that ain't satisfied with the way we run things.'"[19]

Wood not only played up the sinister qualities of Bjornstam's appearance, but also prominently placed the emblems of the Communist party — a hammer and a sickle — on the wall in the background, as a humorous reference to Bjornstam's radical social views.

Interestingly, Wood's initial drawing was milder, showing the handyman with raised eyebrows and an untrimmed mustache, which made his face seem melancholy and timid.[20] In the final drawing, however, Wood played up the sinister elements, although the elegance of the waxed and carefully twisted mustache introduces a hint of self-consciousness and vanity, and makes the illustration more humorous than sinister. These changes made the drawing more dramatic and memorable, although they significantly diverge from the character of the text. The two triptychs of male and female characters complement each other. For example, Vida Sherwin, the practical idealist, balances Raymie Wutherspoon, the impractical idealist; Carol Kennicott, the impractical town booster balances Jim Blausser, the crass town booster; Mrs. Bogart, the socially manipulative trouble-maker, balances Miles Bjornstam, the socially isolated town trouble-maker. In other words, Wood is playing with a variety of symmetrical patterns, which can be expressed through a simple symbolic notation.

The two triptychs are divided according to female (A) and male (B) in the following pattern:

AAA
BBB

In addition, they are divided according to good (A), bad (C), and between good and bad (B) in the following pattern.

ABC
ABC

Finally, they are divided between practical (A), impractical (C) and somewhere between the two (B) in the following pattern:

ABA
CBC

(In essence, the men as a group are somewhat less practical than the women).

Finally, one can group the two lines according to the attraction between the men and women in each line, ranging from strong attraction (A), to indifference (B), to hostility (C). Vida Sherwin and Raymie Wutherspoon are strongly attracted to each other (they marry); Carol Kennicott and Ray Blausser are indifferent; Mrs. Bogart and Miles Bjornstam are actively opposed to each other. This creates the pattern:

ABC
ABC

Finally, Wood devotes a triptych which sums up the society of Gopher Prairie as a whole:

Main Street Mansion
General Practitioner
Village Slums

This triptych is centered on the hands of Dr. Kennicott, who is taking the pulse of a patient. The scene represents a balance of good and bad, since while the action is good, the illness is bad. On the "good" side of this drawing is a Main Street mansion, the summit of Gopher Prairie's social aspirations. On the "bad" side is a village slum, featuring half a dozen privies surrounding a common water pump. Notably, no figures appear in either of the two architectural scenes, and no faces are visible in the scene of Dr. Kennicott. Thus, this group of illustrations takes its subjects out of the realm of personality, to stress broader issues of environment and survival. None of these scenes fits closely with any particular description in the book, although they reinforce its general themes.

The scene of the family doctor, holding the arm of a farmer to take his pulse, is not one that occurs in the novel, although the book contains many descriptions of Dr. Kennicott's generosity to his patients. Notably, Lewis's description of Kennicott's hands does not match Wood's drawing. He states that Kennicott has "thick, capable hands," and notes that his nails are "jagged and ill-shaped from his habit of cutting them with a pocket knife and despising a nail-file as effeminate and urban."[21] No doubt Wood's model, Dr. Bennett, had delicate hands, but Wood could easily have altered this fact if he had wished.

The phrase *General Practitioner* is used in the novel, although it carries a different weight than in Wood's drawing, since it is used apologetically by Kennicott, who declares that, "I don't want to be a plug general practitioner all my life."[22]

Similarly, *Main Stream Mansion* matches only loosely with the description of the Kennicott's house on Main Street:

"A square brown house, rather damp. A screen porch with pillars of thin painted pine surmounted by scrolls and brackets and bumps of jig-sawed wood. No shrubbery to shut off the public gaze. A lugubrious bay-window to the right of the porch. Window curtains of starched cheap lace revealing a pink marble table with a conch shell and a Family Bible." [23]

While Wood's house is brown and he includes porch pillars, he omits most of the other specifics of Lewis's description, such as the scrolls and brackets, the bay window and the lace curtains. Some of the most prominent features of his drawing, such as the dramatic overhang of the roof or the oval window, are his own inventions. Indeed, it is not even clear whether Wood intended to portray the Kennicott's mansion or simply to create a generic picture of a Main Street mansion in Gopher Prairie. If, however, he was attempting the latter, he did so without close reference to Lewis's text. For example, Wood may have been picturing the mansion that Kennicott aspired to — "a house exactly like Sam Clark's…A house resembling the mind of a merchant who votes the party ticket straight and goes to church once a month and owns a good car."[24]

The drawing of a slum, while it picks up hints from Lewis's account, is also largely Wood's invention. Lewis notes that Swede Hollow has "no sewage, no street cleaning," and the prevalence of typhus in the novel suggests poor sanitation.[25] In another passage he declares:

"Wherever as many as three houses are gathered there will be a slum of at least one house. In Gopher Prairie, as the Sam Clarks boasted, "You don't get any of this poverty that you find in cities—always plenty of work—no need of charity—man got to be blame shiftless if he don't get ahead." But now that the summer mask of leaves and grass was gone, Carol discovered misery and dead hope. In a shack of thin boards covered with tarpaper she saw the washerwoman, Mrs. Steinhof, working in gray steam. Outside, her six-year-old boy chopped wood. He had a torn jacket…. His hands were covered with red mittens through which protruded his raw knuckles." [26]

In fact, Wood's drawing is somewhat fantastic, for even in the most squalid of slums it seems unlikely that outhouses would be placed so close to the common water pump.[27]

Interestingly, Wood's drawing of *Village Slums* was delivered two months after the other eight drawings of the series, suggesting that Wood conceived it later than the others. My guess is that after making the other two drawings, Wood recognized that he could create a third triptych, with the addition of this design. One can express this symbolically by laying out the three triptychs in a box, resembling a tic-tac-toe board:

Practical Idealist, The Perfectionist, The Good Influence
Main Street Mansion, General Practitioner, Village Slums
Sentimental Yearner, Booster, The Radical

This set of three triptychs forms a perfect square, with three down and three across, and it can also be diagrammed in simple symbolic notation.

For example, male and female:

AAA
CBC
BBB

Good and bad:

ABC
ABC
ABC

Practical (or desirable in practical terms) and impractical (I rate the scene of hands between the two, since while it is practical to heal a patient it is impractical to become injured or ill):

ABC
ABC
ABC

What is striking is that all of these patterns are symmetrical, although none of them are the same. In other words, whether consciously or not, Wood created characters and scenes that balance each other and that possess a symmetrical logic.

Wood probably did not diagram the qualities he was exploring so rigorously as this, but at an unconscious level he was striving for a network of cross-connections between his drawings, and an overall sense of balance and symmetry.

When we look at Wood's illustrations in this way, we discern that he was creating triptychs that express complex symmetries with each other. To create these symmetries he sometimes needed to alter Lewis's characters. In Grant Wood's scheme, for example, Miles Bjornstam needs to be a villain who parallels Mrs. Bogart, and contrasts with Raymie Wutherspoon and Vida Sherwin. Bringing out the subtleties of his personality, as Wood did in his first drawing, not only created a more muted image, but destroyed the balance of the overall scheme. Both in his selection of characters (such as the obscure Jim Blausser) and in his presentation of them, Wood was willing to stretch the intentions of the text to create a scheme that would work well on its own terms.

Henry Adams

Chapter 8 Notes

[1] My thanks to Lea Rosson DeLong, who invited me to write this essay and kindly shared her own research on Grant Wood. Many of the references in this essay are based on her research.

[2] Audrey Hamilton, "Wood Draws *for Main Street*; Iowa Artist Illustrates Special Edition of Lewis's Novel," *Daily Iowan*, May 22, 1937.

[3] *Main Street*, p. 219.

[4] *Main Street*, p. 356.

[5] Lewis never alludes to Carol's buttons in the novel, although there is a button episode that she participates in. When she is out walking with her child, Hugh, Erik Valborg discovers that one of the child's buttons is undone. "Oh, dear me, he's got a button unbuttoned!" Valborg states. (*Main Street*, 1937, p. 278).

[6] *Main Street*, 1937, p. 52.

[7] *Main Street*, 1937, p. 56.

[8] S. A. N., "The Happy, Busy Toiler in Overalls Who is Grant Wood," *Kansas City Times*, February 14, 1938, Nan Wood Graham Scrapbook, No. 2, p. 81.

[9] Darrell Garwood, *Artist in Iowa, A Life of Grant Wood*, W. W. Norton & Company, Inc., New York 1944, p. 203.

[10] Garwood, *op. cit*, pp. 202-203.

[11] James Denis, p. 122; Wanda Corn, p. 114. Guy Pollock is described in *Main Street*, 1937, p. 127.

[12] *Main Street*, p. 61.

[13] *Main Street*, p. 122.

[14] *Main Street*, pp. 47, 210.

[15] "A Midwest Artist Views 'Main Street,'" *St. Louis Post-Dispatch*, Sunday Magazine, May 23, 1937, p. 1.

[16] *Main Street*, 1937, p. 223.

[17] *Main Street*, 1937, p. 93.

[18] *Main Street*, 1937, p. 258.

[19] *Main Street*, 1937, p. 94.

[20] Dennis, 1975, p. 122.

[21] *Main Street*, 1937, p. 236.

[22] *Main Street*, 1937, p. 142.

[23] *Main, Street*, 1937, p. 24.

[24] *Main Street*, 1937, page 242.

[25] *Main Street*, 1937, p. 93.

[26] *Main Street*, 1937, p. 92.

[27] Wood gave one of his slum drawings to his secretary and assistant Park Reinard. Presumably he did so because a drawing with outhouses was not easily salable, and thus made an appropriate gift. In his description on the drawing he noted that the gift did not quite match with Reinard's personality—clearly a reference to the outhouses. Interestingly, the other drawing by Wood that Reinard owned, a study for *January,* was also a snow scene. Again, Wood may have made the gift because snow scenes were less salable than more cheerful subjects. But is it too fanciful to note that the gift of two such frigid images suggests some element of emotional repression in his relationship with Reinard?

Chapter 9 The Regional Context of *Main Street*: Word and Image

Main Street, Gopher Prairie, Minnesota isn't necessarily an address you'd like to have. Sinclair Lewis's fictional community stands alongside Sherwood Anderson's Winesburg, Ohio, Edgar Lee Masters's Spoon River, Illinois; Edwin Arlington Robinson's Tilbury Town, Maine; and Grace Metalious's Peyton Place, New Hampshire, on the list of prominent American literary dystopias. They are places where dreams die and individuality is crushed, where minds are small and hearts become stunted. In direct contrast to Thornton Wilder's Grover's Corners, which has become a communal imaginative national property, Gopher Prairie is a place you'd rather disown than embrace.

Although the generic "Main Street" identifies streets in countless American towns, Lewis's novel takes on cultural meaning and power in a literary and imaginative context that is particularly Midwestern. While artists like Robinson and Metalious resemble Lewis in their critique of the American small town, part of their impact came from their contradiction and critique of current attitudes and "truths" about New England. Over the course of the nineteenth century—and increasingly so after the Civil War—writers, artists, architects, and historic preservationists began to reshape and idealize New England as the land of tidy white villages and stalwart Yankee farmers that tourists seek out even today. In the face of increasing urbanization, industrialization, and immigration, New Englanders hung on to their past a place where everyone was of Anglo Saxon descent, lived in quaint small towns, worked hard, and led virtuous, moral post-Puritan lives. Not only the region, but the nation invested a great deal of emotional and imaginative energy in this image of New England, and through the colonial revival in architecture and decorative arts it became a popular symbol of what many Americans considered their best historical selves. When writers like Robinson and Metalious suggested that New Englanders were not blissfully exempt from life's troubles but were, in fact, particularly prone to them, they were deliberately denying an established regional identity. In an important way, they were attempting to set the literary record straight about New England, replacing romance with a bleak psychological and emotional realism.

New England authors weren't the only ones with prevailing regional identities and narratives looming over their shoulders, of course. Wallace Stegner in the West and William Faulkner in the South are just two examples of authors who tried to balance local experience with the story-shaping force of regional mythologies. Midwestern writers, however, faced a different imaginative situation in relating themselves to their region. Rather than having to grapple with established regional meanings and images, Midwest writers and artists like Wood and Lewis instead were confronted by a lack of regional mythologies. The emptiness of those sparsely settled Midwestern fields and plains was a blank page, which they could fill out according to their own perceptions. As collective creators of regional meaning, Midwest writers and artists wielded a kind of power that their counterparts in other American regions did not.

The national perception of the Midwest as "fly-over country," devoid of any visual, cultural, or historical sites of interest, is well known, and is a part of the imaginative context within which Midwestern writers and artists create. In critic Diane Quantic's words, "the vast plains' expanses force writers to create meaning from an apparent void,"[1] and this sense of absence, of emptiness, becomes the point from which they start. William Least Heat-Moon's opening impression in his *PrairyErth* of Chase County, Kansas, is of "a most spare landscape, seemingly poor for a reporter to poke into, one appearing thin and minimal in history and texture."[2]

Midwestern writers who try to probe the meaning of their rural and small-town landscapes, often admit to having internalized this sense of meaninglessness. What can one possibly say about such a place when all the interesting and exciting things have happened elsewhere? Lisa Knopp describes how her hometown in Iowa came to appear to her after years of exposure to formal schooling and popular culture: "Gradually, I saw Burlington as the end of the world where nothing had happened or would happen. . . . Since local history wasn't valued and thus wasn't taught (or vice versa), I learned little about where I was from and what it meant to be shaped by such a place."[3] Paul Gruchow has noted about his native Rosewood Township, Minnesota, that its residents "never imagined they were being watched or admired from afar," that "Even the most optimistic inhabitant of Rosewood Township understood its significance to be obscure,"[4] and that children like himself "grew up believing that . . . there was nothing worth seeing in our own tedious flatlands."[5] In the absence of Pilgrims, Revolutionary heroes, Civil War battles, cowboys and Indians, and the sorts of second-hand historical identity that such events and figures can inspire in residents of other regions, writers in the center of the country look around themselves and find nothing more inspiring than the unremarkable lives of their Midwestern neighbors.

And yet, what seems like an absence also offers opportunity, a free field for creation, for small-scale acts of mythmaking on a place-by-place basis. In his "On Writing an Illinois Poem," James McGowan captures the nature of writing about the Midwest, of making something out of what looks like nothing. McGowan's speaker, a three-year resident of

Illinois, remains put off by the state's blank monotony: "the prairie's laid in blocks / and towns are just a smaller grid; / roads meet in perpendicular / and go in only four directions / (though a thousand miles in each)." In his mind, the emptiness of the visual field must be matched by an equivalent cultural and imaginative vacuum: "there is nothing for the mind to climb on; / it grows tassel high and reachable, / grows always grounded, / grows to be brought down in its cycle, / re-grown in old grooves / by these minds, steel-clad, / stores of the dry wisdom of fact and practice, / who dominate the innocent attention / as grain elevators command the highway." Living in Illinois but refusing to identify with it, to forge allegiance with its landscape and culture, the speaker combines imaginative distance with disdain. He shares Knopp's and Gruchow's sense that interesting things happen and interesting people live in some distant corner of the country. The narrator probably read his Lewis and his Anderson, has written off Midwestern minds as small and cramped, and has dismissed Midwestern lives as not worth living.

And yet, he knows that he is wrong: "But yet I understand so few things of this land and people— / flats and facts and squares— / I should not write." Writing "an Illinois poem" entails writing from within, not imposing from without; it cannot be a projection of one's prejudices upon a blank Midwestern screen, but must heed the details of local life, the subtle patterns of local history, and the shared and private contents of local heads. He knows that he is disqualified to write, because he is estranged from what he senses is present around him, but does not participate in: "I think, though, that there is / there must be mystery, dimension, depth— / each citizen his soul, each grid its ghosts— / I've heard of towering substance, strength, imagination, / prairie art, and love— / (and rumors of the circles and the symbols out of sight, / behind thick blinds, / in dark, in woody parlors)."[6]

This is what the Midwestern writer does. Lacking any overarching frameworks of regional identity to embrace or resist, Midwestern writers fill space with home-grown stories, turning the familiar abstract survey grid into a complex mosaic of meaning, converting flatness and emptiness into "mystery, dimension, depth." And what they do for the landscape, they do for its residents as well, giving them a richness, a fullness of "soul," corresponding to that which they find on the land. Midwestern authors may write critically, sometimes harshly, but they write with inside knowledge. In the process, they create a Midwest of the mind to replace the terra incognita that occupies the center of many Americans' national mental maps.

What writers do with words, artists do with visual images, creating scenes and populating them with human figures which neither confirm nor confound viewers' attitudes of the Midwest. Instead, the artists show their viewers that there is *something* out there worthy of serious thought and attention. Which brings us back, finally, to Lewis and Wood, to the interaction and intermingling of the words of the one and the images of the other as they collaborate in the creation of a Minnesota of the mind. Despite Lewis's opening protestation of universality—that Gopher Prairie's "Main Street is the continuation of Main Streets everywhere," that "The story would be the same in Ohio or Montana, in Kansas or Kentucky, or Illinois, and not very differently would it be told Up York State or in the Carolina hills"[7]—his novel takes on a particular Midwestern resonance when viewed in the context outlined above, one in which it makes perfect sense to pair the work of Sinclair Lewis's imagination with that of the regionalist Grant Wood.[8] Despite the common association of *Main Street* with sophisticated satire of small-town small-mindedness and oafish boosterism, it is instructive to remember that the book's subtitle is "The Story of Carol Kennicott." Carol Kennicott is the book's protagonist, who, "though she was Minnesota-born . . . was not an intimate of the prairie villages," but rather had been raised in Mankato (which "in its garden-sheltered streets and aisles of elms is white and green New England reborn") and sent to college in Minneapolis.[9] Though *in* Minnesota, Carol is not *of* Minnesota, and as such bears close resemblance to McGowan's would-be Illinois poet. She has much to learn about the town of Gopher Prairie, where she moves after she marries Dr. Will Kennicott. She fills in the blanks presented by the landscape and its people. The reader shares in Carol's journey, perhaps identifying with her initial inability to conceive of the world's Gopher Prairies as credible places for serious people to live, following her process of discovery, and finally, her qualified acceptance.

Carol's initial inspection of Main Street finds her bemused and bewildered, seeing only the lack of things, unable to find anything, in McGowan's phrase, "for the mind to climb on." "Main Street . . . was too small to absorb her. The broad, straight, unenticing gashes of the streets let in the grasping prairie on every side. She realized the vastness and the emptiness of the land."[10] Appalled by the shabby appearance of both the street's business buildings and the people in and around them, "She wanted to run, fleeing from the encroaching prairie, demanding the security of a great city. Her dreams of creating a beautiful town were ludicrous. Oozing out from every drab wall, she felt a forbidding spirit which she could never conquer."[11] To her mind and eye, Gopher Prairie is antagonistic, something unknowable, to be resisted and rejected rather than understood. Her distance and distaste prefigure those of McGowan's poet: "I must be wrong. People do live here. It *can't* be as ugly as — as I know it is! I must be wrong. But I can't do it. I can't go through with it."[12] But she does. By book's end, after living and working on her own in Washington for a year, she consents to return to her husband and her home. While not glossing over the very real limitations of provincial life — "I do not admit that Main Street is as beautiful as it should be! I do not admit that Gopher Prairie is greater or more generous than Europe!"[13] — she comes to accept the town for what it is, as long as it repays the favor.

"Her active hatred of Gopher Prairie had run out. She saw it now as a toiling new settlement. With sympathy she remembered Kennicott's description of its citizens as 'a lot of pretty good folks, working hard and trying to bring up their families the best they can.' She recalled tenderly the young awkwardness of Main Street and the makeshifts of the little brown cottages; she pitied their shabbiness and isolation; . . . She saw Main Street in the dusty prairie sunset, a line of frontier shanties with solemn lonely people waiting for her, solemn and lonely as an old man who has outlived his friends."

With understanding comes tenderness and compassion—and, at last, a sense of belonging, membership, and local identity. She declares of the town that "I can love it, now," and upon contemplating her return "she again saw Gopher Prairie as her home, waiting for her in the sunset, rimmed round with splendor."[14]

Textured place has supplanted blank space; a chunk of the Midwest that was once an alien Other has now, for better or worse, become a part of who Carol is, and how she sees herself. In contributing illustrations to *Main Street*, Grant Wood drew on his own sense of Midwestern identity. His own experience and immersion in the region reinforces Lewis's Regionalist argument, filling the Midwestern blank with finely rendered depictions of seven of the book's characters and two of its primary settings. Wood did not share Lewis's ambivalence toward the region, as Wanda Corn points out, "What Lewis was apt to indict, Wood was likely to enjoy. Lewis belonged to that generation which had revolted against the village, Wood to the one which had returned to it."[15] However, Wood did enter into the spirit of the novel, producing comic portraits of the smirking religious hypocrite Mrs. Bogart and the portly, pop-eyed booster Jim Blausser. While the illustrations are given generic titles, ("The Radical," "Sentimental Yearner," "Practical Idealist," etc.), Wood based his depictions on actual Midwesterners. He asked seven friends to pose for him and gave them costumes and postures appropriate to their *Main Street* depiction and characterization. The illustrations suggest the wide range of personality and emotional life contained within the Midwest's many Gopher Prairies, encompassed between the "Main Street Mansion" at one social pole and the "Village Slums" at the other.

Wood clearly takes these characters seriously as people, not simply as types. His "Sentimental Yearner," while his skyward gaze and dainty flower might seem comical, communicates a sad tenderness; his "Practical Idealist," Vida Sherwin, shines with earnest energy; the strong compassionate hands of "General Practitioner," Will Kennicott, care for a sick man; the anger and strength of "Radical" Miles Bjornstrom are carefully limned in his eyes, hands, and defiant pose. "Each citizen his soul" appears to have been Wood's goal. Even Carol Kennicott herself, "The Perfectionist," is rendered with more complexity than she is in the book, appearing as others would have seen her—gazing censoriously from behind her curtains, in the town but not yet of it. Wood's vision complements and deepens Lewis's, accomplishing in a visual medium what words, for all their power, cannot: the sense of a rounded person, one whose self emerges through words and gestures as well as thought and action, and, in this case, an engaging sense of just what kinds of people occupy Main Street and what can be lost if one is unable or unwilling to acknowledge their human complexity.

Unlike New England, the West, and the South, the Midwest does not come with a compliment of mental furniture that allows us to throw together quick and easy impressions of its meaning and identity. To a casual reader, *Main Street* might seem only to confer negative stereotypes about the region. But reading it as a story of Carol Kennicott's difficult but gradual emplacement, and especially reading it in light of the sympathetic rendering of Midwestern character that Grant Wood's illustrations provide, reminds us that to think of overarching regional identities in this case is really beside the point. The Midwest reveals itself on its own terms, place by place, and together Lewis and Wood help us understand where and how to look for it.

Kent C. Ryden

Chapter 9 Notes

1. Diane Dufva Quantic, *The Nature of the Place: A Study of Great Plains Fiction* (Lincoln: University of Nebraska Press, 1995), 155.

2. William Least Heat-Moon, *PrairyErth: A Deep Map* (Boston: Houghton Mifflin, 1991), 15.

3. Lisa Knopp, *Field of Vision* (Iowa City: University of Iowa Press, 1996), 7-8.

4. Paul Gruchow, *Grass Roots: The Universe of Home* (Minneapolis: Milkweed Editions, 1995), 10.

5. Gruchow, 135.

6. James McGowan, "On Writing an Illinois Poem," in Robert C. Bray, *Rediscoveries: Literature and Place in Illinois* (Urbana: University of Illinois Press, 1982), vii-viii.

7. Sinclair Lewis, *Main Street* (New York: Penguin, 1985), 8.

8. See Wanda M. Corn, *Grant Wood: The Regionalist Vision* (New Haven: Yale University Press for the Minneapolis Institute of Arts, 1983).

9. Lewis, 13.

10. Lewis, 38.

11. Lewis, 39.

12. Lewis, 42.

13. Lewis, 416.

14. Lewis, 409.

15. Corn, 114.

1891 Grant DeVolson Wood born February 13 near Anamosa (Linn County), Iowa.

1900 Birth of sister Nan, informal archivist and biographer of her brother's life. Nan served as the model for the female figure in *American Gothic.* Wood painted her portrait (*Portrait of Nan*) in 1933 and kept the painting until his death; it was prominently hung in his Iowa City home.

1901 Following the death of his father, Wood moved with his family to the east-central Iowa town of Cedar Rapids where he grew up and was educated in the public schools.

1910 Graduated from Washington High School and left immediately to begin his formal education as an artist. He studied at the Minneapolis School of Design for one summer semester with Ernest Batchelder, then returned to Cedar Rapids.

1911 Returned for another summer semester at the Minneapolis School of Design, then back to Cedar Rapids where he taught at the Rosedale Country School. Wood attended (but did not enroll in) drawing classes at the University of Iowa in Iowa City, about fifty miles away.

1913 Moved to Chicago to work as a designer, mostly in metal forms. He was employed by the Kalo Silversmith's Shop until he formed his own business (1914), the Wolund Shop, also specializing in metal design. Took drawing classes at the School of the Art Institute.

1916 His business having failed, Wood returned to Cedar Rapids to support his mother and sister. In partnership with Paul Hanson, Wood built three houses in Cedar Rapids, one of which became his family's home. He began to develop a local reputation as an artist and designer.

1918 At America's entrance into World War I, Wood joined the Army. He was trained at Camp Dodge, near Des Moines, then sent to Washington D.C. to design camouflage. He survived the influenza epidemic of those years, but suffered an attack of appendicitis which was later incorrectly reported as a case of anthrax.

1919 Returned to Cedar Rapids where he began a career as an art teacher in the Cedar Rapids Public Schools.

First exhibition, with fellow Cedar Rapids artist, Marvin Cone, at local department store, Killian's.

1920 First of four trips to Europe. Accompanied by Cone, Wood spent the summer painting in Paris and vicinity.

Sinclair Lewis published *Main Street,* which became a best seller and established his reputation as a major American novelist and commentator on the Midwest.

1923-24 Second trip to Europe, from fall of 1923 through summer of 1924. Fall, 1923: enrolled at Academie Julian, a loosely organized art school favored by many American artists abroad. He traveled to Italy during the winter, then returned to France. On his return, his most important Cedar Rapids patron, David Turner, offered him a stipend and a studio home in the carriage house of Turner Mortuary. Dubbed "5 Turner Alley," this was Wood's residence — where he produced some of his most important paintings, including *American Gothic* — until he moved to Iowa City in 1934.

1925 Ended his teaching career in the Cedar Rapids Public Schools to concentrate on his art and design, receiving commissions from the local community and becoming an increasingly recognized participant in the artistic and cultural life of Cedar Rapids.

1926 Third trip to Europe, summer. Exhibition of paintings at the Galerie Carmine in Paris. Wood's style at this time was a loosely-brushed impressionistic one with abundant browns, yellows and oranges; his typical subject matter was landscape, especially rural scenes. His European subjects were usually picturesque "sights" of architecture and street scenes.

1928 Fourth and last trip to Europe, this time to Munich, Germany, where he helped fabricate the stained glass window designs for the commission, received the year before, for the Cedar Rapids Veterans Memorial Building. In Munich for four months, Wood observed Flemish and German late Medieval-Early Renaissance painting in museums and may have seen paintings and photographs of German artists associated with the contemporary style known as Neue Sachlichkeit (New Objectivity).

The Little Gallery established in Cedar Rapids. Headed by Edward Rowan (later, an important figure in the federal New Deal art programs), the gallery was Iowa's most important supporter of contemporary art and especially of modern Iowa artists.

1929 Developing a new painting style, Wood gradually abandoned his impressionistic approach for a sharply linear one that focused on local subject matter. The first painting clearly carried out in this new style was a portrait of his mother, *Woman with Plants*, which he showed in the Annual Exhibition of Painting and Sculpture at the Art Institute of Chicago.

1930 Created his most famous work of art, *American Gothic*, which won the Harris medal at the Forty-third Annual Exhibition of Painting and Sculpture and was purchased by the Art Institute of Chicago. The painting was immediately regarded as a distinctly

American, specifically Midwestern, image and began both the fame and the controversy that followed Wood for the rest of his life.

Walter Pritchard Eaton opined in the Boston Herald that Sinclair Lewis should use part of the money from his recently-awarded Nobel Prize in literature to buy *American Gothic*.

1931 Experiencing a burst of productivity, Wood created many works of art, including several of his most important paintings, such as *Appraisal, Midnight Ride of Paul Revere, The Birthplace of Herbert Hoover*, and *Fall Plowing.*

1932 Painted *Daughters of Revolution*, widely interpreted as a "satirical" commentary on American, especially Midwestern, provincialism.

Founded the Stone City Art Colony and School, held in the summer months only. Institutionalizing his Regionalist philosophy, Wood hoped that his Art Colony would evolve into a permanent fixture of regional art — one among many other centers of regional art.

Drew *Study for Self-Portrait*, showing himself as a Midwestern artist, dressed in overalls, with a landscape and a windmill behind him.

1933 Second and last summer session of the Stone City Colony and School. Illustrated book jacket of *In Tragic Life* by Vardis Fisher, his first commission for book or book jacket illustration.

1934 Appointed (in December, 1933) head of the Iowa Public Works of Art Project, a state division of the first of several New Deal art programs during the Depression era. Wood organized a group of artists, including Christian Petersen, John V. Bloom, Arnold Pyle, Lee Allen, Bertrand Adams and Tom Savage, most of whom (except Petersen) had attended Stone City sessions. The group produced the painted and sculpted mural cycles now at Iowa State University in Ames: *When Tillage Begins, Other Arts Follow* and *Breaking the Prairie Sod* were installed in the library; Petersen alone produced the relief sculpture cycle, *The History of Dairying* for the Dairy Industry Building. All used Midwestern, Regionalist subject matter.

Joined the faculty of the Department of Graphic Arts at the University of Iowa where he mainly taught mural painting.

Helped to organize and design the club room of the Society for the Prevention of Cruelty to Speakers, an outgrowth of the Times Club, a group of University of Iowa professors who invited cultural, especially literary, figures to speak on campus. Among the speakers in 1934 was Christopher Morley, an editor at the *Saturday Review of Literature* and a supporter of Wood.

Illustrated book jacket for *Passion Spins the Plot* by Vardis Fisher.

1935 Exhibition at the Lakeside Press Galleries in Chicago. The Lakeside Press, a division of R.R. Donnelley, designed and printed the 1937 Limited Editions Club *Main Street*, illustrated by Grant Wood.

Exhibition at the Ferargil Galleries, his first solo exhibition in New York City.

Published *Revolt Against the City*, a small volume containing an essay on Wood's Regionalist philosophy. The essay is often considered to have been heavily influenced by, and perhaps even partially written by, Wood's colleague at the University of Iowa, Frank Luther Mott, head of the School of Journalism. Mott was the model for the Main Street character, *Booster*. Another colleague in the journalism department and fellow Times Club member, Professor Charles L. Sanders, modeled for *Sentimental Yearner*.

Married Sara Sherman Maxon, a Cedar Rapids native who had a career as a singer. The couple moved to Iowa City where they purchased a nineteenth century house that they began to renovate. The household also included Maxon's son, Arthur, a dentist who joined the faculty of the School of Dentistry at the University, and his wife Dorothy and their child. Arthur served as the model for *The Radical* and Dorothy for *The Perfectionist.*

Illustrated book jacket for *O' Chautauqua* by Thomas Duncan.

Drew *Return from Bohemia,* a self-portrait showing the artist seated at an easel, surrounded by Iowans, intended as a cover illustration for his proposed autobiography of the same name.

In October letter, Wood mentioned for the first time his commission from George Macy of the Limited Editions Club for illustrations for *Main Street*.

1936 Drew all but one of the illustrations for the Limited Editions Club's *Main Street*, a novel of the American Midwest by Sinclair Lewis. The exact date of the commission and the sequence of the drawings is not known.

Exhibited his drawings for the illustrations to *Farm on the Hill,* a children's book by Madelyn Darrough Horn, at the Maynard Walker Galleries in New York.

Exhibited five drawings from the *Main Street* series at the Art Institute of Chicago in their *16th Annual Exhibition. Watercolors, Pastels, Drawings and Monotypes.*

1937 In January, sent his final drawing (*Village Slums*) for the nine illustrations of *Main Street.*

Installed *Breaking the Prairie Sod,* the final section of his Iowa State University mural cycle, *When Tillage Begins, Other Arts Follow.*

The Limited Editions Club edition of *Main Street*, with nine illustrations by Wood, published in May. Reviewed in University of Iowa newspaper, the *Daily Iowan,* where two professors were recognized as models: Frank Luther Mott for *Booster* and Charles L. Sanders for *Sentimental Yearner.*

Began relationship with Associated American Artists, which published and sold his lithographs in editions of 250.

1938 Produced book jacket illustration for *Plowing on Sunday* by Thomas Duncan.

1939 Divorced from Sara Sherman Maxon Wood. Resumed the creation of major paintings, including *Parson Weem's Fable, Haying*, and *New Road.*

1940 Produced book jacket illustration for *Oliver Wiswell* by Kenneth Roberts.

Drew portrait of Henry Wallace, Iowan who had been Secretary of Agriculture in the Franklin D. Roosevelt administration since 1933. The portrait appeared on the cover of *Time* (September 23).

Began leave of absence from teaching duties at the University of Iowa, due largely to disagreements within the Art Department about Wood's art, his career and his teaching practices.

1941 Established a studio at Clear Lake, Iowa, where he produced his last paintings: *Spring in Town* and *Spring in the Country.*

Commissioned by Abbott Laboratories to produce lithograph to be distributed to physicians, *Family Doctor*. The composition was based on his *Main Street* illustration, *General Practitioner*. The model for the hands in both pictures was Dr. A.W. Bennett, Wood's personal physician.

Began treatment for cancer at University of Iowa Hospitals.

1942 Died on February 12, the day before his 51st birthday.

Memorial exhibition in the Fifty-third Annual Exhibition of American Painting and Sculpture at the Art Institute of Chicago, the exhibition series in which he had first won fame with *American Gothic.* Of the *Main Street* drawings, only *The Good Influence* was displayed.

CHECKLIST OF EXHIBITION

The *Main Street* Drawings

Booster, 1936
Charcoal, pencil, and chalk on brown paper, 20 1/2 x 16 inches
Davenport Museum of Art, purchase through the Friends of Art acquisition fund and a gift from Mr. and Mrs. Morris Geifman
Booster reproduced with permission of the Easton Press

General Practitioner, 1936-1937
Pencil, colored pencil, and chalk on light brown paper, 20 1/2 x 16 inches
Collection of Edward Lenkin
General Practitioner reproduced with permission of the Easton Press

The Good Influence, 1936
Graphite, pencil, and watercolor on wove paper adhered to masonite, 20 1/2 x 16 inches
Courtesy of the Pennsylvania Academy of the Fine Arts, Philadelphia. Collections Fund 1952.6.2
The Good Influence reproduced with permission of the Easton Press

Main Street Mansion, 1936-1937
Charcoal, pencil, and chalk on brown paper, 20 1/2 x 15 3/4 inches
Hunter Museum of American Art, Chattanooga, Tennessee, Museum purchase
Main Street Mansion reproduced with permission of the Easton Press

The Perfectionist, 1935-1937
Black and white crayon, graphite, black ink, and white opaque watercolor on brown wove paper, 20 1/2 x 16 inches
The Fine Arts Museum of San Francisco, Gift of Mr. and Mrs. John D. Rockefeller 3rd 1979.7.106
The Perfectionist reproduced with permission of the Easton Press

Practical Idealist, 1935-1937
Charcoal, pencil, and chalk on brown paper, 20 1/2 x 16 inches
Howard F. and Roberta Green Ahmanson
Practical Idealist reproduced with permission of the Easton Press

The Radical, 1936-1937
Charcoal, pencil, and chalk on brown paper, 20 1/2 x 16 inches
Collection of Peter Brady
The Radical reproduced with permission of the Easton Press

Sentimental Yearner, 1936
Pencil, black and white conte crayon, painted white around image, 20 1/2 x 16 inches
The Minneapolis Institute of Arts, Gift of Alan Goldstein
Sentimental Yearner reproduced with permission of the Easton Press

Study for Village Slums, 1935-1937
Charcoal, pencil, and chalk on paperboard, 21 x 16 inches
Smithsonian American Art Museum, Gift of Park and Phyllis Rinard,1991.122.1
Village Slums reproduced with permission of the Easton Press

Village Slums, 1935-1937
Charcoal, pencil, and chalk on brown paper, 20 1/2 x 16 inches
Vance Jordan Fine Art
Village Slums reproduced with permission of the Easton Press

Other works of art

Study for Self Portrait, 1932
Charcoal and pastel on paper, 14 1/2 x 12 inches
Cedar Rapids Museum of Art, Cedar Rapids, Iowa State University Art Association Purchase, 93.11

Return from Bohemia, 1935
Crayon, gouache and pencil on paper, 23 1/2 x 20 inches
Curtis Galleries, Inc., Minneapolis

Information about the drawings is given as provided by the lenders.

Books

Main Street by Sinclair Lewis
Illustrated by Grant Wood
Limited Editions Club, 1937
Book number 143, signed and numbered (in ink) by Grant Wood
Printed above artist's signature: "Of the edition of "Main Street," fifteen hundred copies have been made for the members of the Limited Editions Club at the Lakeside Press, Chicago, under the supervision of W.A. Kittredge; the illustrations having been drawn by Grant Wood, who here signs."
Brunnier Art Museum

Main Street by Sinclair Lewis
The Easton Press, Norwalk, Connecticut, 1965
Text facsimile of 1937 Limited Editions edition
Private collection

Lenders to the Exhibition

The following people and organizations lent works of art to the exhibition *Grant Wood's Main Street.*

Howard F. and Roberta Green Ahmanson
Peter Brady
The Davenport Museum of Art
Fine Arts Museums of San Francisco
Hunter Museum of American Art
Edward J. Lenkin
Minneapolis Institute of Arts
Pennsylvania Academy of the Fine Arts
Smithsonian American Art Museum
Vance Jordan Fine Arts

Donors to *Grant Wood's Main Street*

Grant Wood's Main Street exhibition and publication are sponsored by Howard F. and Roberta Green Ahmanson and Hometown Perry, Iowa.

Photography Credits and Reproduction Rights

Frontispiece
Photograph of Grant Wood in his Iowa City home, c. 1937
Reproduced with permission of the State Historical Society of Iowa–Iowa City

Figure 1
Photograph of Sinclair Lewis, c. 1915
Reproduced with permission of the Minnesota State Historical Society

Figure 2, *43*, 77
Grant Wood
Main Street Mansion, 1936-1937
Charcoal, pencil, and chalk on brown paper, 20 1/2 x 15 3/4 inches
Hunter Museum of American Art, Chattanooga, Tennessee, Museum purchase
Main Street Mansion reproduced with permission of the Easton Press

Figure 3, *44*, 46, 56, 62
Grant Wood
The Perfectionist, 1935-1937
Black and white crayon, graphite, black ink, and white opaque watercolor on brown wove paper, 20 1/2 x 16 inches
The Fine Arts Museum of San Francisco, Gift of Mr. and Mrs. John D. Rockefeller 3rd 1979.7.106
The Perfectionist reproduced with permission of the Easton Press

Figure 4, *48*, 51
Grant Wood
Sentimental Yearner, 1936
Pencil, black and white conte crayon, painted white around image, 20 1/2 x 16 inches
The Minneapolis Institute of Arts, Gift of Alan Goldstein
Sentimental Yearner reproduced with permission of the Easton Press

Figure 5, *54*, 55
Grant Wood
The Radical, 1936-1937
Charcoal, pencil, and chalk on brown paper, 20 1/2 x 16 inches
Collection of Peter Brady
The Radical reproduced with permission of the Easton Press

Figure 6, *58*, 61, 76
Grant Wood
General Practitioner, 1936-1937
Pencil, colored pencil, and chalk on light brown paper, 20 1/2 x 16 inches
Collection of Edward Lenkin
General Practitioner reproduced with permission of the Easton Press

Figure 7, 33, *64*
Grant Wood
The Good Influence, 1936
Graphite, pencil, and watercolor on wove paper adhered to masonite, 20 1/2 x 16 inches
Courtesy of the Pennsylvania Academy of the Fine Arts, Philadelphia. Collections Fund, 1952.6.2
The Good Influence reproduced with permission of the Easton Press

Figure 8, 32, 41, 47, 50, *66*
Grant Wood
Practical Idealist, 1935-1937
Charcoal, pencil, and chalk on brown paper, 20 1/2 x 16 inches
Howard F. and Roberta Green Ahmanson
Practical Idealist reproduced with permission of the Easton Press

Figure 9, *67*, 71
Grant Wood
Booster, 1936
Charcoal, pencil, and chalk on brown paper, 20 1/2 x 16 inches
Davenport Museum of Art, purchase through the Friends of Art acquisition fund and a gift from Mr. and Mrs. Morris Geifman
Booster reproduced with permission of the Easton Press

Figure 10, *72*, 75, 78
Grant Wood
Village Slums, 1935-1937
Charcoal, pencil, and chalk on brown paper, 20 1/2 x 16 inches
Vance Jordan Fine Art
Village Slums reproduced with permission of the Easton Press

Figure 73
Grant Wood
Study for Village Slums, 1935-1937
Charcoal, pencil, and chalk on paperboard, 21 x 16 inches
Smithsonian American Art Museum, Gift of Park and Phyllis Rinard,1991.122.1
Village Slums reproduced with permission of the Easton Press

Figure 11
Photograph of Grant Wood making studies for *Spring in the Country*
Reproduced with permission of the Davenport Museum of Art, Davenport, Iowa

Figure 12
Grant Wood
American Gothic, 1930
Oil on beaverboard, 29 1/4 x 24 1/2 inches
Friends of American Art Collection, 1930.934
© The Art Institute of Chicago and VAGA, New York, NY, reproduction, The Art Institute of Chicago
All rights reserved by The Art Institute of Chicago

Figure 13
Grant Wood
Appraisal, 1931
Oil on composition board, 29 1/2 x 35 1/4 inches
Carnegie-Stout Public Library, Dubuque, Iowa
© Estate of Grant Wood/Licensed by VAGA, New York, NY

Figure 14
Grant Wood
Daughters of Revolution, 1932
Oil on masonite panel, 20 x 40 inches
Cincinnati Art Museum, The Edwin and Virginia Irwin Memorial, 1959.46
© Estate of Grant Wood/Licensed by VAGA, New York, NY

Figure 15
Photograph of Christopher Morley, c. 1934
Reproduced with permission of the State Historical Society of Iowa–Iowa City

Figure 16
Photograph of Clubroom for the Society for the Prevention of Cruelty to Speakers, c. 1934
Reproduced with permission of the State Historical Society of Iowa–Iowa City

Figure 17
Photograph of Grant Wood and Thomas Hart Benton
Reproduced with permission of the State Historical Society of Iowa–Iowa City

Figure 18
Photograph of Thomas Craven
Reproduced with permission of the State Historical Society of Iowa–Iowa City

Figure 19
Photograph of Thomas Duncan and MacKinlay Kantor
Reproduced with permission of the State Historical Society of Iowa–Iowa City

Figure 20
Photograph of William Rose Benet
Reproduced with permission of the the State Historical Society of Iowa–Iowa City

Figure 21
Photograph of the 1937 Limited Editions Club *Main Street*
Photograph courtesy of University Relations, Iowa State University

Figure 22
Photograph of *Practical Idealist* as it appears in the 1937 Limited Editions Club *Main Street*
Practical Idealist reproduced with permission of the Easton Press, photograph courtesy of University Relations, Iowa State University

Figure 23
Photograph of *The Perfectionist* as it appears in the 1937 Limited Editions Club *Main Street*
The Perfectionist reproduced with permission of the Easton Press, photograph courtesy of University Relations, Iowa State University

Figure 24
Booster as it appears in the 1937 Limited Editions Club Main Street
Booster reproduced with permission of the Easton Press, photograph courtesy of University Relations, Iowa State University

Figure 25
Photograph of Charles L. Sanders and Frank Luther Mott, *The Hawkeye*, 1939 (vol. 48), 45
Reproduced with permission of Special Collections, University of Iowa Library

Figure 26
Grant Wood
Engineering, (detail of *When Tillage Begins, Other Arts Follow*), 1934
Oil on canvas, 17 feet 4 inches x 6 feet 3 inches
Commissioned by Iowa State College. Made possible by the Public Works of Art Project (PWAP). Located in Parks Library, Art on Campus Program, University Museums, Iowa State University. U 88.91

Figure 27
Grant Wood
Agriculture, (detail of *When Tillage Begins Other Arts Follow*), 1934
Oil on canvas, 17 feet 4 inches x 6 feet 3 inches
Commissioned by Iowa State College. Made possible by the Public Works of Art Project (PWAP). Located in Parks Library, Art on Campus Program, University Museums, Iowa State University. U 88.91

Figure 28
Grant Wood
Breaking the Prairie Sod, 1936-1937
Oil on canvas, 11 x 41 feet
Located in Parks Library
Art on Campus Collection, University Museums, Iowa State University. U88.68

Figure 29
Photograph of Wood at work on his painting *Haying*, c. 1940-1941
The Hawkeye, 1941 (vol. 50), 22
Reproduced with permission of Special Collections, University of Iowa Library

Figure 30
Grant Wood
Spring in Town, 1941
Oil on panel, 26 x 24 1/2 inches
Swope Art Museum, Terre Haute, Indiana 1941.30

Figure 31
Christian Schad
Sonja, 1928
Oil on canvas, 35 1/2 x 23 1/2 inches
Staatliche Museen zu Berlin-Preußischer Kulturbesitz Nationalgalerie,1997, erworben durch der Verein der Freunde durch die 'Stiftung Ingeborg und Günter Milich, Berlin'.
Photograph by Jörg P. Anders

Figure 34
Grant Wood
Portrait of Nan, 1933
Oil on Masonite panel, 43 1/2 x 28 1/2 inches (oval)
On loan to the Elvehjem Museum of Art, University of Wisconsin-Madison
Collection of William Benton

Figure 35
Christian Schad
Self-Portrait, 1927
Oil on wood, 29 7/8 x 24 1/4 inches
Private Collection

Figure 36
Grant Wood
Sketch for Self Portrait, 1932
Chalk and pencil on paper, 15 1/3 x 12 3/4 inches
Davenport Museum of Art, Davenport, Iowa

Figure 37
Otto Dix
Big City, 1927-1928
Galerie der Stadt Stuttgart

Figure 38
August Sander
Kleinstädterin, c. 1928, from *People of the Twentieth Century*, I/6/13
© 2003 Die Photographische Sammlung/SKStiftung Kultur-August Sander Archiv, Cologne/ARS, NY

Figure 39
August Sander
Der Sturmer oder Revolutionär, 1925, from *People of the Twentieth Century*, I/ST/3
© 2003 Die Photographische Sammlung/SKStiftung Kultur-August Sander Archiv, Cologne/ARS, NY

Figure 40
August Sander
Bildhauerin, 1929, from *People of the Twentieth Century*, III/17/15
© 2003 Die Photographische Sammlung/SKStiftung Kultur-August Sander Archiv, Cologne/ARS, NY

Figure 42
Photograph of the 1937 Limited Editions Club *Main Street*
Photo courtesy of University Relations, Iowa State University

Figure 45
Grant Wood
Home Economics, (detail of *When Tillage Begins Other Arts Follow*), 1934
Oil on canvas, 17 feet 4 inches x 6 feet 3 inches
Commissioned by Iowa State College. Made possible by the Public Works of Art Project (PWAP). Located in Parks Library, Art on Campus Program, University Museums, Iowa State University. U 88.91

Figure 49
Otto Dix
Self Portrait, 1912
Oil and tempera on panel, 29 x 19 1/2 inches
Gift of Robert H. Tannahill
Photograph © 1986 Detroit Institute of Arts
© 2003 Artists Rights Society (ARS), New York / VG Bild-Kunst, Bonn

Figure 52
Photograph of Charles L. Sanders, *The Hawkeye*, 1936 (vol. 45), 55.
Reproduced with permission of Special Collections, University of Iowa Library

Figure 53
Photograph of Charles L. Sanders, *The Hawkeye*, 1941 (vol. 50), 224
Reproduced with permission of Special Collections, University of Iowa Library

Figure 57
Photograph of Dr. Arthur Sherman Maxon, *The Hawkeye*, 1939 (vol. 48), 87
Reproduced with permission of Special Collections, University of Iowa Library

Figure 59
Christian Petersen
Country Doctor, 1936
Painted plaster, 32 x 9 1/2 x 14 1/2 inches
Gift of Helen J. Sebek. UM99.298
Christian Petersen Collection, University Museums, Iowa State University

Figure 60
Samuel Kravitt
Censorship, c. 1935-1936
Photograph reproduced with permission of Mrs. Samuel Kravitt, photograph courtesy of University Relations, Iowa State University

Figure 63
Grant Wood
Family Doctor, 1941
Lithograph, 8 7/8 x 11 7/8 inches
Des Moines Art Center Permanent Collections; purchased by the Mrs. Richard Rollins memorial fund, 1980.19. Photograph by Ray Andrews, Des Moines, IA
Reproduction with permission of the Estate of Grant Wood/Licensed by VAGA, New York, NY

Figure 65
Grant Wood
Adolescence, 1933
Gouache and ink on paper, 24 1/4 x 12 1/2 inches
Collection of Mr. and Mrs. Richard Waitzer, photograph courtesy of Vance Jordan Fine Art
© Estate of Grant Wood/Licensed by VAGA, New York, NY

Figure 68
Photograph of Frank Luther Mott, *The Hawkeye*, 1939 (vol. 48), 45
Reproduced with permission of Special Collections, University of Iowa Library

Figure 69
Photograph of Frank Luther Mott at the S.P.C.S.
Reproduced with permission of Iowa State Historical Society, Iowa City, Iowa

Figure 70
Photograph of Frank Luther Mott, *The Hawkeye*, 1941(vol. 50), 226
Reproduced with permission of Special Collections, University of Iowa Library

Figure 74
Grant Wood
January, 1937
Lithograph on paper, 8 7/8 x 11 7/8 inches
Des Moines Art Center Permanent Collections; bequest of Mrs. Charles Howard by exchange, 1978.34
Reproduction with permission of the Estate of Grant Wood/Licensed by VAGA, New York, NY

Figure *79*
Grant Wood
Study for Self Portrait, 1932
Charcoal and pastel on paper, 14 1/2 x 12 inches
Cedar Rapids Museum of Art, Cedar Rapids, Iowa Art Association Purchase, 93.11
© Estate of Grant Wood/Licensed by VAGA, New York, NY

Figure *80*
Grant Wood
Return from Bohemia, 1935
Crayon, gouache, and pencil on paper, 23 1/2 x 20 inches
Curtis Galleries, Inc., Minneapolis
Reproduced with permission of Curtis Galleries, Inc.
Reproduction with permission of the Estate of Grant Wood/Licensed by VAGA, New York, NY

Figure 81
Photograph of Wood drawing a study for *Spring in the Country*, c. 1940-1941
The Hawkeye, 1943 (vol. 52), 136
Reproduced with permission of Special Collections, University of Iowa Library

University Museums Staff

Lynette L. Pohlman
Director and Chief Curator

Matthew DeLay
Curator of Education and Interpretation

Rachel Hampton
Collections Manager and Public Relations Officer

Janet McMahon
Administrative Specialist

Susan Olson
Development Secretary

Eleanor Ostendorf
Interim Curator, Farm House Museum and Curatorial Program Assistant

Allison Sheridan
Education Assistant and Security Officer

Index

A

B

C

D

F

G

H

I

J

K

L

M

N

O

P

Q

R

S

T

U

V

W

Y